Leading Innovative Organizations Book Series

Leading Innovative Organizations Book Series

Strategic Human Resource Management in Public Organizations

Jonathan H. Westover, Ph.D.
Utah Valley University

Leading Innovative Organizations Book Series

First published in 2023 in Orem, Utah, USA
by HCI Press
as part of Leading Innovative Organizations series

Library of Congress Cataloging-in-Publication Data

Strategic Human Resource Management in Public Organizations / Jonathan H. Westover, editor.
p. cm. -- (Leading Innovative Organizations series)
ISBN: 9798399411385 (HCI Press)
1. Human Resource Management. 2. Leadership. 3. Strategy 4. Public Sector I. Westover, Jonathan H.

Table of Contents

About the Editor

Dr. Jonathan H. Westover is an Associate Professor of Management and Associate Director of the Center for the Study of Ethics at Utah Valley University, specializing in international human resource management, organizational development, and community-engaged experiential learning. He is also a human resource development and performance management consultant. Already a recipient of numerous research, teaching, and service awards and fellowships early in his academic career, Jonathan also recently was named a Fulbright Scholar and was visiting faculty in the MBA program at Belarusian State University (Minsk, Belarus), and he is also a regular visiting faculty member in other graduate public organization programs in the U.S., UK, France, Poland, and China. Prior to his doctoral studies in the Sociology of Work and Organizations, Comparative International Sociology, and International Political Economy (University of Utah), he received his B.S. in Sociology (Research and Analysis emphasis, Public organization Management minor, Korean minor) and MPA (emphasis in Human Resource Management) from the Marriott School of Management at Brigham Young University. He also received graduate certificates in demography and higher education teaching during his time at the University of Utah. His ongoing research examines issues of globalization, labor transformation, work quality characteristics, and the determinants of job satisfaction cross-nationally.

Acknowledgements

This text was created under a Creative Commons Attribution-NonCommercial ShareAlike 3.0 License without attribution as requested by the work's original creator or licensee. I would like to thank the many anonymous individuals who contributed their own wisdom and writing to this edited work. Of course, this text would not be possible without each of their important contributions. Most of all, I would like to publically thank my wife (Jacque) and my six wonderful children (Sara, Amber, Lia, Kaylie, David, and Brayden) for all of their love and support!

Preface

The goal with this book is not only to provide the necessary academic background information but also to present the material with a practitioner's focus on public sector organizations, as well as both large and small public organizationes. The writing style is clear and focused, with clear and concise language that makes the book interesting and understandable to the future HRM professional and manager alike. It is highly likely that any leader will have to take on an HRM role at some point in their careers. This text is useful enough for the HRM professional, but the information presented is also applicable to all managers, supervisors, and executives at any level within any organization. Besides these differences, other key differences include the following:

- This book utilizes a technology focus and shows how HRM activities can be leveraged using technology.
- We have also included a chapter on communication and information about motivational theories. Since communication is a key component of HRM, it makes sense to include it as a full chapter in this book. Human motivation is one of the cornerstones of HR, which is why we include information on this as well.
- Rather than dividing certain chapters, we have combined some chapters to provide the entire picture of related topics at once. For example, in Chapter 6 "Compensation and Benefits in Public Organizations", we discuss both pay and benefits, instead of separating them into two chapters.
- The exercises and cases utilize critical thinking skills and teamwork to help the points come through.
- The Organizational Focus boxes focus on the concepts and how public sector organizations apply these concepts.
- Practical application is the focus of this book. We want you to be able to read the book and apply the concepts. We feel this approach makes the material much more useful, instead of only academic.
- How Would You Handle This? situations in the book utilize critical-thinking skills to think about ethical situations in HRM. Each situation also includes audio examples on how an HRM professional or manager could handle the situation.

These features and pedagogical components make the book easy to read and understand while still maintaining an academic focus.

The organization of the book is intuitive. The book follows the process HR professionals or managers will go through as they ensure they have the right employees at the right time to make sure the organization is productive and successful.

- In Chapter 1 "The Role of Human Resources in Public Organizations", we discuss the role of human resources in public organization and why, in a constantly changing world, the HRM function is key to a successful organization.
- In Chapter 2 "Developing and Implementing Strategic HRM Plans in Public Organizations", we discuss HR strategic plans and how those plans should be developed. Strategic planning is necessary to tie organizational objectives with HRM objectives, but it is also important to have a "people plan" and address the ever-changing work environment.
- In Chapter 3 "Diversity and Multiculturalism in Public Organization", we discuss the diversity aspect of organizations and why multiculturalism is so important to ensuring a healthy organization.
- In Chapter 4 "Recruitment in Public Organizations in Public Organizations", recruitment, the process for getting the most qualified individuals with diverse backgrounds, is the focus. We discuss some of the important laws to consider when hiring people and methods to recruit highly qualified individuals.
- In Chapter 5 "Selection in Public Organizations", we talk about the selection process. Once you have recruited people, you must organize the process that selects the best candidate. This can include interviewing, employment tests, and selecting the criteria by which candidate performance will be measured.
- In Chapter 6 "Compensation and Benefits in Public Organizations", we discuss how you compensate individuals through pay, benefits, vacation time, and other incentives.
- Chapter 7 "Retention and Motivation in Public Organizations" discusses the talent management approach—that is, how you can retain the best employees through retention strategies and motivation techniques.

- The training and development aspect of HRM is likely one of the most important aspects of HRM. After you have gone through the time and effort to recruit, select, and compensate the employee, you will need to ensure career growth through continuing training, which is the focus of Chapter 8 "Training and Development in Public Organizations".
- Since communication is a key component to any and all aspects of HRM, we have a detailed discussion on communication and management style. While some of the information may be covered in other classes on topics in which people (such as HRM) are the focus, a review on communication is important. In Chapter 9 "Successful Employee Communication in Public Organizations", we also discuss management styles, since this is an important form of communication, and in fact, many people leave organizations because of their managers.
- Chapter 10 "Managing Employee Performance in Public Organizations" discusses some of the possible performance issues and how to handle those performance issues. We also discuss employee discipline and how to handle layoffs.
- Chapter 11 "Employee Assessment in Public Organizations" focuses on how to assess performance of the employee. We address performance evaluation systems and methods.
- Most HRM professionals will work with unions, the focus of Chapter 12 " Working with Labor Unions and Employee Relations in Public Organizations". The unionization process, how to negotiate union contracts, and history of labor unions are discussed.
- Employee safety and health are necessary to a productive workplace. Chapter 13 "Safety and Health at Work in Public Organizations" addresses some of the health and safety issues, such as drug use, carpal tunnel, and other issues relating to keeping employees healthy at work.
- Chapter 14 "International HRM in Public Organizations" looks at the differences between international HRM and domestic HRM. We discuss the recruitment, selection, and retention components of international HRM.
- Finally, Chapter 15 "Leading an Ethical Public Organization" looks at issues of organizational governance, ethics, and social responsibility within organizations.

Features

Each chapter contains several staple and innovative features as follows:

- *Opening situation:* The opening situation is used to show how the chapter topics have real-life applications for HR professionals and managers. The short openings are straightforward and show the practical application of the concepts.
- *Learning objectives by section:* Instead of a long list of learning objectives at the front of the chapter, we divide the learning objectives by section and offer exercises and key terms for every section in the book. This is a great way to "self-check" and make sure the key concepts are learned before moving to the next section.
- *How Would You Handle This? situation*: These situations are created to utilize critical-thinking skills that are necessary for strategic HRM. The situations are ethics-based in nature and also include audio that discusses the situation.
- *Figures*: There are numerous figures in every chapter. I think you will find they are clear and focused but are not a series of endless graphs and charts of statistics that are interesting but of little value to learning the key strategic concepts in HRM.
- *Case study*: The case study at the end of every chapter is a good way to make sure students have learned the material. The case presents real-world situations and utilizes HRM knowledge and skills to complete. The case studies are often tied to not only the current chapter but also past chapters to ensure continued application of past concepts.
- *Team activities*: The team activities will sometimes require students to work in small groups but may also involve the entire class. These activities are designed to promote communication, teamwork, and of course, the specific HRM concept, which are all valuable skills in HRM.

Chapter 1:
The Role of Human Resources in Public Organizations

Human Resource Management Day to Day

You have just been hired to work in the human resource department of a small organizational. You heard about the job through a conference you attended, put on by the Society for Human Resource Management (SHRM). Previously, the owner of the organizational, Jennifer, had been doing everything related to human resource management (HRM). You can tell she is a bit critical about paying a good salary for something she was able to juggle all on her own. On your first day, you meet the ten employees and spend several hours with the organizational owner, hoping to get a handle on which human resource processes are already set up.

Shortly after the meeting begins, you see she has a completely different perspective of what HRM is, and you realize it will be your job to educate her on the value of a human resource manager. You look at it as a personal challenge—both to educate her and also to show her the value of this role in the organization.

First, you tell her that HRM is a strategic process having to do with the staffing, compensation, retention, training, and employment law and policies side of the public organization. In other words, your job as human resources (HR) manager will be not only to write policy and procedures and to hire people (the administrative role) but also to use strategic plans to ensure the right people are hired and trained for the right job at the right time. For example, you ask her if she knows what the revenue will be in six months, and Jennifer answers, "Of course. We expect it to increase by 20 percent." You ask, "Have you thought about how many people you will need due to this increase?" Jennifer looks a bit sheepish and says, "No, I guess I haven't gotten that far." Then you ask her about the training programs the organizational offers, the software used to allow employees to access pay information online, and the compensation policies. She responds, "It looks like we have some work to do. I didn't know that human resources involved all of that." You smile at her and start discussing some of the specifics of the public organization, so you can get started right away writing the strategic human resource management plan.

What Is Human Resources?

LEARNING OBJECTIVES

1. Explain the role of HRM in organizations.
2. Define and discuss some of the major HRM activities.

Every organization, large or small, uses a variety of capital to make the public organization work. Capital includes cash, valuables, or goods used to generate income for a public organization. For example, a retail store uses registers and inventory, while a consulting firm may have proprietary software or buildings. No matter the industry, all organizations have one thing in common: they must have people to make their capital work for them. This will be our focus throughout the text: generation of revenue through the use of people's skills and abilities.

What Is HRM?

Human resource management (HRM) is the process of employing people, training them, compensating them, developing policies relating to them, and developing strategies to retain them. As a field, HRM has undergone many changes over the last twenty years, giving it an even more important role in today's organizations. In the past, HRM meant processing payroll, sending birthday gifts to employees, arranging organizational outings, and making sure forms were filled out correctly—in other words, more of an administrative role rather than a strategic role crucial to the success of the organization. Jack Welch, former CEO of General Electric and management guru, sums up the new role of HRM: "Get out of the parties and birthdays and enrollment forms.... Remember, HR is important in good times, HR is defined in hard times." [1]

It's necessary to point out here, at the very beginning of this text, that every manager has some role relating to human resource management. Just because we do not have the title of HR manager doesn't mean we won't perform all or at least some of the HRM tasks. For example, most managers deal with compensation, motivation, and retention of employees—making these aspects not only part of HRM but also part of management. As a result, this book is equally important to someone who wants to be an HR manager and to someone who will manage a public organization.

Human Resource Recall

Have you ever had to work with a human resource department at your job? What was the interaction like? What was the department's role in that specific organization?

The Role of HRM

Keep in mind that many functions of HRM are also tasks other department managers perform, which is what makes this information important, despite the career path taken. Most experts agree on seven main roles that HRM plays in organizations. These are described in the following sections.

Staffing

You need people to perform tasks and get work done in the organization. Even with the most sophisticated machines, humans are still needed. Because of this, one of the major tasks in HRM is staffing. Staffing involves the entire hiring process from posting a job to negotiating a salary package. Within the staffing function, there are four main steps:

1. *Development of a staffing plan.* This plan allows HRM to see how many people they should hire based on revenue expectations.
2. *Development of policies to encourage multiculturalism at work.* Multiculturalism in the workplace is becoming more and more important, as we have many more people from a variety of backgrounds in the workforce.
3. *Recruitment.* This involves finding people to fill the open positions.
4. *Selection.* In this stage, people will be interviewed and selected, and a proper compensation package will be negotiated. This step is followed by training, retention, and motivation.

Development of Workplace Policies

Every organization has policies to ensure fairness and continuity within the organization. One of the jobs of HRM is to develop the verbiage surrounding these policies. In the development of policies, HRM, management, and executives are involved in the process. For example, the HRM professional will likely recognize the need for a policy or a change of policy, seek opinions on the policy, write the policy, and then communicate that policy to employees. It is key to note here that HR departments do not and cannot work alone. Everything they do needs to involve all other departments in the organization. Some examples of workplace policies might be the following:

- Discipline process policy
- Vacation time policy
- Dress code
- Ethics policy
- Internet usage policy

Compensation and Benefits Administration

HRM professionals need to determine that compensation is fair, meets industry standards, and is high enough to entice people to work for the organization.Compensation includes anything the employee receives for his or her work. In addition, HRM professionals need to make sure the pay is comparable to what other people performing similar jobs are being paid. This involves setting up pay systems that take into consideration the number of years with the organization, years of experience, education, and similar aspects. Examples of employee compensation include the following:

- Health Benefits
- Pay
- 401(k) (retirement plans)
- Stock purchase plans
- Vacation time
- Sick leave
- Bonuses
- Tuition reimbursement

Retention

Human resource people must be aware of all the laws that affect the workplace. An HRM professional might work with some of thHRM Retention involves keeping and motivating employees to stay with the organization. Compensation is a major factor in employee retention, but there are other factors as well. Ninety percent of employees leave a organizational for the following reasons:

1. The job they are performing
2. Challenges with their manager
3. Poor fit with organizational culture
4. Poor workplace environment

Despite this, 90 percent of managers think employees leave as a result of pay.[2] As a result, managers often try to change their compensation packages to keep people from leaving, when compensation isn't the reason they are leaving at all.

Training and Development

Once we have spent the time to hire new employees, we want to make sure they not only are trained to do the job but also continue to grow and develop new skills in their job. This results in higher productivity for the organization. Training is also a key component in employee motivation. Employees who feel they are developing their skills tend to be happier in their jobs, which results in increased employee retention. Examples of training programs might include the following:

- Job skils training, such as how to run a particular computer program
- Training on communication
- Team-building activities
- Policy and legal training, such as sexual harassment training and ethics training

Dealing with Laws Affecting Employment

Human resource people must be aware of all the laws that affect the workplace. An HRM professional might work with some of these laws:

- Discrimination laws
- Health-care requirements
- Compensation requirements such as the minimum wage
- Worker safety laws
- Labor laws

The legal environment of HRM is always changing, so HRM must always be aware of changes taking place and then communicate those changes to the entire management organization. Rather than presenting a chapter focused on HRM laws, we will address these laws in each relevant chapter.

Worker Protection

Safety is a major consideration in all organizations. Oftentimes new laws are created with the goal of setting federal or state standards to ensure worker safety. Unions and union contracts can also impact the requirements for worker safety in a workplace. It is up to the human resource manager to be aware of worker protection requirements and ensure the workplace is meeting both federal and union standards. Worker protection issues might include the following:

- Chemical hazards
- Heating and ventilation requirements
- Use of "no fragrance" zones
- Protection of private employee information

Communication

Besides these major roles, good communication skills and excellent management skills are key to successful human resource management as well as general management.

Awareness of External Factors

In addition to managing internal factors, the HR manager needs to consider the outside forces at play that may affect the organization. Outside forces, orexternal factors, are those things the organizational has no direct control over; however, they may be things that could positively or negatively impact human resources. External factors might include the following:

1. Globalization and offshoring
2. Changes to employment law
3. Health-care costs
4. Employee expectations
5. Diversity of the workforce
6. Changing demographics of the workforce
7. A more highly educated workforce
8. Layoffs and downsizing
9. Technology used, such as HR databases
10. Increased use of social networking to distribute information to employees

For example, the recent trend in flexible work schedules (allowing employees to set their own schedules) and telecommuting (allowing employees to work from home or a remote location for a specified period of time, such as one day per week) are external factors that have affected HR. HRM has to be aware of these outside issues, so they can develop policies that meet not only the needs of the organizational but also the needs of the individuals. Another example is the Patient Protection and Affordable Care Act, signed into law in 2010. Compliance with this bill has huge implications for HR. For example, a organizational with more than fifty employees must provide health-care coverage or pay a penalty. Currently, it is estimated that 60 percent of employers offer health-care insurance to their employees.[3] Because health-care insurance will be mandatory, cost concerns as well as using health benefits as a recruitment strategy are big external challenges. Any manager operating without considering outside forces will likely alienate employees, resulting in unmotivated, unhappy workers. Not understanding the external factors can also mean breaking the law, which has a concerning set of implications as well.

One way managers can be aware of the outside forces is to attend conferences and read various articles on the web. For example, the website of the Society for Human Resource Management, SHRM Online,[4] not only has job postings in the field but discusses many contemporary human resource issues that may help the manager make better decisions when it comes to people management.

KEY TAKEAWAYS

- *Capital* includes all resources a organizational uses to generate revenue. Human resources or the people working in the organization are the most important resource.
- *Human resource management* is the process of employing people, training them, compensating them, developing policies relating to the workplace, and developing strategies to retain employees.
- There are seven main responsibilities of HRM managers: staffing, setting policies,*compensation* and benefits, *retention*, training, employment laws, and worker protection. In this book, each of these major areas will be included in a chapter or two.
- In addition to being concerned with the seven internal aspects, HRM managers must keep up to date with changes in the *external environment* that may impact their employees. The trends toward *flexible schedules* and *telecommuting* are examples of external aspects.
- To effectively understand how the external forces might affect human resources, it is important for the HR manager to read the HR literature, attend conferences, and utilize other ways to stay up to date with new laws, trends, and policies.

EXERCISES

1. State arguments for and against the following statement: there are other things more valuable in an organization besides the people who work there.
2. Of the seven tasks an HR manager does, which do you think is the most challenging? Why?

---

[1] Kristen B. Frasch, David Shadovitz, and Jared Shelly, "There's No Whining in HR," *Human Resource Executive Online*, June 30, 2009, accessed September 24, 2010,http://www.hreonline.com/HRE/story.jsp?storyId=227738167.

[2] Leigh Rivenbark, "The 7 Hidden Reasons Why Employees Leave," *HR Magazine*, May 2005, accessed October 10, 2010,http://findarticles.com/p/articles/mi_m3495/is_5_50/ai_n1372140 6.

[3] Peter Cappelli, "HR Implications of Healthcare Reform," *Human Resource Executive Online*,March 29, 2010, accessed August 18, 2011, http://www.hreonline.com/HRE/story.jsp?storyId=379096509.

[4] Society for Human Resource Management, accessed August 18, 2011,http://www.shrm.org/Pages/default.aspx.

1.2 Skills Needed for HRM

LEARNING OBJECTIVES

1. Explain the professional and personal skills needed to be successful in HRM.
2. Be able to define human resource management and the certifications that can be achieved in this profession.

One of the major factors of a successful manager or human resource (HR) manager is an array of skills to deal with a variety of situations. It simply isn't enough to have knowledge of HR, such as knowing which forms need to be filled out. It takes multiple skills to create and manage people, as well as a cutting-edge human resource department.

The first skill needed is organization. The need for this skill makes sense, given that you are managing people's pay, benefits, and careers. Having organized files on your computer and good time-management skills are crucial for success in any job, but especially if you take on a role in human resources.

Like most jobs, being able to multitask—that is, work on more than one task at a time—is important in managing human resources. A typical person managing human resources may have to deal with an employee issue one minute, then switch and deal with recruiting. Unlike many management positions, which only focus on one task or one part of the public organization, human resources focuses on all areas of the public organization, where multitasking is a must.

As trite as it may sound, people skills are necessary in any type of management and perhaps might be the most important skills for achieving success at any job. Being able to manage a variety of personalities, deal with conflict, and coach others are all in the realm of people management. The ability to communicate goes along with people skills. The ability to communicate good news (hiring a new employee), bad news (layoffs), and everything in between, such as changes to policy, makes for an excellent manager and human resource management (HRM) professional.

Keys to a successful career in HRM or management include understanding specific job areas, such as managing the employee database, understanding employment laws, and knowing how to write and develop a strategic plan that aligns with the public organization. All these skills will be discussed in this book.

A strategic mind-set as an HR professional is a key skill as well. A person with a strategic mind-set can plan far in advance and look at trends that could affect the environment in which the public organization is operating. Too often, managers focus on their own area and not enough on the public organization as a whole. The strategic HR professional is able to not only work within his or her area but also understand how HR fits into the bigger picture of the public organization.

Ethics and a sense of fairness are also necessary in human resources. Ethics is a concept that examines the moral rights and wrongs of a certain situation. Consider the fact that many HR managers negotiate salary and union contracts and manage conflict. In addition, HR managers have the task of ensuring compliance with ethics standards within the organization. Many HR managers are required to work with highly confidential information, such as salary information, so a sense of ethics when managing this information is essential.

HUMAN RESOURCE RECALL

Think of your current skills. Are there personal or professional skills you would like to work on?

Finally, while we can list a few skills that are important, understanding the particular public organization, knowing the public organization strategy, and being able to think critically about how HR can align itself with the strategy are ways to ensure HR departments are critical parts of the public organization. HR is a specialized area, much like accounting or finance. However, many individuals are placed in HR roles without having the specific knowledge to do the job. Oftentimes people with excellent skills are promoted to management and then expected (if the organizational is small) to perform recruiting, hiring, and compensation tasks. This is the reason we will refer to management and HR management interchangeably throughout the chapters. In addition, these skills are important for HRM professionals and managers alike.

Having said that, for those of you wanting a career in HRM, there are three exams you can take to show your mastery of HRM material:

1. *Professional in Human Resources (PHR).* To take this exam, an HR professional must have at least two years' experience. The exam is four hours long and consists of 225 multiple-choice questions in a variety of areas. Twelve percent of the test focuses on strategic management, 26 percent on workforce planning, 17 percent on human resource development, 16 percent on rewards, 22 percent on employee and labor relations, and 7 percent on risk management. The application process for taking the exam is given on the Human Resource Certification Institute website at http://www.hrci.org.
2. *Senior Professional in Human Resources (SPHR).* This exam is designed for HR professionals who focus on designing and planning, rather than actual implementation. It is recommended that the person taking this exam has six to eight years of experience and oversees and manages an HR department. In this test, the greater focus is on the strategic aspect of HRM.
3. *Global Professional in Human Resources (GPHR).* This exam is for HR professionals who perform many of their tasks on a global level and whose organizations often work across borders. This exam is three hours long, with 165 multiple-choice questions. A person with two years of professional experience can take the certification test. However, because the test has the international aspect, someone who designs HR-related programs and processes to achieve public organization goals would be best suited to earn this certification.

The benefits of achieving certifications are great. In addition to demonstrating the abilities of the HR professional, certification allows the professional to be more marketable in a very competitive field.

Most organizations need a human resource department or a manager with HR skills. The industries and job titles are so varied that it is possible only to list general job titles in human resources:

1. Recruiter
2. Compensation analyst
3. Human resources assistant
4. Employee relations manager
5. Benefits manager
6. Work-life coordinator
7. Training and development manager
8. Human resources manager
9. Vice president for human resources
10. This is not an exhaustive list, but it can be a starting point for research on this career path.

KEY TAKEAWAYS

- There are a number of skills crucial to human resource management. First, being able to organize and multitask is necessary. In this job, files must be managed, and an HR manager is constantly working in different areas of the public organization.
- Communication skills are necessary in HRM as well. The ability to present good and bad news, work with

a variety of personalities, and coach employees is important in HRM.

- Specific job skills, such as computer skills, knowledge of employment law, writing and developing strategic plans, and general critical-thinking skills are important in any type of management, but especially in human resource management.
- A sense of fairness and strong ethics will make for the best HR manager. Because HR works with a variety of departments to manage conflict and negotiate union contracts and salary, the HR professional needs ethics skills and the ability to maintain confidentiality.
- Since one of the major responsibilities of an HR department is to align the HR strategic plan with the public organization strategic plan, critical and creative thinking, as well as writing, are skills that will benefit the HR manager as well.
- Many people find themselves in the role of HR manager, so we will use the termHR manager throughout this book. However, many other types of managers also perform the tasks of recruiting, selecting, and compensating, making this book and the skills listed in this section applicable to all majors.
- Certification exams can be taken to make you more marketable in the field of HRM. These certifications are offered by the HR Certification Institute (HRCI).

EXERCISE

1. What are your perceptions of what an HR manager does on a day-to-day basis? Research this job title and describe your findings. Is this the type of job you expected?

1.3 Today's HRM Challenges

LEARNING OBJECTIVE

1. Identify and explain some of the challenges associated with HRM.

All departments within an organization must prove their value and contributions to the overall public organization strategy, and the same is true with HRM. As organizations are becoming more concerned with cutting costs, HRM departments must show the value they add to the organization through alignment with public organization objectives. Being able to add value starts with understanding some of the challenges of public organizationes and finding ways to reduce a negative impact on the public organization. This section will discuss some of the HRM challenges, and the rest of this text will dive into greater detail about how to manage these challenges.

Containing Costs

If you were to ask most public organization owners what their biggest challenges are, they will likely tell you that cost management is a major factor to the success or failure of their public organization. In most public organizationes today, the people part of the public organization is the most likely place for cuts when the economy isn't doing well.

Consider the expenses that involve the people part of any public organization:

1. Health-care benefits
2. Training costs
3. Hiring process costs
4. And many more…

These costs cut into the bottom line of any public organization. The trick is to figure out how much, how many, or how often benefits should be offered, without sacrificing employee motivation. A organizational can cut costs by not offering benefits or 401(k) plans, but if its goal is to hire the best people, a hiring package without these items will most certainly not get the best people. Containment of costs, therefore, is a balancing act. An HR manager must offer as much as he or she can to attract and retain employees, but not offer too much, as this can put pressure on the organizational's bottom line. We will discuss ways to alleviate this concern throughout this book.

For example, there are three ways to cut costs associated with health care:

1. Shift more of the cost of health care to employees
2. Reduce the benefits offered to cut costs
3. Change or better negotiate the plan to reduce health-care costs

Health care costs organizations approximately $4,003 per year for a single employee and $9,764 for families. This equals roughly 83 percent and 73 percent of total health-care costs for single employees and employees with families,_[1] respectively. One possible strategy for containment for health-care plans is to implement a cafeteria plan.Cafeteria plans started becoming popular in the 1980s and have become standard in many organizations._[2] This type of plan gives all employees a minimum level of benefits and a set amount to spend on flexible benefits, such as additional health care or vacation time. It creates more flexible benefits, allowing the employee, based on his or her family situation, to choose which benefits are right for them. For example, a mother of two may choose to spend her flexible benefits on health care for her children, while a single, childless female may opt for more vacation days. In other words, these plans offer flexibility, while saving money, too.

Another way to contain costs is by offering training. While this may seem counterintuitive, as training does cost money up front, it can actually save money in the long run. Consider how expensive a sexual harassment lawsuit or wrongful termination lawsuit might be. For example, a Sonic Drive-In was investigated by the Equal Opportunity Employment Commission (EEOC) on behalf of seventy women who worked there, and it was found that a manager at one of the stores subjected the victims to inappropriate touching and comments. This lawsuit cost the organization $2 million.[3] Some simple training up front (costing less than the lawsuit) likely would have prevented this from happening. Training employees and management on how to work within the law, thereby reducing legal exposure, is a great way for HR to cut costs for the organization as a whole.

The hiring process and the cost of turnover in an organization can be very expensive. Turnover refers to the number of employees who leave a organizational in a particular period of time. By creating a recruiting and selection process with cost containment in mind, HR can contribute directly to cost-containment strategies organizational wide. In fact, the cost of hiring an employee or replacing an old one (turnover) can be as high as $9,777 for a position that pays $60,000.[4] By hiring smart the first time, HR managers can contain costs for their organization.

In a survey reported on by the Sales and Marketing Management newsletter,[5] 85 percent of managers say that ineffective communication is the cause of lost revenue. E mail, instant messaging, text messages, and meetings are all examples of communication in public organization. An understanding of communication styles, personality styles, and channels of communication can help us be more effective in our communications, resulting in cost containment. In HRM, we can help ensure our people have the tools to communicate better, and contain costs and save dollars in doing so.

One cost-containment strategy for US public organizationes has been offshoring. Offshoringrefers to the movement of jobs overseas to contain costs. It is estimated that 3.3 million US jobs will be moved overseas by 2015.[6] According to the US Census Bureau, most of these jobs are Information Technology (IT) jobs as well as manufacturing jobs. This issue is unique to HR, as the responsibility for developing training for new workers and laying off domestic workers will often fall under the realm of HRM.

Of course, cost containment isn't only up to HRM and managers, but as organizations look at various ways to contain costs, human resources can certainly provide solutions.

Technology

Technology has greatly impacted human resources and will continue to do so as new technology is developed. Through use of technology, many organizations have virtual workforces that perform tasks from nearly all corners of the world. When employees are not located just down the hall, management of these human resources creates some unique challenges. For example, technology creates an even greater need to have multicultural or diversity understanding. Since many people will work with individuals from across the globe, cultural sensitivity and understanding is the only way to ensure the use of technology results in increased productivity rather than decreased productivity due to miscommunications.

Technology also creates a workforce that expects to be mobile. Because of the ability to work from home or anywhere else, many employees may request and even demand a flexible schedule to meet their own family and personal needs. Productivity can be a concern for all managers in the area of flextime, and another challenge is the fairness to other workers when one person is offered a flexible schedule.

Many organizations, however, are going a step further and creating virtual organizations, which don't have a physical location (cost containment) and allow all employees to work from home or the location of their choice. As you can imagine, this creates concerns over productivity and communication within the organization.

The use of smartphones and social networking has impacted human resources, as many organizations now disseminate information to employees via these methods. Of course, technology changes constantly, so the methods used today will likely be different one year or even six months from now. The large variety of databases available to perform HR tasks is mind boggling. For example, databases are used to track employee data, compensation, and training. There are also databases available to track the recruiting and hiring processes.

Of course, the major challenge with technology is its constantly changing nature, which can impact all practices in HRM.

HOW WOULD YOU HANDLE THIS?

Too Many Friends

You are the HR manager for a small organizational, consisting of twenty-three people plus the two owners, Steve and Corey. Every time you go into Steve's office, you see he is on Facebook. Because he is Facebook friends with several people in the organization, you have also heard he constantly updates his status and uploads pictures during work time. Then, at meetings, Steve will ask employees if they saw the pictures he recently uploaded from his vacation, weekend, or backpacking trip. One employee, Sam, comes to you with a concern about this. "I am just trying to do my job, but I feel if I don't look at his photos, he may not think I am a good employee," she says. How would you handle this?

Cyberloafing, a term used to describe lost productivity as a result of an employee using a work computer for personal reasons, is another concern created by technology. One study performed by Nucleus Research found that the average worker uses Facebook for fifteen minutes per day, which results in an average loss of 1.5 percent of productivity.[7] Some workers, in fact, use Facebook over two hours per day during working hours. Restricting or blocking access to the Internet, however, can result in angry employees and impact motivation at work.

Technology can create additional stress for workers. Increased job demands, constant change, constant e-mailing and texting, and the physical aspects of sitting in front of a computer can be not only stressful but also physically harmful to employees.

The Economy

Tough economic times in a country usually results in tough times for public organization, too. High unemployment and layoffs are clearly HRM and managerial issues. If a human resource manager works for a unionized organizational, union contracts are the guiding source when having to downsize owing to a tough economy.

Besides union restrictions, legal restrictions on who is let go and the process followed to let someone go should be on the forefront of any manager's mind when he or she is required to lay off people because of a poor economy. Dealing with performance issues and measuring performance can be considerations when it is necessary to lay off employees.

Likewise, in a growth economy, the HR manager may experience a different kind of stress. Massive hiring to meet demand might occur if the economy is doing well. For example, McDonald's restaurants had to fill six hundred positions throughout Las Vegas and held hiring day events in 2010._[8] Imagine the process of hiring this many people in a short period of time The same recruiting and selection processes used under normal circumstances will be helpful in mass hiring situations.

The Changing and Diverse Workforce

Human resources should be aware that the workforce is constantly changing. For example, in the 2010 census, the national population was 308,745,538, with 99,531,000 in 2010 working full time, down from 2008 when 106,648,000 were working full time._[9] For full-time workers, the average weekly salary was higher the more educated the worker.

ORGANIZATIONAL FOCUS

Multigenerational is here to stay, and Xerox is the leader in recruiting of Generation Y talent. This age group has been moving into the labor market over the last six years, and this major demographic change, along with the retirement of baby boomers, has many organizations thinking. Organizational organizations know they must find out where their new stars are coming from. In recruiting this new talent, Xerox isn't looking to old methods, because they know each generation is different. For example, Xerox developed the "Express Yourself" recruiting campaign, which is geared around a core value of this generation, to develop solutions and change. Joe Hammill, the director of talent acquisition, says, "Gen Y is very important. Xerox and other organizations view this emerging workforce as the future of our organization."_[10] Besides the new recruiting campaign, recruiters are working at what they term "core colleges"—that is, those that produce the kind of talent they need. For example, they developed recruitment campaigns with specific institutions such as the Rochester Institute of Technology because of its strong engineering and printing science programs. On their organizational website, they have a specific tab for the recent college graduate, emphasizing core values of this generation, including the ability to contribute, support, and build skills. With its understanding of multicultural generations, Xerox has created a talent pool for years to come.

It is expected that over the next ten years, over 40 percent of the workforce will retire, and there will not be enough younger workers to take the jobs once held by the retiring workforce.[11] In fact, the American Society of Training and Development says that in the next twenty years, seventy-six million Americans will retire, and only forty-six million will replace them. As you can imagine, this will create a unique staffing obstacle for human resources and managers alike, as they try to find talented people in a pool that doesn't have enough people to perform necessary jobs. The reason for this increase in retirement is the aging baby boomers. Baby boomers can be defined as those born between the years 1946 and 1964, according to the Census Bureau. They are called the baby boomers because there was a large increase of babies born after soldiers came back from World War II. Baby boomers account for seventy-six million people in the United States in 2011, the same year in which the first of the baby boomers have started to retire.

The impact of the baby boomer generation on our country and on human resource management is huge. First, the retirement of baby boomers results in a loss of a major part of the working population, and there are not enough people to fill those jobs that are left vacant. Second, the baby boomers' knowledge is lost upon their retirement. Much of this knowledge isn't formalized or written down, but it contributes to the success of public organization. Third, elderly people are living longer, and this results in higher health-care costs for all currently in the workforce. It is estimated that three out of five baby boomers do not have enough money saved for retirement,[12] meaning that many of them will depend on Social Security payments to meet basic needs. However, since the Social Security system is a pay-as-you-go system (i.e., those paying into the system now are paying for current retirees), there may not be enough current workers to cover the current Social Security needs. In fact, in 1950 there were 16 workers to support each Social Security beneficiary, but today there are only 3.3 workers supporting each beneficiary.[13] The implications can mean that more will be paid by current workers to support retirees.

As a result of the aging workforce, human resources should keep abreast of changes in Social Security legislation and health-care costs. In addition, human resource managers should review current workers' skill levels and monitor retirements and skills lost upon those retirements, which is part of strategic planning. Having knowledge about current workers and skills, as well as predicting future workforce needs, will be necessary to deal with the challenges of an aging workforce.

HUMAN RESOURCE RECALL

Have you ever worked in a multigenerational organization? What were some of the challenges in working with people who may have grown up in a different era?

Another challenge, besides lack of workers, is the multigenerational workforce. Employees between the ages of seventeen and sixty-eight have different values and different expectations of their jobs. Any manager who tries to manage these workers from varying generations will likely have some challenges. Even compensation preferences are different among generations. For example, the traditional baby boomer built a career during a time of pensions and strongly held values of longevity and loyalty to a organizational. Compare the benefit needs of this person to someone who is younger and expects to save through a 401(k) plan, and it is clear that the needs and expectations are different.[14] Throughout this book, we will discuss compensation and motivational strategies for the multigenerational workforce.

Diversity refers to age, disability, race, sex, national origin, and religion. Each of these components makes up the productive workforce, and each employee has different needs, wants, and goals. This is why it is imperative for the HRM professional to understand how to motivate the workforce, while ensuring that no laws are broken.

Ethics

A discussion of ethics is necessary when considering challenges of human resources. Much of the discussion surrounding ethics happened after the early to mid-2000s, when several organizations were found to have engaged in gross unethical and illegal conduct, resulting in the loss of billions of dollars from shareholders. Consider the statistics: only 25 percent of employees trusted their CEO to tell the truth, and 80 percent of people said that employers have a moral responsibility to society.[15] Based on these numbers, an ethical workplace is important not only for shareholder satisfaction but for employee satisfaction as well. Organizations are seeing the value of implementing ethics codes within the public organization.

Many human resource departments have the responsibility of designing codes of ethics and developing policies for ethical decision making. Some organizations hire ethics officers to specifically focus on this area of the public organization. Out of four hundred organizations surveyed, 48 percent had an ethics officer, who reported to either the CEO or the HR executive._[16] According to Steve Miranda, chief human resources officer for the Society for Human Resource Management (SHRM), "[the presence of an ethics officer] provides a high-level individual with positional authority who can ensure that policies, practices, and guidelines are effectively communicated across the organization."_[17]

For example, the insurance organizational Allstate recently hired a chief ethics and compliance officer (CECO) who offers a series of workshops geared toward leaders in the organization, because they believe that maintaining high ethical standards starts at the top of an organization. In addition, the CECO monitors reports of ethics complaints within the organization and trains employees on the code of ethics or code of conduct.[18] A code of ethics is an outline that explains the expected ethical behavior of employees. For example, General Electric (GE) has a sixty-four-page code of conduct that outlines the expected ethics, defines them, and provides information on penalties for not adhering to the code. The code of conduct is presented below. Of course, simply having a written code of ethics does little to encourage positive behavior, so many organizations (such as GE) offer stiff penalties for ethics violations. Developing policies, monitoring behavior, and informing people of ethics are necessary to ensure a fair and legal public organization.

The following is an outline of GE's code of conduct:_[19]

- Obey the applicable laws and regulations governing our public organization conduct worldwide.
- Be honest, fair, and trustworthy in all your GE activities and relationships.
- Avoid all conflicts of interest between work and personal affairs.
- Foster an atmosphere in which fair employment practices extend to every member of the diverse GE community.
- Strive to create a safe workplace and to protect the environment.
- Through leadership at all levels, sustain a culture where ethical conduct is recognized, valued, and exemplified by all employees.

KEY TAKEAWAYS

- One of the most important aspects to productive HRM is to ensure the department adds value to the rest of the organization, based on the organization's strategic plan.
- One of the major challenges of HRM is containment of costs. This can be done in several ways, for example, in the way health care and benefits are offered. Many organizations are developing cafeteria plans that satisfy the employee and help contain costs.
- HRM can also contain costs by developing and managing training programs and ensuring employees are well trained to be productive in the job.
- Hiring is a very expensive part of human resources, and therefore HRM should take steps to ensure they are hiring the right people for the job the first time.Turnover is a term used to describe the departure of an employee.
- Poor communication results in wasting time and resources. We can communicate better by understanding communication channels, personalities, and styles.
- Technology is also a challenge to be met by human resources. For example, employees may request alternative work schedules because they can use technology at home to get their work done.
- Because technology is part of our work life, cyberloafing, or employees spending too much time on the Internet, creates new challenges for managers. Technology can also create challenges such as workplace stress and lack of work-life balance.
- The economy is a major factor in human resource management. HR managers, no matter what the state of the economy, must plan effectively to make sure they have the right number of workers at the right time. When we deal with a down economy, the legal and union implications of layoffs must be considered, and in an up economy, hiring of workers to meet the internal demand is necessary.
- The retirement of baby boomers is creating a gap in the workplace, related to not only the number of people available but also the skills people have.Multigenerational organizations, or organizations with workers of a variety of ages, must find ways to motivate employees, even though those employees may have different needs. HR must be aware of this and continually plan for the challenge of a changing workforce. Diversity in the workplace is an important challenge in human resource management.
- Ethics and monitoring of ethical behavior are also challenges in HRM. Setting ethical standards and monitoring ethical behavior, including developing

a code of conduct, is a must for any successful public organization.

EXERCISES

1. Research the various generations: baby boomers, Generation X, and the Y Generation (millennials). Compare and contrast five differences between the generations. How might these differences impact HRM?
2. Review news articles on the current state of the economy. Which aspects of these articles do you think can relate to HRM?

---

[1] "Use Three Strategies to Cut Health Care Costs," Public organization Management Daily, September 9, 2010, accessed October 10, 2010,http://www.public organizationmanagementdaily.com/articles/23381/1/Use-3-strategies-to-cut-health-care-costs/Page1.html.
[2] Mary Allen, "Benefits, Buffet Style—Flexible Plans," Nation's Public organization, January 1997, accessed October 1, 2010, http://findarticles.com/p/articles/mi_m1154/is_v75/ai_4587731.
[3] "LL Sonic Settles EEOC Lawsuit for $2 Million," Valencia County News Bulletin, June 23, 2011.
[4] James Del Monte, "Cost of Hiring and Turnover," JDA Professional Services, Inc., 2010, accessed October 1, 2010, http://www.jdapsi.com/Client/articles/coh.
[5] "The Cost of Poor Communications," Sales and Marketing, December 22, 2006, accessed October 1, 2010, http://www.allpublic organization.com/marketing-advertising/4278862-1.html.
[6] Vivek Agrawal and Diana Farrell, "Who Wins in Offshoring?" in "Global Directions," special issue, McKinsey Quarterly, (2003): 36–41,https://www.mckinseyquarterly.com/Who_wins_in_offshoring_1363.
[7] "Facebook Use Cuts Productivity at Work," Economic Times, July 25, 2009, accessed October 4, 2010, http://economictimes.indiatimes.com/tech/internet/Facebook-use-cuts-productivity-at-work-Study/articleshow/4818848.cms.
[8] "McDonald's Readies for Massive Hiring Spree," Fox 5 News, Las Vegas, May 2010, accessed October 5, 2010, http://www.fox5vegas.com/news/23661640/detail.html (site discontinued).
[9] Bureau of Labor Statistics, Current Population Survey Report, accessed July 7, 2011,http://www.bls.gov/cps/earnings.htm#education.
[10] Stephanie Armour, "Generation Y: They've Arrived at Work with a New Attitude," USA Today, November 6, 2005.
[11] Alvaro Fernandez, "Training the Aging Workforce," SharpBrains, August 10, 2007, accessed October 6, 2010, http://www.sharpbrains.com/blog/2007/08/10/training-the-aging-workforce-and-their-brains.
[12] Joe Weisenthal, "3 of 5 Baby Boomers Don't Have Enough for Retirement," Public organization Insider Magazine, August 16, 2010, http://www.public organizationinsider.com/boomers-cutting-back-2010-8.
[13] Brenda Wenning, "Baby Boomer Retirement May Be a Bust," Metrowest News Daily, March 21, 2010.
[14] Michelle Capezza, "Employee Benefits in a Multigenerational Workplace," EpsteinBeckerGreen, August 12, 2010, accessed October 6, 2010,http://www.ebglaw.com/showNewsletter.aspx?Show=13313.
[15] Strategic Management Partners, "Unethical Statistics Announced At Public organization Leaders Event," news release, http://www.consult-smp.com/archives/2005/02/unethical_stati.html, accessed August 31, 2011.
[16] Mark McGraw, "The HR-Ethics Alliance," HR Executive Online, June 16, 2011, accessed July 7, 2011, http://www.hreonline.com/HRE/story.jsp?storyId=533339153.
[17] Mark McGraw, "The HR-Ethics Alliance," HR Executive Online, June 16, 2011, accessed July 7, 2011, http://www.hreonline.com/HRE/story.jsp?storyId=533339153, brackets in the original.
[18] Mark McGraw, "The HR-Ethics Alliance," HR Executive Online, June 16, 2011, accessed July 7, 2011, http://www.hreonline.com/HRE/story.jsp?storyId=533339153.
[19] "The Spirit and the Letter," General Electric Organizational, accessed August 10, 2011,http://files.georganizational.com/gecom/citizenship/pdfs/TheSpirit&TheLetter.pdf.

1.4 Cases and Problems

CHAPTER SUMMARY

- Human resource management is the process of employing people, training them, compensating them, developing policies relating to the workplace, and developing strategies to retain employees. Three certification exams, which are offered by the Human Resource Certification Institute, can be taken to show HRM skills and become more marketable.
- Human resource management involves seven main areas: (1) staffing, (2) workplace policies, (3) benefits and compensation, (4) retention, (5) training, (6) employment laws, and (7) employee protection.
- Human resource managers need many different types of skills. Being able to organize, multitask, and communicate effectively, as well as having specific job skills, such as how to run a particular computer program, and a sense of fairness and ethics, is crucial to a successful career in HRM.
- There are many contemporary challenges associated with HRM. First, it is up to everyone in the organization to contain costs. HR managers need to look at their individual departments and demonstrate the necessity and value of their functions to the organization. HR managers can also help contain costs in several ways, such as managing benefits plans and compensation and providing training.
- The fast-changing nature of technology is also a challenge in HRM. As new technologies are developed, employees may be able to implement innovative ways of working such as flextime. HR managers are also responsible for developing policies dealing with cyberloafing and other workplace time wasters revolving around technology. Employee stress and lack of work-life balance are also greatly influenced by technology.

- Awareness of the changes in the economy allows the human resource manager to adequately plan for reductions and additions to the workforce.
- The aging and changing workforce is our final factor. As baby boomers retire, there likely will not be enough people to replace them, and many of the skills the baby boomers have may be lost. In addition, having to work with multiple generations at once can create challenges as different expectations and needs arise from multigenerational workforces.

CHAPTER CASE

Changes, Changes

Jennifer, the owner and manager of a organizational with ten employees, has hired you to take over the HRM function so she can focus on other areas of her public organization. During your first two weeks, you find out that the organizational has been greatly affected by the up economy and is expected to experience overall revenue growth by 10 percent over the next three years, with some quarters seeing growth as high as 30 percent. However, five of the ten workers are expected to retire within three years. These workers have been with the organization since the beginning and provide a unique historical perspective of the organizational. The other five workers are of diverse ages.

In addition to these changes, Jennifer believes they may be able to save costs by allowing employees to telecommute one to two days per week. She has some concerns about productivity if she allows employees to work from home. Despite these concerns, Jennifer has even considered closing down the physical office and making her organizational a virtual organization, but she wonders how such a major change will affect the ability to communicate and worker motivation.

Jennifer shares with you her thoughts about the costs of health care on the organization. She has considered cutting benefits entirely and having her employees work for her on a contract basis, instead of being full-time employees. She isn't sure if this would be a good choice.

Jennifer schedules a meeting with you to discuss some of her thoughts. To prepare for the meeting, you perform research so you can impress your new boss with recommendations on the challenges presented.

1. Point out which changes are occurring in the public organization that affect HRM.
2. What are some considerations the organizational and HR should be aware of when making changes related to this case study?
3. What would the initial steps be to start planning for these changes?
4. What would your role be in implementing these changes? What would Jennifer's role be?

TEAM ACTIVITIES

1. In a group of two to three people, research possible career paths in HRM and prepare a PowerPoint presentation to discuss your findings.
2. Interview an HR manager and discuss his or her career path, skills, and daily tasks. Present your findings to your class.

NOTES:

NOTES:

Chapter 2:
Developing and Implementing Strategic HRM Plans in Public Organizations

The Value of Planning

James stumbled into his position as the human resource manager. He had been working for Techno, Inc. for three years, and when the organizational grew, James moved from a management position into a human resource management position. Techno, Inc. is a technology and software consulting organizational for the music industry.

James didn't have a good handle on how to effectively run a human resources (HR) department, so for much of the time he tried to figure it out as he went. When Techno started seeing rapid growth, he hired thirty people within a one-month period to meet the demand. Proud of his ability to accomplish his task of meeting the public organization's current needs, James was rather pleased with himself. He had spent numerous hours mulling over recruitment strategies, putting together excellent compensation plans, and then eventually sifting through résumés as a small part of the hiring process. Now the organization had the right number of people needed to carry out its projects.

Fast forward five months, however, and it turned out the rapid growth was only temporary. James met with the executives of the public organization who told him the contracts they had acquired were finished, and there wasn't enough new work coming in to make payroll next month if they didn't let some people go. James felt frustrated because he had gone through so much effort to hire people, and now they would be laid off. Never mind the costs of hiring and training his department had taken on to make this happen. As James sat with the executives to determine who should be laid off, he felt sad for the people who had given up other jobs just five months before, only to be laid off.

After the meeting, James reflected on this situation and realized that if he had spoken with the executives of the organizational sooner, they would have shared information on the duration of the contracts, and he likely would have hired people differently, perhaps on a contract basis rather than on a full-time basis. He also considered the fact that the organization could have hired an outsourcing organizational to recruit workers for him. As Jason mulled this over, he realized that he needed a strategic plan to make sure his department was meeting the needs of the organization. He vowed to work with the organizational executives to find out more about the organizational's strategic plan and then develop a human resource
management (HRM) strategic plan to make sure Techno, Inc. has the right number of workers with the right skills, at the right time in the future.

2.1 Strategic Planning

LEARNING OBJECTIVES

1. Explain the differences been HRM and personnel management.
2. Be able to define the steps in HRM strategic planning.

In the past, human resource management (HRM) was called the personnel department. In the past, the personnel department hired people and dealt with the hiring paperwork and processes. It is believed the first human resource department was created in 1901 by the National Cash Register Organizational (NCR). The organizational faced a major strike but eventually defeated the union after a lockout. After this difficult battle, the organizational president decided to improve worker relations by organizing a personnel department to handle grievances, discharges, safety concerns, and other employee issues. The department also kept track of new legislation surrounding laws impacting the organization. Many other organizations were coming to the same realization that a department was necessary to create employee satisfaction, which resulted in more productivity. In 1913, Henry Ford saw employee turnover at 380 percent and tried to ease the turnover by increasing wages from $2.50 to $5.00, even though $2.50 was fair during this time period._[1] Of course, this approach didn't work for long, and these large organizations began to understand they had to do more than hire and fire if they were going to meet customer demand.

More recently, however, the personnel department has divided into human resource management and human resource development, as these functions have evolved over the century. HRM is not only crucial to an organization's success, but it should be part of the overall organizational's strategic plan, because so many public organizationes today depend on people to earn profits. Strategic planning plays an important role in how productive the organization is.

Table 2.1 Examples of Differences between Personnel Management and HRM

Personnel Management Focus	**HRM Focus**
Administering of policies	Helping to achieve strategic goals through people
Stand-alone programs, such as training	HRM training programs that are integrated with organizational's mission and values
Personnel department responsible for managing people	Line managers share joint responsibility in all areas of people hiring and management
Creates a cost within an organization	Contributes to the profit objectives of the organization

Most people agree that the following duties normally fall under HRM. Each of these aspects has its own part within the overall strategic plan of the organization:

1. *Staffing.* Staffing includes the development of a strategic plan to determine how many people you might need to hire. Based on the strategic plan, HRM then performs the hiring process to recruit and select the right people for the right jobs.
2. *Basic workplace policies.* Development of policies to help reach the strategic plan's goals is the job of HRM. After the policies have been developed, communication of these policies on safety, security, scheduling, vacation times, and flextime schedules should be developed by the HR department. Of course, the HR managers work closely with supervisors in organizations to develop these policies. Workplace policies will be addressed throughout the book.
3. *Compensation and benefits.* In addition to paychecks, 401(k) plans, health benefits, and other perks are usually the responsibility of an HR manager.
4. *Retention.* Assessment of employees and strategizing on how to retain the best employees is a task that HR managers oversee, but other managers in the organization will also provide input.
5. *Training and development.* Helping new employees develop skills needed for their jobs and helping current employees grow their skills are also tasks for which the HRM department is responsible. Determination of training needs and development and implementation of training programs are important tasks in any organization. Succession planning includes handling the departure of managers and making current employees ready to take on managerial roles when a manager does leave.
6. *Regulatory issues and worker safety.* Keeping up to date on new regulations relating to employment, health care, and other issues is generally a responsibility that falls on the HRM department.

In smaller organizations, the manager or owner is likely performing the HRM functions.[2] They hire people, train them, and determine how much they should be paid. Larger organizations ultimately perform the same tasks, but because they have more employees, they can afford to employ specialists, or human resource managers, to handle these areas of the public organization. As a result, it is highly likely that you, as a manager or entrepreneur, will be performing HRM tasks, hence the value in understanding the strategic components of HRM.

HRM vs. Personnel Management

Human resource strategy is an elaborate and systematic plan of action developed by a human resource department. This definition tells us that an HR strategy includes detailed pathways to implement HRM strategic plans and HR plans. Think of theHRM strategic plan as the major objectives the organization wants to achieve, and the HR plan as the specific activities carried out to achieve the strategic plan. In other words, the strategic plan may include long-term goals, while the HR plan may include short-term objectives that are tied to the overall strategic plan. As mentioned at the beginning of this chapter, human resource departments in the past were called personnel departments. This term implies that the department provided "support" for the rest of the organization. Organizations now understand that the human side of the public organization is the most important asset in any public organization (especially in this global economy), and therefore HR has much more importance than it did twenty years ago. While personnel management mostly involved activities surrounding the hiring process and legal compliance, human resources involves much more, including strategic planning, which is the focus of this chapter. The Ulrich HR model, a common way to look at HRM strategic planning, provides an overall view of the role of HRM in the organization. His model is said to have started the movement that changed the view of HR; no longer merely a functional area, HR became more of a partnership within the organization. While his model has changed over the years, the current model looks at alignment of HR activities with the overall global public organization strategy to form a strategic partnership.[3] His newly revised model looks at five main areas of HR:

1. *Strategic partner.* Partnership with the entire organization to ensure alignment of the HR function with the needs of the organization.
2. *Change agent.* The skill to anticipate and respond to change within the HR function, but as a organizational as a whole.
3. *Administrative expert and functional expert.* The ability to understand and implement policies, procedures, and processes that relate to the HR strategic plan.
4. *Human capital developer.* Means to develop talent that is projected to be needed in the future.
5. *Employee advocate.* Works for employees currently within the organization.

According to Ulrich,[4] implementation of this model must happen with an understanding of the overall organizational objectives, problems, challenges, and opportunities. For example, the HR professional must understand the dynamic nature of the HRM environment, such as changes in labor markets, organizational culture and values, customers, shareholders, and the economy. Once this occurs, HR can determine how best to meet the needs of the organization within these five main areas.

HRM AS A STRATEGIC COMPONENT OF THE PUBLIC ORGANIZATION

Keeping the Ulrich model in mind, consider these four aspects when creating a good HRM strategic plan:

1. Make it applicable. Often people spend an inordinate amount of time developing plans, but the plans sit in a file somewhere and are never actually used. A good strategic plan should be the guiding principles for the HRM function. It should be reviewed and changed as aspects of the public organization change. Involvement of all members in the HR department (if it's a larger department) and communication among everyone within the department will make the plan better.
2. Be a strategic partner. Alignment of organizational values in the HRM strategic plan should be a major objective of the plan. In addition, the HRM strategic plan should be aligned with the mission and objectives of the organization as a whole. For example, if the mission of the organization is to promote social responsibility, then the HRM strategic plan should address this in the hiring criteria.
3. Involve people. An HRM strategic plan cannot be written alone. The plan should involve everyone in the organization. For example, as the plan develops, the HR manager should meet with various people in departments and find out what skills the best employees have. Then the HR manager can make sure the people recruited and interviewed have similar qualities as the best people already doing the job. In addition, the HR manager will likely want to meet with the financial department and executives who do the budgeting, so they can determine human resource needs and recruit the right number of people at the right times. In addition, once the HR department determines what is needed, communicating a plan can gain positive feedback that ensures the plan is aligned with the public organization objectives.
4. Understand how technology can be used. Organizations oftentimes do not have the money or the inclination to research software and find budget-friendly options for implementation. People are sometimes nervous about new technology. However, the best organizations are those that embrace technology and find the right technology uses for their public organizationes. There are thousands of HRM software options that can make the HRM processes faster, easier, and more effective. Good strategic plans address this aspect.

HR managers know the public organization and therefore know the needs of the public organization and can develop a plan to meet those needs. They also stay on top of current events, so they know what is happening globally that could affect their strategic plan. If they find out, for example, that an economic downturn is looming, they will adjust their strategic plan. In other words, the strategic plan needs to be a living document, one that changes as the public organization and the world changes.

HUMAN RESOURCE RECALL

Have you ever looked at your organization's strategic plan? What areas does the plan address?

The Steps to Strategic Plan Creation

HRM strategic plans must have several elements to be successful. There should be a distinction made here: the HRM strategic plan is different from the HR plan. Think of the HRM strategic plan as the major objectives the organization wants to achieve, while the HR plan consists of the detailed plans to ensure the strategic plan is achieved. Oftentimes the strategic plan is viewed as just another report that must be written. Rather than jumping in and writing it without much thought, it is best to give the plan careful consideration.

Table 2.2 Lifecycle Stages and HRM Strategy

Life Cycle Stage	Staffing	Compensation	Training and Development	Labor / Employee Relations
Introduction	Attract best technical and professional talent.	Meet or exceed labor market rates to attract needed talent.	Define future skill requirements and begin establishing career ladders.	Set basic employee-relations philosophy of organization.
Growth	Recruit adequate numbers and mix of qualifying workers. Plan management succession. Manage rapid internal labor market movements.	Meet external market but consider internal equity effects. Establish formal compensation structures.	Mold effective management team through management development and organizational development.	Maintain labor peace, employee motivation, and morale.
Maturity	Encourage sufficient turnover to minimize layoffs and provide new openings. Encourage mobility as reorganizations shift jobs around.	Control compensation costs.	Maintain flexibility and skills of an aging workforce.	Control labor costs and maintain labor peace. Improve productivity.
Decline	Plan and implement workforce reductions and reallocations; downsizing and outplacement may occur during this stage.	Implement tighter cost control.	Implement retraining and career consulting services.	Improve productivity and achieve flexibility in work rules. Negotiate job security and employment-adjustment policies.

Source: Seattle University Presentation, accessed July 11, 2011, http://fac-staff.seattleu.edu/gprussia/web/mgt383/HR%20Planning1.ppt

Conduct a Strategic Analysis

A strategic analysis looks at three aspects of the individual HRM department:

1. Understanding of the organizational mission and values. It is impossible to plan for HRM if one does not know the values and missions of the organization. As we have already addressed in this chapter, it is imperative for the HR manager to align department objectives with organizational objectives. It is worthwhile to sit down with organizational executives, management, and supervisors to make sure you have a good understanding of the organizational mission and values.
2. Another important aspect is the understanding of the organizational life cycle. You may have learned about the life cycle in marketing or other public organization classes, and this applies to HRM, too. An organizational life cycle refers to the introduction, growth, maturity, and decline of the organization, which can vary over time. For example,

   when the organization first begins, it is in the introduction phase, and a different staffing, compensation, training, and labor/employee relations strategy may be necessary to align HRM with the organization's goals. This might be opposed to an organization that is struggling to stay in public organization and is in the decline phase. That same organization, however, can create a new product, for example, which might again put the organization in the growth phase. Table 2.2 "Lifecycle Stages and HRM Strategy" explains some of the strategies that may be different depending on the organizational life cycle.
3. Understanding of the HRM department mission and values. HRM departments must develop their own departmental mission and values. These guiding principles for the department will change as the organizational's overall mission and values change. Often the mission statement is a list of what the department does, which is less of a strategic approach. Brainstorming about HR goals, values, and priorities is a good way to start. The mission statement should express how an organization's human resources help that organization meet the public organization goals. A poor mission statement might read as follows: "The human resource department at Techno, Inc. provides resources to hiring managers and develops compensation plans

and other services to assist the employees of our organizational."

4. A strategic statement that expresses how human resources help the organization might read as follows: "HR's responsibility is to ensure that our human resources are more talented and motivated than our competitors', giving us a competitive advantage. This will be achieved by monitoring our turnover rates, compensation, and organizational sales data and comparing that data to our competitors."_[5] When the mission statement is written in this way, it is easier to take a strategic approach with the HR planning process.
5. Understanding of the challenges facing the department. HRM managers cannot deal with change quickly if they are not able to predict changes. As a result, the HRM manager should know what upcoming challenges may be faced to make plans to deal with those challenges better when they come along. This makes the strategic plan and HRM plan much more usable.

Identify Strategic HR Issues

In this step, the HRM professionals will analyze the challenges addressed in the first step. For example, the department may see that it is not strategically aligned with the organizational's mission and values and opt to make changes to its departmental mission and values as a result of this information.

Many organizations and departments will use a strategic planning tool that identifies strengths, weaknesses, opportunities, and threats (SWOT analysis) to determine some of the issues they are facing. Once this analysis is performed for the public organization, HR can align itself with the needs of the public organization by understanding the public organization strategy. See Table 2.3 "Sample HR Department SWOT Analysis for Techno, Inc." for an example of how a organizational's SWOT analysis can be used to develop a SWOT analysis for the HR department.

Once the alignment of the organizational SWOT is completed, HR can develop its own SWOT analysis to determine the gaps between HR's strategic plan and the organizational's strategic plan. For example, if the HR manager finds that a department's strength is its numerous training programs, this is something the organization should continue doing. If a weakness is the organization's lack of consistent compensation throughout all job titles, then the opportunity to review and revise the compensation policies presents itself. In other words, the organizational's SWOT analysis provides a basis to address some of the issues in the organization, but it can be whittled down to also address issues within the department.

Table 2.3 Sample HR Department SWOT Analysis for Techno, Inc.

Strengths	Hiring talented people
	Organizational growth
	Technology implementation for public organization processes
	Excellent relationship between HRM and management/executives
Weaknesses	No strategic plan for HRM
	No planning for up/down cycles
	No formal training processes
	Lacking of software needed to manage public organization processes, including go-to-market staffing strategies
Opportunities	Development of HRM staffing plan to meet industry growth
	HRM software purchase to manage training, staffing, assessment needs for an unpredictable public organization cycle
	Continue development of HRM and executive relationship by attendance and participation in key meetings and decision-making processes
	Develop training programs and outside development opportunities to continue development of in-house marketing expertise
Threats	Economy
	Changing technology

Prioritize Issues and Actions

Based on the data gathered in the last step, the HRM manager should prioritize the goals and then put action plans together to deal with these challenges. For example, if an organization identifies that they lack a comprehensive training program, plans should be developed that address this need. An important aspect of this step is the involvement of the management and executives in the organization. Once you have a list of issues you will address, discuss them with the management and executives, as they may see other issues or other priorities differently than you. Remember, to be effective, HRM must work with the organization and assist the organization in meeting goals. This should be considered in every aspect of HRM planning.

Draw Up an HRM Plan

Once the HRM manager has met with executives and management, and priorities have been agreed upon, the plans are ready to be developed. Sometimes organizations have great strategic plans, but when the development of the details occurs, it can be difficult to align the strategic plan with the more detailed plans. An HRM manager should always refer to the overall strategic plan before developing the HRM strategic plan and HR plans.

Even if a organizational does not have an HR department, HRM strategic plans and HR plans should still be developed by management. By developing and monitoring these plans, the organization can ensure the right processes are implemented to meet the ever-changing needs of the organization. The strategic plan looks at the organization as a whole, the HRM strategic plan looks at the department as a whole, and the HR plan addresses specific issues in the human resource department.

KEY TAKEAWAYS

- Personnel management and HRM are different ways of looking at the job duties of human resources. Twenty years ago, personnel management focused on administrative aspects. HRM today involves a strategic process, which requires working with other departments, managers, and executives to be effective and meet the needs of the organization.
- In general, HRM focuses on several main areas, which include staffing, policy development, compensation and benefits, retention issues, training and development, and regulatory issues and worker protection.
- To be effective, the HR manager needs to utilize technology and involve others.
- As part of strategic planning, HRM should conduct a strategic analysis, identify HR issues, determine and prioritize actions, and then draw up the HRM plan.

EXERCISES

1. What is the difference between HR plans and HRM strategic plans? How are they the same? How are they different?
2. Of the areas of focus in HRM, which one do you think is the most important? Rank them and discuss the reasons for your rankings.

---

[1] Michael Losey, "HR Comes of Age," HR Magazine, March 15, 1998, accessed July 11, 2011,http://findarticles.com/p/articles/mi_m3495/is_n3_v43/ai_20514399.
[2] Jan de Kok and Lorraine M. Uhlaner, "Organization Context and Human Resource Management in the Small Firm" (Tinbergen Institute Discussion Papers 01-038/3, Tinbergen Institute, 2001), accessed August 13, 2011, http://ideas.repec.org/s/dgr/uvatin.html.
[3] David Ulrich and Wayne Brockbank, The HR Value Proposition (Boston: Harvard Public organization Press, 2005), 9–14.
[4] David Ulrich, "Evaluating the Ulrich Model," Acerta, 2011, accessed July 11, 2011,http://www.goingforhr.be/extras/web-specials/hr-according-to-dave-ulrich#ppt_2135261.
[5] Gary Kaufman, "How to Fix HR," Harvard Public organization Review, September 2006, accessed July 11, 2011, http://hbr.org/2006/09/how-to-fix-hr/ar/1.

2.2 Writing the HRM Plan

LEARNING OBJECTIVE

1. Describe the steps in the development of an HRM plan.

The writing of an HRM strategic plan should be based on the strategic plans of the organization and of the department. Once the strategic plan is written, the HR professional can begin work on the HR plan. This is different from the strategic plan in that it is more detailed and more focused on the short term.

HOW WOULD YOU HANDLE THIS?

Compensation Is a Touchy Subject

As the HR manager, you have access to sensitive data, such as pay information. As you are looking at pay for each employee in the marketing department, you notice that two employees with the same job title and performing the same job are earning different amounts of money. As you dig deeper, you notice the employee who has been with the organizational for the least amount of time is actually getting paid more than the person with longer tenure. A brief look at the performance evaluations shows they are both star performers. You determine that two different managers hired the employees, and one manager is no longer with the organization. How would you handle this?

Figure 2.3

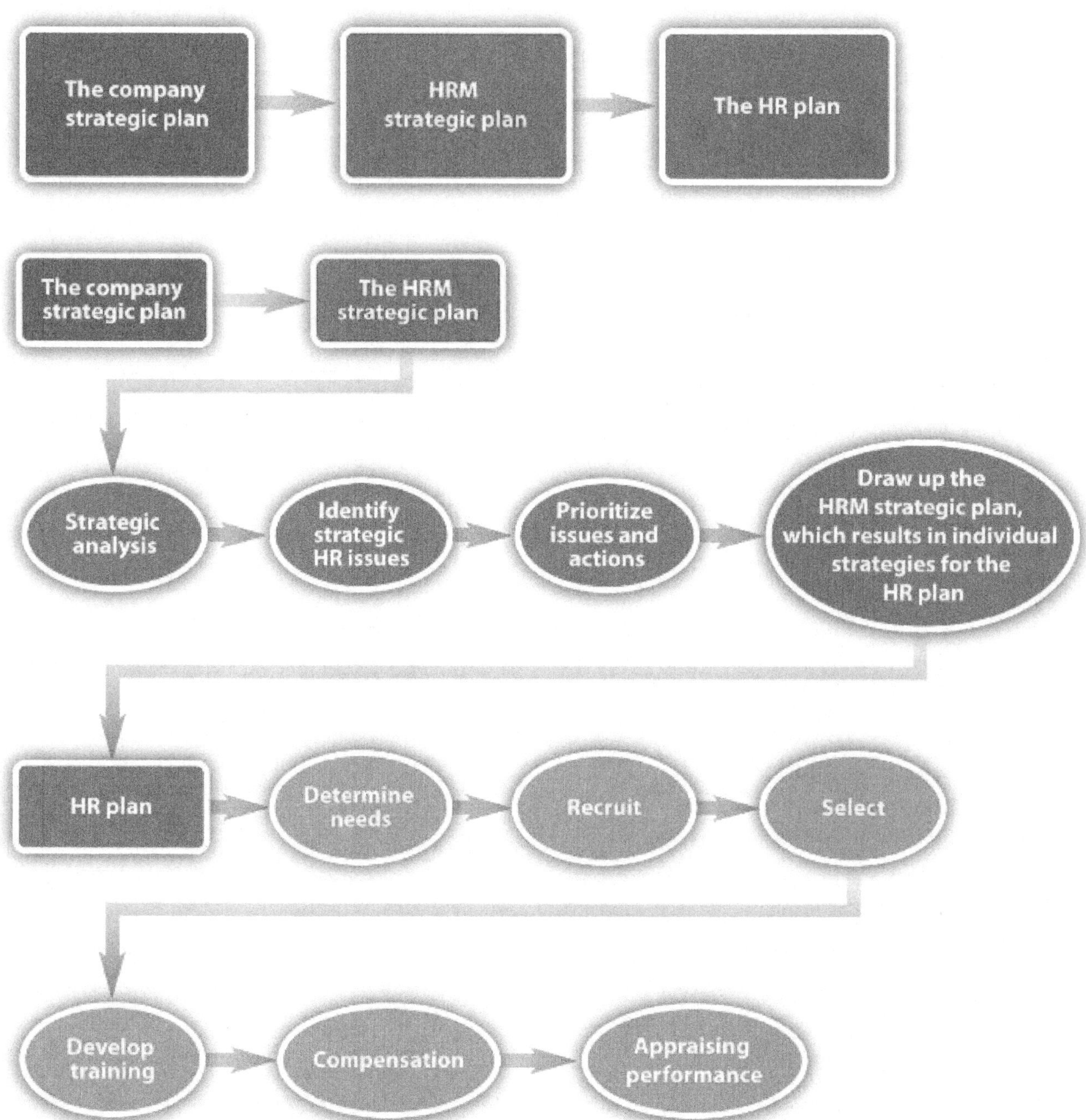

The six parts of the HRM plan include the following:

1. *Determine human resource needs.* This part is heavily involved with the strategic plan. What growth or decline is expected in the organization? How will this impact your workforce? What is the economic situation? What are your forecasted sales for next year?
2. *Determine recruiting strategy.* Once you have a plan in place, it's necessary to write down a strategy addressing how you will recruit the right people at the right time.
3. *Select employees.* The selection process consists of the interviewing and hiring process.
4. *Develop training.* Based on the strategic plan, what training needs are arising? Is there new software that everyone must learn? Are there problems in handling conflict? Whatever the training topics are, the HR manager should address plans to offer training in the HRM plan.
5. *Determine compensation.* In this aspect of the HRM plan, the manager must determine pay scales and other compensation such as health care, bonuses, and other perks.

6. *Appraise performance.* Sets of standards need to be developed so you know how to rate the performance of your employees and continue with their development.

Determine Human Resource Needs

The first part of an HR plan will consist of determining how many people are needed. This step involves looking at organizational operations over the last year and asking a lot of questions:

1. Were enough people hired?
2. Did you have to scramble to hire people at the last minute?
3. What are the skills your current employees possess?
4. What skills do your employees need to gain to keep up with technology?
5. Who is retiring soon? Do you have someone to replace them?
6. What are the sales forecasts? How might this affect your hiring?

These are the questions to answer in this first step of the HR plan process. As you can imagine, this cannot be done alone. Involvement of other departments, managers, and executives should take place to obtain an accurate estimate of staffing needs for now and in the future.

Many HR managers will prepare an inventory of all current employees, which includes their educational level and abilities. This gives the HR manager the big picture on what current employees can do. It can serve as a tool to develop employees' skills and abilities, if you know where they are currently in their development. For example, by taking an inventory, you may find out that Richard is going to retire next year, but no one in his department has been identified or trained to take over his role. Keeping the inventory helps you know where gaps might exist and allows you to plan for these gaps.

HR managers will also look closely at all job components and will analyze each job. By doing this analysis, they can get a better picture of what kinds of skills are needed to perform a job successfully. Once the HR manager has performed the needs assessment and knows exactly how many people, and in what positions and time frame they need to be hired, he or she can get to work on recruiting, which is also called astaffing plan.

Recruit

Recruitment is an important job of the HR manager. Knowing how many people to hire, what skills they should possess, and hiring them when the time is right are major challenges in the area of recruiting. Hiring individuals who have not only the skills to do the job but also the attitude, personality, and fit can be the biggest challenge in recruiting. Depending on the type of job you are hiring for, you might place traditional advertisements on the web or use social networking sites as an avenue. Some organizations offer bonuses to employees who refer friends. No matter where you decide to recruit, it is important to keep in mind that the recruiting process should be fair and equitable and diversity should be considered.

Depending on availability and time, some organizations may choose to outsource their recruiting processes. For some types of high-level positions, a head hunter will be used to recruit people nationally and internationally. A head hunter is a person who specializes in matching jobs with people, and they usually work only with high-level positions. Another option is to use an agency that specializes in hiring people for a variety of positions, including temporary and permanent positions. Some organizations decide to hire temporary employees because they anticipate only a short-term need, and it can be less expensive to hire someone for only a specified period of time.

No matter how it is done, recruitment is the process of obtaining résumés of people interested in the job. In our next step, we review those résumés, interview, and select the best person for the job.

Select

After you have reviewed résumés for a position, now is the time to work toward selecting the right person for the job. Numerous studies have been done, and while they have various results, the majority of studies say it costs an average of $45,000 to hire a new manager.[1] While this may seem exaggerated, consider the following items that contribute to the cost:

1. Time to review résumés
2. Time to interview candidates
3. Interview expenses for candidates
4. Possible travel expenses for new hire or recruiter
5. Possible relocation expenses for new hire
6. Additional bookkeeping, payroll, 401(k), and so forth
7. Additional record keeping for government agencies
8. Increased unemployment insurance costs
9. Costs related to lack of productivity while new employee gets up to speed

Because it is so expensive to hire, it is important to do it right. First, résumés are reviewed and people who closely match the right skills are selected for interviews. Many organizations perform phone interviews first so they can further narrow the field. The HR manager is generally responsible for setting up the interviews and determining the interview schedule for a particular candidate. Usually, the more senior the position is, the longer the interview process takes, even up to eight weeks.[2] After the interviews are conducted, there may be reference checks, background checks, or testing that will need to be performed before an offer is made to the new employee. HR managers are generally responsible for this aspect. Once the applicant has met all criteria, the HR manager will offer the selected person the position. At this point, salary, benefits, and vacation time may be negotiated. Compensation is the next step in HR management.

Determine Compensation

What you decide to pay people is much more difficult than it seems. Pay systems must be developed that motivate employees and embody fairness to everyone working at the organization. However, organizations cannot offer every benefit and perk because budgets always have constraints. Even governmental agencies need to be concerned with compensation as part of their HR plan. For example, in 2011, Illinois State University gave salary increases of 3 percent to all faculty, despite state budget cuts in other areas. They reasoned that the pay increase was needed because of the competitive nature of hiring and retaining faculty and staff. The university president said, "Our employees have had a very good year and hopefully this is a good shot in the arm that will keep our morale high."[3]

The process in determining the right pay for the right job can have many variables, in addition to keeping morale high. First, as we have already discussed, the organization life cycle can determine the pay strategy for the organization. The supply and demand of those skills in the market, economy, region, or area in which the public organization is located is a determining factor in compensation strategy. For example, a organizational operating in Seattle may pay higher for the same job than their division in Missoula, Montana, because the cost of living is higher in Seattle. The HR manager is always researching to ensure the pay is fair and at market value. Employees can develop their skills while getting paid for it. Training is the next step in the HR planning process.

Develop Training

Once we have planned our staffing, recruited people, selected employees, and then compensated them, we want to make sure our new employees are successful. One way we can ensure success is by training our employees in three main areas:

1. *Organizational culture.* A organizational culture is the organization's way of doing things. Every organizational does things a bit differently, and by understanding the organizational culture, the employee will be set up for success. Usually this type of training is performed at an orientation, when an employee is first hired. Topics might include how to request time off, dress codes, and processes.
2. *Skills needed for the job.* If you work for a retail store, your employees need to know how to use the register. If you have sales staff, they need to have product knowledge to do the job. If your organizational uses particular software, training is needed in this area.
3. *Human relations skills.* These are non-job-specific skills your employees need not only to do their jobs but also to make them all-around successful employees. Skills needed include communication skills and interviewing potential employees.

Perform a Performance Appraisal

The last thing an HR manager should plan is the performance appraisal. Aperformance appraisal is a method by which job performance is measured. The performance appraisal can be called many different things, such as the following:

1. Employee appraisal
2. Performance review
3. 360 review
4. Career development review

No matter what the name, these appraisals can be very beneficial in motivating and rewarding employees. The performance evaluation includes metrics on which the employee is measured. These metrics should be based on the job description, both of which the HR manager develops. Various types of rating systems can be used, and it's usually up to the HR manager to develop these as well as employee evaluation forms. The HR manager also usually ensures that every manager in the organization is trained on how to fill out the evaluation forms, but more importantly, how to discuss job performance with the employee. Then the HR manager tracks the due dates of performance appraisals and sends out e-mails to those managers letting them know it is almost time to write an evaluation.

HUMAN RESOURCE RECALL

Have you ever been given a performance evaluation? What was the process and the outcome?

KEY TAKEAWAYS

- Human resource planning is a process that is part of the strategic plan. It involves addressing specific needs within the organization, based on the organizational's strategic direction.
- The first step in HR planning is determining current and future human resource needs. In this step, current employees, available employees in the market, and future needs are all analyzed and developed.
- In the second step of the process, once we know how many people we will need to hire, we can begin to determine the best methods for recruiting the people we need. Sometimes an organization will use head hunters to find the best person for the job.
- After the recruiting process is finished, the HR manager will begin the selection process. This involves setting up interviews and selecting the right person for the job. This can be an expensive process, so we always want to hire the right person from the beginning.
- HR managers also need to work through compensation plans, including salary, bonus, and other benefits, such as health care. This aspect is important, since most organizations want to use compensation to attract and retain the best employees.
- The HR manager also develops training programs to ensure the people hired have the tools to be able to do their jobs successfully.

EXERCISES

1. Of the parts of HR planning, which do you think is most difficult, and why? Which would you enjoy the most, and why?
2. Why is it important to plan your staffing before you start to hire people?
3. What is the significance of training? Why do we need it in organizations?

---

[1] Susan Herman, Hiring Right: A Practical Guide (Thousand Oaks, CA: Sage, 1993), xv.
[2] John Crant, "How Long Does an Interview Process Take?" Jobsinminneapolis.com, December 2, 2009, accessed October 28, 2010,http://www.jobsinminneapolis.com/articles/title/How-Long-Does-an-Interview-Process-Take/3500/422.
[3] Stephanie Pawlowski, "Illinois State University to Get Salary Bump," WJBC Radio, July 11, 2011, accessed July 11, 2011, http://wjbc.com/illinois-state-university-faculty-to-get-salary-bump.

2.3 Tips in HRM Planning

LEARNING OBJECTIVE

1. Explain the aspects needed to create a usable and successful HRM plan.

As you have learned from this chapter, human resource strategic planning involves understanding your organizational's strategic plan and HR's role in the organization. The planning aspect meets the needs of the strategic plan by knowing how many people should be hired, how many people are needed, and what kind of training they need to meet the goals of the organization. This section gives some tips on successful HR strategic planning.

ORGANIZATIONAL FOCUS

Like many Organizational organizations throughout the world, IBM in India finds that picking the best prospects for job postings isn't always easy. By using advanced analytics, however, it aims to connect the strategic plan, staffing needs, and the hiring process using a simple tool. The project was originally developed to assign people to projects internally at IBM, but IBM found this tool able to not only extract essential details like the number of years of experience but also make qualitative judgments, such as how good the person actually is for the job._[1] This makes the software unique, as most résumé-scanning software programs can only search for specific keywords and are not able to assess the job fit or tie the criteria directly to the overall strategic plan. The project uses IBM India's spoken web technology, in which the prospective employee answers a few questions, creating the equivalent of voice résumé. Then using these voice résumés, the hiring manager can easily search for those prospects who meet the needs of the organization and the objectives of the strategic plan.

Some of the challenges noted with this software include the recognition of language and dialect issues. However, the IBM human resources solution is still one of the most sophisticated of such tools to be developed. "Services is very people-intensive. Today, there is talk of a war for talent, but attracting the right kind of people is a challenge, yet unemployment is very high. Our solution applies sophisticated analytics to workforce management," says Manish Gupta, director at IBM Research-India._[2]

It is likely that this is only the beginning of the types of technology that allow HR professionals to tie their HR plans directly to a strategic plan with the touch of a few buttons.

Link HRM Strategic Plan to Organizational Plan

Understanding the nature of the public organization is key to being successful in creating a strategic plan for HRM. Because every public organization is different, the needs of the public organization may change, depending on the economy, the season, and societal changes in our country. HR managers need to understand all these aspects of the public organization to better predict how many people are needed, what types of training are needed, and how to compensate people, for example. The strategic plan that the HR manager writes should address these issues. To address these issues, the HR manager should develop the departmental goals and HR plans based on the overall goals of the organization. In other words, HR should not operate alone but in tandem with the other parts of the organization. The HRM plan should reflect this.

Monitor the Plan Constantly

Oftentimes a great strategic plan is written, taking lots of time, but isn't actually put into practice for a variety of reasons, such as the following:

1. The plan wasn't developed so that it could be useful.
2. The plan wasn't communicated with management and others in the HRM department.
3. The plan did not meet the budget guidelines of the organization.
4. The plan did not match the strategic outcomes of the organization.
5. There was lack of knowledge on how to actually implement it.

There is no point in developing a plan that isn't going to be used. Developing the plan and then making changes as necessary are important to making it a valuable asset for the organization. A strategic plan should be a living document, in that it changes as organizational or external factors change. People can get too attached to a specific plan or way of doing things and then find it hard to change. The plan needs to change constantly or it won't be of value.

Measure It

A good strategic plan and HR plan should discuss the way "success" will be measured. For example, rather than writing, "Meet the hiring needs of the organization," be more specific: "Based on sales forecasts from our sales department, hire ten people this quarter with the skills to meet our ten job openings." This is a goal that is specific enough to be measured. These types of quantitative data also make it easier to show the relationship between HR and the organization, and better yet, to show how HR adds value to the bottom line. Likewise, if a organizational has a strategic objective to be a safe workplace, you might include a goal to "develop training to meet the needs of the organization." While this is a great goal, how will this be measured? How will you know if you did what you were supposed to do? It might be difficult to measure this with such a general statement. On the other hand, a goal to "develop a safety training workshop and have all employees complete it by the end of the year" is specific and can be measured at the end to determine success.

HUMAN RESOURCE RECALL

What are some of your personal goals? Are these goals measureable?

Sometimes Change Is Necessary

It can be difficult to base an entire plan on forecasted numbers. As a result, an HRM department that is willing to change quickly to meet the needs of the organization proves its worthiness. Consider a sales forecast that called for fifteen new hires, but you find out months later the organization is having a hard time making payroll. Upon digging deeper, you find the sales forecasts were overexaggerated, and now you have fifteen people you don't really need. By monitoring the changes constantly (usually done by asking lots of questions to other departments), you can be sure you are able to change your strategic plan as they come.

Be Aware of Legislative Changes

One of the major challenges in HRM is having an awareness of what is happening from a legal perspective. Because most budgets are based on certain current laws, knowing when the law changes and how it will affect department budgets and planning (such as compensation planning) will create a more solid strategic plan. For example, if the minimum wage goes up in your state and you have minimum wage workers, reworking the budget and communicating this change to your accounting team is imperative in providing value to the organization. We will discuss various legislation throughout this book.

KEY TAKEAWAYS

- As has been the theme throughout this chapter, any HRM plan should be directly linked to the strategic plan of the organization.
- A plan should be constantly updated and revised as things in the organization change.

- A good strategic plan provides tools to determine whether you met the goal. Any plan should have measureable goals so the connection to success is obvious.
- Changes in a strategic plan and in goal setting are necessary as the internal and external environments change. An HR manager should always be aware of changes in forecasts, for example, so the plan can change, too.
- Legislative changes may impact strategic plans and budgets as well. It's important to make sure HR managers are keeping up on these changes and communicating them.

EXERCISES

1. What are some ways an HR manager can keep up on legislative changes? Do a web search and list specific publications that may help keep the HR manager aware of changes.
2. Why is it important to be able to measure strategic plans? What might happen if you don't?

---

[1] Sridhar Chari, "IBM Automates Parsing of Resumes," iStock Analyst, July 11, 2011, accessed July 11, 2011, http://www.istockanalyst.com/public organization/news/5283887/ibm-automates-parsing-of-resumes.
[2] Sridhar Chari, "IBM Automates Parsing of Resumes," iStock Analyst, July 11, 2011, accessed July 11, 2011, http://www.istockanalyst.com/public organization/news/5283887/ibm-automates-parsing-of-resumes.

2.4 Cases and Problems

CHAPTER SUMMARY

- Human resource management was once called the personnel department. In the past, hiring people and working with hiring paperwork was this department's job. Today, the HRM department has a much broader role, and as a result, HR managers must align their strategies with the organizational's strategies.
- Functions that fall under HRM today include staffing, creation of workplace policies, compensation and benefits, retention, training and development, and working with regulatory issues and worker protection.
- Human resource strategy is a set of elaborate and systematic plans of action. The organizational objectives and goals should be aligned with the objectives and goals of the individual departments.
- The steps to creating an HRM strategic plan include conducting a strategic analysis. This entails having an understanding of the values and mission of the organization, so you can align your departmental strategy in the same way.
- The second step is to identify any HR issues that might impact the public organization.
- The third step, based on the information from the first and second steps, is to prioritize issues and take action. Finally, the HRM professional will draw up the HRM plan.
- The HRM plan consists of six steps. The first is to determine the needs of the organization based on sales forecasts, for example. Then the HR professional will recruit and select the right person for the job. HRM develops training and development to help better the skills of existing employees and new employees, too. The HR manager will then determine compensation and appraise performance of employees. Each of these parts of the HRM plan is discussed in its own separate chapter in greater detail.
- As things in the organization change, the strategic plan should also change.
- To make the most from a strategic plan, it's important to write the goals in a way that makes them measurable.

CHAPTER CASE

We Merged…Now What?

Earlier this month, your organizational, a running equipment designer and manufacturer called Runners Paradise, merged with a smaller clothing design organizational called ActiveLeak. Your organizational initiated the buyout because of the excellent design team at ActiveLeak and their brand recognition, specifically for their MP3-integrated running shorts. Runners Paradise has thirty-five employees and ActiveLeak has ten employees. At ActiveLeak, the owner, who often was too busy doing other tasks, handled the HRM roles. As a result, ActiveLeak has no strategic plan, and you are wondering if you should develop a strategic plan, given this change. Here are the things you have accomplished so far:

- Reviewed compensation and adjusted salaries for the sake of fairness. Communicated this to all affected employees.
- Developed job requirements for current and new jobs.
- Had each old and new employee fill out a skills inventory Excel document, which has been merged into a database.
- From this point, you are not sure what to do to fully integrate the new organization.

1. Why should you develop an HRM strategic plan?
2. Which components of your HR plan will you have to change?

3. What additional information would you need to create an action plan for these changes?

TEAM ACTIVITIES

1. Work in a group of three to five people. Choose a organizational and perform a SWOT analysis on that organization and be prepared to present it to the class.
2. Based on the SWOT analysis you performed in the first question, develop new objectives for the organization.

NOTES:

NOTES:

Chapter 3: Diversity and Multiculturalism in Public Organizations

Hiring Multicultural

On a Tuesday afternoon, as you are getting ready to go to lunch, you receive an e-mail from your human resources (HR) manager about the need to hire a new project manager, and there is a $500 bonus for referring a friend who successfully joins the organizational. Immediately, you e-mail your friend Daniel, because you know he would be great for the job. Daniel is eventually hired for the position, and a few months later a new e-mail goes out asking for friend recommendations for a new position. You and Daniel both recommend someone, and eventually that person gets hired. Over the next year, hiring notices are not advertised externally as the organization has had good luck with this hiring practice. Seems like a great way to recruit new people, doesn't it? It can be, but it also can be a detriment to the diversity and multiculturalism of the workplace. How, you might wonder?

While not true across the board, people have a tendency to spend time with people who are like themselves, in race, income level, and other aspects of diversity such as sexual orientation. In fact, according to the National Institute of Child Health and Human Development and a study published in the American Journal of Sociology, it is much more likely that someone will name a person in their own race as a friend than someone of a different race._[1] Likewise, even from a young age, people tend to choose friends who are of the same race. As a result, when you recommend Daniel for a position, it is highly likely that Daniel is similar, from a diversity perspective, to you. Then, when Daniel recommends someone for a job, it is highly likely that he, too, is recommending someone with similar characteristics as you both. This obviously creates a lack of multicultural diversity in the workplace, which can mean lost profits for organizations.

---

[1] James Moody, "Race, School Integration, and Friendship Segregation in America," American Journal of Sociology 107, no. 3 (2001): 679–719.

3.1 Diversity and Multiculturalism

LEARNING OBJECTIVES

1. Define, explain, and identify your own power and privilege.
2. Provide reasoning as to why diversity is important to maintain profitability.

Many people use the terms diversity and multiculturalism interchangeably, when in fact, there are major differences between the two. Diversity is defined as the differences between people. These differences can include race, gender, sexual orientation, religion, background, socioeconomic status, and much more. Diversity, when talking about it from the human resource management (HRM) perspective, tends to focus more on a set of policies to meet compliance standards. The Equal Employment Opportunity Commission (EEOC) oversees complaints in this area.

Multiculturalism goes deeper than diversity by focusing on inclusiveness, understanding, and respect, and also by looking at unequal power in society. In a report called "The 2007 State of Workplace Diversity Management Report,"_[1] most HR managers said that diversity in the workplace is

1. not well defined or understood at work,
2. focuses too much on compliance, and
3. places too much emphasis on gender and ethnicity.

This chapter focuses on the advantages of a diverse workplace and discusses multiculturalism at work and the compliance aspect of diversity.

Power and Privilege

As defined in this chapter, diversity focuses on the "otherness" or differences between individuals and has a goal of making sure, through policies, that everyone is treated the same. While this is the legal and the right thing to do, multiculturalism looks at a system of advantages based on race, gender, and sexual orientation calledpower and privilege. In this system, the advantages are based on a system in which one race, gender, and sexual orientation is predominant in setting societal rules and norms.

The interesting thing about power and privilege is that if you have it, you may not initially recognize it, which is why we can call it invisible privilege. Here are some examples:

1. *Race privilege.* Let's say you (a Caucasian) and your friend (an African American) are having dinner together, and when the bill comes, the server gives the check to you. While this may not seem like a big issue, it assumes you (being Caucasian) are the person paying for the meal. This type of invisible privilege may not seem to matter if

you have that privilege, but if you don't, it can be infuriating.

2. *Social class privilege.* When Hurricane Katrina hit New Orleans in 2005, many people from outside the storm area wondered why so many people stayed in the city, not even thinking about the fact that some people couldn't afford the gas to put in their car to leave the city.
3. *Gender privilege.* This refers to privileges one gender has over another—for example, the assumption that a female will change her name to her husband's when they get married.
4. *Sexual orientation privilege.* If I am heterosexual, I can put a picture of my partner on my desk without worrying about what others think. I can talk about our vacations together or experiences we've had without worrying what someone might think about my relationship. This is not the case for many gay, lesbian, and transgendered people and their partners.

Oftentimes the privilege we have is considered invisible, because it can be hard to recognize one's own privilege based on race, gender, or social class. Many people utilize the color-blind approach, which says, "I treat everyone the same" or "I don't see people's skin color." In this case, the person is showing invisible privilege and thus ignoring the privileges he or she receives because of race, gender, or social class. While it appears this approach would value all people equally, it doesn't, because people's different needs, assets, and perspectives are disregarded by not acknowledging differences.[2]

Another important aspect of power and privilege is the fact that we may have privilege in one area and not another. For example, I am a Caucasian female, which certainly gives me race privilege but not gender privilege. Important to note here is that the idea of power and privilege is not about "white male bashing" but understanding our own stereotypes and systems of advantage so we can be more inclusive with our coworkers, employees, and managers.

So what does this all mean in relation to HRM? It means we can combine the understanding of certain systems that allow for power and privilege, and by understanding we may be able to eliminate or at least minimize these issues. Besides this, one of the best things we can do for our organizations is to have a diverse workforce, with people from a variety of perspectives. This diversity leads to profitability and the ability to better serve customers.

HUMAN RESOURCE RECALL

Take this week to examine your own power and privilege as a result of gender, race, or social class. Notice how people treat you because of your skin color, gender, or how you dress and talk.

STEREOTYPES AND THE EFFECT ON PRIVILEGE

This video discusses some racial stereotypes and white privilege through "on the street" interviews.
Please view this video at http://www.youtube.com/watch?v=Q1wztUJ4VVE.

Why Diversity and Multiculturalism?

When many people look at diversity and multiculturalism, they think that someone's gender, skin color, or social class shouldn't matter. So diversity can help us with policies to prevent discrimination, while multiculturalism can help us gain a deeper understanding of the differences between people. Hopefully, over time, rather than look at diversity as attaining numerical goals or complying with the law, we can combine the concepts to create better workplaces. Although many books discuss laws relating to diversity, not many actually describe why diversity is necessary in the workplace. Here are a few main reasons:

1. It is the law.
2. We can better serve customers by offering a broader range of services, such as being able to speak a variety of languages and understanding other cultures.
3. We can better communicate with one another (saving time and money) and customers.
4. With a multicultural perspective, we can create better ideas and solutions.

ORGANIZATIONAL FOCUS

Hilton is one of the most recognized names in the hotel industry. Hilton employs 130,000 people in 3,750 hotels in 84 countries. The hotel chain, with some locations franchised, focuses on diversity and inclusion as part of its operations. First, it has a director of global diversity and inclusion, who plays a key role in executing the Hilton global diversity and inclusion efforts, which are focused on culture, talent, workplace, and marketplace diversity strategies. Each Hilton brand must establish its own diversity performance goals and initiatives, which are monitored by the diversity council. The diversity council is made up of the organizational board of directors, the CEO, and vice president of human resources. At any given time, Hilton has thirty or more diversity initiatives in place,[3] which are managed by the diversity council.

Hilton has created several diversity programs within the communities in which the hotels operate. For example, Hilton was one of the first hotel chains to develop an outreach program to educate minority and female entrepreneurs for franchise investments. One part of the program includes invitation-only seminars that discuss what it takes to be a successful hotel owner. Hilton says its diversity seminars are driven by the fact that it wants employees to reflect the diversity of the customers.

In addition to the outreach program, Hilton partners with historically black colleges and universities for recruiting, which creates an effective tie to jobs once students graduate. It has developed a supplier tracking system, so it knows the total number of supplier payments made and how many of those suppliers are female or minorities. William A. Holland, the vice president for workforce planning and analysis says, "It takes leadership to make diversity work, and our diversity initiative comes from the highest levels of our organization."_[4]

Promoting a multicultural work environment isn't just the law. Through a diverse work environment and multicultural understanding, organizations can attain greater profitability. A study by Cedric Herring called Does Diversity Pay?_[5] reveals that diversity does, in fact, pay. The study found those public organizationes with greater racial diversity reporter higher sales revenues, more customers, larger market shares, and greater relative profits than those with more homogeneous workforces. Other research on the topic by Scott Page, the author of The Difference: How the Power of Diversity Creates Better Groups, Firms, Schools, and Societies_[6] ended up with similar results. Page found that people from varied backgrounds are more effective at working together than those who are from similar backgrounds, because they offer different approaches and perspectives in the development of solutions. Often people believe that diversity is about checking a box or only providing window dressing to gain more customers, but this isn't the case. As put by Eric Foss, chairperson and CEO of Pepsi Beverages Organizational, "It's not a fad. It's not an idea of the month. It's central and it's linked very directly to public organization strategy."_[7] A study by the late Roy Adler of Pepperdine University shows similar results. His 19-year study of 215 Organizational organizations shows a strong correlation between female executives and high profitability._[8] Another study, conducted by Project Equality, found that organizations that rated low on equal opportunity issues earned 7.9 percent profit, while those who rated highest with more equal opportunities resulted in 18.3 percent profit._[9] These numbers show that diversity and multiculturalism certainly is not a fad, but a way of doing public organization that better serves customers and results in higher profits.

As managers, we need to recognize this and develop policies that recognize not only the importance of diversity but the importance of nurturing multicultural understanding in the workplace. Many employees, however, may be resistant to a discussion on diversity and multiculturalism. Much of this may have to do with their own power and privilege, but some resistance may be related to the discomfort people may feel when faced with the realization that change is a necessity and the cultural makeup of the workplace is changing. Some people may feel "We've always done it this way" and are less willing to change to the new ways of doing things.

Perhaps one of the best diversity statements by a Organizational organizational was made by Jose Manuel Souto, the CFO for Visa in Latin America. He says, "A diverse workforce is critical to providing the best service to our global clients, supporting our public organization initiatives, and creating a workplace environment that promotes respect and fairness."[10]

KEY TAKEAWAYS

- Diversity is the real or perceived differences between individuals. This can include race, gender, sexual orientation, size, cultural background, and much more.
- Multiculturalism is a term that is similar to diversity, but it focuses on development of a greater understanding of how power in society can be unequal due to race, gender, sexual orientation, power, and privilege.
- Power and privilege is a system of advantages based on one's race, gender, and sexual orientation. This system can often be invisible (to those who have it), which results in one race or gender having unequal power in the workplace. Of course, this unequal power results in unfairness, which may be of legal concern.
- Diversity is important to the success of organizations. Many studies have shown a direct link between the amount of diversity in a workplace and the organizational's success.

EXERCISES

1. Perform an Internet search to find a specific diversity policy for an organization. What is the

policy? From what you know of the organization, do you believe they follow this policy in reality?
2. Visit the website http://www.diversityinc.com and find their latest "top 50 list." What criteria are used to appear on this list? What are the top five organizations for the current year?

---

[1] Society for Human Resource Management, The 2007 State of Workplace Diversity Management Report, March 2008, accessed August 3, 2011,http://www.shrm.org/Publications/HRNews/Pages/DiversityPublicorganizationImperative.aspx.
[2] Victoria C. Plaut, Kecia M. Thomas, and Matt J. Goren, "Is Multiculturalism or Color Blindness Better for Minorities?" Psychological Science 20, no. 4 (2009): 444–46.
[3] Jason Forsythe, "Leading with Diversity," New York Times, 2005, accessed July 13, 2011,http://www.nytimes.com/marketing/jobmarket/diversity/hilton.html.
[4] Jason Forsythe, "Leading with Diversity," New York Times, 2005, accessed July 13, 2011,http://www.nytimes.com/marketing/jobmarket/diversity/hilton.html.
[5] Cedric Herring, "Does Diversity Pay? Racial Composition of Firms and the Public organization Case for Diversity" (paper presented at the annual meeting of the American Sociological Association, Montreal, Canada, August 11, 2006), accessed May 5, 2009,http://citation.allacademic.com/meta/p_mla_apa_research_citation/1/0/1/7/9/pages101792/p101792-1.php.
[6] Scott E. Page, The Difference: How the Power of Diversity Creates Better Groups, Firms, Schools, and Societies (Princeton, NJ: Princeton University Press, 2007).
[7] William J. Holstein, "Diversity is Even More Important in Hard Times," New York Times, February 13, 2009, accessed August 25, 2011,http://www.nytimes.com/2009/02/14/public organization/14interview.html.
[8] Roy Adler, "Women in the Executive Suite Correlate to High Profits," Glass Ceiling Research Center.
[9] Melissa Lauber, "Studies Show That Diversity in Workplace Is Profitable," Project Equality, n.d., accessed July 11, 2011, http://www.villagelife.org/news/archives/diversity.html.
[10] National Latina Public organization Women Association, "Women and Minorities on Organizational Boards Still Lags Far Behind National Population," accessed August 24, 2011,http://nlbwa.org/component/content/article/64-nationalnews/137-procon-and-asian-global-sourcing-conference.

3.2 Diversity Plans

LEARNING OBJECTIVES

1. Be able to apply strategies to create a multicultural work environment and diversity plans.
2. Be able to create an HR plan with diversity considerations.

While state and federal laws must be followed to ensure multiculturalism, the culture of the organizational and the way the organization operates can contribute to the nurturing of a multicultural environment (or not). Most organizations have a formalized and written antidiscrimination and harassment policy. For example, Zappos's policy states, "The diversity of Zappos' employees is a tremendous asset. We are firmly committed to providing equal opportunity in all aspects of employment and will not tolerate any illegal discrimination or harassment. Examples of such behavior include derogatory comments based on racial or ethnic characteristics and unwelcome sexual advances. Please refer to the applicable sections of the Employee Handbook for further guidance."[1]

Implementing a policy is an excellent first step, but what is important is how the organizational acts on those formalized processes and written policies. Let's say, for example, an organization has a published policy on inclusion of those with physical disabilities, but much "schmoozing" and relationship development with managers takes place on the golf course on Friday afternoons. While the policy states the organizational doesn't discriminate, their actions and "traditions" show otherwise and do discriminate against those with disabilities. If this is where the informal work and relationship building take place, an entire group could be left out of this process, likely resulting in lower pay and promotion rates. Likewise, organizations that have a "beer Friday" environment may discriminate against those whose religions do not condone drinking alcohol. While none of these situations are examples of blatant discrimination, a organizational's culture can contribute to an environment that is exclusive rather than inclusive.

Many organizations have developed diversity management plans that are tied to the written diversity policy of the organization. In fact, in many larger organizations, such as Hilton, manager- or director-level positions have been created to specifically manage diversity plans and programs. Josh Greenberg, a researcher in the area of workplace diversity, contends that organizations with specific diversity plans tend to be able to facilitate changes more quickly than organizations without diversity plans.[2] He says there are three main steps to creating diversity plans:

1. *Assessment of diversity.* Employee satisfaction surveys, discussions, and open forums that can provide insight into the challenges and obstacles to diversity. Inclusion of all workers for input is necessary to create a useful plan.
2. *Development of the diversity plan.* Based on step 1, a series of attainable and measurable goals should be developed regarding workplace diversity.
3. *Implementation of the plan.* The commitment of executives and management is necessary. Formulating action plans based on the goals developed in step 2 and assignment

of implementation and measurement of those plans must follow. The action plan should be the responsibility of the entire organization, not just the director of diversity or human resources.

Recruitment and Selection

Sometimes organizations do not mean to be exclusive or discriminatory, but their practices are discriminatory and illegal. For example, the Equal Employment Opportunity Commission (EEOC) says it is illegal to publish a job advertisement that shows a preference for a particular type of person or discourages someone from applying for a job. For example, a Facebook post that says "recent college graduates wanted" might be inclusive to a younger group and discouraging to a diverse (older) workforce, not making the post multicultural. Another example might be the reliance on word-of-mouth advertisement for job openings. Suppose you have a mostly Hispanic workforce and use word of mouth for recruitment. It is likely that most new hires will also be Hispanic. This is also illegal, but perhaps a consideration is the lack of diversity you will have in your workplace with these recruitment methods.

Make sure that job announcements aren't posted only for your Facebook friends to see; post them in a variety of places to gain the largest and most diverse response.

We address discrimination in the selection process ina future chapter, a mention of the four-fifths rule here is important to determine how we can quantitatively evaluate discrimination in our selection practices. One way to calculate possible discrimination is by using the four-fifths rule, or 80 percent rule. The rule states that a selection rate for any race, sex, or ethnic group that is less than four-fifths of the rate for the group with the highest rate could be regarded as adverse impact.Adverse impact refers to employment practices that may appear to be neutral but have a discriminatory effect on a protected group. For example, let's assume 100 women and 500 men applied to be firefighters. Let's say 20 of those women were hired and 250 men were hired. To determine adverse impact based on the four-fifths rule, calculate the following:

- Selection rate for women: 20 percent
- Selection rate for men: 50 percent
- Then divide the highest selection rate: .20/.50 = .4

Because .4, or 40 percent, is less than four-fifths, there may be adverse impact in the selection process for firefighters.

Testing

If employment tests are required, a test must be in direct relation to the job. For example, an organization that uses a personality test in hiring must be able to show that the personality test results are nondiscriminatory and do not exclude a population.

In addition, if a reasonable accommodation is needed, such as an interpreter, and it does not cause financial difficulty for the organization, this should be granted.

Also consider the type of test and how it might exclude a certain group of people, such as those who don't speak English as a first language.

Pay and Promotion

Development of policies related to pay and promotion is key to fairness in a multicultural situation. It is widely published that women make about 77 percent of what men earn for similar jobs._[3] Many studies have tried to determine a cause for this pay inequity, and here are some of the possible reasons studied and researched:

1. *Hours worked.* Studies have said that women tend to work fewer hours because of child-care and housework expectations.
2. *Occupational choice.* A study performed by Anne York at Meredith College_[4]found that women tend to choose careers that pay less because they are worried about balancing family and career. In addition, numerous studies show that women choose careers on the basis of gender stereotypes (e.g., nurse, teacher) and that this leads to lower pay.
3. *Stereotypes.* The concept of male bias is a possibility. In many studies, people were more likely to choose male doctors over female doctors, even when experience and education were the same._[5] There appears to be a perception that men may be more competent in certain types of jobs.
4. *Maternity and family leave.* Women leaving the workforce for a short or extended period of time may affect the perception of promotability in the workplace.
5. *Salary negotiation.* A study performed by Bowles and Babcock_[6] showed that men were eight times more likely to negotiate salary than women. In addition, when women did negotiate, they received lower monetary returns. Consider a study performed by Cornell University, which found that women were often negatively affected in their job when they negotiated salary, as compared to men not being viewed negatively after negotiations.

Whatever the reason for pay difference, all managers should be aware of these differences when hiring and promoting. Allowing managers to determine the pay for their employees can also bring out negative stereotypes—and lead to breaking of the law. Determining a set pay schedule for all new and promoted employees can help remedy this situation.

A factor in promotions can also be the mentor-mentee relationship. Most individuals in organizations will have an informal mentor who helps them "through the ranks." Traditionally, this informal mentor relationship results in someone "pairing up" with another who has similar physical characteristics, is the same gender, or has a similar mind-set. As a result, if the organization has, for example, mostly men, it is likely the female will not be informally mentored, which can result in lack of promotion. Likewise, if the workforce consists of mostly Caucasian females, it is likely the African American male may not develop an informal mentor relationship with his female counterparts. Development of a formal mentorship program to ensure that everyone has a mentor is one way to alleviate this situation.

Now What?

Now that you have an awareness of the aspects of HR that could be affected by multiculturalism, you may consider what steps you can take to create a more multicultural workplace. The first step would be to create a diversity plan, as discussed earlier in this section. The second step would be to look at the operation of the HR department and to figure out what departmental measures can be taken to promote diversity.

HR, for example, can provide a training series on power and privilege and how it relates to the workplace. Awareness is the first step to creating a truly multicultural environment. Once employees recognize their own power and privilege, the training could be developed to include laws related to diversity, and discussions on bias can take place. Then discussions can be held on how to improve HR plans such as job analysis, recruitment, and selection to create a multicultural work environment. Rather than thinking about this training as one of many objectives that must be accomplished, think about the training from the conversation perspective. Getting the conversation started is the first step in this personal and professional development process for employees.

Some of the aspects to creating a training focused on multiculturalism might include the following:

1. Build a cultural knowledge about customs, religions, and histories.
2. Discuss treatment of people based on them as individuals, rather than as part of a "group," which can result in stereotyping.
3. Teach employees to listen actively, which can help raise cultural awareness.
4. Train employees to rethink current policies and how those policies might be exclusive to a certain group.
5. Work on resistance to change. Many employees think, "This is the way we have always done it, and now we have to change it because we have a group of ____ working here now."
6. Does your leadership team have a multiculturalism perspective? Are many ethnic backgrounds and other multicultural traits represented?

While these suggestions may not eliminate power and privilege, the ability to talk about differences and expectations can be a key ingredient to creating a more inclusive environment. Sometimes this type of training can help people evaluate their perceptions. For example, suppose a complaint came through that a woman was making derogatory sexual comments to only one group of men in an organization. When talked to about it, she said she made comments to the "techies" because she thought the comments would provide them a needed confidence boost, but she generally wouldn't make those types of comments. This is an example of her perception ("techies" need confidence boosts from women) followed by her action (the comments) on this perception. When we assume our perceptions are correct, we are usually wrong. Training can get people to consider their emotions, stereotypes, and expectations. Besides training, asking ourselves a series of important questions can be the start to making diversity and multiculturalism work. The University of California, San Francisco human resource department lists some of these questions, which are shown in the sidebar.

THINGS TO CONSIDER WHEN CREATING A MULTICULTURAL AND DIVERSE WORK ENVIRONMENT

- Do you test your assumptions before acting on them?
- Do you believe there is only one right way of doing things, or that there are a number of valid ways that accomplish the same goal? Do you convey that to staff?
- Do you have honest relationships with each staff member you supervise? Are you comfortable with each of them? Do you know what motivates them, what their goals are, and how they like to be recognized?
- Are you able to give negative feedback to someone who is culturally different from you?

- When you have open positions, do you insist on a diverse screening committee and make additional outreach efforts to ensure that a diverse pool of candidates has applied?
- When you hire a new employee, do you not only explain job responsibilities and expectations clearly but orient the person to the campus and department culture and unwritten rules?
- Do you rigorously examine your unit's existing policies, practices, and procedures to ensure that they do not differentially impact different groups? When they do, do you change them?
- Are you willing to listen to constructive feedback from your staff about ways to improve the work environment? Do you implement staff suggestions and acknowledge their contribution?
- Do you take immediate action with people you supervise when they behave in ways that show disrespect for others in the workplace, such as inappropriate jokes and offensive terms?
- Do you make good faith efforts to meet your affirmative action goals?
- Do you have a good understanding of institutional isms such as racism and sexism and how they manifest themselves in the workplace?
- Do you ensure that assignments and opportunities for advancement are accessible to everyone?
- What policies, practices, and ways of thinking have differential impact on different groups?
- What organizational changes should be made to meet the needs of a diverse workforce?

Source: University of California, San Francisco, "Managing Diversity in the Workplace," chap. 12 in Guide to Managing Human Resources, accessed July 11, 2011, http://ucsfhr.ucsf.edu/index.php/pubs/hrguidearticle/chapter-12-managing-diversity-in-the-workplace/#684.

HUMAN RESOURCE RECALL

Why is multiculturalism important in the workplace? What is your role, as an employee in your organization, to ensure a diverse workforce?

HOW WOULD YOU HANDLE THIS?

Refer a Friend

Your manager is very concerned about the cost of hiring the three new people you need. As a result, she doesn't want to post the advertisement in a variety of places; she thinks it's best to just use a "refer a friend" recruitment strategy. When she moves forward with this strategy, ten people turn in résumés. Upon looking further, it appears all applicants went to the same private religious college and graduated around the same time. You are concerned that this method of recruitment lacks diversity. How would you handle this with your manager?

How Would You Handle This?

KEY TAKEAWAYS

- Oftentimes there are cultural aspects to an organization that make it resistant to an inclusive environment. These are often not obvious, but it is important to be aware of how your own organizational culture impacts multiculturalism.
- One way to begin the discussion within your organization is to create diversity action plans, for which the entire organizational is responsible and for which HR is the change agent. In addition to organizationalwide initiatives, HR can also look within its own HR plans to see where it may be able to change.
- In recruitment, awareness of how and where you post announcements is crucial.
- Testing should be fair and unbiased and shouldn't negatively impact someone based on race, national origin, gender, social class, or educational level.
- There are many reasons for differences in pay. Development of a set pay scale can alleviate some of the issues surrounding unfair pay, especially between men and women.
- Formal mentorship programs can create multicultural understanding and can ensure people do not stick with their own race or gender when helping someone move up the ranks in an organization.

EXERCISES

1. What are some things we can do, personally, to be more multiculturally efficient?
2. What are the advantages of having a set pay scale? What are the disadvantages?

---

[1] Zappos.com, accessed August 25, 2011, http://about.zappos.com/our-unique-culture/zappos-core-values/build-open-and-honest-relationships-communication.

[2] Josh Greenberg, "Diversity in the Workplace: Benefits, Challenges, Solutions," The Multicultural Advantage, 2004, accessed July 12, 2011,http://www.multiculturaladvantage.com/recruit/diversity/Diversity-in-the-Workplace-Benefits-Challenges-Solutions.asp.

[3] National Committee on Pay Equity, accessed August 25, 2011,http://www.iwpr.org/initiatives/pay-equity-and-discrimination/#publications.

[4] E. Anne York, "Gender Differences in the College and Career Aspirations of High School Valedictorians," Journal of Advanced Academics 19, no. 4 (Summer 2008): 578–600,http://eric.ed.gov/ERICWebPortal/detail?accno=EJ822323.

[5] David R. Hekman, Karl Aquino and Brad P. Owens, "An Examination of Whether and How Racial and Gender Biases Influence Customer

Satisfaction," Academy of Management Journal53, no. 2 (April 2010): 238–264.
[6] Hannah Riley Bowles and Linda Babcock, "When Doesn't It Hurt Her to Ask? Framing and Justification Reduce the Social Risks of Initiating Compensation" (paper presented at IACM 21st Annual Conference, December 14, 2008): accessed August 25, 2011,http://papers.ssrn.com/sol3/papers.cfm?abstract_id=1316162.

3.3 Multiculturalism and the Law

LEARNING OBJECTIVES

1. Define the role of the Equal Employment Opportunity Commission (EEOC).
2. Explain the various types of laws covered by the EEOC.

As we already know, it is in an organization's best interest to hire and promote a multicultural and diverse workforce. Sometimes though, people are still discriminated against at work. As a result, a federal agency has been established to ensure employees have a place to file complaints should they feel discriminated against.

Equal Employment Opportunity Commission (EEOC)
The Equal Employment Opportunity Commission (EEOC) is a federal agency charged with the task of enforcing federal employment discrimination laws. The laws include those that protect people from discrimination in all areas of employment, such as discrimination based on race, color, religion, sex, national origin, age, and disability. People who have filed a discrimination charge are also protected against discrimination under the EEOC. Employers with at least fifteen employees (twenty for age discrimination) are covered under the EEOC. This agency covers not only discrimination in hiring but also discrimination in all types of work situations such as firing, promotions, harassment, training, wages, and benefits. The EEOC has the authority to investigate charges of discrimination against employers. The agency investigates the claims, makes a finding, and then tries to settle the charge. If they are unsuccessful in settling the charge, the EEOC has the right to file a lawsuit on behalf of the complainants. The EEOC has headquarters in Washington, DC, with fifty-three field offices throughout the United States.

If a organizational has more than one hundred employees, a form called the EEO-1 must be filled out yearly. This form confirms the demographics of an organization based on different job categories._[1] An organization that employs more than fifty people and works for the federal government must also file an EEO-1 yearly, with the deadline normally in September. In addition, organizations must post the EEOC notice, which you have probably seen before, perhaps in the organizational break room. Finally, organizations should keep on file records such as hiring statistics in the event of an EEOC investigation.

It is necessary to mention here that while there is a legal compliance concern, as discussed before, it is in the organizational's best interest to hire a diverse workforce. So while we can discuss the legal aspects, remember that the purpose of having a diverse workforce is not just to meet EEOC requirements but to create a better, more profitable workplace that better serves customers.

Table 3.1 How the EEOC Process Works and Requirements for Employers

Requirements by EEOC
Post Federal and State EEOC notices
File yearly report called EEO-1
Keep copies of documents on file
Process for Investigation
1. The EEOC complaint is filed.
2. The EEOC notifies the organization of the charges.
3. The EEOC acts as a mediator between the employee and the employer to find a solution.
4. If step 3 is unsuccessful, the EEOC will initiate an investigation.
5. The EEOC makes a determination, and then the employer has the option of remedying the situation or face a potential lawsuit.

EEOC Federal Legislation
While the EEOC is the larger governing body, many pieces of legislation relating to multicultural practices are part of the EEOC family of laws. Many of these laws began with Title VII of the Civil Rights Act in 1964. This act, enforced by the EEOC, covers several areas in which discrimination was rampant. However, abona fide occupational qualification (BFOQ) is a quality or attribute employers are allowed to consider when making decisions during the selection process. Examples of BFOQs are a maximum age limit for airline pilots for safety reasons and a Christian college's requirement that the president of the college be Christian.

EEOC laws relate specifically to the following and are discussed in detail in future chapters on "Recruitment" and "Selection":

1. Age

2. Disability
3. Equal pay
4. Genetic information
5. National origin
6. Pregnancy
7. Race/color
8. Religion
9. Retaliation
10. Sex
11. Sexual harassment

Age

Age discrimination involves treating someone less favorably because of his or her age. Created in 1967, the Age Discrimination in Employment Act (ADEA) is enforced by the EEOC. This law covers people who are age forty or older. It does not cover favoring an older worker over a younger worker, if the older worker is forty years or older. The law covers any aspect of employment such as hiring, firing, pay, job assignments, promotions, layoffs, training, fringe benefits, and any other condition or term of employment.

The law also goes deeper by forbidding harassment of someone based on age. While simple teasing or offhand comments are not covered, more serious offensive remarks about age are covered by this EEOC law.

Disability

The Americans with Disabilities Act (ADA) prohibits discrimination against those with disabilities and is enforced by the EEOC. Discrimination based on disability means treating a qualified person unfavorably because of a disability. For example, if someone has AIDS that is controlled, the employee cannot be treated unfavorably. The law requires an employer to provide reasonable accommodation to an employee or applicant with a disability, unless this accommodation would cause significant difficulty or expense for the employer. A reasonable accommodation is defined by the EEOC as any change in the work environment or in the way things are customarily done that enables an individual with a disability to enjoy equal employment opportunities. A reasonable accommodation might include making the workplace accessible for wheelchair use or providing equipment for someone who is hearing or vision impaired.

This law does not mean that organizations are required to hire unqualified people. The law specifically states the person must be qualified for the job and have a disability defined by the law. A disability defined by the law can include the following:

1. Physical or mental condition that limits a major life activity (walking, talking, seeing, hearing, or learning)
2. History of a disability (e.g., cancer that is in remission)
3. Physical or mental impairment that is not transitory (lasting or expected to last less than six months)

The law places limits on employers when it comes to asking job applicants questions about medical history or asking a person to take a medical exam.

Equal Pay/Compensation

The basis of this law is that people are paid the same for the same type of work, and the law specifically addresses gender pay differences. Rather than job title, job content is used to determine if the job is the same work. In addition to covering salary, it deals with overtime pay, bonus, stock options, profit sharing, and other types of bonus plans such as vacation and holiday pay. If inequality in pay is found, the employer cannot reduce the wages of either sex to equalize the pay.
An employee who files an equal pay charge has the option to go directly to court rather than the EEOC.

Genetic Information

This law is one of the newer EEOC laws, which took effect in November 2009. The EEOC's definition of genetic information includes family medical information or information about the manifestation of a disease or disorder in an individual's family. For example, an employer cannot discriminate against an employee whose family has a history of diabetes or cancer. This information could be used to discriminate against an employee who has an increased risk of getting a disease and may make health-care costs more expensive for the organization.

In addition, the employer is not allowed to seek out genetic information by requesting, requiring, or purchasing this information. However, there are some situations in which receiving this information would not be illegal:

1. A manager or supervisor overhears an employee talking about a family member's illness.
2. Information is received based on wellness programs offered on a voluntary basis.
3. If the information is required as documentation to receive benefits for the Family and Medical Leave Act (FMLA).
4. If the information is commercial, such as the appearance of information in a newspaper, as long as the employer is not specifically searching those sources for the purpose of finding genetic information.

5. If genetic information is required through a monitoring program that looks at the biological effects of toxic substances in the workplace.
6. For those professions that require DNA testing, such as law enforcement agencies. In this case, the genetic information may only be used for analysis in relation to the specific case at hand.

This law also covers how information about genetics should be kept. For example, genetic information must be kept separate from an employee's regular file.

National Origin

It is illegal to treat people unfavorably because they are from a particular country or part of the world, because of their accent, or because they appear to be of a particular descent (even if they are not). The law protecting employees based on national origin refers to all aspects of employment: hiring, firing, pay, job assignments, promotions, layoffs, training, and fringe benefits. An employer can require an employee to speak English only if it is necessary to perform the job effectively. An English-only policy is allowed only if it is needed to ensure the safe or efficient operations of the employer's public organization. An employer may not base an employment decision on a foreign accent, unless the accent seriously interferes with job performance.

Pregnancy

This section of the EEOC refers to the unfavorable treatment of a woman because of pregnancy, childbirth, or a medical condition related to pregnancy or childbirth. The Pregnancy Discrimination Act of 1978, added to the Civil Rights Act of 1964, is enforced by the EEOC. The female who is unable to perform her job owing to pregnancy must be treated the same as other temporarily disabled employees. For example, modified tasks or alternative assignments should be offered. This law refers not only to hiring but also to firing, pay, job assignments, promotions, layoffs, training, and fringe benefits. In addition to this law against discrimination of pregnant women, theFamily and Medical Leave Act (FMLA) is enforced by the US Department of Labor._[2] The FMLA requires organizations with fifty or more employees to provide twelve weeks of unpaid leave for the following:

1. Birth and care of a newborn child
2. Care of an adopted child
3. Care for immediate family members (spouse, child, or parent) with a serious health condition
4. Medical leave for the employee who is unable to work because of a serious health condition

In addition to the organizational size requirement, the employee must have worked at least 1,250 hours over the past 12 months.

Race/Color

This type of discrimination refers to treating someone unfavorably because he or she is of a certain race or because of certain characteristics associated with race. These characteristics might include hair texture, skin color, or facial features. Discrimination can occur when the person discriminating is the same race or color of the person who is being discriminated against. EEOC law also protects people who are married to or associated with someone of a certain race or color. As with the other types of antidiscrimination laws we have discussed, this law refers not only to the initial hiring but also to firing, pay, job assignments, promotions, layoffs, training, and fringe benefits.

Religion

This part of the EEOC refers to treating a person unfavorably because of their religious beliefs. This law requires a organizational to reasonably accommodate an employee's religious beliefs or practices, unless doing so would burden the organization's operations. For example, allowing flexible scheduling during certain religious periods of time might be considered a reasonable accommodation. This law also covers accommodations in dress and grooming, such as a headscarf, religious dress, or uncut hair and a beard in the case of a Sikh. Ideally, the employee or applicant would notify the employer that he or she needs such an accommodation for religious reasons, and then a discussion of the request would occur. If it wouldn't pose hardship, the employer should honor the request. If the request might cause a safety issue, decrease efficiency, or infringe on the rights of other employees, it may not be honored.

Sex and Sexual Harassment

Sex discrimination involves treating someone unfavorably because of their sex. As with all EEOC laws, this relates to hiring, firing, pay, job assignments, promotions, layoffs, training, and fringe benefits. This law directly ties into sexual harassment laws, which include unwelcome sexual advances, requests for sexual favors, and other verbal or physical harassment of a sexual nature. The victim can be male or female, and sexual harassment can occur female to female, female to male, male to female, and male to male.

Retaliation

In all the laws mentioned, the EEOC set of laws makes it illegal to fire, demote, harass, or retaliate against people because they filed a charge of discrimination, complained about discrimination, or participated in employment discrimination proceedings. Perhaps one of the most high-profile sexual harassment and retaliation cases was that of Sanders v. Thomas. Isiah Thomas, then coach of the New York Knicks, fired Anucha Browne Sanders because she hired an attorney to file sexual harassment claims charges. The jury awarded Browne Sanders $11.6 million in punitive charges because of the hostile work environment Thomas created and another $5.6 million because Browne Sanders was fired for complaining._[3] A portion of the lawsuit was to be paid by Madison Square Garden and James Dolan, chairman of Cablevision, the parent organizational of Madison Square Garden and the Knicks. Browne Sanders's lawyers successfully argued that the inner workings of Madison Square Garden were hostile and lewd, and that the former marketing executive of the organization subjected her to hostility and sexual advances. Thomas left the organization as coach and president in 2008. As in this case, there are large financial and public relations penalties not only for sexual harassment but for retaliation after a harassment suit has been filed.

All types of discrimination and laws affecting multiculturalism are a key aspect for HR managers and managers to understand.

Military Service

The Uniformed Services Employment and Reemployment Rights Act (USERR) protects people who serve or have served in the armed forces, Reserves, National Guard, or other uniformed services. The act ensures these individuals are not disadvantaged in their civilian careers because of their service. It also requires they be reemployed in their civilian jobs upon return to service and prohibits discrimination based on past, present, or future military service.

HUMAN RESOURCE RECALL

What types of discrimination (under the EEOC) do you think are the most common and why? Have you ever experienced discrimination in the workplace, at school, or in extracurricular activities? Explain.

KEY TAKEAWAYS

- The Equal Employment Opportunity Commission (EEOC) is a federal agency charged with the development and enforcement of laws relating to multiculturalism and diversity in the workplace.
- The EEOC covers discrimination based on several areas. Organizations cannot discriminate based on age; EEOC law covers people who are forty years or older.
- Employers cannot discriminate against people with disabilities and must provide reasonable accommodations, such as the addition of a wheelchair ramp to accommodate those with disabilities.
- Equal pay refers to the fact people should legally be paid the same amount for performing the same type of work, even if the job title is different.
- The newest addition to EEOC law prohibits discrimination based on genetic information, such as a history of cancer in a family.
- Unfavorable treatment of people because they are from a particular country or part of the world or have an accent is covered by the EEOC. An organization cannot require people to speak English, unless it is a requirement for the job or needed for safety and efficient operation of the organization.
- Women can't be discriminated against because they are pregnant. The inability to perform certain tasks due to pregnancy should be treated as a temporary disability; accommodation can be in the form of modified tasks or alternative assignments.
- The EEOC protects people from discrimination based on their race or color.
- Religion is also an aspect of the EEOC family of laws. The protection of religion doesn't allow for discrimination; accommodations include modifications of work schedules or dress to be made for religious reasons.
- Discrimination on the basis of sex is illegal and covered by the EEOC. Sexual harassment is also covered by the EEOC and states that all people, regardless of sex, should work in a harassment-free environment.
- Retaliation is also illegal. An organization cannot retaliate against anyone who has filed a complaint with the EEOC or a discrimination lawsuit.
- The US Department of Labor oversees some aspects of EEOC laws, such as theFamily and Medical Leave Act (FMLA). This act requires organizations to give twelve weeks of unpaid leave in the event of an adoption, a birth, or a need to provide care to sick family members.

EXERCISES

1. Visit the EEOC website at http://www.eeoc.gov and explain the methods an employee can use in filing a complaint with the EEOC.
2. If an employer is found to have discriminated, what are some "remedies" listed on the EEOC website?

---

[1] Equal Opportunity Employment Commission, 2011 EEO-1 Survey, accessed December 20, 2010, http://www.eeoc.gov/employers/eeo1survey.
[2] US Department of Labor, Leave Benefits: Family and Medical Leave, US Department of Labor, accessed December 20, 2010, http://www.dol.gov/dol/topic/benefits-leave/fmla.htm.
[3] Michael Schmidt, "Jury Awards $11.6 Million to Former Knicks Executive," New York Times,October 2, 2007, accessed July 12, 2011,http://www.nytimes.com/2007/10/02/sports/basketball/03garden-cnd.html.

3.4 Cases and Problems

CHAPTER SUMMARY

- Diversity is the real or perceived differences between individuals. Diversity can include race, gender, sexual orientation, size, cultural background, and many other differences. Multiculturalism is similar to diversity but focuses on the development of a greater understanding of how power in society can be unequal because of race, gender, sexual orientation, power, and privilege.
- Power and privilege is a system of advantages based on one's race, gender, and sexual orientation. This system can often be invisible (to those who have it), which results in one race or gender having unequal power in the workplace. Of course, this unequal power results in unfairness, which may be a legal concern.
- Diversity is important to the success of organizations. Many studies have shown a direct link between the amount of diversity in a workplace and the success of the organizational.
- Oftentimes there are cultural aspects to an organization that make it resistant to an inclusive environment. These are often not obvious, but awareness of how your own organizational culture impacts multiculturalism is important. Job announcements, testing, and pay differences are organizational culture components that can create exclusive environments.
- In recruitment, awareness of how and where you post announcements is crucial. Development of a set pay scale can alleviate some of the issues surrounding unfair pay, especially between men and women.
- Formal mentorship programs can create multicultural understanding and ensure people do not stick with their own race or gender when helping someone move up the ranks in an organization.
- The Equal Employment Opportunity Commission (EEOC) is a federal agency charged with development and enforcement of laws relating to multiculturalism and diversity in the workplace.
- The EEOC covers discrimination based on several areas. Organizations cannot discriminate based on age—that is, against someone who is forty or older. They also can't discriminate against people with disabilities or on the basis of race, genetic information, national origin, gender, or religion.
- Retaliation is also illegal, based on EEOC laws. An organization cannot retaliate against anyone who has filed a complaint with the EEOC or a discrimination lawsuit.
- The US Department of Labor oversees some aspects of EEOC laws, such as theFamily and Medical Leave Act (FMLA). This act requires organizations to give twelve weeks of unpaid leave in the event of an adoption, birth, or caregiving of sick family members.

CHAPTER CASE

But…It's Our Organizational Culture!

You are the HR manager for a fifty-person firm that specializes in the development and marketing of plastics technologies. When you were hired, you felt the organizational had little idea what you should be paid and just made up a number, which you were able to negotiate to a slightly higher salary. While you have been on the job for three months, you have noticed a few concerning things in the area of multiculturalism, besides the way your salary was offered. The following are some of those items:

1. You know that some of the sales team, including the sales manager, get together once a month to have drinks at a strip club.
2. A Hispanic worker left the organization, and in his exit interview, he complained of not seeing a path toward promotion.
3. The only room available for breast-feeding mothers is the women's restroom.
4. The organization has a policy of offering $200 to any employee who refers a friend, as long as the friend is hired and stays at least six months.
5. The manufacturing floor has an English-only policy.
6. You have heard managers refer to those wearing turbans in a derogatory way.

What do you think needs to be done to create a more inclusive environment, without losing the culture of the organizational? What suggestions would you make to those involved in each of the situations?

TEAM ACTIVITY

1. In groups, research recent high-profile cases involving diversity or multiculturalism. Prepare a five-minute presentation on the case to present to classmates.

NOTES:

NOTES:

Chapter 4:
Recruitment in Public Organizations

Keeping Up with Growth

Over the last two years, the organizational where Melinda works as HR manager, Dragon Enterprises, has seen plenty of growth. Much of this growth has created a need for a strategic, specific recruiting processes. In the past, Dragon Enterprises recruited simply on the basis of the applications they received, rather than actively searching for the right person for the job. The first thing Melinda did when arriving at the organizational was to develop a job analysis questionnaire, which she had all employees fill out using the website SurveyMonkey. The goal was to create a job analysis for each position that existed at the organizational. This happened to be the point where the organization started seeing rapid growth, as a result of increased demand for the types of parts the organizational sells. Luckily, since Melinda followed the industry closely and worked closely with management, part of her strategic outline planned for the hiring of several new positions, so she was mostly ready for it. Keeping in mind the Equal Employment Opportunity Commission (EEOC) laws and the organizational's position on a diverse workforce, Melinda set out to write new job descriptions for the job analysis she had performed. She knew the job analysis should be tied to the job description, and both of these should be tied to the job qualifications. Obviously, to recruit for these positions, she needed to develop a recruitment plan. Over the next year, the organization needed to hire three more floor management positions, three office positions, and fifteen factory floor positions. Next, she needed to determine a time line to recruit candidates and a method by which to accept the applications she would receive. After sharing this time line with her colleague, the chief operating officer, she went to work recruiting. She sent an e-mail to all employees asking them to refer a friend and receive a $500 bonus. Next, part of her strategy was to try to find very specialized talent in management to fill those positions. For this, she thought working with a recruiting organizational might be the best way to go. She also used her Twitter and Facebook accounts to broadcast the job openings. After a three-week period, Melinda had 54 applications for the management positions, 78 for the office positions, and 110 for the factory floor positions. Pleased with the way recruiting had gone, she started reviewing the résumés to continue with the selection process.

4.1 The Recruitment Process

LEARNING OBJECTIVES

1. Discuss the need for forecasting human resource needs and techniques for forecasting.
2. Be able to explain the steps to an effective recruitment strategy.
3. Be able to develop a job analysis and job description.

The recruitment process is an important part of human resource management (HRM). It isn't done without proper strategic planning. Recruitment is defined as a process that provides the organization with a pool of qualified job candidates from which to choose. Before organizations recruit, they must implement proper staffing plans and forecasting to determine how many people they will need. The basis of the forecast will be the annual budget of the organization and the short- to long-term plans of the organization—for example, the possibility of expansion. In addition to this, the organizational life cycle will be a factor. Forecasting is based on both internal and external factors. Internal factors include the following:

1. Budget constraints
2. Expected or trend of employee separations
3. Production levels
4. Sales increases or decreases
5. Global expansion plans
6. External factors might include the following:
7. Changes in technology
8. Changes in laws
9. Unemployment rates
10. Shifts in population
11. Shifts in urban, suburban, and rural areas
12. Competition

Once the forecasting data are gathered and analyzed, the HR professional can see where gaps exist and then begin to recruit individuals with the right skills, education, and backgrounds. This section will discuss this step in HR planning.

Recruitment Strategy

Although it might seem easy, recruitment of the right talent, at the right place and at the right time, takes skill and practice, but more importantly, it takes strategic planning. An understanding of the labor market and the factors determining the relevant aspects of the labor market is key to being strategic about your recruiting processes.

Based on this information, when a job opening occurs, the HRM professional should be ready to fill that position. Here are the aspects of developing a recruitment strategy:

1. Refer to a staffing plan.
2. Confirm the job analysis is correct through questionnaires.
3. Write the job description and job specifications.
4. Have a bidding system to recruit and review internal candidate qualifications for possible promotions.
5. Determine the best recruitment strategies for the position.
6. Implement a recruiting strategy.

The first step in the recruitment process is acknowledgment of a job opening. At this time, the manager and/or the HRM look at the job description for the job opening (assuming it isn't a new job).

Assuming the job analysis and job description are ready, an organization may decide to look at internal candidates' qualifications first. Internal candidates are people who are already working for the organizational. If an internal candidate meets the qualifications, this person might be encouraged to apply for the job, and the job opening may not be published. Many organizations have formal job posting procedures andbidding systems in place for internal candidates. For example, job postings may be sent to a listserv or other avenue so all employees have access to them. However, the advantage of publishing open positions to everyone in and outside the organizational is to ensure the organization is diverse.

Then the best recruiting strategies for the type of position are determined. For example, for a high-level executive position, it may be decided to hire an outside head-hunting firm. For an entry-level position, advertising on social networking websites might be the best strategy. Most organizations will use a variety of methods to obtain the best results.

Another consideration is how the recruiting process will be managed under constraining circumstances such as a short deadline or a low number of applications. In addition, establishing a protocol for how applications and résumés will be processed will save time later. For example, some HRM professionals may use software such as Microsoft Excel to communicate the time line of the hiring process to key managers.

Once these tasks are accomplished, the hope is that you will have a diverse group of people to interview (called the selection process). Before this is done, though, it is important to have information to ensure the right people are recruited. This is where the job analysis and job description come in.

Job Analysis and Job Descriptions

The job analysis is a formal system developed to determine what tasks people actually perform in their jobs. The purpose of a job analysis is to ensure creation of the right fit between the job and the employee and to determine how employee performance will be assessed. A major part of the job analysis includes research, which may mean reviewing job responsibilities of current employees, researching job descriptions for similar jobs with competitors, and analyzing any new responsibilities that need to be accomplished by the person with the position. According to research by Hackman and Oldham,[1] a job diagnostic survey should be used to diagnose job characteristics prior to any redesign of a job.

Figure 4.1 Process for Writing the Job Analysis

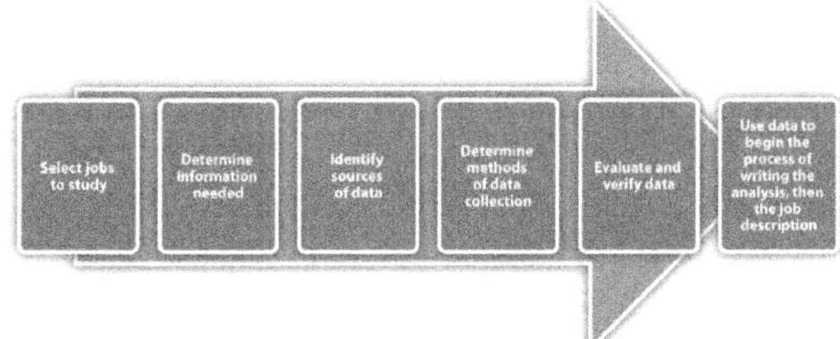

To start writing a job analysis, data need to be gathered and analyzed, keeping in mind Hackman and Oldham's model. Figure 4.1 "Process for Writing the Job Analysis"shows the process of writing a job analysis. Please note, though, that a job analysis is different from a job design. Job design refers to how a job can be modified or changed to be more effective—for example, changing tasks as new technology becomes available.

The information gathered from the job analysis is used to develop both the job description and the job specifications. A job description is a list of tasks, duties, and responsibilities of a job. Job specifications, on the other hand, discuss the skills and abilities the person must have to perform the job. The two are tied together, as job descriptions are usually written to include job specifications. A job analysis must be performed first, and then based on that data, we can successfully write the job description and job specifications. Think of the analysis as "everything an employee is required and expected to do."

Two types of job analyses can be performed: a task-based analysis and a competency- or skills-based analysis. A task-based analysis focuses on the duties of the job, as opposed to a competency-based analysis, which focuses on the specific knowledge and abilities an employee must have to perform the job. An example of a task-based analysis might include information on the following:

1. Write performance evaluations for employees.
2. Prepare reports.
3. Answer incoming phone calls.
4. Assist customers with product questions.
5. Cold-call three customers a day.

With task job analysis, the specific tasks are listed and it is clear. With competency based, it is less clear and more objective. However, competency-based analysis might be more appropriate for specific, high-level positions. For example, a competency-based analysis might include the following:

1. Able to utilize data analysis tools
2. Able to work within teams
3. Adaptable
4. Innovative

You can clearly see the difference between the two. The focus of task-based analyses is the job duties required, while the focus of competency-based analyses is on how a person can apply their skills to perform the job. One is not better than the other but is simply used for different purposes and different types of jobs. For example, a task-based analysis might be used for a receptionist, while a competency-based analysis might be used for a vice president of sales position. Consider the legal implications, however, of which job analysis is used. Because a competency-based job analysis is more subjective, it might be more difficult to tell whether someone has met the criteria.

Once you have decided if a competency-based or task-based analysis is more appropriate for the job, you can prepare to write the job analysis. Of course, this isn't something that should be done alone. Feedback from managers should be taken into consideration to make this task useful in all levels of the organization. Organization is a key component to preparing for your job analysis. For example, will you perform an analysis on all jobs in the organization or just focus on one department? Once you have determined how you will conduct the analysis, a tool to conduct the analysis should be chosen. Most organizations use questionnaires (online or hard copy) to determine the duties of each job title. Some organizations will use face-to-face interviews to perform this task, depending on time constraints and the size of the organization. A job analysis questionnaire usually includes the following types of questions, obviously depending on the type of industry:

1. Employee information such as job title, how long in position, education level, how many years of experience in the industry
2. Key tasks and responsibilities
3. Decision making and problem solving: this section asks employees to list situations in which problems needed to be solved and the types of decisions made or solutions provided.
4. Level of contact with colleagues, managers, outside vendors, and customers
5. Physical demands of the job, such as the amount of heavy lifting or ability to see, hear, or walk
6. Personal abilities required to do the job—that is, personal characteristics needed to perform well in this position
7. Specific skills required to do the job—for example, the ability to run a particular computer program
8. Certifications to perform the job

Once all employees (or the ones you have identified) have completed the questionnaire, you can organize the data, which is helpful in creating job descriptions. If there is more than one person completing a questionnaire for one job title, the data should be combined to create one job analysis for one job title. There are a number of software packages available to help human resources perform this task, such as AutoGOJA.

Once the job analysis has been completed, it is time to write the job description and specifications, using the data you collected. Job descriptions should always include the following components:

1. Job functions (the tasks the employee performs)
2. Knowledge, skills, and abilities (what an employee is expected to know and be able to do, as well as personal attributes)
3. Education and experience required
4. Physical requirements of the job (ability to lift, see, or hear, for example)

Once the job description has been written, obtaining approval from the hiring manager is the next step. Then the

HR professional can begin to recruit for the position. Before we discuss specific recruitment strategies, we should address the law and how it relates to hiring.

TIPS TO WRITING A GOOD JOB DESCRIPTION

- Be sure to include the pertinent information:
    - Title
    - Department
    - Reports to
    - Duties and responsibilities
    - terms of employment
    - qualifications needed
- Think of the job description as a snapshot of the job.
- Communicate clearly and concisely.
- Make sure the job description is interesting to the right candidate applying for the job.
- Avoid acronyms.
- Don't try to fit all job aspects into the job description.
- Proofread the job description.

HUMAN RESOURCE RECALL

Does your current job or past job have a job description? Did it closely match the tasks you actually performed?

KEY TAKEAWAYS

- The recruitment process provides the organization with a pool of qualified applicants.
- Some organizations choose to hire internal candidates—that is, candidates who are already working for the organization. However, diversity is a consideration here as well.
- A job analysis is a systematic approach to determine what a person actually does in his or her job. This process might involve a questionnaire to all employees. Based on this analysis, an accurate job description and job specifications can be written. A job description lists the components of the job, while job specifications list the requirements to perform the job.

EXERCISES

1. Do an Internet search for "job description." Review three different job descriptions and then answer the following questions for each of the jobs:
    a. What are the job specifications?
    b. Are the physical demands mentioned?
    c. Is the job description task based or competency based?
    d. How might you change this job description to obtain more qualified candidates?

Why do the five steps of the recruitment process require input from other parts of the organization? How might you handle a situation in which the employees or management are reluctant to complete a job analysis?

---

[1] J. Richard Hackman and Greg R. Oldham, "Motivation through the Design of Work: Test of a Theory," Organizational Behavior and Human Performance 16, no. 2 (August 1976): 250–79.

4.2 The Law and Recruitment

LEARNING OBJECTIVE

1. Explain the Immigration Reform and Control Act (IRCA), Patriot Act, and equal employment opportunity (EEO) laws and how they relate to recruiting.

One of the most important parts of HRM is to know and apply the law in all activities the HR department handles. Specifically with hiring processes, the law is very clear on a fair hiring that is inclusive to all individuals applying for a job. The laws discussed here are applied specifically to the recruiting of new employees.

Immigration Reform and Control Act

The Immigration Reform and Control Act (IRCA) was adopted by Congress in 1986.[1] This law requires employers to attest to their employees' immigration status. It also makes it illegal to hire or recruit illegal immigrants. The purpose of this law is to preserve jobs for those who have legal documentation to work in the United States. The implications for human resources lie in the recruitment process, because before entering employees into the selection process (interviewing, for example), it is important to know they are eligible to work in the United States. This is why many application forms ask, "Are you legally able to work in the United States?" Dealing with the IRCA is a balancing act, however, because organizations cannot discriminate against legal aliens seeking work in the United States.

The IRCA relates not only to workers you hire but also to subcontractors. In a subcontractor situation (e.g., your organization hires an outside firm to clean the building after hours), your organization can still be held liable if it is determined your organization exercises control over how and when the subcontractors perform their jobs. In 2005, undocumented janitorial workers sued Walmart, arguing that the contracting organizational they worked for didn't pay them a minimum wage.[2] Because the retailer controlled many of the details of their work, Walmart was considered to be a coemployer, and as a result, Walmart was held responsible not only for back wages but for the fact their subcontractor had hired undocumented workers.

HR professionals must verify both the identity and employment eligibility of all employees, even if they are temporary employees. The INS I-9 form (Employment Eligibility Verification form) is the reporting form that determines the identity and legal work status of a worker.
If an audit is performed on your organizational, you would be required to show I-9 forms for all your workers. If an employer hires temporary workers, it is important to manage data on when work visas are to expire, to ensure compliance. Organizations that hire illegal workers can be penalized $100 to $1,000 per hire. There is a software solution for management of this process, such as HR Data Manager. Once all data about workers are inputted, the manager is sent reminders if work authorization visas are about to expire. Employers are required to have the employee fill out the I-9 form on their first day of work, and the second section must be filled out within three days after the first day of employment. The documentation must be kept on file three years after the date of hire or for one year after termination. Some states, though, require the I-9 form be kept on file for as long as the person is employed with the organization.

In 2010, new rules about the electronic storage of forms were developed. The US Department of Homeland Security said that employees can have these forms electronically signed and stored.

Patriot Act

In response to the September 11, 2001, terrorist attacks against the United States, thePatriot Act was signed, introducing legislative changes to enhance the federal government's ability to conduct domestic and international investigations and surveillance activities. As a result, employers needed to implement new procedures to maintain employee privacy rights while also creating a system that allowed for release of information requested by the government.

The act also amended the Electronic Communications Privacy Act, allowing the federal government easier access to electronic communications. For example, only a search warrant is required for the government to access voice mail and e-mail messages.

The act also amended the Foreign Intelligence Surveillance Act. The government is allowed to view communications if an employee is suspected of terrorism, and the government does not have to reveal this surveillance to the employer.
It is prudent for HR professionals and managers to let potential employees know of these new requirements, before the hiring process begins.

HOW WOULD YOU HANDLE THIS?

Wrong Job Description

Aimee, a highly motivated salesperson, has come to you with a complaint. She states that she had her performance evaluation, but all the items on her evaluation didn't relate to her actual job. In the past two years, she explains, her job has changed because of the increase of new public organization development using technology. How would you handle this? How Would You Handle This?

EEO Set of Laws

The Equal Employment Opportunity Commission (EEOC) is a federal agency charged with the task of enforcing federal employment discrimination laws. While there are restrictions on the type of organizational covered (organizations with at least fifteen employees), the EEOC requires collection of data and investigates discrimination claims, again, for organizations with more than fifteen employees.

Under EEO law related to the recruitment process, employers cannot discriminate based on age (forty years or older), disability, genetic information, national origin, sex, pregnancy, race, and religion. In a job announcement, organizations usually have an EEO statement. Here are some examples:

1. (Organizational name) is fully committed to Equal Employment Opportunity and to attracting, retaining, developing, and promoting the most qualified employees without regard to their race, gender, color, religion, sexual orientation, national origin, age, physical or mental disability, citizenship status, veteran status, or any other characteristic prohibited by state or local law. We are dedicated to providing a work environment free from discrimination and harassment, and where employees are treated with respect and dignity.
2. (Organizational name) does not unlawfully discriminate on the basis of race, color, religion, national origin, age, height, weight, marital status, familial status, handicap/disability, sexual orientation, or veteran status in employment or the provision of services, and provides,

upon request, reasonable accommodation including auxiliary aids and services necessary to afford individuals with disabilities an equal opportunity to participate in all programs and activities.
3. It is the policy of (college name), in full accordance with the law, not to discriminate in employment, student admissions, and student services on the basis of race, color, religion, age, political affiliation or belief, sex, national origin, ancestry, disability, place of birth, general education development certification (GED), marital status, sexual orientation, gender identity or expression, veteran status, or any other legally protected classification. (College name) recognizes its responsibility to promote the principles of equal opportunity for employment, student admissions, and student services taking active steps to recruit minorities and women.
4. (Organizational name) will not discriminate against or harass any employee or applicant for employment on the basis of race, color, creed, religion, national origin, sex, sexual orientation, disability, age, marital status, or status with regard to public assistance. (Organizational name) will take affirmative action to ensure that all practices are free of such discrimination. Such employment practices include, but are not limited to, the following: hiring, upgrading, demotion, transfer, recruitment or recruitment advertising, selection, layoff, disciplinary action, termination, rates of pay or other forms of compensation, and selection for training.

In addition to including the EEO policy in the job announcement, HR is required to post notices of EEOC policies in a visible part of the work environment (such as the break room).

Although the EEOC laws in hiring are clear about discrimination, an exception may occur, called the bona fide occupational qualification (BFOQ). BFOQ is a quality or attribute that is reasonably necessary to the normal operation of the public organization and that can be used when considering applicants. To obtain a BFOQ exception, a organizational must prove that a particular person could not perform the job duties because of sex, age, religion, disability, and national origin. Examples of BFOQ exceptions might include the following:

1. A private religious school may require a faculty member to be of the same denomination.
2. Mandatory retirement is required for airline pilots at a certain age.
3. A clothing store that sells male clothing is allowed to hire only male models.
4. If an essence of a restaurant relies on one sex versus another (e.g., Hooters), they may not be required to hire male servers.

However, many arguments for BFOQ would not be considered valid. For example, race has never been a BFOQ, nor has customers' having a preference for a particular gender. Generally speaking, when going through the recruitment process and writing job descriptions, assuming a BFOQ would apply might be a mistake. Seeking legal council before writing a job description would be prudent.

Other aspects to consider in the development of the job description are disparate impact and disparate treatment. These are the two ways to classify employment discrimination cases. Disparate impact occurs when an organization discriminates through the use of a process, affecting a protected group as a whole, rather than consciously intending to discriminate. Some examples of disparate impact might include the following:

1. Requirement of a high school diploma, which may not be important to employment, could discriminate against racial groups
2. A height requirement, which could limit the ability of women or persons of certain races to apply for the position
3. Written tests that do not relate directly to the job
4. Awarding of pay raises on the basis of, say, fewer than five years of experience, which could discriminate against people older than forty

Disparate treatment, when one person is intentionally treated differently than another, does not necessarily impact the larger protected group as a whole, as in disparate impact. The challenge in these cases is to determine if someone was treated differently because of their race or gender or if there was another reason for the different treatment. Here are two examples:

1. Both a male and a female miss work, and the female is fired but the male is not.
2. A organizational does not hire people of a certain race or gender, without a BFOQ.

HUMAN RESOURCE RECALL

Can you think of other examples of disparate impact that might affect a certain protected group of people under EEOC?

KEY TAKEAWAYS

- IRCA stands for Immigration and Reform Act. This law requires all employers to determine eligibility of an employee to work in the United States. The reporting form is called an I-9 and must be completed and kept on file (paper or electronic) for at least three years, but some states require this documentation to be kept on file for the duration of the employee's period of employment.
- The Patriot Act allows the government access to data that would normally be considered private—for example, an employee's records and work voice mails and e-mails (without the organizational's consent). The HR professional might consider letting employees know of the compliance with this law.
- The EEOC is a federal agency charged with ensuring discrimination does not occur in the workplace. They oversee the equal employment opportunity (EEO) set of laws. Organizations must post EEO laws in a visible location at their workplace and also include them on job announcements.
- Related to the EEOC, the bona fide occupational qualification (BFOQ) makes it legal to discriminate in hiring based on special circumstances—for example, requiring the retirement of airline pilots at a certain age due to safety concerns.
- Disparate impact refers to a policy that may limit a protected EEO group from receiving fair treatment. Disparate impact might include a test or requirement that negatively impacts someone based on protected group status. An example is requiring a high school diploma, which may not directly impact the job. Disparate treatment refers to discrimination against an individual, such as the hiring of one person over another based on race or gender.

EXERCISES

1. Describe the difference between disparate treatment and disparate impact.
2. Explain a situation (other than the ones described in this section) in which a BFOQ might be appropriate. Then research to see if in the past this reasoning has been accepted as a BFOQ.

---

[1] U.S. Citizenship and Immigration Services website. Accessed January 17, 2011.http://www.uscis.gov/portal/site/uscis/menuitem.5af9bb95919f35e66f614176543f6d1a/?vgnextchannel=b328194d3e88d010VgnVCM10000048f3d6a1RCRD&vgnextoid=04a295c4f635f010VgnVCM1000000ecd190aRCRD.

[2] Zavala v. Wal-Mart, No. 03-5309, DC NJ (2005).

4.3 Recruitment Strategies

LEARNING OBJECTIVE

1. Explain the various strategies that can be used in recruitment.

Now that we have discussed development of the job analysis, job description, and job specifications, and you are aware of the laws relating to recruitment, it is time to start recruiting. It is important to mention, though, that a recruitment plan should be in place. This plan can be informal, but you should outline where you plan to recruit and your expected time lines. For example, if one of your methods is to submit an ad to a trade publication website, you should know their deadlines. Also of consideration is to ensure you are recruiting from a variety of sources to ensure diversity. Lastly, consider the economic situation of the country. With high unemployment, you may receive hundreds of applications for one job. In an up economy, you may not receive many applications and should consider using a variety of sources.

Some organizations, such as Southwest Airlines, are known for their innovative recruitment methods. Southwest looks for "the right kind of people" and are less focused on the skills than on the personality of the individual.[1] When Southwest recruits, it looks for positive team players that match the underdog, quirky organizational culture. Applicants are observed in group interviews, and those who exhibit encouragement for their fellow applicants are usually those who continue with the recruitment process. This section will discuss some of the ways Southwest and many other Organizational organizations find this kind of talent.

Figure 4.5 Overview of the Steps to the Recruitment Process

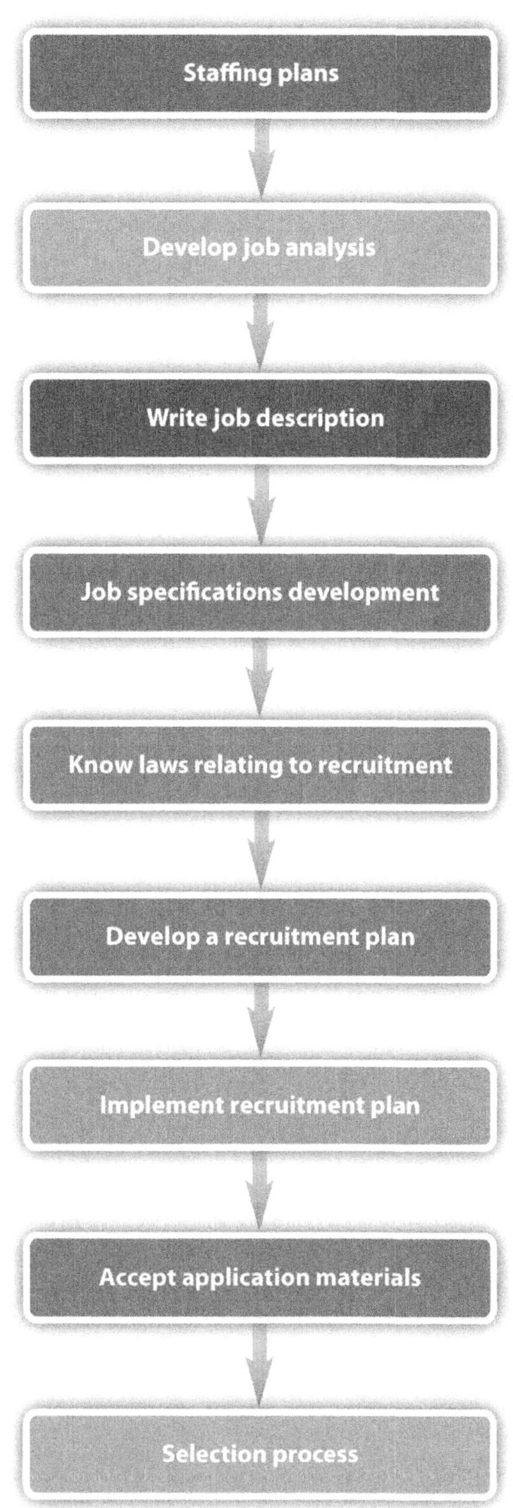

Recruiters

Some organizations choose to have specific individuals working for them who focus solely on the recruiting function of HR. Recruiters use similar sources to recruit individuals, such as professional organizations, websites, and other methods discussed in this chapter. Recruiters are excellent at networking and usually attend many events where possible candidates will be present. Recruiters keep a constant pipeline of possible candidates in case a position should arise that would be a good match. There are three main types of recruiters:

1. *Executive search firm.* These organizations are focused on high-level positions, such as management and CEO roles. They typically charge 10–20 percent of the first year salary, so they can be quite expensive. However, they do much of the upfront work, sending candidates who meet the qualifications.
2. *Temporary recruitment or staffing firm.* Suppose your receptionist is going on medical leave and you need to hire somebody to replace him, but you don't want a long-term hire. You can utilize the services of a temporary recruitment firm to send you qualified candidates who are willing to work shorter contracts. Usually, the firm pays the salary of the employee and the organizational pays the recruitment firm, so you don't have to add this person to your payroll. If the person does a good job, there may be opportunities for you to offer him or her a full-time, permanent position. Kelly Services, Manpower, and Snelling Staffing Services are examples of staffing firms.
3. *Organizational recruiter.* A organizational recruiter is an employee within a organizational who focuses entirely on recruiting for his or her organizational. Organizational recruiters are employed by the organizational for which they are recruiting. This type of recruiter may be focused on a specific area, such as technical recruiting.
4. *A contingent recruiter* is paid only when the recruiter starts working, which is often the case with temporary recruitment or staffing firms. A retained recruiter gets paid up front (in full or a portion of the fee) to perform a specific search for a organizational.

While the HR professional, when using recruiters, may not be responsible for the details of managing the search process, he or she is still responsible for managing the process and the recruiters. The job analysis, job description, and job specifications still need to be developed and candidates will still need to be interviewed.

ORGANIZATIONAL FOCUS

In 2009, when Amazon purchased Zappos for 10 million shares of Amazon stock (roughly $900 million in 2009), the strategic move for Amazon didn't change the hiring and recruiting culture of Zappos. Zappos, again voted one of the best one hundred organizations to work for by CNN Money [2] believes it all starts with the people they hire. The recruiting staff always asks, "On a scale of 1–10, how weird do you think you are?" This question ties directly to the organizational's strategic plan and core value number three, which is "create fun and a little weirdness." Zappos recruits people who not only have the technical abilities for the job but also are a good culture fit for the organization. Once hired, new employees go through two weeks of training. At the end of the training, newly hired employees are given "the offer." The offer is $2,000 to quit on the spot. This ensures Zappos has committed people who have the desire to work with the organization, which all begins with the recruiting process.

Campus Recruiting

Colleges and universities can be excellent sources of new candidates, usually at entry-level positions. Consider technical colleges that teach cooking, automotive technology, or cosmetology. These can be great sources of people with specialized training in a specific area. Universities can provide people that may lack actual experience but have formal training in a specific field. Many organizations use their campus recruiting programs to develop new talent, who will eventually develop into managers.

For this type of program to work, it requires the establishment of relationships with campus communities, such as campus career services departments. It can also require time to attend campus events, such as job fairs. IBM, for example, has an excellent campus recruiting program. For IBM, recruiting out of college ensures a large number of people to grow with the organization. [3]

Setting up a formal internship program might also be a way to utilize college and university contacts. Walgreens, for example, partners with Apollo College to recruit interns; this can result in full-time employment for the motivated intern and money saved for Walgreens by having a constant flow of talent.

Professional Associations

Professional associations are usually nonprofit organizations whose goal is to further a particular profession. Almost every profession has its own professional organization. For example, in the field of human resources, the Society for Human Resource Management allows organizations to post jobs relating to HR. The American Marketing Association, also a professional organization, allows job postings as well. Usually, there is a fee involved, and membership in this association may be required to post jobs. Here are some examples of professional associations:

1. Professional Nursing Association
2. Society of Women Engineers
3. International Federation of Accountants
4. Institute of Management Consultants
5. United Professional Sales Association
6. National Lawyers Guild
7. National Organization of Minority Architects
8. International Federation of Journalists (union)
9. International Metalworkers Federation (union)
10. Association of Flight Attendants (union)

Labor unions can also be excellent sources of candidates, and some unions also allow job postings on their website. The key to using this as a successful recruitment strategy is to identify the organizations that relate to your public organization and to develop relationships with members in these organizations. This type of networking can help introduce you to people in your industry who may be looking for a job or know of someone who needs a job.

HUMAN RESOURCE RECALL

What do you think is the best way to determine the right set of recruitment methods for your organization? What methods would be best for your current job?

Websites

If you have ever had to look for a job, you know there are numerous websites to help you do that. From the HR perspective, there are many options to place an ad, most of which are inexpensive. The downside to this method is the immense number of résumés you may receive from these websites, all of which may or may not be qualified. Many organizations, to combat this, implement software that searches for keywords in résumés, which can help combat this problem. Some examples of websites might include the following:

- Your own organizational website
- Yahoo HotJobs
- Monster
- CareerBuilder
- JobCentral

Social Media

Facebook, Twitter, LinkedIn, YouTube, and MySpace are excellent places to obtain a media presence to attract a variety of workers. In 2007, Sodexo, which provides services such as food service and facilities management, started using social media to help spread the word about their organizational culture. Since then, they have saved $300,000 on traditional recruiting methods._[4] Sodexo's fifty recruiters share updates on Twitter about their excellent organizational culture. Use of this media has driven traffic to the careers page on Sodexo's website, from 52,000 to 181,000.

The goal of using social media as a recruiting tool is to create a buzz about your organization, share stories of successful employees, and tout an interesting culture. Even smaller organizations can utilize this technology by posting job openings as their status updates. This technique is relatively inexpensive, but there are some things to consider. For example, tweeting about a job opening might spark interest in some candidates, but the trick is to show your personality as an employer early on. According to Bruce Morton of Allegis Group Services, using social media is about getting engaged and having conversations with people before they're even thinking about you as an employer._[5] Debbie Fisher, an HR manager for a large advertising agency, Campbell Mithun, says that while tweeting may be a good way to recruit people who can be open about their job hunt, using tools such as LinkedIn might be a better way to obtain more seasoned candidates who cannot be open about their search for a new job, because of their current employment situation. She says that LinkedIn has given people permission to put their résumé online without fear of retribution from current employers.

Creativity with a social media campaign also counts. Campbell Mithun hired thirteen interns over the summer using a unique twist on social media. They asked interested candidates to submit thirteen tweets over thirteen days and chose the interns based on their creativity.

Many organizations, including Zappos, use YouTube videos to promote the organizational. Within the videos is a link that directs viewers to the organizational's website to apply for a position in the organizational.

Facebook allows free job postings in Facebook Marketplace, and the organizational Facebook page can also be used as a recruiting tool. Some organizations decide to use Facebook ads, which are paid on a "per click" or per impression (how many people potentially see the ad) basis. Facebook ad technology allows specific regions and Facebook keywords to be targeted._[6] Some individuals even use their personal Facebook page to post status updates listing job opportunities and asking people to respond privately if they are interested.

Events

Many organizations, such as Microsoft, hold events annually to allow people to network and learn about new technologies. Microsoft's Professional Developer Conference (PDC), usually held in July, hosts thousands of web developers and other professionals looking to update their skills and meet new people.

Some organizations, such as Choice Career Fairs, host job fairs all over the country; participating in this type of job fair may be an excellent way to meet a large variety of candidates. Other events may not be specifically for recruiting, but attending these events may allow you to meet people who could possibly fill a position or future position. For example, in the world of fashion, Fashion Group International (FGI) hosts events internationally on a weekly basis, which may allow the opportunity to meet qualified candidates.

Special/Specific Interest Groups (SIGs)

Special/specific interest groups (SIGs), which may require membership of individuals, focus on specific topics for members. Often SIGs will have areas for job posting, or a variety of discussion boards where jobs can be posted. For example, the Women in Project Management SIG provides news on project management and also has a place for job advertisements. Other examples of SIGs might include the following:

- Oracle Developer SIG
- African American Medical Librarians Alliance SIG
- American Marketing Association Global Marketing SIG
- Special Interest Group for Accounting Information Systems (SIG-ASYS)
- Junior Lawyer SIG
- Recruiting using SIGs can be a great way to target a specific group of people who are trained in a specific area or who have a certain specialty.

Referrals

Most recruiting plans include asking current employees, "Who do you know?" The quality of referred applicants is usually high, since most people would not recommend someone they thought incapable of doing the job. E-mailing a job opening to current employees and offering incentives to refer a friend can be a quick way of recruiting individuals. Due to the success of most formalized referral programs, it is suggested that a program be part of the overall HRM strategic plan and recruitment strategy. However, be wary of using referrals as the only method for recruitment, as this can lead to lack of diversity in a workplace. Nepotism means a preference for hiring relatives of current employees, which can also lead to lack of diversity and management issues in the workplace.

Table 4.1 Advantages and Disadvantages of Recruiting Methods

Recruitment Method	Advantages	Disadvantages
Outside recruiters, executive search firms, and temporary employment agencies	Can be time saving	Expensive
		Less control over final candidates to be interviewed
Campus recruiting/educational institutions	Can hire people to grow with the organization	Time consuming
	Plentiful source of talent	Only appropriate for certain types of experience levels
Professional organizations and associations	Industry specific	May be a fee to place an ad
	Networking	May be time-consuming to network
Websites/Internet recruiting	Diversity friendly	Could be too broad
	Low cost	Be prepared to deal with hundreds of résumés
	Quick	
Social media	Inexpensive	Time consuming
		Overwhelming response
Events	Access to specific target markets of candidates	Can be expensive
		May not be the right target market
SIG	Industry specific	Research required for specific SIGS tied to jobs
Referrals	Higher quality people	Concern for lack of diversity
	Retention	Nepotism
Unsolicited résumés and applications	Inexpensive, especially with time-saving keyword résumé search software	Time consuming
Internet and/or traditional advertisements	Can target a specific audience	Can be expensive
Employee leasing	For smaller organizations, it means someone does not have to administer compensation and benefits, as this is handled by leasing organizational	Possible costs
	Can be a good alternative to temporary employment if the job is permanent	Less control of who interviews for the position
Public employment agencies	The potential ability to recruit a more diverse workforce	May receive many résumés, which can be time-consuming
	No cost, since it's a government agency	
	2,300 points of service nationwide	
Labor unions	Access to specialized skills	May not apply to some jobs or industries; Builds relationship

For example, the University of Washington offers $1,200 any time a current employee successfully refers a friend to work at their medical centers. Usually, most incentives require the new employee to be hired and stay a specified period of time. Some examples of incentives that can be used to refer a friend might include the following:

- A gift card to the employee
- A financial incentive
- Raffles for most referrals

These types of programs are called employee referral programs (ERPs) and tend to generate one of the highest returns on investment per hire.[7] To make an ERP program effective, some key components should be put into place:

1. Communicate the program to existing employees.
2. Track the success of the program using metrics of successful hires.
3. Be aware of the administrative aspect and the time it takes to implement the program effectively.
4. Set measureable goals up front for a specialized program.

Accenture recently won the ERE Media Award for one of the most innovative ERPs. Its program has increased new hires from referrals from 14 percent to 32 percent, and employee awareness of the program jumped from just 20 percent to 99 percent.[8] The uniqueness of their program lies with the reward the employee receives. Instead of offering personal financial compensation, Accenture makes a donation to the charity of the employee's choice, such as a local elementary school. Their program also seeks to decrease casual referrals, so the employee is asked to fill out an online form to explain the skills of the individual they are referring. The organizational has also developed a website where current employees can go to track the progress of referrals. In addition, employee referral applications are flagged online and fast-tracked through the process—in fact, every referral is acted upon. As you can see, Accenture has made their ERP a success through the use of strategic planning in the recruitment process.

Costs of Recruitment

Part of recruitment planning includes budgeting the cost of finding applicants. For example, let's say you have three positions you need to fill, with one being a temporary hire. You have determined your advertising costs will be $400, and your temporary agency costs will be approximately $700 for the month. You expect at least one of the two positions will be recruited as a referral, so you will pay a referral bonus of $500. Here is how you can calculate the cost of recruitment for the month:

cost per hire = advertising costs + recruiter costs + referral costs + social media costs + event costs.

$400 + $700 + $500 = $1600/3 = $533 recruitment cost per hire.

In addition, when we look at how effective our recruiting methods are, we can look at a figure called the yield ratio. A yield ratio is the percentage of applicants from one source who make it to the next stage in the selection process (e.g., they get an interview). For example, if you received two hundred résumés from a professional organization ad you placed, and fifty-two of those make it to the interview state, this means a 26 percent yield (52/200). By using these calculations, we can determine the best place to recruit for a particular position. Note, too, that some yield ratios may vary for particular jobs, and a higher yield ratio must also consider the cost of that method, too. For an entry-level job, campus recruiting may yield a better ratio than, say, a organizational recruiter, but the organizational recruiter may have higher cost per hires.

After we have finished the recruiting process, we can begin the selection process.

KEY TAKEAWAYS

- HR professionals must have a recruiting plan before posting any job description. The plan should outline where the job announcements will be posted and how the management of candidate materials, such as résumés, will occur. Part of the plan should also include the expected cost of recruitment.
- Many organizations use recruiters. Recruiters can be executive recruiters, which means an outside firm performs the search. For temporary positions, a temporary or staffing firm such as Kelly Services might be used. Organizational recruiters work for the organization and function as a part of the HR team.
- Campus recruiting can be an effective way of recruiting for entry-level positions. This type of recruiting may require considerable effort in developing relationships with college campuses.
- Almost every profession has at least one professional association. Posting announcements on their websites can be an effective way of targeting for a specific job.

- Most organizations will also use their own website for job postings, as well as other websites such as Monster and CareerBuilder.
- Social media is also a popular way to recruit. Usage of websites such as Twitter and Facebook can get the word out about a specific job opening, or give information about the organizational, which can result in more traffic being directed to the organizational's website.
- Recruiting at special events such as job fairs is another option. Some organizations have specific job fairs for their organizational, depending on the size. Others may attend industry or job-specific fairs to recruit specific individuals.
- SIGs, or special/specific interest groups, are usually very specialized. For example, female project managers may have an interest group that includes a discussion board for posting of job announcements.
- Employee referrals can be a great way to get interest for a posted position. Usually, incentives are offered to the employee for referring people they know. However, diversity can be an issue, as can nepotism.
- Our last consideration in the recruitment process is recruitment costs. We can determine this by looking at the total amount we have spent on all recruiting efforts compared to the number of hires. A yield ratio is used to determine how effective recruiting efforts are in one area. For example, we can look at the number of total applicants received from a particular form of media, and divide that by the number of those applicants who make it to the next step in the process (e.g., they receive an interview).

EXERCISES

1. Perform an Internet search on professional associations for your particular career choice. List at least three associations, and discuss recruiting options listed on their websites (e.g., do they have discussion boards or job advertisements links?).
2. Have you ever experienced nepotism in the workplace? If yes, describe the experience. What do you think are the upsides and downsides to asking current employees to refer someone they know?

---

[1] W. P. Carey, "Employees First: Strategy for Success," Knowledge @ W. P. Carey, W. P. Carey School of Public organization, Arizona State University, June 26, 2008, accessed July 11, 2011,http://knowledge.wpcarey.asu.edu/article.cfm?articleid=1620.
[2] Cheryl Sowa, "Going Above and Beyond," America's Best, September/October 2008, accessed July 11, 2011, http://www.americasbestorganizations.com/magazine/articles/going-above-and-beyond.aspx.
[3] "University Students," IBM, n.d., accessed January 17, 2011, http://www-03.ibm.com/employment/start_university.html.
[4] Sodexo, "Sodexo Earns SNCR Excellent Award for Innovative Use of Social Media," news release, December 2, 2009, accessed January 17, 2011,http://www.sodexousa.com/usen/newsroom/press/press09/sncrexcellenceaward.asp.
[5] Anna Lindow, "How to Use Social Media for Recruiting," Mashable, June 11, 2011, accessed July 12, 2011, http://mashable.com/2011/06/11/social-media-recruiting.
[6] Tiffany Black, "How to Use Social Media as a Recruiting Tool," Inc., April 22, 2010, accessed July 12, 2011, http://www.inc.com/guides/2010/04/social-media-recruiting.html.
[7] Dave Lefkow, "Improving Your Employee Referral Program and Justifying Your Investment," ERE.net, February 21, 2002, accessed July 12, 2011,http://www.ere.net/2002/02/21/improving-your-employee-referral-program-and-justifying-your-investment.
[8] John Sullivan, "Amazing Practices in Recruiting—ERE Award Winners 2009," pt. 1, ERE.net, April 13, 2009, accessed July 12, 2011, http://www.ere.net/2009/04/13/amazing-practices-in-recruiting-ere-award-winners-2009-part-1-of-2.

4.4 Cases and Problems

CHAPTER SUMMARY

- The recruitment process provides the organization with a pool of qualified applicants.
- Some organizations choose to hire internal candidates—that is, candidates who are already working for the organization. However, diversity is a consideration here as well.
- A job analysis is a systematic approach to determine what a person actually does in his or her job. This process might involve a questionnaire to all employees. Based on this analysis, an accurate job description and job specifications can be written. A job description lists the components of the job, while job specifications list the requirements to perform the job.
- IRCA stands for Immigration and Reform Act. This law requires all employers to determine eligibility of an employee to work in the United States. The reporting form is called an I-9 and must be completed and kept on file (paper or electronic) for at least three years, but some states require this documentation to be kept on file for the duration of the employee's period of employment.
- The Patriot Act allows the government access to data that would normally be considered private, for example, an employee's records and work voice mails and e-mails (without the organizational's consent). The HR professional might consider letting employees know of the compliance with this law.
- The Equal Employment Opportunity Commission (EEOC) is a federal agency charged with ensuring discrimination does not occur in the workplace. They

oversee the EEO set of laws. Organizations must post EEO laws in a visible location at their workplace and also include them on job announcements.

- Related to the EEOC, the bona fide occupational qualification (BFOQ) makes it legal to discriminate in hiring based on special circumstances, for example, requiring the retirement of airline pilots at a certain age due to safety concerns.
- Disparate impact refers to a policy that may limit a protected EEO group from receiving fair treatment. Disparate impact might include a test or requirement that negatively impacts someone based on protected group status. An example is requiring a high school diploma, which may not directly impact the job.Disparate treatment refers to discrimination against an individual, such as the hiring of one person over another based on race or gender.
- HR professionals must have a recruiting plan before posting any job description.
- Many organizations use recruiters. Recruiters can be executive recruiters, which means an outside firm performs the search. For temporary positions, a temporary or staffing firm such as Kelly Services might be used. Organizational recruiters work for the organization and function as a part of the HR team.
- Campus recruiting can be an effective way of recruiting for entry-level positions. This type of recruiting may require considerable effort in developing relationships with college campuses.
- Almost every profession has at least one professional association. Posting announcements on their websites can be an effective way of targeting for a specific job.
- Most organizations will also use their own website for job postings, as well as other websites such as Monster and CareerBuilder.
- Social media is also a popular way to recruit. Usage of websites such as Twitter and Facebook can get the word out about a specific job opening, or give information about the organizational, which can result in more traffic being directed to the organizational's website.
- Recruiting at special events such as job fairs is another option. Some organizations have specific job fairs for their organizational, depending on the size. Others may attend industry or job specific fairs to recruit specific individuals.
- SIGs or special/specific interest groups are usually very specialized. For example, female project managers may have an interest group that includes a discussion board for posting of job announcements.
- Employee referrals can be a great way to get interest for a posted position. Usually, incentives are offered to the employee for referring people they know. However, diversity can be an issue, as can nepotism.
- Our last consideration in the recruitment process is recruitment costs. We can determine this by looking at the total amount we have spent on all recruiting efforts compared to the number of hires. A yield ratio is used to determine how effective recruiting efforts are in one area. For example, we can look at the number of total applicants received from a particular form of media, and divide that by the number of those applicants who make it to the next step in the process (e.g., they receive an interview).

CHAPTER CASE

Recruitment Statistics

As the assistant to the human resources director at Tally Group, you normally answer phones and set appointments for the director. You are interested in developing skills in HRM, and one day, your HR director presents you with a great opportunity for you to show what you can do. She asks you to analyze last year's recruitment data to determine which methods have worked best. As you look at the data, you aren't sure how to start, but you remember something on this from your HRM class in college. After reviewing the data in your book, you feel confident to analyze these numbers. Please go ahead and perform calculations on these numbers, then provide answers to the questions that follow.

Table 4.2 Tally Group Recruiting Numbers, 2012

Method	Total Number Recruited	Yearly Cost ($)
Temporary placement firms	8	3,200
Campus recruiting	2	1,500
Professional association ads	10	4,500
Social media/organizational website	33	300
Job fair	3	500
Referrals	26	26,000

1. Prepare a report summarizing your findings for the recruitment cost per hire and yield ratio for each type of recruiting method.
2. Make a recommendation to your human resource director on where the department should spend more of its time recruiting.

TEAM ACTIVITIES

1. Students should be in teams of four or five. Choose a recruitment method from Table 4.2 "Tally Group Recruiting Numbers, 2012"and perform research on additional advantages and disadvantages of that method and then present ideas to the class.
2. Visit the Dictionary of Occupational Titles(http://www.occupationalinfo.org) and view the list of job titles presented on the website. Create a sample job description for a job title of your team's choice.

NOTES:

NOTES:

Chapter 5: Selection in Public Organizations

The Interview

Many of us have or will sit in a waiting room with our best clothes on awaiting a job (or school) interview. You can feel your palms sweat and thoughts race as you wait for your name to be called. You look around at the office environment and imagine yourself walking through those doors everyday. People walk by and smile, and overall, you have a really good first impression of the organization. You hope they like you. You tell yourself to remember to smile, while recalling all your experience that makes you the perfect person for this job. A moment of self-doubt may occur, as you wonder about the abilities of the other people being interviewed and hope you have more experience and make a better impression than they do. You hear your name, stand up, and give a firm handshake to the HR manager. The interview has begun.

As she walks you back to a conference room, you think you see encouraging smiles as you pass by people. She asks you to take a chair and then tells you what the interview process will be like. She then asks the first question, "Tell me about yourself." As you start discussing your experience, you feel yourself relax, just a little bit. After the interview finishes, she asks you to take a quick cognitive test, which you feel good about. She tells you she will be doing reference checks and will let you know by early next week.

To get to this point, the hiring manager may have reviewed hundreds of résumés and developed criteria she would use for selection of the right person for the job. She has probably planned a time line for hiring, developed hiring criteria, determined a compensation package for the job, and enlisted help of other managers to interview candidates. She may have even performed a number of phone interviews before bringing only a few of the best candidates in for interviews. It is likely she has certain qualities in mind that she is hoping you or another candidate will possess. Much work goes into the process of hiring someone, with selection being an important step in that process. A hiring process done correctly is time-consuming and precise. The interviewer should already have questions determined and should be ready to sell the organization to the candidate as well. This chapter will discuss the main components to the selection process.

5.1 The Selection Process

LEARNING OBJECTIVE

1. Be able to name and discuss the steps in the selection process.

Figure 5.2 The Selection Process at a Glance

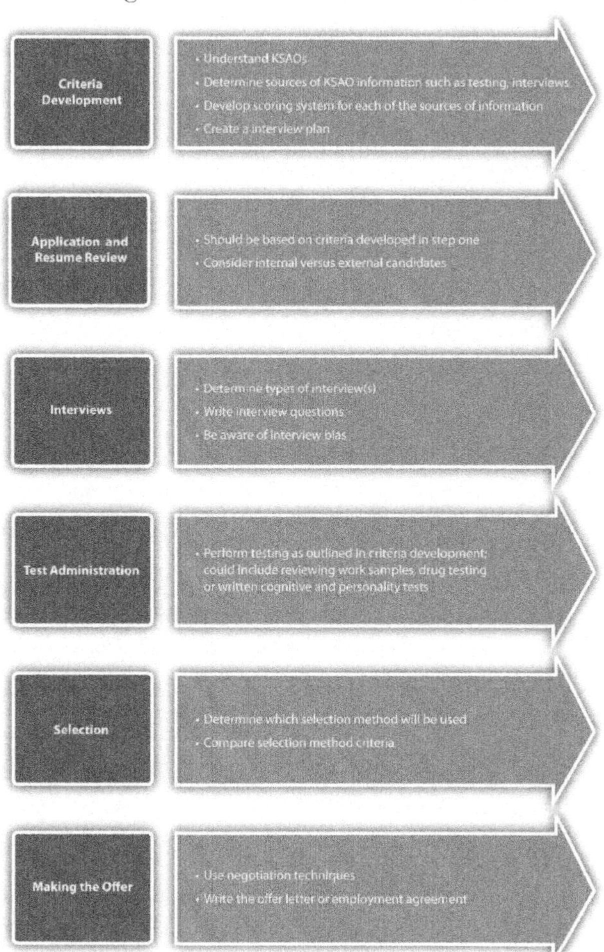

Once you have developed your recruitment plan, recruited people, and now have plenty of people to choose from, you can begin the selection process. The selection processrefers to the steps involved in choosing people who have the right qualifications to fill a current or future job opening. Usually, managers and supervisors will be ultimately responsible for the hiring of individuals, but the role of human resource management (HRM) is to define and guide managers in this process. The selection process is expensive. The time for all involved in the hiring process to review résumés, weight the applications, and interview the best candidates takes away time (and costs money) that those individuals could spend on other activities. In addition, there are the costs of testing candidates and bringing them in from out of town for interviews. In fact, the US Department of Labor and Statistics estimates the combined direct and indirect cost of hiring someone new can reach upwards of $40,000.[1] Because of the high cost, it is important to hire the right person from the beginning and ensure a fair selection process. For example, the Austin, Texas, fire department calculated it would cost $150,000 to reinterview candidates, after the interview questions were leaked to the public, giving some candidates possibly unfair advantages in the interview process.[2]

The selection process consists of five distinct aspects:

1. Criteria development. All individuals involved in the hiring process should be properly trained on the steps for interviewing, including developing criteria, reviewing résumés, developing interview questions, and weighting the candidates.
2. The first aspect to selection is planning the interview process, which includes criteria development. Criteria development means determining which sources of information will be used and how those sources will be scored during the interview. The criteria should be related directly to the job analysis and the job specifications. In fact, some aspects of the job analysis and job specifications may be the actual criteria. In addition to this, include things like personality or cultural fit, which would also be part of criteria development. This process usually involves discussing which skills, abilities, and personal characteristics are required to be successful at any given job. By developing the criteria before reviewing any résumés, the HR manager or manager can be sure he or she is being fair in selecting people to interview. Some organizations may need to develop an application or a biographical information sheet. Most of these are completed online and should include information about the candidate, education, and previous job experience.
3. Application and résumé review. Once the criteria have been developed (step one), applications can be reviewed. People have different methods of going through this process, but there are also computer programs that can search for keywords in résumés and narrow down the number of résumés that must be looked at and reviewed.
4. Interviewing. After the HR manager and/or manager have determined which applications meet the minimum criteria, he or she must select those people to be interviewed. Most people do not have time to review twenty or thirty candidates, so the field is sometimes narrowed even further with a phone interview.
5. Test administration. Any number of tests may be administered before a hiring decision is made. These include drug tests, physical tests, personality tests, and cognitive tests. Some organizations also perform reference checks, credit report checks, and background checks. Once the field of candidates has been narrowed down, tests can be administered.
6. Making the offer. The last step in the selection process is to offer a position to the chosen candidate. Development of an offer via e-mail or letter is sometimes a more formal part of this process. Compensation and benefits will be defined in an offer.

ORGANIZATIONAL FOCUS

In a 2010 interview,[3] Robert Selander, then CEO of MasterCard, cited presence as one of the most important aspects to acing an interview. He describes how, in any large organization, an employee will be expected to engage with a variety of stakeholders, from a member of Congress to a contractor replacing the carpet in the building. He says that a good employee—at any level of the organization—should be able to communicate well but also be able to communicate to a variety of stakeholders. Selander also says he will always ask the candidate about his or her weaknesses, but more importantly, how the candidate plans to address those weaknesses to make sure they do not become a barrier to success. He always asks the question "What can you do for us?" When asked if he could pose only one interview question, what would it be, his answer was, "Share with me two situations, work related that you are proud of, where something was achieved based on your own personal initiative and the other where the achievement was a result of the team getting something done that you could not have done alone." In other words, Selander is looking for not only personal ability but the ability to work within a team to accomplish tasks. Selander offers advice to new college grads: try to find an organization where you can be involved and see all aspects of the public organization and be provided training to help you with certain skills that will be needed.

HUMAN RESOURCE RECALL

When was the last time you interviewed for a job? Did the process seem to flow smoothly? Why or why not?

KEY TAKEAWAYS

- The selection process refers to the steps involved in choosing someone who has the right qualifications to fill a current or future job opening.
- There are five main steps in the selection process. First, criteria are developed to determine how the person will be chosen. Second is a review of the applications and résumés, often done via a computer program that can find keywords. Next is interviewing the employee. The last steps involve testing, such as a personality test or drug test, and then finally, making the offer to the right candidate.

EXERCISE

1. What components are included in the selection process? Which one do you think is the most important?

---

[1] Leroy Hamm, "Pre-Employment Testing," IHD Corporation, n.d., accessed August 2, 2011,http://www.ihdcorp.com/articles-hr/pre-employment-testing.htm.

[2] KVUE News, "Re-Interview Process to Cost $150,000," June 23, 2011, accessed August 2, 2011, http://www.kvue.com/news/local/AFD--124452379.html.

[3] Adam Bryant, "The X Factor When Hiring? Call It Presence," June 26, 2010, New York Times, accessed July 12, 2011, http://www.nytimes.com/2010/06/27/public organization/27corner.html?scp=1&sq=Selander&st=cse&pagewanted=1.

5.2 Criteria Development and Résumé Review

LEARNING OBJECTIVES

1. Be able to explain why criteria development is an important part of the selection process.
2. Give examples of types of criteria that can be developed.
3. Describe the advantages and disadvantages of internal and external candidates.

Before we begin to review résumés and applications, we must have a clear idea of the person we want to hire for the position. Obviously, the job specifications will help us know the minimum qualifications, such as education level and years of experience. However, additional criteria might include the attitude of the potential hire, the ability to take initiative, and other important personal characteristics and professional abilities that may not always be demonstrated in an application or résumé. A specific score on a personality test, quality of work samples, and other tools to determine qualifications should be included as part of the criteria. In other words, knowing exactly what you want before you even begin the process of looking through résumés will make this process much easier. In human resources, this is called KSAOs, or knowledge, skills, abilities, and other personal characteristics that make a person successful on the job. Some organizations, such as the United States Department of Veterans Affairs, require applicants to address each one of the KSAOs listed in the job position within their cover letter. [1]

Criteria Development Considerations

Many HR professionals and managers develop the criteria for hiring, as well as the interview questions, before reviewing any résumés. This allows for a streamlined process with specific guidelines already set before reviewing a résumé. For example, criteria for a project management job might include the following:

1. Two years of experience managing a $2 million or more project budget
2. A bachelor's degree in public organization or closely related field
3. Ability to work on multiple projects at once
4. Problem-solving ability
5. Conflict-management ability
6. Ability to manage a team of five to six diverse workers
7. Score of at least a 70 on cognitive ability test
8. Score of excellent from most recent employer

By setting criteria ahead of time, the hiring team has a clear picture of exactly what qualifications they are looking for. As a result, it is easier to determine who should move forward in the selection process. For example, if someone does not have a bachelor's degree, given this is a criterion, their application materials can be filed away, perhaps for another job opening. Likewise, the HR manager can include those résumés with two or more years of experience and bachelor's degree in the interview pile and then develop interview questions that show the candidates' problem-solving, multitasking, and conflict-management abilities.

Résumé parsing or résumé scanning software is readily available and can make the initial screening easier. For example, Sovren software allows the HR manager to include keywords such as bachelor's degree or management. This software scans all received résumés and selects the ones that have the keywords. While it still may be necessary to review résumés, this type of software can save time having to look through résumés that obviously do not meet the minimum qualifications.

Validity and Reliablity

The validity refers to how useful the tool is to measure a person's attributes for a specific job opening. A tool may include any and all of the following:

1. Résumé-scanning software
2. Reference checks
3. Cognitive ability tests
4. Work samples
5. Credit reports
6. Biographical information blanks
7. Weighted application forms
8. Personality tests
9. Interview questions

Biographical information blanks (BIBs) are a useful part of the application process. A BIB is a series of questions about a person's history that may have shaped his or her behavior. The BIB can be scored in the same way as an interview or a résumé, assuming the organization knows which types of answers are predictable for success in a given job. Similarly, a weighted application form involves selecting an employee characteristic to be measured and then identifying which questions on the application predict the desired behavior. Then scores are assigned to each predictor. Of course, the development of the scoring should be determined before any résumés and application forms have been reviewed. In other words, any tool you use to determine someone's qualifications for a job should have validity to determine they are the right fit for the job.

Reliability refers to the degree in which other selection techniques yield similar data over time. For example, if you ask the same interview question of every applicant for the project management position, and the "right" answer always yields similar, positive results, such as the hiring of a successful employee every time, the question would be considered reliable. An example of an unreliable test might occur with reference checks. Most candidates would not include a reference on their résumé who might give them a poor review, making this a less reliable method for determining skills and abilities of applicants.

Fit Issues

Fit includes not only the right technical expertise, education, and experience but also fit in organizational culture and team culture. For example, at Facebook headquarters in Palo Alto, California, engineers are selected based on their willingness to take risks, as risk taking is nurtured at Facebook.[2] In addition to this component of their organizational culture, the organizational looks for the "hacker" personality, because a hacker is someone who finds ways around the constraints placed upon a system. At Zappos, the organizational culture is one focused on customer service and the willingness of people to provide the best customer service in all aspects of the public organization. At Amazon, the huge online retailer, a core value in their organizational culture is a focus on developing leaders to grow with the organization. If a potential candidate is not interested in long-term career growth, he or she might not be deemed an appropriate strategic fit with the organization. In today's organizations, most people are required to work within teams. As a result, fit within a team is as important as organizational culture fit. Microsoft, for example, does an immense amount of teamwork. The organizational is structured so that there are marketers, accountants, developers, and many others working on one product at a time. As a result, Microsoft looks for not only organizational culture fit but also fit with other team members.

Reviewing Résumés

Once we have developed our criteria for a specific job, we can begin the review process. Everyone prefers to perform this differently. For example, all the hiring decision makers may review all résumés, list the people they would like to meet in person, and then compare the lists. Another method might be to rate each candidate and interview only those above a certain score. Obviously, much of the process will depend on the organization's size and the type of job. None of this process can be done fairly without first setting criteria for the job.

When looking at résumés to determine whom to interview, a manager should be concerned with the concepts of disparate impact and disparate treatment. Disparate impact is unintended discrimination against a protected group as a whole through the use of a particular requirement. Disparate impact may be present in the interviewing process, as well as other employment-related processes such as pay raises and promotions. For example, a requirement of being able to lift 110 pounds might be considered as having disparate impact on women, unless the job requires this ability. Every criteria developed should be closely considered to see if it might have disparate impact on a protected group of individuals. For example, the requirement of a certain credit score might have a negative impact on immigrants, who may not have a well-developed credit rating. However, if being able to manage money is an important requirement of the job, this requirement might not be discriminatory.

Disparate treatment in hiring might include not interviewing a candidate because of one's perception about the candidate's age, race, or gender.

Table 5.1 Possible Advantages and Disadvantages of Hiring an Internal versus an External Candidate

	Advantages	Disadvantages
Internal Candidates	Rewards contributions of current staff	Can produce "inbreeding," which may reduce diversity and difference perspectives
	Can be cost effective, as opposed to using a traditional recruitment strategy	May cause political infighting between people to obtain the promotions
	Can improve morale	Can create bad feelings if an internal candidate applies for a job and doesn't get it
	Knowing the past performance of the candidate can assist in knowing if they meet the criteria	
External Candidates	Brings new talent into the organizational	Implementation of recruitment strategy can be expensive
	Can help an organization obtain diversity goals	Can cause morale problems for internal candidates
	New ideas and insight brought into the organizational	Can take longer for training and orientation

The last consideration is the hiring of internal versus external candidates. Aninternal candidate is someone who already works within the organization, while anexternal candidate is someone who works outside the organization. A bidding process may occur to notify internal candidates of open positions. Generally speaking, it is best to go through a formal interview process with all candidates, even if they work within the organization. This way, an HR professional can be assured that disparate treatment does not occur because of favoritism. For example, a senior executive of your organization just left, and you believe the manager in that department is qualified to take over the position. Suppose, though, that the manager has been lobbying you for the job for some time and has even taken you out to lunch to talk about the job. While this person has maintained high visibility and lobbied for the promotion, there may be equally qualified internal candidates who did not use the same lobbying techniques. Automatically offering the position to this internal candidate might undermine others who are equally qualified. So while hiring internally can be a motivator, making assumptions about a particular person may not be a motivator to others. This is why it is best, even if you hire internally, to post a formal job announcement listing the job description and job qualifications, so everyone in the organization can have an equal opportunity to apply for the job.

Once you have completed the criteria for the particular job and narrowed down the field, you can begin the interview process.

HOW WOULD YOU HANDLE THIS?

Poor Interviewer
As the assistant to the HR manager, one of your jobs is to help managers get ready to interview candidates. When you offer help to Johnathan, he says he has interviewed hundreds of people and doesn't need your help in planning the interview process. When you sit in the interview with him, he asks inappropriate questions that you don't feel really assess the abilities of a candidate. How would you handle this?
How Would You Handle This?

KEY TAKEAWAYS

- The first step in selection is to begin reviewing résumés. Even before you do this, though, it is important to develop criteria that each candidate will be measured against. This can come from the job description as well as the job qualifications.
- Other tools, such as cognitive ability tests, credit checks, and personality tests, can be used to determine qualifications. When developing your criteria for interviewing, determine the level the applicant needs to meet to meet the minimum criteria, for example, a minimum score on a personality test.
- We should be concerned with validity and reliability of measurement tools.Validity refers to how valid the test is, that is, how well a test measures a candidate's abilities to do a job. Reliability refers to which selection techniques yield similar data or results over time. It is important to choose the right measurement tool used to determine whether the candidate meets the criteria.

- Setting criteria before the interview process starts ensures that disparate impactor disparate treatment does not occur in the interview process.
- When hiring, there is the option of internal and external candidates. Each has its own set of advantages and disadvantages. Internal candidates may be able to "hit the ground running," but external candidates may come in with new perspectives. Even if an internal candidate seems to be the best hire, it is best to still perform the process of posting the job and interviewing, since other less vocal employees might be qualified internal candidates as well. In other words, don't assume one person is the obvious choice for the promotion.

EXERCISES

1. Develop criteria for the position of a retail salesperson working in teams.
2. Describe the advantages and disadvantages of hiring an internal and external candidate. Give an example of when you don't think an external candidate should be considered for a position.
3. How can development of criteria or minimum standards help in a case of disparate treatment accusations?

---

[1] "What Are KSAs?" US Department of Veterans Affairs, accessed August 2, 2011,http://www.va.gov/jobs/hiring/apply/ksa.asp.
[2] Ellen McGirt, "Most Innovative Organizations," Fast Organizational, February 2010, accessed July 12, 2011, http://www.fastorganizational.com/mic/2010/profile/facebook.

5.3 Interviewing

LEARNING OBJECTIVES

1. Explain the various types of interviews and interview questions.
2. Discuss interview methods and potential mistakes in interviewing candidates.
3. Explain the interview process.

Interviewing people costs money. As a result, after candidates are selected, good use of time is critical to making sure the interview process allows for selection of the right candidate. In an unstructured interview, questions are changed to match the specific applicant; for example, questions about the candidate's background in relation to their résumé might be used. In a structured interview, there is a set of standardized questions based on the job analysis, not on individual candidates' résumés. While a structured interview might seem the best option to find out about a particular candidate, the bigger concern is that the interview revolves around the specific job for which the candidate is interviewing. In a structured interview, the expected or desired answers are determined ahead of time, which allows the interviewer to rate responses as the candidate provides answers. This allows for a fair interview process, according to the US Office of Personnel Management._[1] For purposes of this section, we will assume that all interviews you perform will be structured, unless otherwise noted.

Types of Interviews

Interview processes can be time-consuming, so it makes sense to choose the right type of interview(s) for the individual job. Some jobs, for example, may necessitate only one interview, while another may necessitate a telephone interview and at least one or two traditional interviews. Keep in mind, though, that there will likely be other methods with which to evaluate a candidate's potential, such as testing. Here are different types of interviews:

1. *Traditional interview.* This type of interview normally takes place in the office. It consists of the interviewer and the candidate, and a series of questions are asked and answered.
2. *Telephone interview.* A telephone interview is often used to narrow the list of people receiving a traditional interview. It can be used to determine salary requirements or other data that might automatically rule out giving someone a traditional interview. For example, if you receive two hundred résumés and narrow these down to twenty-five, it is still unrealistic to interview twenty-five people in person. At this point, you may decide to conduct phone interviews of those twenty-five, which could narrow the in-person interviews to a more manageable ten or so people.
3. *Panel interview.* A panel interview occurs when several people are interviewing one candidate at the same time. While this type of interview can be nerve racking for the candidate, it can also be a more effective use of time. Consider some organizations who require three to four people to interview candidates for a job. It would be unrealistic to ask the candidate to come in for three or four interviews, so it makes sense for them to be interviewed by everyone at once.
4. *Information interview.* Informational interviews are usually used when there is no specific job opening, but the candidate is exploring possibilities in a given career field. The advantage to conducting these types of interviews is the ability to find great people ahead of a job opening.
5. *Meal interviews.* Many organizations offer to take the candidate to lunch or dinner for the interview. This can

allow for a more casual meeting where, as the interviewer, you might be able to gather more information about the person, such as their manners and treatment of waitstaff. This type of interview might be considered an unstructured interview, since it would tend to be more of a conversation as opposed to a session consisting of specific questions and answers.

6. *Group interview.* In a group interview, two or more candidates interview at the same time. This type of interview can be an excellent source of information if you need to know how they may relate to other people in their job.
7. *Video interviews.* Video interviews are the same as traditional interviews, except that video technology is used. This can be cost saving if one or more of your candidates are from out of town. Skype, for example, allows free video calls. An interview may not feel the same as a traditional interview, but the same information can be gathered about the candidate.
8. *Nondirective interview* (sometimes called an unstructured interview).In a nondirective interview, the candidate essentially leads the discussion. Some very general questions that are planned ahead of time may be asked, but the candidate spends more time talking than the interviewer. The questions may be more open ended; for example, instead of asking, "Do you like working with customers?" you may ask, "What did you like best about your last job?" The advantage of this type of interview is that it can give candidates a good chance to show their abilities; however, the downside is that it may be hard to compare potential candidates, since questions are not set in advance. It relies on more of a "gut feeling" approach.

It is likely you may use one or more of these types of interviews. For example, you may conduct phone interviews, then do a meal interview, and follow up with a traditional interview, depending on the type of job.

Interview Questions

Most interviews consist of many types of questions, but they usually lean toward situational interviews or behavior description interviews. A situational interview is one in which the candidate is given a sample situation and is asked how he or she might deal with the situation. In a behavior description interview, the candidate is asked questions about what he or she actually did in a variety of given situations. The assumption in this type of interview is that someone's past experience or actions are an indicator of future behavior. These types of questions, as opposed to the old "tell me about yourself" questions, tend to assist the interviewer in knowing how a person would handle or has handled situations. These interview styles also use a structured method and provide a better basis for decision making. Examples of situational interview questions might include the following:

1. If you saw someone stealing from the organizational, what would you do?
2. One of your employees is performing poorly, but you know he has some personal home issues he is dealing with. How would you handle complaints from his colleagues about lack of performance?
3. A coworker has told you she called in sick three days last week because she actually decided to take a vacation. What would you do?
4. You are rolling out a new sales plan on Tuesday, which is really important to ensure success in your organization. When you present it, the team is lukewarm on the plan. What would you do?
5. You disagree with your supervisor on her handling of a situation. What would you do?
6. Examples of behavior description interview questions might include the following:
7. Tell me about a time you had to make a hard decision. How did you handle this process?
8. Give an example of how you handled an angry customer.
9. Do you show leadership in your current or past job? What would be an example of a situation in which you did this?
10. What accomplishments have given you the most pride and why?
11. What plans have you made to achieve your career goals?

As you already know, there are many types of interview questions that would be considered illegal. Here are some examples:

1. *National origin.* You cannot ask seemingly innocent questions such as "That's a beautiful name, where is your family from?" This could indicate national origin, which could result in bias. You also cannot ask questions about citizenship, except by asking if a candidate is legally allowed to work in the United States. Questions about the first language of the candidate shouldn't be asked, either. However, asking "Do you have any language abilities that would be helpful in this job?" or "Are you authorized to work in the United States?" would be acceptable.
2. *Age.* You cannot ask someone how old they are, and it is best to avoid questions that might indicate age, such as "When did you graduate from high school?" However, asking "Are you over 18?" is acceptable.

3. *Marital status.* You can't ask direct questions about marital status or ages of children. An alternative may be to ask, "Do you have any restrictions on your ability to travel, since this job requires 50 percent travel?"
4. *Religion.* It's illegal to ask candidates about their religious affiliation or to ask questions that may indicate a religion-affiliated school or university.
5. *Disabilities.* You may not directly ask if the person has disabilities or recent illnesses. You can ask if the candidate is able to perform the functions of the job with or without reasonable accommodations.
6. *Criminal record.* While it is fine to perform a criminal record check, asking a candidate if they have ever been arrested is not appropriate; however, questions about convictions and guilty pleadings are acceptable.
7. *Personal questions.* Avoid asking personal questions, such as questions about social organizations or clubs, unless they relate to the job.

Besides these questions, any specific questions about weight, height, gender, and arrest record (as opposed to allowable questions about criminal convictions) should be avoided.

HR professionals and managers should be aware of their own body language in an interview. Some habits, such as nodding, can make the candidate think they are on the right track when answering a question. Also, be aware of ahalo effect or reverse halo effect. This occurs when an interviewer becomes biased because of one positive or negative trait a candidate possesses. Interview bias can occur in almost any interview situation. Interview bias is when an interviewer makes assumptions about the candidate that may not be accurate._[2] These assumptions can be detrimental to an interview process. Contrast bias is a type of bias that occurs when comparing one candidate to others. It can result in one person looking particularly strong in an area, when in fact they look strong compared to the other candidates.

A gut feeling bias is when an interviewer relies on an intuitive feeling about a candidate. Generalization bias can occur when an interviewer assumes that how someone behaves in an interview is how they always behave. For example, if a candidate is very nervous and stutters while talking, an assumption may be made that he or she always stutters. Another important bias called cultural noise bias occurs when a candidate thinks he or she knows what the interviewer wants to hear and answers the questions based on that assumption. Nonverbal behavior bias occurs when an interviewer likes an answer and smiles and nods, sending the wrong signal to the candidate. A similar to me bias (which could be considered discriminatory) results when an interviewer has a preference for a candidate because he or she views that person as having similar attributes as themselves. Finally, recency bias occurs when the interviewer remembers candidates interviewed most recently more so than the other candidates.

HUMAN RESOURCE RECALL

What are the dangers of a reverse halo effect? *A halo effect occurs when a desirable trait makes us believe all traits possessed by the candidate are desirable. This can be a major danger in interviewing candidates.*

Interview Process

Once the criteria have been selected and interview questions developed, it is time to start interviewing people. Your interviewing plan can determine the direction and process that should be followed:

1. Recruit new candidates.
2. Establish criteria for which candidates will be rated.
3. Develop interview questions based on the analysis.
4. Set a time line for interviewing and decision making.
5. Connect schedules with others involved in the interview process.
6. Set up the interviews with candidates and set up any testing procedures.
7. Interview the candidates and perform any necessary testing.
8. Once all results are back, meet with the hiring team to discuss each candidate and make a decision based on the established criteria.
9. Put together an offer for the candidate.

As you can see, a large part of the interviewing process is planning. For example, consider the hiring manager who doesn't know exactly the type of person and skills she is looking to hire but sets up interviews anyway. It is difficult, if not impossible, to determine who should be hired if you don't know what you are looking for in the first place. In addition, utilizing time lines for interviewing can help keep everyone involved on track and ensure the chosen candidate starts work in a timely manner. Here are some tips to consider when working with the interview process:

1. Make sure everyone is trained on the interviewing process. Allowing someone who has poor interviewing skills to conduct the interview will likely not result in the best candidate. In a worst-case scenario, someone could ask an illegal question, and once hired, the candidate can sue the organization. UCLA researchers_[3]calculated that plaintiffs win about half of hiring discrimination cases

that go to trial, sometimes because of interviewers asking illegal questions. For example, "I see you speak Spanish, where did you study it?" is a seemingly harmless question that could be indirectly asking a candidate his or her ethnic background. To avoid such issues, it's important to train managers in the proper interviewing process.

2. Listen to the candidate and try to develop a rapport with them. Understand how nervous they must be and try to put them at ease.
3. Be realistic about the job. Do not try to paint a "rosy" picture of all aspects of the job. Being honest up front helps a candidate know exactly what they will be in for when they begin their job.
4. Be aware of your own stereotypes and do not let them affect how you view a potential candidate.
5. Watch your own body language during the interview and that of the candidate. Body language is a powerful tool in seeing if someone is the right fit for a job. For example, Scott Simmons, vice president at Crist|Kolder, interviewed someone for a CFO position. The candidate had a great résumé, but during the interview, he offered a dead-fish handshake, slouched, and fidgeted in his chair. The candidate didn't make eye contact and mumbled responses, and, of course, he didn't get the job,[4] because his body language did not portray the expectations for the job position.
6. Stick to your criteria for hiring. Do not ask questions that have not been predetermined in your criteria.
7. Learn to manage disagreement and determine a fair process if not everyone on the interviewing team agrees on who should be hired.

Once you have successfully managed the interview process, it is time to make the decision.

HUMAN RESOURCE RECALL

Can you think of a time when the interviewer was not properly trained? What were the results?

KEY TAKEAWAYS

- Traditional, telephone, panel, informational, meal, group, and video are types of interviews. A combination of several of these may be used to determine the best candidate for the job. A structured interview format means the questions are determined ahead of time, and unstructured means the questions are based on the individual applicant. The advantage of a structured interview is that all candidates are rated on the same criteria. Before interviewing occurs, criteria and questions for a structured interview should be developed.
- Interview questions can revolve around situational questions orbehavioral questions. Situational questions focus on asking someone what they would do in a given situation, while behavioral questions ask candidates what they have done in certain situations.
- Interview questions about national origin, marital status, age, religion, and disabilities are illegal. To avoid any legal issues, it is important for interviewers to be trained on which questions cannot be asked. The halo effect, which assumes that one desirable trait means all traits are desirable, should also be avoided.
- The process involved in interviewing a person includes the following steps: recruit new candidates; establish criteria for which candidates will be rated; develop interview questions based on the analysis; set a time line for interviewing and decision making; connect schedules with others involved in the interview process; set up interviews with candidates and set up any testing procedures; interview the candidates and perform any necessary testing; and once all results are back, meet with the hiring team to discuss each candidate and make a decision based on the established criteria; then finally, put together an offer for the candidate.
- Developing a rapport, being honest, and managing the interview process are tips to having a successful interview.

EXERCISES

1. With a partner, develop a list of five examples (not already given in the chapter) of situational and behavioral interview questions.
2. Why is it important to determine criteria and interview questions before bringing someone in for an interview?
3. Visit Monster.com and find two examples of job postings that ask those with criminal records not to apply. Do you think, given the type of job, this is a reasonable criteria?

---

[1] "Structured Interviews: A Practical Guide," US Office of Personnel Management, September 2008, accessed January 25, 2011,https://apps.opm.gov/ADT/ContentFiles/SIGuide09.08.08.pdf.
[2] Jeff Lipschultz, "Don't Be a Victim of Interview Bias," Career Builder, June 15, 2010, accessed July 12, 2011, http://jobs.aol.com/articles/2010/06/15/interview-bias/.

[3] Mark Hanricks, "3 Interview Questions That Could Cost You $1 Million," BNET, March 8, 2011, accessed August 2, 2011, http://www.bnet.com/blog/public organization-myths/3-interview-questions-that-could-cost-your-organizational-1-million/791.
[4] Scott Reeves, "Is Your Body Betraying You in Job Interviews?" Forbes, February 2006, accessed August 2, 2011, http://www.forbes.com/2006/02/15/employment-careers-interviews-cx_sr_0216bizbasics.html.

5.4 Testing and Selecting

LEARNING OBJECTIVES

1. Explain the types of tests that can be administered as part of the selection process.
2. Be able to discuss the types of selection models.

Besides the interview, we can also look at several other aspects that may predict success on the job. If any test is to be criteria for measuring a candidate, this should be communicated to each person interviewing, and criteria should be developed on specific test scores and expectations before interviewing and testing begins.

Testing

A variety of tests may be given upon successful completion of an interview. These employment tests can gauge a person's KSAOs in relation to another candidate. The major categories of tests include the following:

1. Cognitive ability tests
2. Personality tests
3. Physical ability tests
4. Job knowledge tests
5. Work sample

A number of written tests can be administered. A cognitive ability test can measure reasoning skills, math skills, and verbal skills. An aptitude test measures a person's ability to learn new skills, while an achievement test measures someone's current knowledge. Depending on the type of job, one or both will be better suited.

A cognitive ability test measures intelligences, such as numerical ability and reasoning. The Scholastic Aptitude Test (SAT) is an example of a cognitive ability test. It is important to note that some cognitive ability tests can have disparate impact. For example, in EEOC v. Ford Motor Co. and United Automobile Workers of America, African Americans were rejected from an apprentice program after taking a cognitive test known as the Apprenticeship Training Selection System (ATSS).[1] The test showed significant disparate impact on African Americans, and it was then replaced by a different selection procedure, after costing Ford $8.55 million. Some sample test categories might include the following:

1. Reasoning questions
2. Mathematical questions and calculations
3. Verbal and/or vocabulary skills

Aptitude tests can measure things such as mechanical aptitude and clerical aptitude (e.g., speed of typing or ability to use a particular computer program). Usually, an aptitude test asks specific questions related to the requirements of the job. To become a New York City police offer, for example, an aptitude test is required before an application will be considered. The written exam is given as a computerized test at a computerized testing center in the city. The test measures cognitive skills and observational skills (aptitude test) required for the job.[2]

Personality tests such as Meyers-Briggs and the "Big Five" personality factors may be measured and then compared with successful employee scores. For example, The University of Missouri Health Care system recently launched a patient satisfaction initiative as part of its strategic plan. The plan includes training for current employees and personality testing for nursing, managerial, and physician candidates.[3] The goal of the test is to assess talent and to see if the candidate has the potential to meet the expectations of patients. They hired a private organizational, Talent Plus, who conducts the test via phone interviews. However, many organizations administer tests themselves, and some tests are free and can be administered online.

The Big Five personality test looks at extroversion, agreeableness, conscientiousness, neuroticism, and openness. Self-assessment statements might include the following:

1. I have an assertive personality.
2. I am generally trusting.
3. I am not always confident in my abilities.
4. I have a hard time dealing with change.

Some institutions also require physical ability tests; for example, to earn a position in a fire department, you may have to be able to carry one hundred pounds up three flights of stairs. If you use tests in your hiring processes, the key to making them useful is to determine a minimum standard or expectation, specifically related to the requirements of the job. An HR manager should also consider the legality of such tests. In the EEOC v. Dial Corp. case,[4] women were disproportionately rejected for entry-level positions. Prior to the test, 46 percent of hires were women, but after implementation of the test, only 15 percent of the new hires were women. The Equal Employment Opportunity Commission (EEOC) established that the test was considerably more difficult than the job, resulting in disparate impact. Physical ability tests need to show direct correlation with the job duties.

A job knowledge test measures the candidate's level of understanding about a particular job. For example, a job knowledge test may require an engineer to write code in a given period of time or may ask candidates to solve a case study problem related to the job.

Work sample tests ask candidates to show examples of work they have already done. In the advertising public organization, this may include a portfolio of designs, or for a project manager, this can include past project plans or budgets. When applying for a pharmaceutical representative position, a "brag book" might be required._[5] A brag book is a list of recommendation letters, awards, and achievements that the candidate shares with the interviewer. Work sample tests can be a useful way to test for KSAOs. These work samples can often be a good indicator of someone's abilities in a specific area. As always, before looking at samples, the interviewer should have specific criteria or expectations developed so each candidate can be measured fairly.

Once the interview is completed and testing occurs, other methods of checking KSAOs, including checking references, driving records, and credit history, can be performed. Some organizations even use Facebook as a way of gauging the candidate's professionalism.

Reference checking is essential to verify a candidate's background. It is an added assurance that the candidate's abilities are parallel with what you were told in the interview. While employment dates and job titles can be verified with previous employers, many employers will not verify more than what can be verified in the employment record because of privacy laws. However, if you do find someone who is willing to discuss more than just dates and job titles, a list of questions is appropriate. Some of these questions might include the following:

1. What was the title and responsibilities of the position the candidate had while at your organizational?
2. Do you think the candidate was qualified to assume those responsibilities?
3. Does this person show up on time and have good attendance?
4. Would you consider this person a team player?
5. What are the three strongest and weakest characteristics of this candidate?
6. Would you rehire this person?

If a candidate will be driving a organizational car or vehicle, such as a UPS truck, driving records may be checked. Criminal background checks may also be used if the position will include interaction with the public. If the position requires handling of money, a credit check may be required, although a written notice is required to be given to the candidate before the credit check is carried out. In addition, written permission must be provided to the credit agency, and the applicants must receive a copy of the report and a copy of their rights under the Consumer Credit Reporting Reform Act (CCRRA). All these types of tests can be used to determine if someone has been honest about their past employment.
Some organizations require drug testing, which causes some debate. While some organizations say this is a safety issue (and pay lower insurance premiums), others say it is an invasion of privacy. As long as drug tests are administered for a defensible reason (safety), many organizations will continue to require them. Some organizations will also require physical examinations to ensure the candidate can perform the tasks required. A final form of testing is the honesty test. A number of "what would you do" questions are asked. The challenge with this type of test is that many people know the "right" answer but may not be honest in their responses.

Forty-five percent of organizations use social networking such as Facebook, Twitter, or LinkedIn to gather information about potential candidates._[6] See Table 5.2 "Reasons Why Employers Acted upon Data Found on Social Networking Sites" for the types of data found on social networking sites that disqualified candidates, according to an article by Fast Organizational. This can be an effective method to see the kind of image the candidate portrays in his or her personal time.

Selection Methods
A clinical selection approach is probably the most common selection method, and it involves all who will be making the decision to hire a candidate. The decision makers review the data and, based on what they learn from the candidate and the information available to them, decide who should be hired for a job. Because interviewers have a different perception about the strengths of a candidate, this method leaves room for error. One consideration is disparate treatment, in which one's biases may result in not hiring candidates based on their age, race, or gender. One way to

handle this and limit the personal stereotypes and perceptions of the interviewers is to use astatistical method in hiring.

Table 5.2 Reasons Why Employers Acted upon Data Found on Social Networking Sites

Provocative or inappropriate photos or info	53%
Drinking or drug use	44%
Badmouthing previous employer, colleague, or client	35%
Poor communication skills	29%
Discriminatory comments	26%
Lied about qualifications	24%
Leaked confidential information about previous job	20%

Source: Kit Eaton "If You're Applying for a Job, Censor Your Facebook Page," Fast Organizational, August 19, 2009, accessed January 27, 2011,http://www.fastorganizational.com/blog/kit-eaton/technomix/if-youre-applying-job-censor-your-facebook-page.

In the statistical method, a selection model is developed that assigns scores and gives more weight to specific factors, if necessary. For example, for some jobs, the ability to work in a team might be more important, while in others, knowledge of a specific computer program is more important. In this case, a weight can be assigned to each of the job criteria listed. For example, if the job is a project manager, ability to work with the client might be more important than how someone dresses for the interview. So, in the example shown in Figure 5.4 "Sample Selection Model, with Sample Scores and Weighting Filled In", dress is weighted 1, while being able to give bad news to a client is weighted 5. In the example, the rating is multiplied by the weight to get the score for the particular job criteria. This method allows for a fairer process and can limit disparate treatment, although it may not limit disparate impact. A statistical method may work like this: you and the hiring team review the job analysis and job description and then determine the criteria for the job. You assign weights for each area and score ranges for each aspect of the criteria, rate candidates on each area as they interview, and then score tests or examine work samples. Once each hiring manager has scored each candidate, the hiring team can compare scores in each area and hopefully hire the best person in the best way. A sample candidate selection model is included in Figure 5.4 "Sample Selection Model, with Sample Scores and Weighting Filled In".

With the statistical approach, there is more objectivity than with the clinical approach. Statistical approaches include the compensatory model, multiple cutoff model, and the multiple hurdle model. In the compensatory model, a similar method of scoring is used as the weighted model but permits a high score in an important area to make up for a lower score in another area. In our Figure 5.4 "Sample Selection Model, with Sample Scores and Weighting Filled In" example, ability to give bad news to a client might outweigh a test score. These decisions would be made before the interviews happen.

Figure 5.4 Sample Selection Model, with Sample Scores and Weighting Filled In

Job Criteria	Rating*	Weight**	Total	Comments
Dress	4	1	4	Candidate dressed appropriately.
Personality	2	5	10	Did not seem excited about the job.
Interview questions				
Give an example of a time you showed leadership.	3	3	9	Descriptive but didn't seem to have experience required.
Give an example of when you had to give bad news to a client.	0	5	0	Has never had to do this.
Tell us how you have worked well in a team.	5	4	20	Great example of teamwork given.
Score on cognitive ability test.	78	5	390	Meets minimum required score of 70.
Work sample rating.	5	5	25	Excellent work samples.
			458	

***Rating system of 1-5, with 5 being the highest**
****Weighting of 1-5, with 5 being the most important**

A multiple cutoff model requires that a candidate has a minimum score level on all selection criteria. In our Figure 5.4 "Sample Selection Model, with Sample Scores and Weighting Filled In" example, the candidate may be required to have a score of at least 2 out of 5 on each criteria. If this was the case, the candidate in Figure 5.4 "Sample Selection Model, with Sample Scores and Weighting Filled In" scored low on "bad news to a client," meaning he or she wouldn't get the job in a multiple cutoff model. In themultiple hurdle model, only candidates with high (preset) scores go to the next stages of the selection process. For example, the expectations might be to score a 4 on at least three of the items in Figure 5.4 "Sample Selection Model, with Sample Scores and Weighting Filled In". If this were the case, this candidate might make it to the next level of the selection process, since he or she scored at least a 4 on three criteria areas.

Once the discussion on whom to hire has occurred and a person has been selected, the final phase of the process is to make an offer to the candidate.

KEY TAKEAWAYS

- Once the interview process is complete, some organizations use other means of measuring candidates. For example, work samples are an excellent way of seeing how someone might perform at your organizational.
- An aptitude test or achievement test can be given. An aptitude test measures how well someone might be able to do something, while an achievement test measures what the candidate already knows. Tests that measure cognitive ability and personality are examples.
- Some organizations also perform drug tests and physical tests. A physical test might consist of being able to lift a certain amount of weight, if required for the job. Honesty tests are also given; these measure the honesty level of the candidate. However, these tests may not be reliable, since someone can guess the "right" answer.
- Facebook, Twitter, and other social networking websites are also used to gather information about a candidate. Calling references is another option.
- Every person interviewing the candidate should have a selection model; this method utilizes a statistical approach as opposed to a clinical approach. The selection table lists the criteria on the left and asks interviewers to provide a rating for each. This method can allow for a more consistent way of measuring candidates.

EXERCISES

1. Develop a sample candidate selection for your current job.
2. Visit your or another person's Facebook page. Consider the content from an interviewer's point of view. Should anything be removed or changed?

---

[1] "Employment Tests and Selection Procedures," US Equal Employment Opportunity Commission, accessed August 2, 2011,http://www.eeoc.gov/policy/docs/factemployment_procedures.html
[2] "Exam Schedule," New York Police Department, accessed August 2, 2011,http://www.nypdrecruit.com/exam-center/exam-overview.
[3] Janese Silvey, "MU Health Care to Renew Satisfaction Effort," Columbia Daily Tribune, August 2, 2011, accessed August 2, 2011,http://www.columbiatribune.com/news/2011/aug/02/mu-health-care-to-renew-satisfaction-effort/.
[4] "Employment Tests and Selection Procedures," US Equal Employment Opportunity Commission, accessed August 2, 2011,http://www.eeoc.gov/policy/docs/factemployment_procedures.html
.
[5] Katharine Hansen, "So, You Want to Get into Paramedical Sales?" n.d., Quintessential Careers, accessed August 2, 2011,http://www.quintcareers.com/pharmaceutical_sales_careers.html.
[6] Kit Eaton, "If You're Applying for a Job, Censor Your Facebook Page," Fast Organizational, August 19, 2009, accessed January 27, 2011, http://www.fastorganizational.com/blog/kit-eaton/technomix/if-youre-applying-job-censor-your-facebook-page.

5.5 Making the Offer

LEARNING OBJECTIVE

1. Explain the steps in making the offer to the candidate.

Oftentimes once the decision is made to hire a candidate, HR professionals feel their job is finished. But making the offer to the chosen candidate can be equally as important as the interview process. If the offer is not handled properly, you can lose the candidate, or if the candidates takes the job, he or she could start off on the wrong foot.

According to Paul Falcone, vice president for human resources at the Organizational organizational Time Warner, detailed information should be asked of the candidate before the offer is even made.[1] He says that as soon as the offer is made, power is shifted to the candidate. To handle this, he suggests asking salary questions in the interview, including the following:

1. "If we were to make a job offer today, when would you be in a position to accept or reject the offer?" If the candidate answers "right now," this indicates they do not have other job offers on the table or if they do, you are their first choice.
2. "At what point, dollar wise, would you accept our job offer and at what point, dollar wise would you reject the offer?" The advantage of using this strategy is that it gets to the point of understanding the candidate's expectations. If the interviewee does not respond right away, you can clarify by asking, "I am asking this question because I would like to gauge your interest level. Share with me the ideal salary offer versus at what point you would be willing to walk away from this opportunity."

Asking these questions can assist in qualifying candidates, based on salary expectations. For example, if a candidate requests 20 percent more than you are able to pay for the job, this discussion can be had before the offer is even made, perhaps making this candidate no longer viable.

Once you have determined in the interview process that the salary expectation is in the range of what you can offer, the first step is to make the offer as soon as the decision is made. In a tight labor market, waiting a week or two may impact your ability to hire your first choice. You probably already have a salary range in mind and can begin to narrow down the offer based on the individual's KSAOs. Based on the range of salary you can offer, consider the following questions when making the offer to a candidate:

- What is the scarcity of the particular skills set?
- What are the "going" wages in your geographic area?
- What are the current economic conditions?
- What is the current pay for similar positions in your organization?
- What is your organizational compensation strategy?
- What is the fair market value of the job?
- What is the level of the job within the organization?
- What are your budget constraints?
- How soon will the employee be productive in the organization?
- Are there other candidates equally qualified that might have lower salary expectations?
- What are the national and regional unemployment rates?
- If you cannot pay more, can you offer other perks such as a signing bonus or flexible work schedule?

Once the offer has been made, it is reasonable to give the candidate some time to decide, but not too long, as this can result in losing other candidates should this candidate reject the job offer. It is likely the candidate may come back and ask for higher salary or benefits. Some tips to successfully negotiate are included below and in Video 5.4:

1. Be prepared. Know exactly what you can and can't offer.
2. Explain the career growth the organization can provide.
3. Address the benefits of the candidate's joining the organization.
4. Discuss the entire offer, including other benefits offered to the employee.
5. View the negotiation as a win-win situation.
6. Be able to provide salary research of similar positions and competitors for the same job title.
7. Use the trading technique. For example, "I cannot offer you the salary you are requesting right now, but what if we were able to review salary at your six-month performance review, assuming ____ objectives are met?"

Once the phone call is made and the candidate accepts the offer, an e-mail or formal letter should follow, outlining details of the employment agreement. The employment agreement or offer letter should include the following:

1. Job title
2. Salary
3. Other compensation, such as bonuses or stock options
4. Benefits, such as health-care coverage, 401(k)
5. Vacation time/paid holidays
6. Start date
7. Noncompete agreement expectations
8. Additional considerations such as relocation expenses

Once the pay and benefits package has been successfully negotiated and the offer letter (or e-mail) sent, you should clarify acceptance details in writing and receive confirmation of the start date. It is not unusual for people in higher-level positions to need a month or even two to transition from their old jobs. During this period, make sure to stay in touch and even complete the new hire paperwork in the meantime.

KEY TAKEAWAYS

- The HR professional's job isn't finished once the selection is made. The next step is to actually make the offer. This step is important, because if it isn't done properly, you could lose the candidate or have ill feelings at the onset of the employment relationship.
- Once you have made the decision to hire someone, make the offer to the candidate right away. Normally this is done through a phone call and a follow-up e-mail, outlining the details of the offer.
- It is not unusual for someone to negotiate salary or benefits. Know how far you can negotiate and also be aware of how your current employees will be affected if you offer this person a higher salary.
- If you are having trouble coming to an agreement, be creative in what you can offer; for example, offer flextime instead of higher pay.

EXERCISE

1. Research "salary negotiation" on the Internet. What tips are provided for job seekers? Do you think these same tips could apply to the HR professional? Why or why not?

---

[1] Paul Falcone, "The New Hire: Five Questions to Ask before Making the Job Offer," n.d., Monster.com, accessed July 13, 2011, http://hiring.monster.com/hr/hr-best-practices/recruiting-hiring-advice/acquiring-job-candidates/making-a-job-offer.aspx.

5.6 Cases and Problems

CHAPTER SUMMARY

- The selection process refers to the steps involved in choosing someone who has the right qualifications to fill a current or future job opening.
- There are five main steps in the selection process. First, criteria should be developed to determine how the

person will be chosen. Second, a review of the applications and résumés is conducted, often via a computer program that can find keywords. Next, interview the employee. The last steps involve administering tests, such as a personality test or drug test, and making the offer to the right candidate.

- The first step in selection is to review résumés. Even before you do this, though, it is important to develop criteria against which each candidate will be measured. Criteria can come from the job description as well as the job qualifications.
- Other tools, such as cognitive ability tests, credit checks, or personality tests, can be used to determine qualifications. When developing your criteria for interviewing, determine the level the applicant needs to meet to meet the minimum criteria—for example, a minimum score for a personality test.
- We should be concerned with validity and reliability of measurement tools.Validity refers to how valid the test is—that is, how well a test measures a candidate's abilities to do a job. Reliability refers to which selection techniques yield similar data or results over time. It is important to choose the right measurement tool used to determine whether the candidate meets the criteria.
- Use of criteria before the interview process starts is also important to make sure disparate impact or disparate treatment do not occur in the interview process.
- When hiring, there is the option of internal and external candidates. Each has its own set of advantages and disadvantages. Internal candidates may be able to "hit the ground running" but external candidates may come in with new perspectives. Even if an internal candidate seems to be the best hire, it is best to still perform the process of posting the job and interviewing, since other less vocal employees might be qualified internal candidates as well. In other words, don't assume one person is the obvious choice for the promotion.
- Traditional, telephone, panel, informational, meal, group, and video are types of interviews. A combination of several of these may be used to determine the best candidate for the job. A structured interview format means the questions are determined ahead of time, and unstructured means the questions are based on the individual applicant. The advantage of a structured interview is that all candidates are rated on the same criteria. Before interviewing occurs, criteria and questions for a structured interview should be developed.
- Interview questions can revolve around situational questions or behavioral questions. Situational questions focus on asking someone what they would do in a given situation, while behavioral questions ask candidates what they would have done in certain situations.
- Interview questions about national origin, marital status, age, religion, and disabilities are illegal. To avoid any legal issues, it is important for interviewers to be trained on which questions cannot be asked. The halo effect, which assumes that one desirable trait means all traits are desirable, should also be avoided.
- The process involved in interviewing a person includes the following steps: recruit new candidates; establish criteria for which candidates will be rated; develop interview questions based on the analysis; set a time line for interviewing and decision making; connect schedules with others involved in the interview process; set up interviews with candidates and set up any testing procedures; interview the candidates and perform any necessary testing; and once all results are back, meet with the hiring team to discuss each candidate and make a decision based on the established criteria. Finally, put together an offer for the candidate.
- Developing a rapport, being honest, and managing the interview process are tips to having a successful interview.
- Once the interview process is complete, some organizations use other means of measuring candidates. For example, work samples are an excellent way of seeing how someone might perform at your organizational.
- An aptitude test or achievement test can be given. An aptitude test measures how well someone might be able to do something, while an achievement test measures what the candidate already knows. Tests that measure cognitive ability and personality are examples.
- Some organizations also perform drug tests and physical tests. A physical test might consist of being able to lift a certain amount of weight, if required for the job. Honesty tests are also given, which measure the honesty level of the candidate. However, these tests may not be reliable, since someone can guess the "right" answer.
- Facebook, Twitter, and other social networking websites are used to gather information about a candidate. Calling references is another option.
- Every person interviewing the candidate should have a selection model; this method utilizes a statistical approach as opposed to a clinical approach. The selection table lists the criteria on the left and asks interviewers to provide a rating for each. This method can allow for a more consistent way of measuring candidates.

- The job of the HR professional isn't finished once the selection is made. The next step is to make the offer. This step is important, because if it isn't done properly, you could lose the candidate or have ill feelings at the onset of the employment relationship.
- Once you have made the decision to hire someone, make the offer to the candidate right away. Normally this is done through a phone call and a follow-up e-mail, outlining the details of the offer.
- It is not unusual for someone to negotiate salary or benefits. Know how far you can negotiate, and also be aware of how your current employees will be affected if you offer this person a higher salary.
- If you are having trouble coming to an agreement, be creative in what you can offer; for example, offer flextime instead of higher pay.

CHAPTER CASE

The Four-Fifths Rule

The four-fifths rule is a way of measuring adverse impact in selection processes of organizations. It works like this: assume your organization requires a cognitive test for employment. You set a test score of 70 as the required pass rate for the candidate to be considered for an interview. Based on our numbers, if 50 percent of men passed this test with a score of 70, then four-fifths or 40 percent of women should also be able to pass the test. You might calculate it like this:

Gender	Total who scored 70 or above	Total who took the test	Percent
Male	52	62	83.8 or 84% passed
Female	36	58	62.07 or 62%

If you divide the total of who scored above 70 by the total number who took the test, it shows the percentage of 84 percent passed the test. If you divide the number of women who passed by the total number of women who took the test, you come up with 62 percent. Then divide 62 percent by 84 percent (62/84 = 73.8%). The resulting 74 percent means that it is below the 80 percent or the four-fifths rule, and this test could be considered to have disparate impact.

52/62 = 84% of men who took the test passed the test36/58 = 62% of women who took the test passed the test62/84 = 73.8%, less than 80%, which could show disparate impact
This is only an indicator as to how the selection process works for the organization, and other factors, such as sample size, can impact the reliability of this test. Using the tables below, please calculate possible disparate impact and then answer the questions that follow.

National Origin	Passing Test Score	Total Number Taking the Test	Percent
Caucasians	56	89	
Minority groups	48	62	

Age	Passing Test Score	Total Number Taking the Test	Percent
People under 40	28	52	
People over 40	23	61	

Gender	Passing Test Score	Total Number Taking the Test	Percent
Male	71	82	
Female	64	85	

1. Please calculate the above numbers using the four-fifths rule. Based on your calculation:
   a. Which group or groups might be affected negatively by this test?
   b. What would be your considerations before changing any selection tools based on this data?
   c. How might you change your selection process to ensure disparate impact isn't occurring at your organization?

TEAM ACTIVITY

1. In a team of two, take the Big Five personality test online (http://www.outofservice.com/bigfive/) and compare scores.
2. Assume you are hiring a retail salesperson and plan to administer the same Big Five personality test you took above. In your team, develop minimum percentile scores for each of the five areas that would be acceptable for your new hire.

NOTES:

NOTES:

Chapter 6:
Compensation and Benefits in Public Organizations

Matching Compensation with Core Values

As you sit down to review the compensation package your organizational offers, one thing that stands out is that your compensation package no longer matches the core values of your organization. When your organization merged five years ago with a similar firm that specializes in online shoe retailing, your organizational had to hire hundreds of people to keep up with growth. As a result—and what happens with many organizations—the compensation plans are not revised and revisited as they should be. The core values your organizational adopted from the merging organizational focused on customer service, freedom to work where employees felt they could be most productive, and continuing education of employees, whether or not the education was related to the organization. The compensation package, providing the basic salary, health benefits, and 401(k) plans, seems a bit old-fashioned for the type of organizational yours has become.

After reviewing your organizational's strategic plan and your human resource management (HRM) strategic plan, you begin to develop a compensation plan that includes salary, health benefits, and 401(k) plans, but you feel it might be smart to better meet the needs of your employees by making some changes to these existing plans. For example, you are considering implementing a team bonus program for high customer service ratings and coverage for alternative forms of medicine, such as acupuncture and massage. Instead of guessing what employees would like to see in their compensation packages, you decide to develop a compensation survey to assess what benefits are most important to your employees. As you begin this task, you know it will be a lot of work, but it's important to the continued recruitment, retention, and motivation of your current employees.

6.1 Goals of a Compensation Plan

LEARNING OBJECTIVE

1. Be able to explain the goals of a compensation plan.

So far, we have discussed the process for strategic plan development and the recruitment and selection process. The next aspect of HRM is to develop compensation plans that will help in the recruitment and retention of employees. This is the topic of this chapter.

Most of us, no matter how much we like our jobs, would not do them without a compensation package. When we think of compensation, often we think of only our paycheck, but compensation in terms of HRM is much broader. A compensation package can include pay, health-care benefits, and other benefits such as 401(k) plans, which will all be discussed in this chapter. Before we discuss specifics, you should be aware of courses and certifications that can be earned through the WorldatWork Society of Certified Professionals, specifically related to compensation (other certifications will be discussed in their respective chapters). WorldatWork offers several certifications in the area of compensation:

- Certified Compensation Professional (CCP)
- Certified Benefits Professional (CBP)
- Certified Sales Compensation Professional (CSCP)
- Certified Executive Compensation Professional (CECP)

These certifications involve taking a multiple-choice exam online or at one of the WorldatWork testing locations. The exams test for knowledge, experience, and skills in each of the compensation certification areas and can be a valuable asset to you when applying for HR positions.

The certifications are based on many of the aspects of this chapter, including understanding the goals of compensation packages for employees, which is our focus for this section. First, the compensation package should be positive enough to attract the best people for the job. An organization that does not pay as well as others within the same industry will likely not be able to attract the best candidates, resulting in a poorer overall organizational performance.

Once the best employees and talent come to work for your organization, you want the compensation to be competitive enough to motivate people to stay with your organization. Although we know that compensation packages are not the only thing that motivates people, compensation is a key component.

Third, compensation can be used to improve morale, motivation, and satisfaction among employees. If employees are not satisfied, this can result not only in higher turnover but also in poor quality of work for those employees who do stay. A proper compensation plan can also increase loyalty in the organization.

Pay systems can also be used to reward individual or team performance and encourage employees to work at their own peak performance. In fact, in the 2011 list of the Best Organizations to Work For by Fortune magazine, all the organizations who topped the list (SAS and Boston Consulting Group, for example) had satisfied employees—not only with their pay, but their entire benefits package.[1]

With an appropriate pay system, organizations find that customer service is better because employees are happier. In addition, having fairly compensated, motivated employees not only adds to the bottom line of the organization but also facilitates organizational growth and expansion. Motivated employees can also save the organizational money indirectly, by not taking sick days when the employee isn't really sick, and organizations with good pay packages find fewer disability claims as well.

So far, our focus on HRM has been a strategic focus, and the same should be true for development of compensation packages. Before the package is developed for employees, it's key to understand the role compensation plays in the bottom line of the organization. For example, in 2010, the US military spent 22 percent of its budget on personnel salaries.[2] One-fifth of the total budget—or more—is not uncommon for most US organizations, depending on the industry. As a result, it is easy to see why the compensation plan should be an important aspect of the overall HRM strategic plan. The next few sections will detail the aspects of creating the right compensation packages: for your organization, including legal considerations.

HUMAN RESOURCE RECALL

If you have had or currently have a job, do you feel the compensation plan motivated you? Why or why not?

KEY TAKEAWAYS

- A compensation package is an important part of the overall strategic HRM plan, since much of the organizational budget is for employee compensation.
- A compensation package can include salary, bonuses, health-care plans, and a variety of other types of compensation.
- The goals of compensation are to attract people to work for your organization and to retain people who are already working in the organization.
- Compensation is also used to motivate employees to work at their peak performance and improve morale.
- Employees who are fairly compensated tend to provide better customer service, which can result in organizational growth and development.

EXERCISE

1. Visit a website that gives salary information for a variety of jobs, such ashttp://www.salary.com. Using the search box, type in your ideal job and research salary information. What is the median salary for the job you searched? What is the lowest salary you would be willing to accept for this job? At which point would you be completely satisfied with the pay for this job?

---

[1] "100 Best Organizations to Work For," CNN Money, accessed February 11, 2011,http://money.cnn.com/magazines/fortune/bestorganizations/2011/snapshots/1.html?iid=EL.

[2] US Department of Defense, Financial Summary Tables, May 2009, accessed February 11, 2011, http://comptroller.defense.gov/defbudget/fy2010/fy2010_summary_tables_whole.pdf.

6.2 Developing a Compensation Package

LEARNING OBJECTIVES

1. Be able to explain the internal and external considerations of compensation package development.
2. Know how to develop a compensation philosophy.

There are a few basic aspects of compensation packages we should discuss before moving into the specific aspects of compensation. These foundations can assist in the development of a compensation strategy that meets the goals of your organization and is in line with your strategic plan.
Before beginning work on your compensation packages, some analysis should be done to determine your organization's philosophy in regard to compensation. Before development of your compensation philosophies, there are some basic questions to address on your current compensation packages.

2. From the employee's perspective, what is a fair wage?
3. Are wages too high to achieve financial health in your organization?
4. Do managers and employees know and buy-into your compensation philosophy?
5. Does the pay scale reflect the importance of various job titles within the organization?
6. Is your compensation good enough to retain employees?

7. Are state and federal laws being met with your compensation package?
8. Is your compensation philosophy keeping in line with labor market changes, industry changes, and organizational changes?

Once these basic questions are addressed, we can see where we might have "holes" in our compensation package and begin to develop new philosophies in line with our strategic plan, which benefits the organization. Some possible compensation policies might include the following:

1. Are salaries higher or lower depending on the location of the public organization? For example, orthopedic surgeons are paid higher in the North Central states ($537,000) than in Hawaii ($250,000), according to the Medscape Physical report of 2011._[1] Reasons could include cost of living in the area and fewer qualified people in a given area, giving them leverage to ask for a higher salary.
2. Are salaries lower or higher than the average in your region or area? If the salary is lower, what other benefits will the employee receive to make up for this difference? For example, wages might not be as high, but offering flextime or free day care might offset the lower salary.
3. Should there be a specific pay scale for each position in the organization, or should salaries be negotiated on an individual basis? If there is no set pay scale, how can you ensure individual salary offers are fair and nondiscriminatory?
4. What balance of salary and other rewards, such as bonuses, should be part of your compensation package? For example, some organizations prefer to offer a lower salary, but through bonuses and profit sharing, the employee has the potential to earn more.
5. When giving raises, will the employee's tenure be a factor, or will pay increases be merit based only, or a combination of both?

Let's discuss some internal and external factors in determining compensation in more detail.

Internal and External Pay Factors

One major internal factor is the compensation strategy the organizational has decided to use. Sixty-two percent of organizations have a written, documented compensation policy._[2]

Some organizations choose a market compensation policy, market plus, or market minus philosophy. A market compensation policy is to pay the going rate for a particular job, within a particular market based on research and salary studies. The organization that uses a market plus philosophy will determine the going rate and add a percentage to that rate, such as 5 percent. So if a particular job category median pays $57,000, the organization with a market plus of 5 percent philosophy will pay $59,850. A market minus philosophy pays a particular percentage less than the market; so in our example, if a organizational pays 5 percent less, the same job would pay $54,150. The University of Arizona, for example, posts its compensation philosophy on its website:_[3]

In order to fulfill its mission, the University of Arizona shall maintain a compensation program directed toward attracting, retaining, and rewarding a qualified and diverse workforce. Within the boundaries of financial feasibility, employee compensation shall be externally competitive and internally equitable, and shall be based upon performance as recognized within the work unit.

In addition to their compensation philosophy, the university lists compensation objectives, such as "average salaries will be targeted at the average salary levels of employees in comparable positions in our various labor markets." This is an example of a market compensation policy.

An example of an organization with a market plus philosophy is Cisco Systems, listed as one of the top-paying organizations on Fortune's annual list._[4] For example, they pay $131,716 for software engineers, while at Yahoo! software engineers are paid an average of $101,669, using a market philosophy. The pay at Cisco reflects its compensation philosophy and objectives:

Cisco operates in the extremely competitive and rapidly changing high-technology industry. The Board's Compensation Committee believes that the compensation programs for the executive officers should be designed to attract, motivate, and retain talented executives responsible for the success of Cisco and should be determined within a framework based on the achievement of designated financial targets, individual contribution, customer satisfaction, and financial performance relative to that of Cisco's competitors. Within this overall philosophy, the Compensation Committee's objectives are to do the following:

- Offer a total compensation program that is flexible and takes into consideration the compensation practices of a group of specifically identified peer organizations and other selected organizations with which Cisco competes for executive talent

- Provide annual variable cash incentive awards that take into account Cisco's overall financial performance in terms of designated organizational objectives, as well as individual contributions and a measure of customer satisfaction
- Align the financial interests of executive officers with those of shareholders by providing appropriate long-term, equity-based incentives

An example of an organization with a market minus philosophy is Whole Foods. The executive compensation for Whole Foods is a maximum of nineteen times the average store worker (or $608,000), very low by Organizational executive pay standards, which average 343 times.[5] According to John Mackey, Whole Foods CEO, paying on a market minus philosophy makes good public organization sense: "Fewer things harm an organization's morale more than great disparities in compensation. When a workplace is perceived as unfair and greedy, it begins to destroy the social fabric of the organization."[6] Another example of an organization with a market minus philosophy is Southwest Airlines. Despite the lower pay (and more hours), the organization boasts just a 1.4 percent turnover rate, which can be attributed not to pay but to the workplace culture and, as a result, loyalty to the organizational.[7]

There are many reasons why an organization would choose one philosophy over another. A market minus philosophy may tie into the organizational's core values, as in Whole Foods, or it may be because the types of jobs require an unskilled workforce that may be easier and less expensive to replace. A organizational may use a market plus philosophy because the industry's cutting-edge nature requires the best and the brightest.

Other internal pay factors might include the employer's ability to pay, the type of industry, and the value of the employee and the particular job to the organization. In addition, the presence of a union can lead to mandated pay scales.

External pay factors can include the current economic state. For example, in June 2011, the US unemployment rate was 9.2 percent, which is quite high for the country. As a result of surplus workers, compensation may be reduced within organizations because of oversupply of workers. Inflation and cost of living in a given area can also determine compensation in a given market.

Once an organization has looked at the internal and external forces affecting pay, it can begin to develop a pay system within the organization.

KEY TAKEAWAYS

- Before beginning work on a pay system, some general questions need to be answered. Important starting points include questions ranging from what is a fair wage from the employees' perspectives to how much can be paid but still retain financial health.
- After some pay questions are answered, a pay philosophy must be developed, based on internal and external factors. Some organizations implement a market compensation philosophy, which pays the going market rate for a job. Other organizations may decide to utilize a market plus philosophy, which pays higher than the average. A organizational could decide its pay philosophy is a market minus philosophy, which pays less than the market rate. For example, an organization may decide to pay lower salaries but offer more benefits.
- Once these tasks are done, the HR manager can then build a pay system that works for the size and industry of the organization.

EXERCISE

1. Think of your current organization or a past organization. What do you think their pay policy is/was? Describe and analyze whether you think it was or is effective. If you haven't worked before, perform an Internet search on pay policies and describe/analyze the pay policy of an organization.

---

[1] Laura Miller, "9 Statistics on Orthopedic Surgeon Compensation by Location," OS Review, May 25, 2011, accessed August 3, 2011,http://www.beckersorthopedicandspine.com/orthopedic-spine-practices-improving-profits/item/4061-9-statistics-on-2010-orthopedic-surgeon-compensation-by-location.
[2] Dow Scott, "Survey of Compensation Policies and Practices," WorldatWork, accessed July 23, 2011, http://www.worldatwork.org/waw/research/html/comppol03.html.
[3] University of Arizona, "Compensation Philosophy," accessed July 23, 2011,http://www.hr.arizona.edu/compensation_philosophy.
[4] "Top 25 Paying Organizations," Fortune, accessed July 23, 2011,http://money.cnn.com/galleries/2011/pf/jobs/1101/gallery.best_organizations_top_paying.fortune/14.html.
[5] Ted Allen, "AFL-CIO Defends Pay Equality Disclosure Mandate," ISS (blog), July 19, 2011, accessed July 23, 2011, http://blog.riskmetrics.com/gov/2011/07/afl-cio-defends-pay-equity-disclosure-mandate-1.html.
[6] Susanna Hamner and Tom McNichol, "Ripping Up the Rules of Management," CNN Money, n.d., accessed July 23,

2011,http://money.cnn.com/galleries/2007/biz2/0705/gallery.contrarians.biz2/3.html.

[7] Kelly Eggers, "Why It's OK to Be Paid Less," Fins Technology, n.d., accessed July 23, 2011,http://it-jobs.fins.com/Articles/SB130816636352923783/Why-It-s-Okay -to-Get-Paid-Less.

6.3 Types of Pay Systems

LEARNING OBJECTIVES

1. Explain types of job evaluation systems and their uses.
2. Be able to define and discuss the types of pay systems and factors determining the type of pay system used.
3. Know the laws relating to compensation.

Once you have determined your compensation strategy based on internal and external factors, you will need to evaluate jobs, develop a pay system, and consider pay theories when making decisions. Next, you will determine the mix of pay you will use, taking into consideration legal implications.

Figure 6.2 The Process for Implementing Compensation Strategy

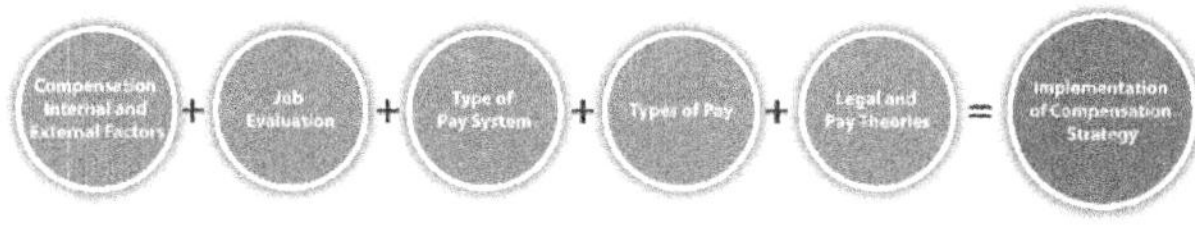

Job Evaluation Systems

As mentioned when we discussed internal and external factors, the value of the job is a major factor when determining pay. There are several ways to determine the value of a job through job evaluation. Job evaluation is defined as the process of determining the relative worth of jobs to determine pay structure. Job evaluation can help us determine if pay is equitable and fair among our employees. There are several ways to perform a job evaluation. One of the simplest methods, used by smaller organizations or within individual departments, is a job ranking system. In this type of evaluation, job titles are listed and ranked in order of importance to the organization. Apaired comparison can also occur, in which individual jobs are compared with every other job, based on a ranking system, and an overall score is given for each job, determining the highest-valued job to the lowest-valued job. For example, in Table 6.1 "Example of a Paired Comparison for a Job Evaluation", four jobs are compared based on a ranking of 0, 1, or 2. Zero indicates the job is less important than the one being compared, 1 means the job is about the same, and 2 means the job is more important. When the scores are added up, it is a quick way to see which jobs are of more importance to the organization. Of course, any person creating these rankings should be familiar with the duties of all the jobs. While this method may provide reasonably good results because of its simplicity, it doesn't compare differences between jobs, which may have received the same rank of importance.

Table 6.1 Example of a Paired Comparison for a Job Evaluation

Job	Receptionist	Project Manager	Account Manager	Sales	Director
Receptionist	X	0	0	0	0 = 4th
Project Administrative Assistant	1	X	0	0	1 = 3rd
Account Manager	2	1	X	0	3 = 2nd
Sales Director	2	2	2	X	6 = 1st

Based on the paired ranking system, the sales director should have a higher salary than the project administrative assistant, because the ranking for that job is higher. Likewise, a receptionist should be paid less than the project administrative assistant because this job ranks lower.

In a job classification system, every job is classified and grouped based on the knowledge and skills required for the job, years of experience, and amount of authority for that job. The US military is perhaps the best known for this type of classification system. The navy, for example, has job classification codes, such as HM (hospitalman). Then the jobs are divided into specialties, such as HM-8483, the classification for surgical technologist, and HM-8451 for a hospitalman-X-ray technician. The federal government and most state governments use this type of system. Tied to each job are the basic function, characteristics, and typical work of that job classification, along with pay range data.

Another type of job evaluation system is the point-factor system, which determines the value of a job by calculating the total points assigned to it. The points given to a specific job are called compensable factors. These can range from leadership ability to specific responsibilities and skills required for the job. Once the compensable factors are determined, each is given a weight compared to the importance of this skill or ability to the organization. When this system is applied to every job in the organization, expected compensable factors for each job are listed, along with corresponding points to determine which jobs have the most relative importance within the organization. Tompkins County in New York uses a point-factor system. Some of their compensable factors include the following:

1. Knowledge
2. Autonomy
3. Supervision
4. Psychological demands
5. Interpersonal skills
6. Internal and external contacts

In this point-factor system, autonomy ranks the highest and is given a weight of twenty-nine, while knowledge is given a rate of twenty, for example. Each of the compensable factors has a narrative that explains how points should be distributed for each factor. In this system, one hundred points are given for knowledge for a bachelor's degree and two to three years of experience, and eighty points are given if an employee has an associate's degree or high school diploma and two to three years of experience. The points are then multiplied by the weight (for knowledge, the weight is twenty) to give a final score on that compensable factor. After a score is developed for each, the employee is placed on the appropriate pay level for his or her score.

Another option for job evaluation is called the Hay profile method. This proprietary job evaluation method focuses on three factors called know-how, problem solving, and accountability. Within these factors are specific statements such as "procedural proficiency." Each of these statements is given a point value in each category of know-how, problem solving, and accountability. Then job descriptions are reviewed and assigned a set of statements that most accurately reflect the job. The point values for each of the statements are added for each job description, providing a quantitative basis for job evaluation and eventually, compensation. An advantage of this method is its quantitative nature, but a disadvantage is the expense of performing an elaborate job evaluation.

Pay Systems

Once you have performed a job evaluation, you can move to the third step, which we call pay grading. This is the process of setting the pay scale for specific jobs or types of jobs.

The first method to pay grade is to develop a variety of pay grade levels. Figure 6.4 "Sample Pay Scale for General Federal Jobs"shows an example. Then once the levels are developed, each job is assigned a pay grade. When employees receive raises, their raises stay within the range of their individual pay grade, until they receive a promotion that may result in a higher pay grade. The advantage of this type of system is fairness. Everyone performing the same job is within a given range and there is little room for pay discrimination to occur. However, since the system is rigid, it may not be appropriate for some organizations in hiring the best people. Organizations that operate in several cities might use a pay grade scale, but they may add percentages based on where someone lives. For example, the cost of living in Spokane, Washington, is much lower than in New York City. If an organization has offices in both places, it may choose to add a percentage pay adjustment for people living within a geographic area—for example, 10 percent higher in New York.

One of the downsides to pay grading is the possible lack of motivation for employees to work harder. They know even if they perform tasks outside their job description, their pay level or pay grade will be the same. This can incubate a stagnant environment. Sometimes this system can also create too many levels of hierarchy. For large organizations, this may work fine, but smaller, more agile organizations may use other methods to determine pay structure. For example, some organizations have moved to adelayering and banding process, which cuts down the number of pay levels within the organization. General Electric delayered pay grades in the mid-1990s because it found that employees were less likely to take a reassignment that was at a lower pay grade, even though the assignment might have been a good development opportunity.[1] So, delayering enables a broader range of pay and more flexibility within each level. Sometimes this type of process also occurs when a organizational downsizes. Let's assume a organizational with five hundred employees has traditionally used a pay grade model but decided to move to a more flexible model. Rather than have, say, thirty pay levels, it may reduce this to five or six levels, with greater salary differentials within the grades themselves. This allows organizations to better reward performance, while still having a basic model for hiring managers to follow.

Rather than use a pay grade scale, some organizations use a going rate model. In this model, analysis of the going rate for a particular job at a particular time is considered when creating the compensation package. This model can work well if market pressures or labor supply-and-demand pressures greatly impact your particular public organization. For example, if you need to attract the best project managers, but more are already employed (lack of supply)—and most organizations are paying $75,000 for this position—you will likely need to pay the same or more, because of labor supply and demand. Many tools are available, such as salarywizard.com, to provide going rate information on particular jobs in every region of the United States.

Another pay model is the management fit model. In this model, each manager makes a decision about who should be paid what when that person is hired. The downside to this model may be potential discrimination, halo effects, and resentment within the organization. Of course, these factors can create morale issues, the exact thing we want to avoid when compensating employees.

In addition to the pay level models we just looked at, other considerations might include the following:

1. *Skill-based pay.* With a skill-based pay system, salary levels are based on an employee's skills, as opposed to job title. This method is implemented similarly to the pay grade model, but rather than job title, a set of skills is assigned a particular pay grade.
2. *Competency-based pay.* Rather than looking at specific skills, the competency-based approach looks at the employee's traits or characteristics as opposed to a specific skills set. This model focuses more on what the employee can become as opposed to the skills he or she already has.
3. *Broadbanding.* Broadbanding is similar to a pay grade system, except all jobs in a particular category are assigned a specific pay category. For example, everyone working in customer service, or all administrative assistants (regardless of department), are paid within the same general band. McDonald's uses this compensation philosophy in their organizational offices, stating that it allows for flexibility in terms of pay, movement, and growth of employees._[2]
4. *Variable pay system.* This type of system provides employees with a pay basis but then links the attainment of certain goals or achievements directly to their pay. For example, a salesperson may receive a certain base pay but earn more if he or she meets the sales quota.

HOW WOULD YOU HANDLE THIS?

You have been working for your organization for five years. After lots of hard work, you are promoted to sales manager. One of your first tasks is to develop goals for your sales team, then create a budget based on these goals. First, you look at the salaries of all the sales staff to find major pay discrepancies. Some salespeople, who perform equally well, are paid much lower than some sales staff whom you consider to be nonperformers. As you dig deeper, you see this is a problem throughout the sales team. You are worried this might affect motivation for your team if they find out what others are making. How would you handle this?
How Would You Handle This?

Pay Theories

Now that we have discussed pay systems, it is important to look at some theories on pay that can be helpful to know when choosing the type of pay system your organization will use.

The *equity theory* is concerned with the relational satisfaction employees get from pay and inputs they provide to the organization. It says that people will evaluate their own compensation by comparing their compensation to others' compensation and their inputs to others' inputs. In other words, people will look at their own compensation packages and at their own inputs (the work performed) and compare that with others. If they perceive this to be unfair, in that another person is paid more but they believe that person is doing less work, motivational issues can occur. For example, people may reduce their own inputs and not work as hard. Employees may also decide to leave the organization as a result of the perceived inequity. In HR, this is an important theory to understand, because even if someone is being paid fairly, they will always compare their own pay to that of others in the organization. The key here is perception, in that the fairness is based entirely on what the employee sees, not what may be the actual reality. Even though HR or management may feel employees are being paid fairly, this may not be the employee's belief. In HR, we need to look at two factors related to pay equity: external pay equity and internal pay equity. External pay equity refers to what other people in similar organizations are being paid for a similar job. Internal pay equity focuses on employees within the same organization. Within the same organization, employees may look at higher level jobs, lower level jobs, and years with the organization to make their decision on pay equity. Consider Walmart, for example. In 2010, Michael Duke, CEO of Walmart, earned roughly $35 million in salary and other compensation,_[3] while employees earned minimum wage or slightly higher in their respective states. While Walmart contends that its wages are competitive in local markets, the retail giant makes no apologies for the pay difference, citing the need for a specialized skill set to be able to be the CEO of a Organizational organizational. There are hundreds of articles addressing the issue of pay equity between upper level managers and employees of an organization. To make a compensation strategy work, the perceived inputs (the work) and outputs (the pay) need to match fairly.

The *expectancy theory* is another key theory in relation to pay. The expectancy theory says that employees will put in as much work as they expect to receive. In other words, if the employee perceives they are going to be paid favorably, they will work to achieve the outcomes. If they believe the rewards do not equal the amount of effort, they may not work as hard. The reinforcement theory, developed by Edward L. Thorndike,[4] says that if high performance is followed by some reward, that desired behavior will likely occur in the future. Likewise, if high performance isn't followed by a reward, it is less likely the high performance will occur in the future. Consider an extreme example of the reinforcement theory in the world of finance. On Wall Street, bonuses for traders and bankers are a major part of their salary. The average bonus in 2010 was $128,530,[5] which does not take into account specific commissions on trades, which can greatly increase total compensation. One interesting consideration is the ethical implications of certain pay structures, particularly commission and bonus plans. For example, after the US government bailed out American International Group (AIG) with $170 billion in 2009, it was reported AIG would still provide some $165 million in bonuses to the same public organization unit that brought the organizational to near collapse, because of contractual issues. Traditionally, a bonus structure is designed to reward performance, rather than be a guaranteed part of the compensation plan, as was the case with AIG. Bonus and commission plans should be utilized to drive desired behavior and act as a reward for the desired behavior, as the reinforcement theory states.

All these theories provide us information to make better decisions when developing our own pay systems. Other considerations are discussed next.

Pay Decision Considerations

Besides the motivational aspect of creating a pay structure, there are some other considerations. First, the size of the organization and the expected expansion of the organization will be a factor. For example, if you are the HR manager for a ten-person organizational, you likely use a going rate or management fit model. While this is appropriate for your organizational today, as your organization grows, it may be prudent to develop a more formal pay structure. Ascentium Corporation, based in Seattle, Washington, found this to be the case. When the organizational started with fewer than fifteen employees, a management fit model was used. As the organizational ballooned to over five hundred employees in four cities, a pay banding model had to be put into place for fairness.

If your organization also operates overseas, a consideration is how domestic workers will be paid in comparison to the global market. One strategy is to develop a centralized compensation system, which would be one pay system for all employees, regardless of where they live. The downside to this is that the cost of living may be much less in some countries, making the centralized system possibly unfair to employees who live and work in more expensive countries. Another consideration is in what currency employees will be paid. Most US organizations pay even their overseas workers in dollars, and not in the local currency where the employee is working. Currency valuation fluctuations could cause challenges in this regard.[6]

How you communicate your pay system is extremely important to enhance the motivation that can be created by fair and equitable wage. In addition, where possible, asking for participation from your employees through the use of pay attitude surveys, for example, can create a transparent compensation process, resulting in higher performing employees.

Organizations should develop market pay surveys and review their wages constantly to ensure the organization is within expected ranges for the industry.

HUMAN RESOURCE RECALL

Why do you think a transparent compensation policy is so important to motivating a workforce?

Types of Pay

After a pay system has been developed, we can begin to look at specific methods of paying our employees. Remember that when we talk about compensation, we are referring to not only an actual paycheck but additional types of compensation, such as incentive plans that include bonuses and profit sharing. We can divide our total pay system into three categories: pay, incentives, and other types of compensation. Pay is the hourly, weekly, or monthly salary an employee earns. An incentive, often called a pay-for-performance incentive, is given for meeting certain performance standards, such as meeting sales targets. The advantage to incentive pay is that organizational goals can be linked directly to employee goals, resulting in higher pay for the employee and goal achievement by the organization. The following are desirable traits of incentive plans:

- Clearly communicated
- Attainable but challenging
- Easily understandable
- Tied to organizational goals

Table 6.3 Types of Pay

Pay	Attributes
Salary	Fixed compensation calculated on a weekly, biweekly, or monthly basis. No extra pay for overtime work.
Hourly Wage	Employees are paid on the basis of number of hours worked.
Piecework System	Employees are paid based on the number of items that are produced.
Types of Incentive Plans	Attributes
Commission Plans	An employee may or may not receive a salary but will be paid extra (e.g., a percentage for every sale made).
Bonus Plans	Extra pay for meeting or beating some goal previously determined. Bonus plans can consist of monetary compensation, but also other forms such as time off or gift certificates.
Profit-Sharing Plans	Annual bonuses paid to employees based on the amount of profit the organization earned.
Stock Options	When an employee is given the right to purchase organizational stock at a particular rate in time. Please note that a stock "option" is different from the actual giving of stock, since the option infers the employee will buy the stock at a set rate, obviously, usually cheaper than the going rate.
Other Types of Compensation	Attributes
Fringe Benefits	This can include a variety of options. Sick leave, paid vacation time, health club memberships, daycare services.
Health Benefits	Most organizations provide health and dental care benefits for employees. In addition, disability and life insurance benefits are offered.
401(k) Plans	Some organizations provide a retirement plan for employees. The organizational would work with a financial organization to set up the plan so employees can save money, and often, organizations will "match" a percentage of what the employee contributes to the plan.

Table 6.3 "Types of Pay" illustrates the three types of compensation.

Most organizations use a combination of pay, incentives, and other compensation, as outlined in Table 6.3 "Types of Pay" , to develop the total compensation package.

Laws Relating to Pay

As you have already guessed from our earlier chapter discussions, people cannot be discriminated against when it comes to development of pay systems. One issue hotly debated is the issue of comparable worth. Comparable worth states that people should be given similar pay if they are performing the same type of job. Evidence over the years shows this isn't the case, with women earning less than men in many industries. On average, a woman earns 79 cents for every $1.00 a man earns. For women of color, the gap is wider at 69 cents for African-American women and 59 cents for Latina women._[7] Many publications state that women earn less than men for a few reasons:

1. Women work fewer hours because of family care and maternity leave.
2. The career path or job choice of women tends to be lower as a whole.
3. There is a bias favoring men as the "breadwinners," and therefore they are paid more.
4. Women are valued less than men in the workplace.
5. Women don't negotiate salaries as well as men do.

While the reasons are certainly debatable, there is evidence that young women (without children) entering the workforce actually earn more than their male counterparts, owing to higher levels of education._[8] The EEOC covers discrimination in the workplace, including pay discrimination based on race, color, religion, sex, and national origin. The Equal Pay Act of 1963 makes it illegal to pay different wages to men and women if they perform equal work in the same workplace.

More recent legislation on pay includes the Lilly Ledbetter Fair Pay Act of 2009, the first law signed by President Obama. This bill amends the Civil Rights Act stating that the 180-day statute of limitations for filing an equal pay lawsuit regarding pay discrimination resets with each discriminatory paycheck. The bill stemmed from a lawsuit against Goodyear Tire and Rubber Organizational by Lilly Ledbetter, who claimed that her nineteen-year career at the organizational consisted of unfair pay, compared to male workers in the organization. Her complaint was time barred by the US Supreme Court, and the new act addressed the time (180 days) constraint in which people have to file claims.

The Fair Labor Standards Act, or FLSA, was established in 1938 and set a minimum wage for jobs, overtime laws, and child labor laws. FLSA divides workers into exempt and nonexempt status, and jobs under exempt status do not fall under the FLSA guidelines. An exempt employee is usually paid a salary and includes executive, professional, outside sales, and administrative positions. A nonexempt employee is usually an hourly employee. For nonexempt employees, some states may implement a higher minimum wage than that established by the federal government. For example, in 2011, the minimum wage is $8.67 per hour in Washington State, while the federal minimum wage is $7.25 per hour. Obviously, as an HR manager or manager, it is your responsibility to ensure everyone is being paid the minimum wage. This law also requires overtime pay if employees work over forty hours per week. Organizations must also post the FLSA poster in a visible part of the workplace, outlining these laws.

Child labor also falls under FLSA. The goal of these laws is to protect the education of children, prohibit the employment of children in dangerous jobs, and limit the number of working hours of children during the school year and other times of the year._[9]

According to the FLSA, tipped employees are those earning $30 or more per month in tips, such as servers in a restaurant. Employers whose employees receive more than $30 in tips may consider tips as part of wages, but they also must pay $2.12 an hour in direct wages. They must also be able to show that the employee receives at least the applicable minimum wage. If the tips and direct wage do not meet the minimum wage, the employer must pay the difference.

Also relating to pay is the Federal Unemployment Tax Act (FUTA). FUTA provides for payments of unemployment compensation to workers who have lost their jobs. Most employers pay a federal and a state unemployment tax, and portions of these funds go toward unemployment benefits should the worker lose his or her job.

TheFederal Employees Compensation Act (FECA) provide s federal employees injured in the performance of their jobs compensation benefits, such as disability. Please note that this is elective for private organizations but required of federal agencies.

KEY TAKEAWAYS

- A job evaluation system should be used to determine the relative value of one job to another. This is the first step in setting up a pay system.
- Several types of pay systems can be implemented. A pay grade system sets up specific pay levels for particular jobs, while a going rate system looks at the pay through the industry for a certain job title. Management fit gives maximum flexibility for managers to pay what they think someone should earn.
- HR managers can also develop pay systems based on skills and competency and utilize broadbanding, which is similar to pay grades. Another option might include variable pay.
- There are several motivational theories in regard to pay. First, the equity theorysays that people will evaluate their own satisfaction with their compensation by comparing it to others' compensation. The expectancy theory says people will put in only as much work as they expect to receive in rewards. Finally, thereinforcement theory says if high performance is followed by a reward, high performance is likely to happen in the future.
- Other pay considerations include the size of the organization, whether the organizational is global, and the level of communication and employee involvement in compensation. HR managers should always be aware of what others are paying in the industry by performing market surveys.
- There are several laws pertaining to pay. Of course, the EEOC ensures that pay is fair for all and does not discriminate. FLSA sets a minimum wage and establishes standards for child labor. FUTA requires employers to pay unemployment taxes on

employees. FECA ensures that federal employees receive certain benefits.

EXERCISES

1. Name and describe three considerations in developing a pay system. Which do you think is best?
2. Which pay theory do you think is the most important when developing your pay system? Why?
3. Visit http://www.dol.gov/dol/topic/wages/minimumwage.htm (please note that sometimes web address change so you may need to search for the information), which publishes minimum wage data for the United States. View the map and compare your state with the federal minimum wage. Is it higher or lower? Which two states have the highest minimum wage? The lowest?

---

[1] Gerald Ferris, Handbook of Human Resource Management (Cambridge, MA: Blackwell, 1995).
[2] McDonald's Corporation, "Your Pay and Rewards," accessed July 23, 2011,http://www.aboutmcdonalds.com/mcd/organizational_careers/benefits/highlights_of_what_we_offer/pay_and_rewards.html.
[3] Alice Gomstyn, "Walmart CEO Pay," ABC News Money, July 2, 1010, accessed July 23, 2011, http://abcnews.go.com/Public organization/walmart-ceo-pay-hour-workers-year/story?id=11067470.
[4] Indiana University, "Edward L. Thorndike," accessed February 14, 2011,http://www.indiana.edu/~intell/ethorndike.shtml.
[5] Aaron Smith, "The 2010 Wall Street Bonus," CNN Money, February 24, 2011, accessed July 23, 2011, http://money.cnn.com/2011/02/24/news/economy/wall_street_bonus/index.htm.
[6] Bobby Watson, "Global Pay Systems, Compensation in Support of a Multinational Strategy," Compensation Benefits Review 37, no. 1 (2005): 33–36.
[7] National Organization for Women, "Facts about Pay Equity," accessed February 15, 2011,http://www.now.org/issues/economic/factsheet.html.
[8] Conor Dougherty, "Young Women's Pay Exceeds Male Peers," Wall Street Journal, September 1, 2010.
[9] US Department of Labor, "Child Labor," accessed February 15, 2011,http://www.dol.gov/whd/childlabor.htm.

6.4 Other Types of Compensation

LEARNING OBJECTIVE

1. Explain the various types of benefits that can be offered to employees.

As you already know, there is more to a compensation package than just pay. There are many other aspects to the creation of a good compensation package, including not only pay but incentive pay and other types of compensation. First, we will discuss benefits that are mandated by the federal government, and then we will discuss types of voluntary benefits, including both incentive pay and other types of compensation.

Mandated: Social Security and Medicare

The Social Security Act of 1935 requires employers to withdraw funds from workers' paychecks to pay for retirement benefits. This is called a payroll tax. Please note that all organizations are legally compelled to offer this benefit. After several revisions, we now call this OASDHI or the Old Age, Survivors, Disability, and Health Insurance Program. To be insured, employees must work forty quarters, with a minimum of $1,000 earned per quarter. Once this money is put aside, anyone born after 1960 will receive benefits at 67. The OASDHI tax in 2011 is 4.2 percent on earnings for employees, up to $106,800 and 6.2 percent for the employer up to the same limits. This covers both retirement income as well as medical benefits, called Medicare, once the employee reaches retirement age.

Mandated: Unemployment Insurance and Workers' Compensation

Unemployment insurance is required under the Social Security Act of 1935 and is also called the Federal Unemployment Tax Act (FUTA). This program's goals include providing some lost income for employees during involuntary unemployment, helping workers find a new job, incentivizing employers to continue employment, and developing worker skills if they are laid off. The majority of this plan is funded by employers' payroll taxes, which account for .8 percent per employee. The rate is actually 6.2 percent of compensation, but employers are allowed a tax credit for these payments, which results in the net .8 percent. With this benefit, employees receive unemployment benefits and/or job training when they are laid off or let go from a current job. However, employees would be ineligible to receive these benefits if they quit their job, as it must be involuntary. Just like Social Security, this payroll tax on employers is required. Some employers also offer workers' compensation benefits. If an employee is hurt on the job, he or she would receive certain benefits, such as a percentage of pay. Jobs are classified into risk levels, and obviously the higher the risk level, the higher the cost of insurance. This is not a federally mandated program, but for some occupations in some states, it may be a requirement.

Mandated: COBRA

While the government does not require organizations to provide health-care and medical benefits to employees, theConsolidated Omnibus Budget Reconciliation Act (COBRA) requires organizations to allow employees to extend their group coverage for up to thirty-six months. The restrictions for this plan include the requirement of a qualifying event that would mean a loss of benefits, such as termination or reduction in hours. For example, if an employee works forty hours a week with medical insurance, but the schedule is reduced to twenty hours, no longer qualifying him or her for benefits, COBRA would be an option.

Voluntary: Incentive Pay Systems

As we discussed earlier, there are several types of incentive pay systems that can be tied directly to public organization objectives and the employees' ability to help the organizational meet those objectives. They include commissions, bonuses, profit sharing, stock options, team pay, and merit pay.

Commissions are usually calculated on the basis of a percentage and earned based on the achievement of specific targets that have been agreed upon by the employee and employer. For example, many salespeople receive commissions from each item sold. Many commission incentive plans require employees to meet a minimum level of sales, who then are paid a comission on each sale beyond the minimum. Astraight commission plan is one in which the employee receives no base pay and entire pay is based on meeting sales goals. Many plans, however, include a base payand commission for each sale. Base pay is the guaranteed salary the employee earns.

Several types of bonuses can be given to employees as incentive pay. Meeting certain organizational goals or successfully completing a project or other objectives can be tied to a bonus, which is a one-time payment to an employee. A spot bonus is an unplanned bonus given to an employee for meeting a certain objective. These types of bonuses do not always have to be money; they can be other forms such as a gift certificate or trip. Fifty-eight percent of WorldatWork members_[1] said that they provide spot bonuses to employees for special recognition above and beyond work performance.

Some organizations choose to reward employees financially when the organization as a whole performs well, through the use of profit sharing as an incentive. For example, if an organization has a profit-sharing program of 2 percent for employees, the employees would earn 2 percent of the overall profit of the organizational. As you have guessed, this can be an excellent incentive for employees to both work as a team and also monitor their own personal performance so as not to let down the team. For example, in 2011, US automaker General Motors gave one of its highest profit-sharing payouts ever. Forty-five thousand employees received $189 million in a profit-sharing bonus, which equaled about $4,200 per person._[2] While profit sharing can be a great incentive, it can also be a large expense that should be carefully considered.

Employee ownership of the organization is similar to profit sharing but with a few key differences. In this type of plan, employees are granted stock options, which allow the employees to buy stock at a fixed price. Then if the stock goes up in value, the employee earns the difference between what he or she paid and the value of the stock. With this type of incentive, employees are encouraged to act in the best interest of the organization. Some plans, called employee stock ownership plans, are different from stock options, in that in these plans the employee is given stock as reward for performance.

In a smaller organization, team pay or group incentives can be popular. In this type of plan, if the group meets a specified goal, such as the increase of sales by 10 percent, the entire group receives a reward, which can consist of additional pay or bonus. Please note that this is different from individualized bonuses, discussed earlier, since the incentive is a reward for the group as opposed for the individual.

Merit pay is a pay program that links pay to how well the employee performs within the job, and it is normally tied to performance appraisals. Merit base is normally an annual pay increase tied to performance. The problem with merit pay is that it may only be received once per year, limiting incentive flexibility. To make merit pay work, performance guidelines should be predetermined. Some organizations offer cost of living annual increases (COLAs), which is not tied to merit but is given to employees as an annual inflationary increase.

ORGANIZATIONAL FOCUS

While the cost of health insurance premiums may be going up for most Americans, these premiums do not hit the individual employee's pocketbook at Microsoft. Microsoft, based in Redmond, Washington, finds itself once again on the Fortune500 Best Organizations to Work For list in several areas, including paying for 100 percent of employees' health-care premiums._[3] In addition to cutting this cost for employees, Microsoft also offers domestic partner benefits, one of the first Fortune500 organizations to do so. In 2005, Microsoft also began to offer partial coverage for transgender surgery to its existing health-care coverage, which earned Microsoft the highest attainable score by the Human Rights Campaign (HRC) Equality Index._[4] Microsoft also promotes fitness and wellness as part of its health-care plan, providing an on-site fitness center and subsidized gym memberships.

Voluntary: Medical Insurance

According to the Bureau of Labor Statistics, 62 percent of organizations in 2010 offered health-care benefits to employees._[5] The yearly cost for employee medical insurance averages $9,552, according to the 2009 Towers Perrin survey._[6] With such a significant cost to organizations, it is up to HR managers to contain these costs, while not negatively affecting employee motivation. Medical insurance usually includes hospital expenses, surgical expenses, and routine health-care visits. Most insurance plans also allow for wellness visits and other alternative care (e.g., massage and acupuncture) within the plans. Many employers also offer vision and dental care benefits as part of their benefits packages. Disability insurance is also provided by some employers as well. We will discuss each of these in detail next. One important law to keep in mind regarding medical insurance is the Health Insurance Portability and Accountability Act (HIPAA) of 1996. It provides federal protections for personal health information held by covered entities, such as employers. In other words, employers cannot divulge or share health care information they may have on an employee.

As the HR professional, it will likely be your responsibility to choose the health-care plan that best meets the needs of your employees. Some options include the following:

1. *Fee-for-service plans.* In this type of plan, people pay for medical expenses out of pocket, and then are reimbursed for the benefit level. For example, if your insurance plan covers doctor visits, you could see any doctor, pay the bill, and then submit payment to your insurer for reimbursement. Most organizations will have a base plan, which covers more serious issues requiring hospitalization, while the major medical part of the plan would cover routine services, such as doctor's visits. As you can imagine, the disadvantage of this type of plan can be twofold: first, the initial expense for the employee, and second, the time it may take to receive reimbursement for employees. Remember that medical insurance can help retain and motivate employees and help you recruit new employees, so consideration of the disadvantages is important.
2. *Health maintenance organizations (HMOs).* The HMO will likely have greater coverage than the fee-for-service plan, but it limits the ability of employees to see the doctors they choose. There may be a limited number of physicians and specialists for the employee to see, and going outside the plan and seeing another doctor may result in an out-of-pocket expense for the employee. Most HMOs cover a wide range of medical issues and will usually require a copayment by the employee. Some may have minimum deductibles they must meet before the HMO will cover in full. For example, if you are part of an HMO with a deductible of $500 and copayments of $25, you would need to see the doctor for a value of $500 (paid out of pocket) before you can begin to just make the $25 copayment for visits. Some HMOs will not allow members to see a specialist, such as a dermatologist, without prior approval from the primary care physician.
3. *Preferred provider organization (PPO).* This type of medical plan is similar to HMOs but allows employees to see a physician outside the network. They will likely still have to pay a deductible as mentioned above, but PPOs do allow employees more freedom to see specialists, such as dermatologists.

When choosing the best type of plan for your organization, the following aspects should be considered:

1. The cost of the plan
2. The type of coverage
3. The quality of the care
4. Administration of the plan

First, the cost is usually a major consideration for the HR professional. Developing a budget for health-care costs, initiating bids from possible providers, and then negotiating those bids is a key factor in controlling this cost for employers.

Second, asking for employees' opinions about the type of coverage they would prefer is a way to ensure your plan meets the needs of your employees. Next, consider the quality of care your employees will receive and, finally, how simple will the plan be for your HR department to administer. For example, many HMO plans offer fully automated and online services for employees, making them easy to administer.

Disability insurance provides income to individuals (usually a portion of their salary) should they be injured or need long-term care resulting from an illness. Short-term disability insurance (STD) provides benefits to someone if they are unable to work for six months or less, while long-term disability insurance (LTD) covers the employee for a longer period of time. Normally, disability insurance provides income to the employee that is 60–80 percent of their normal salary.

Voluntary: 401(k) Plans

As the scenery of the workforce has changed, benefits have changed, too. One such recent change is the movement of employee pension plans to 401(k) plans. While some organizations still offer pension plans, such plans are far more rare. A pension plan is a set dollar amount an employee will receive when they retire from their organization. This type of plan was popular when most people worked their entire life at the same organizational. However, many pension plans have gone bankrupt, and the United States has an agency to protect people from losing pension benefits. ThePension Benefit Guaranty Corporation (PBGC) was created by the Employee Retirement Income Security Act (ERISA) to protect pension benefits in private sector pension plans. If a pension plan ends or isn't able to pay all benefits, PBGC's insurance program pays the benefit that should have been provided. Financing for this plan comes from insurance premiums paid by the organizations whose plans PBGC protects.

As more mobility in the workplace has occurred, most organizations no longer offer pension plans, but instead, they offer 401(k) plans. While a pension plan can motivate employee loyalty, 401(k) plans are far more popular. According to the US Bureau of Labor Statistics, employer-provided retirement plans, such as 401(k) plans, were available to 74 percent of all full-time workers in the United States,_[7] while 39 percent of part-time workers had access to retirement benefits.

A 401(k) plan is a plan set up by the organization in which employees directly deposit money from their paycheck. The funds are tax deferred for the employee until retirement. If an employee leaves the job, their 401(k) plan goes with them. As an extra incentive, many organizations offer to match what the employee puts into the plan, usually based on a percentage. For example, an employee can sign up to contribute 5 percent of salary into a 401(k) plan, and the organizational will contribute the same amount. Most organizations require a vesting period—that is, a certain time period, such as a year, before the employer will match the funds contributed.

Usually, 401(k) plans are easy to administer, after the initial setup has occurred. If the employer is matching employee contributions, the expense of such a plan can be great, but it also increases employee retention. Some considerations when choosing a 401(k) plan are as follows:

1. Is the vendor trustworthy?
2. Does the vendor allow employees to change their investments and account information online?
3. How much are the management fees?

It is first important to make sure the vendor you are considering for administration of your 401(k) plan has a positive reputation and also provides ease of access for your employees. For example, most 401(k) plans allow employees to change their address online and move investments from a stock to a bond. Twenty-four-hour access has become the expectation of most employees, and as a result, this is a major consideration before choosing a plan. Most 401(k) plans charge a fee to manage the investments of your employees. The management fees can vary greatly, so receiving a number of bids and comparing these fees is important to ensure your employees are getting the best deal.

It is important to mention the Employee Retirement Income Security Act (ERISA) here, as this relates directly to administration of your 401(k) plan. First, ERISA does not require employers to offer a pension or 401(k) plan, but for those who do, it requires them to meet certain standards when administering this type of plan. Some of these standards include the following:

1. Requires participants receive specific information about the plan, such as plan features and funding
2. Sets minimum standards for participation and vesting
3. Requires accountability of plan's fiduciary responsibilities
4. Requires payment of certain benefits, should the plan be terminated

Voluntary: Paid Time Off

Time off is a benefit we should address, since this type of benefit varies greatly, especially in other parts of the world. French organizations, for example, are mandated by law to provide five weeks of paid vacation time to employees._[8] In the United States, the number of days off provided is a major budget item worth considering. Here are the general types of time off:

- **Paid Holidays**
- Many organizations offer a set number of paid holidays, such as New Year's Day, Memorial Day, Christmas, Independence Day, and Thanksgiving.
- **Sick Leave**

The number of sick leave days can vary greatly among employers. The average in the United States is 8.4 paid sick days offered to employees per year._[9]

Paid Vacation

With full-time employment, many organizations also offer paid vacation to employees, and it is generally expected as part of the compensation package. According to a survey performed by Salary.com, the average number of paid vacation days in the United States is nine days for one year of service, fourteen days for five years of service, and seventeen days for ten years of service to the organization.[10]

Organizations vary greatly in how vacation time is accrued. Some organizations give one hour for a certain number of days worked, while others require a waiting period before earning any paid time off (PTO). In addition, some organizations allow their employees to carry over unused vacation time from one year to the next, while other employees must use their vacation every year or risk losing it.

Paid Time Off (PTO)

One option is to provide a set number of days off, which can be used for vacation time, holidays, and/or sick leave.

To promote longevity, some organizations offer paid (or for example, 60 percent of salary paid) sabbaticals. For example, after five years of employment, the employee may take a paid sabbatical for one month.

A Final Note on Compensation and Benefits Strategy

When creating your compensation plan, of course the ability to recruit and retain should be an important factor. But also, consideration of your workforce needs is crucial to any successful compensation plan. The first step in development of a plan is to ask the employees what they care about. Some employees would rather receive more pay with fewer benefits or better benefits with fewer days off. Surveying the employees allows you, as the HR professional, to better understand the needs of your specific workforce. Once you have developed your plan, understand that it may change to best meet the needs of your public organization as it changes over time.

Once the plan is developed, communicating the plan with your employees is also essential. Inform your employees via an HR blog, e-mails, and traditional methods such as face to face. Your employees might not always be aware of the benefits cost to the organizational, so making sure they know is your responsibility. For example, if you pay for 80 percent of the medical insurance premiums, let your employees know. This type of communication can go a long way to allowing the employees to see their value to you within the organization.

KEY TAKEAWAYS

- Before beginning work on a pay system, some general questions need to be answered. Questions such as what is a fair wage from the employee's perspective and how much can be paid but still retain financial health are important starting points.
- After some pay questions are answered, development of a pay philosophy must be developed. For example, an organization may decide to pay lower salaries but offer more benefits.
- Once these tasks are done, the HR manager can then build a pay system that works for the size and industry of the organization.
- Besides salary, one of the biggest expenses for compensation is medical benefits. These can include health benefits, vision, dental, and disability benefits.
- Social Security and unemployment insurance are both required by federal law. Both are paid as a percentage of income by the employee and employer.
- Depending on the state, workers' compensation might be a requirement. A percentage is paid on behalf of the employee in case he or she is hurt on the job.
- A mandatory benefit, COBRA was enacted to allow employees to continue their health insurance coverage, even if they leave their job.
- There are three main types of health-care plans. A fee-based plan allows the insured to see any doctor and submit reimbursement after a visit. An HMO plan restricts employees to certain doctors and facilities and may require a copayment and/or deductibles. A PPO plan is similar to the HMO but allows for more flexibility in which providers the employee can see.
- Pension funds were once popular, but as people tend to change jobs more, 401(k) plans are becoming more popular, since they can move with the employee.
- Profit sharing is a benefit in which employees receive a percentage of profit the organization earns. Stock ownership plans are plans in which employees can purchase stock or are granted stock and become an owner in the organization.
- Team rewards are also a popular way to motivate employees. These can be in the form of compensation if a group or the organizational meets certain target goals.
- Paid time off, or PTO, can come in the form of holidays, vacation time, and sick leave. Usually,

employees earn more days as they stay with the organizational.

- Communication with employees is key to a successful benefits strategy.

EXERCISES

1. Of the benefits we discussed, which ones are required by law? Which are not?
2. Research current Federal Insurance Contributions Act (FICA) tax rates and Social Security limits, as these change frequently. Write down each of these rates and be prepared to share in class.
3. Describe the considerations when developing medical benefits. Which do you think would be the most important to you as the HR manager?
4. Visit websites of three organizations you might be interested in working for. Review the incentives they offer and be prepared to discuss your findings in class.

---

[1] WorldatWork, "Spot Bonus Survey," July 2000, accessed July 23, 2011, http://www.worldatwork.org/waw/research/html/spotbonus-home.html.
[2] Nick Bunkley, "GM Workers to Get $189 Million in Profit Sharing," New York Times, February 14, 2011, accessed February 21, 2011,http://www.nytimes.com/2011/02/15/public organization/15auto.html?_r=2&ref=public organization.
[3] "100 Best Organizations to Work For," Fortune, accessed July 21, 2011,http://money.cnn.com/magazines/fortune/bestorganizations/2010/snapshots/51.html.
[4] Gay, Lesbian, Bisexual, and Transgender Employees at Microsoft (GLEAM), Microsoft website, accessed July 21, 2011,http://www.microsoft.com/about/diversity/en/us/programs/ergen/gleam.aspx.
[5] Bureau of Labor Statistics, "Employee Benefits Survey," 2010, accessed July 23, 2011, http://www.bls.gov/ncs/ebs/benefits/2010/ownership/private/table01a.htm.
[6] Towers Watson, "2009 Health Care Cost Survey Reveals High-Performing Organizations Gain Health Dividend,"
[7] US Bureau of Labor Statistics, "Employee Benefits in the United States: March 2010," news release, July 27, 2010, accessed September 12, 2011,http://www.bls.gov/ncs/ebs/sp/ebnr0016.txt.
[8] Rebecca Leung, "France: Less Work, More Time Off," CBS News, February 11, 2009, accessed July 23, 2011,http://www.cbsnews.com/stories/2005/06/27/60II/main704571.shtml.
[9] HRM Guide, "Sick Day Entitlement Survey," accessed February 21, 2011,http://www.hrmguide.com/health/sick-entitlement.htm.
[10] Jessica Yang, "Paid Time Off from Work Survey," Salary.com, accessed September 15, 2011, http://www.salary.com/Articles/ArticleDetail.asp?part=par088.

6.5 Cases and Problems

CHAPTER SUMMARY

- A compensation package is an important part of the overall strategic HRM plan, since much of the organizational budget is for employee compensation.
- A compensation package can include salary, bonuses, health-care plans, and a variety of other types of compensation.
- The goals of compensation are first to attract people to work for your organization. Second, they can be used to retain people who are already working in the organization.
- Compensation is also used to motivate employees to work at their peak performance and improve morale of the organization.
- Employees who are fairly compensated tend to provide better customer service, which can result in organizational growth and development.
- Several types of pay systems can be implemented. A pay grade system sets up specific pay levels for particular jobs, while a going rate system looks at the pay throughout the industry for a certain job title. Management fit gives maximum flexibility for managers to pay what they think someone should earn.
- HR managers can also develop pay systems based on skills and competency and utilize a broadbanding approach, which is similar to pay grades. Another option might include variable pay.
- There are several motivational theories in regard to pay. First, the equity theory says that people will evaluate their own satisfaction with their compensation by comparing it to others' compensation. The expectancy theory says people will put in only as much work as they expect to receive in rewards. Finally, the reinforcement theory says that if high performance is followed by a reward, high performance is likely to happen in the future.
- Other pay considerations include the size of the organization, whether the organizational is global, and the level of communication and employee involvement in compensation. HR managers should always be aware of what others are paying in the industry by performing market surveys.
- There are several laws pertaining to pay. Of course, the Equal Employment Opportunity Commission (EEOC) ensures that pay is fair for all and does not discriminate. The Fair Labor Standards Act (FLSA) sets a minimum wage and establishes standards for child labor. The Federal Unemployment Tax Act (FUTA) requires employers to pay unemployment taxes on employees. TheFederal Employees Compensation

Act (FECA) ensures that federal employees receive certain benefits.

- Besides salary, one of the biggest expenses for compensation is medical benefits. These can include health benefits, vision, dental, and disability benefits.
- The Consolidated Omnibus Budget Reconciliation Act(COBRA) was enacted to allow employees to continue their health insurance coverage, even if they leave their job.
- There are three main types of health-care plans. A fee-based plan allows the insured to see any doctor and submit reimbursement after a visit. An HMO plan restricts employees to certain doctors and facilities and may require a copayment and/or deductibles. A PPO plan is similar to the HMO but allows for more flexibility in which providers the employee can see.
- Pension funds were once popular, but as people tend to change jobs more, 401(k) plans are becoming more popular, since they can move with the employee.
- Profit sharing is a benefit in which employees receive a percentage of profit the organization earns. Stock ownership plans are plans in which employees can purchase stock or are granted stock and become an owner in the organization.
- Team rewards are also a popular way to motivate employees. These can be in the form of compensation if a group or the organizational meets certain target goals.
- Social Security and unemployment insurance are both required by federal law. Both are paid as a percentage of income by the employee and employer.
- Depending on the state, workers' compensation might be a requirement. A percentage is paid on behalf of the employee in case he or she is hurt on the job.
- Paid time off, or PTO, can come in the form of holidays, vacation time, and sick leave. Usually, employees earn more days as they stay with the organizational.
- Communication with employees is key to a successful benefits strategy. This includes communication before implementing the plan as well as communication about the plan.

CHAPTER CASE

PTO: Too Little or Too Much?

You just finished analyzing information for the current compensation and benefits program. You find that some changes should be made, as the majority of employees (you have 120 employees) are not happy with what is being offered. In fact, the plan had not been revised in over fifteen years, making it dated and definitely ready for some changes. One of the major points of contention is the PTO the organization offers. Employees feel the current system of sick time and vacation time offers too few options. For example, one employee says, "I often come to work sick, so I can still have my vacation time for my vacation." Another employee says, "I have given nine years to this organization, but I receive only three days more than someone who has just started." Here is the current PTO offering:

1+ year	7 days
5+years	10 days
10+ years	14 days

1. What cost considerations would you take into account when revising this part of your compensation plan?
2. What other considerations would you take into account when developing a new PTO plan?
3. Propose a new plan and estimate the cost of your plan on an Excel spreadsheet. Be prepared to present to the board of directors.

TEAM ACTIVITY

1. Work in teams of four or five. Assume your organization is expanding and wants to open a sales office overseas. What compensation factors would be a concern? Brainstorm a list and be prepared to present to the rest of the class.
2. Go to http://www.bls.gov/oco/ and review the information on the Occupational Outlook Handbook in teams of three. Pick three different jobs under the management category and record their average salary. Discuss reasons for the pay difference between the jobs you choose.

NOTES:

NOTES:

Chapter 7: Retention and Motivation in Public Organizations

Dissatisfaction Isn't Always about Pay
As an HR consultant, your job normally involves reviewing HR strategic plans and systems of small to medium size organizations, then making recommendations on how to improve. Most of the organizations you work with do not have large HR departments, and they find it less expensive to hire you than to hire a full-time person.

Your current client, Pacific Books, is a small online retailer with forty-seven employees. Pacific Books has had some challenges, and as the economy has improved, several employees have quit. They want you to look into this issue and provide a plan to improve retention.

Pacific Books currently has just one person managing payroll and benefits. The individual managers in the organization are the ones who handle other HR aspects, such as recruiting and developing compensation plans. As you speak with the managers and the payroll and benefits manager, it is clear employees are not happy working for this organization. You are concerned that if the organizational does not improve its employee retention, they will spend an excessive amount of time trying to recruit and train new people, so retention of the current employees is important.

As with most HR issues, rather than just guessing what employees want, you develop a survey to send to all employees, including management. You developed the survey on SurveyMonkey and asked employee satisfaction questions surrounding pay and benefits. However, you know that there are many other things that can cause someone to be unhappy at work, so to take this survey a step further, you decide to ask questions about the type of work employees are doing, management style, and work-life balance. Then you send out a link to all employees, giving them one week to take the survey.

When the results come in, they are astounding. Out of the forty-seven employees, forty-three selected "dissatisfied" on at least four or more areas of the five-question survey. While some employees are not happy with pay and benefits, the results say that other areas of the organization are actually what are causing the dissatisfaction. Employees are feeling micromanaged and do not have freedom over their time. There are also questions of favoritism by some managers for some employees, who always seem to get the "best" projects.

When you sit down with the CEO to discuss the survey results, at first she defends the organization by saying the organizational offers the highest salaries and best benefits in the industry, and she doesn't understand how someone can be dissatisfied. You explain to her that employee retention and motivation is partly about pay and benefits, but it includes other aspects of the employee's job, too. She listens intently and then asks you to develop a retention and motivation plan that can improve the organization.

7.1 The Costs of Turnover

LEARNING OBJECTIVES

1. Be able identify the difference between direct and indirect turnover costs.
2. Describe some of the reasons why employees leave.
3. Explain the components of a retention plan.

According to the book Keeping the People Who Keep You in Public organization by Leigh Branham,[1] the cost of losing an employee can range from 25 percent to 200 percent of that employee's salary. Some of the costs cited revolve around customer service disruption and loss of morale among other employees, burnout of other employees, and the costs of hiring someone new. Losing an employee is called turnover.
There are two types of turnover, voluntary turnover and involuntary turnover. Voluntary turnover is the type of turnover that is initiated by the employee for many different reasons. Voluntary turnover can be somewhat predicted and addressed in HR, the focus of this chapter. Involuntary turnover is where the employee has no choice in their termination—for example, employer-initiated due to nonperformance.

It has been suggested that replacement of an employee who is paid $8 per hour can range upwards of $4,000.[2] Turnover can be calculated by separations during the time period (month)/total number of employees midmonth × 100 = the percentage of turnover. For example, let's assume there were three separations during the month of August and 115 employees midmonth. We can calculate turnover in this scenario by 3/115 × 100 = 2.6% turnover rate.

This gives us the overall turnover rate for our organization. We may want to calculate turnover rates based on region or department to gather more specific data. For example, let's say of the three separations, two were in the accounting department. We have ten people in the accounting department. We can calculate that by accounting: 2/10 × 100 = 20% turnover rate.

The turnover rate in accounting is alarmingly high compared to our organizational turnover rate. There may be something happening in this department to cause unusual turnover.

Table 7.1 Turnover Costs

Direct	Indirect
Recruitment costs	Lost knowledge
Advertising costs for new position	Loss of productivity while new employee is brought up to speed
Orientation and training of new employee	Cost associated with lack of motivation prior to leaving
Severance costs	
Testing costs	
Time to interview new replacements	
Time to recruit and train new hires	Cost associated with loss of trade secrets

In HR, we can separate the costs associated with turnover into indirect costs and direct costs. Direct turnover costs include the cost of leaving, replacement costs, and transition costs, while indirect turnover costs include the loss of production and reduced performance. The following are some examples of turnover costs: [3]

- Recruitment of replacements
- Administrative hiring costs
- Lost productivity associated with the time between the loss of the employee and hiring of replacement
- Lost productivity due to a new employee learning the job
- Lost productivity associated with coworkers helping the new employee
- Costs of training
- Costs associated with the employee's lack of motivation prior to leaving
- Sometimes, the costs of trade secrets and proprietary information shared by the employee who leaves
- Public relations costs

To avoid these costs, development of retention plans is an important function of the HR strategic plan. Retention plans outline the strategies the organization will use to reduce turnover and address employee motivation.

Reasons for Voluntary Turnover

Figure 7.2 Common Reasons for Employee Turnover

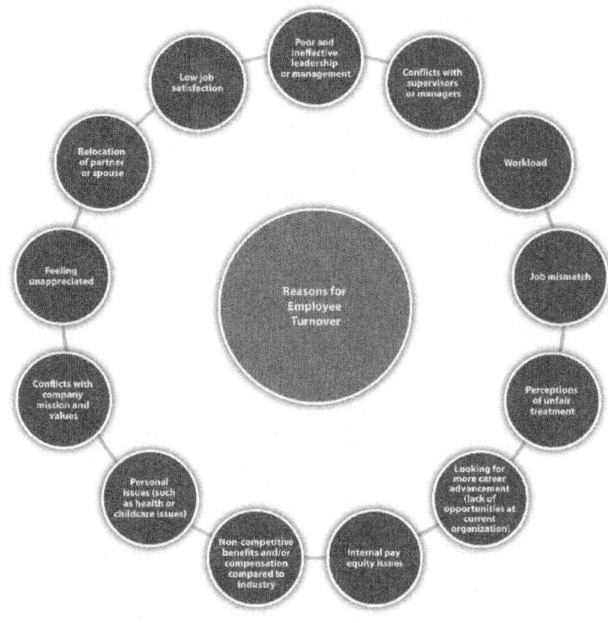

Before we discuss specific details on retention planning, it is important to address the reasons why people choose to leave an organization to begin with. One mistake HR professionals and managers make is to assume people leave solely on the basis of their unhappiness with their compensation packages.

Once we find out what can cause voluntary turnover, we can develop retention strategies to reduce turnover. Some of the common reasons employees leave organizations can include the following:

1. *A poor match between the job and the skills of the employee.* This issue is directly related to the recruitment process. When a poor match occurs, it can cause frustration for the employee and for the manager. Ensuring the recruitment phase is viable and sound is a first step to making sure the right match between job and skills occurs.
2. *Lack of growth.* Some employees feel "stuck" in their job and don't see a way to have upward mobility in the organization. Implementing a training plan and developing a clearly defined path to job growth is a way to combat this reason for leaving.

3. *Internal pay equity.* Some employees, while they may not feel dissatisfied with their own pay initially, may feel dissatisfaction when comparing their pay with others.
4. *Management.* Many employees cite management as their reason for leaving. This can be attributed to overmanaging (micromanaging) people, managers not being fair or playing favorites, lack of or poor communication by managers, and unrealistic expectations of managers.
5. *Workload.* Some employees feel their workloads are too heavy, resulting in employees being spread thin and lacking satisfaction from their jobs, and possibly, lack of work-life balance as a result.
6. *We know that some people will move or perhaps their family situation changes.* This type of turnover is normal and expected. Figure 7.2 "Common Reasons for Employee Turnover" shows other examples of why people leave organizations.

As HR professionals and managers, we want to be sure we have plans in place to keep our best people. One such plan is the retention plan.

HUMAN RESOURCE RECALL

Do you feel your current or past organization did a good job of reducing turnover? Why or why not

KEY TAKEAWAYS

- Retaining employees is an important component to a healthy organization. Losing an employee is called turnover. Turnover can be very expensive to an organization, which is why it is important to develop retention plans to manage turnover.
- Voluntary turnover is turnover that is initiated by the employee, whileinvoluntary turnover is initiated by the organization for various reasons such as nonperformance.
- Direct turnover costs and indirect turnover costs can include the costs associated with employee replacement, declining employee morale, or lost customers.
- Some of the reasons why employees leave can include a poor match between job and skills, no growth potential, pay inequity among employees, the fairness and communication style of management, and heavy workloads.

EXERCISE

1. Perform an Internet search of average employee turnover cost and report findings from at least three different industries or organizations.

---

[1] Leigh Branham, Keeping the People Who Keep You in Public organization (New York: American Management Association, 2000), 6.
[2] Noel Paiement "It Will Cost You $4,000 to Replace Just One $8 per Hour Employee," Charity Village, July 13, 2009, accessed August 30, 2011,http://www.charityvillage.com/cv/research/rhr50.html.
[3] Carl. P. Maertz, Jr. and M. A. Campion, "25 Years of Voluntary Turnover Research: A Review and Critique," in International Review of Industrial and Organizational Psychology, vol. 13, ed. Cary L. Cooper and Ivan T. Robertson (London: John Wiley, 1998), 49–86.

7.2 Retention Plans

LEARNING OBJECTIVES

1. Be able to discuss some of the theories on job satisfaction and dissatisfaction.
2. Explain the components of a retention plan.

Figure 7.4 HR Components of a HPWS

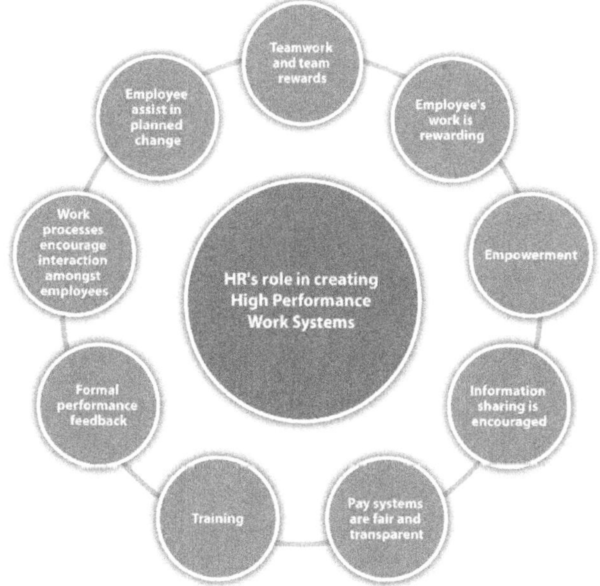

Effective high-performance work systems (HPWS) is the name given to a set of systematic HR practices that create an environment where the employee has greater involvement and responsibility for the success of the organization. A high-performance work system is a strategic approach to many of the things we do in HR, including retention. Generally speaking, a HPWS gets employees involved in conceiving, designing, and implementing processes that are better for the organizational and better for the employee, which increases retention. Figure 7.4 "HR Components of a HPWS"gives an example of HR's part in creating these systems.

Keeping HPWS in mind, we can begin to develop retention plans. The first step in this process is to understand some of the theories on job satisfaction and dissatisfaction. Next, we can gather data as to the satisfaction level of our current employees. Then we can begin to implement specific strategies for employee retention.

Theories on Job Dissatisfaction

There are a number of theories that attempt to describe what makes a satisfied employee versus an unsatisfied employee. While you may have learned about these theories in another class, such as organizational behavior, they are worth a review here to help us better understand employee satisfaction from an HR perspective.

Progression of Job Withdrawal

Figure 7.5 Process of Job Withdrawal

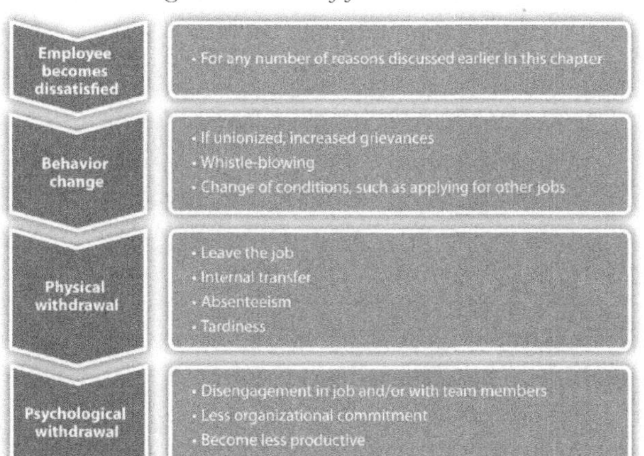

The first step to developing a retention plan is understanding some of the theories surrounding job satisfaction. One of the basic theories is the progression of job withdrawal theory, developed by Dan Farrell and James Petersen.[1] It says that people develop a set of behaviors in succession to avoid their work situation. These behaviors include behavior change, physical withdrawal, and psychological withdrawal.

Within the behavior change area, an employee will first try to change the situation that is causing the dissatisfaction. For example, if the employee is unhappy with the management style, he or she might consider asking for a department move. In the physical withdrawal phase, the employee does one of the following:

- Leaves the job
- Takes an internal transfer
- Starts to become absent or tardy

If an employee is unable to leave the job situation, he or she will experience psychological withdrawal. They will become disengaged and may show less job involvement and commitment to the organization, which can create large costs to the organization, such as dissatisfied customers.

Hawthorne Studies

Between 1927 and 1932, a series of experiments were conducted by Elton Mayo in the Western Electric Hawthorne Works organizational in Illinois.[2] Mayo developed these experiments to see how the physical and environmental factors of the workplace, such as lighting and break times, would affect employee motivation.

This was some of the first research performed that looked at human motivation at work. His results were surprising, as he found that no matter which experiments were performed, worker output improved. His conclusion and explanation for this was the simple fact the workers were happy to receive attention from researchers who expressed interest in them. As a result, these experiments, scheduled to last one year, extended to five years to increase the knowledge base about human motivation.

The implication of this research applies to HR and managers even today. It tells us that our retention plans must include training and other activities that make the employee feel valued.

Maslow's Hierarchy of Needs

In 1943, Abraham Maslow developed what was known as the theory of human motivation.[3] His theory was developed in an attempt to explain human motivation. According to Maslow, there is a hierarchy of five needs, and as one level of need is satisfied, it will no longer be a motivator. In other words, people start at the bottom of the hierarchy and work their way up. Maslow's hierarchy consists of the following:

- Self-actualization needs
- Esteem needs
- Social needs
- Safety needs
- Physiological needs

Physiological needs are our most basic needs, including food, water, and shelter. Safety needs at work might include feeling safe in the actual physical environment, or job security. As humans, we have the basic need to spend time with others.

Esteem needs refer to the need we have to feel good about ourselves. Finally, self-actualization needs are the needs we have to better ourselves.

The implications of his research tell us, for example, that as long as an employee's physiological needs are met, increased pay may not be a motivator. Likewise, employees should be motivated at work by having all needs met. Needs might include, for example, fair pay, safety standards at work, opportunities to socialize, compliments to help raise our esteem, and training opportunities to further develop ourselves.

Herzberg Two-Factor Theory

In 1959, Frederick Herzberg published The Motivation to Work,_[4] which described his studies to determine which aspects in a work environment caused satisfaction or dissatisfaction. He performed interviews in which employees were asked what pleased and displeased them about their work. From his research, he developed the motivation-hygiene theory to explain these results.

The things that satisfied the employees were motivators, while the dissatisfiers were the hygiene factors. He further said the hygiene factors were not necessarily motivators, but if not present in the work environment, they would actually cause demotivation. In other words, the hygiene factors are expected and assumed, while they may not necessarily motivate.

His research showed the following as the top six motivation factors:

1. Achievement
2. Recognition
3. The work itself
4. Responsibility
5. Advancement
6. Growth

The following were the top six hygiene factors:

1. Organizational policies
2. Supervision
3. Relationship with manager
4. Work conditions
5. Salary
6. Relationship with peers

The implication of this research is clear. Salary, for example, is on the hygiene factor list. Fair pay is expected, but it doesn't actually motivate someone to do a better job. On the other hand, programs to further develop employees, such as management training programs, would be considered a motivator. Therefore, our retention plans should be focused on the area of fair salary of course, but if they take the direction of Herzberg's motivational factors, the actual motivators tend to be the work and recognition surrounding the work performed.

McGregor

Douglas McGregor proposed the X-Y theory in his 1960 book called The Human Side of Enterprise._[5] McGregor's theory gives us a starting point to understanding how management style can impact the retention of employees. His theory suggests two fundamental approaches to managing people. Theory X managers, who have an authoritarian management style, have the following fundamental management beliefs:

- The average person dislikes work and will avoid it.
- Most people need to be threatened with punishment to work toward organizational goals.
- The average person needs to be directed.
- Most workers will avoid responsibility.

Theory Y managers, on the other hand, have the following beliefs:

- Most people want to make an effort at work.
- People will apply self-control and self-direction in pursuit of organizational objectives.
- Commitment to objectives is a function of expected rewards received.
- People usually accept and actually welcome responsibility.
- Most workers will use imagination and ingenuity in solving organizational problems.

As you can see, these two belief systems have a large variance, and managers who manage under the X theory may have a more difficult time retaining workers and may see higher turnover rates. As a result, it is our job in HR to provide training opportunities in the area of management, so our managers can help motivate the employees. Training is a large part of the retention plan.

HUMAN RESOURCE RECALL

What are the disadvantages of taking a theory X approach with your employees?

Carrot and Stick

It is unknown for sure where this term was first used, although some believe it was coined in the 1700s during the Seven Years' War. In public organization today, the stick approach refers to "poking and prodding" to get employees to do something. The carrot approach refers to the offering of some reward or incentive to motivate employees. Many organizations use the stick approach, as in the following examples:

- If you don't increase your sales by 10 percent, you will be fired.
- Everyone will have to take a pay cut if we don't produce 15 percent more than we are currently producing.
- As you can see, the stick approach takes a punitive look at retention, and we know this may motivate for a short period of time, but not in the long term.
- The carrot approach might include the following:
- If you increase sales by 10 percent, you will receive a bonus.
- If production increases by 15 percent, the entire team will receive an extra day off next month.

The carrot approach takes a much more positive approach to employee motivation but still may not be effective. For example, this approach can actually demotivate employees if they do not feel the goal is achievable. Also, if organizations use this as the only motivational technique, ignoring physiological rewards such as career growth, this could be a detriment as well. This approach is used as a retention method, usually as part of a compensation plan.

All the employee satisfaction theories we have discussed have implications for the development of our retention plans and reduction of turnover. These theories can be intertwined into the specific retention strategies we will implement.

Sources of Employee Satisfaction Data

After we have an understanding of why employees leave and employee satisfaction theories, research is our next step in developing a retention plan that will work for your organization. There isn't a "one size fits all" approach to retention planning, so the research component is essential to formulate a plan that will make a difference in turnover rates.

Research can be performed in two ways. First, exit interviews of employees who are leaving the organization can provide important retention information. Anexit interview is an interview performed by HR or a manager that seeks information as to what the employee liked at the organization and what they see should be improved. Exit interviews can be a valuable way to gather information about employee satisfaction and can serve as a starting point for determining any retention issues that may exist in the organization. However, the exit survey data should be reviewed over longer periods of time with several employees, so we can be sure we are not making retention plans based on the feedback of only a few people.

SAMPLE EXIT INTERVIEW QUESTIONS

1. What is your primary reason for leaving?
2. What did you like most about your job?
3. What did you like least about your job?
4. Did you feel there was room for growth in your job?
5. What incentives did you utilize while at our organizational?
6. Which incentives would you change and why?
7. Did you have enough training to do your job effectively?

The second way to perform research is through employee satisfaction surveys. A standardized and widely used measure of job satisfaction is thejob descriptive index (JDI) survey. While JDI was initially developed in 1969 at Bowling Green State University, it has gone through extensive revisions, the most recent one in 2009. JDI looks at five aspects of job satisfaction, including present job, present pay, opportunities for promotion, supervision, and coworkers.[6] Each of the five facets contains nine or eighteen questions; the survey can be given in whole or measure only one facet. The value of the scale is that an HR manager can measure job satisfaction over a period of time and compare current results to past results and even compare job satisfaction at their organizational versus their industry. This allows the HR manager to consider changes in the organization, such as a change in compensation structure, and see how job satisfaction is impacted by the change.

Any type of survey can provide information on the employee's satisfaction with their manager, workload, and other satisfaction and motivational issues. A few things should be considered when developing an employee satisfaction survey:

1. Communicate the purpose and goal of the survey.
2. Once the survey is complete, communicate what changes have been made as a result of the survey.
3. Assure employees their responses will be anonymous and private.
4. Involve management and leadership in the survey development.
5. Ask clear, concise questions that get at the root of morale issues.

Once data have been gathered and analyzed, we can formulate our retention plans. Our plan should always be tied to the strategic goals of the organization and the HPWS previously developed, and awareness of motivational theories should be coupled with the plans. Here are the components of a retention plan:

1. JDI survey results, other survey results, and exit interview findings
2. Current retention plans, strengths, and weaknesses
3. Goals of a retention plan (e.g., reduce turnover by 10 percent)
4. Individual strategies to meet retention and turnover reduction goals.
5. Budgeting. An understanding of how your retention plans will impact the payroll budget is important. See Video 7.2 for an example on how to calculate turnover costs and compare those to costs saved with an effective retention strategy.

KEY TAKEAWAYS

- A high-performance work system (HPWS) is a set of systematic HR practices that create an environment where the employee has greater involvement and responsibility for the success of the organization. The overall organizational strategy should impact the HPWS HR develops in regard to retention.
- Retention plans are developed to address employee turnover, resulting in a more effective organization.
- The first step in developing a retention plan is to use exit interviews and/or surveys to find out the satisfaction level of employees. Once you have the data, you can begin to write the plan, making sure it is tied to the organizational objectives.
- A standardized and widely used measure of job satisfaction is the JDI survey, or the Job Descriptive Index. While JDI was initially developed in 1969 at Bowling Green State University, it has gone through extensive revisions, the most recent one in 2009. JDI looks at five aspects of job satisfaction, including present job, present pay, opportunities for promotion, supervision, and coworkers.[7]
- A retention plan normally consists of survey and exit interview analysis, any current plans and strengths and weaknesses of those plans, the goal of the retention plan, and finally, the specific strategies to be implemented.
- There are many motivation theories that attempt to explain people's motivation or lack of motivation at work.
- The Hawthorne studies were a series of studies beginning in 1927 that initially looked at physical environments but found that people tended to be more motivated when they felt cared about. The implications to retention are clear, in that employees should feel cared about and developed within the organization.
- Maslow's theory on motivation says that if someone already has a need met, giving them something to meet more of that need will no longer motivate. Maslow divided the needs into physiological, safety, social, esteem, and self-actualization needs. Many organizations only motivate based on the low-level needs, such as pay. Development of training opportunities, for example, can motivate employees on high-level self-actualization needs.
- Herzberg developed motivational theories based on actual motivation factors and hygiene factors. Hygiene factors are those things that are expected in the workplace and will demotivate employees when absent but will not actually motivate when present. If managers try to motivate only on the basis of hygiene factors, turnover can be high. Motivation on both of his factors is key to a good retention plan.
- McGregor's theory on motivation looked at managers' attitudes toward employees. He found that theory X managers had more of a negative view of employees, while theory Y managers had a more positive view. Providing training to the managers in our organization can be a key retention strategy based on McGregor's theory.
- The carrot-and-stick approach means you can get someone to do something by prodding or by offering some incentive to motivate them to do the work. This theory implies these are the only two methods to motivate, which of course, we know isn't true. The implication of this in our retention plan is such that we must utilize a variety of methods to retain employees.

EXERCISES

1. What types of things will motivate you in your career? Name at least five things. Where would these fit on Maslow's hierarchy of needs and Herzberg's two-factor theory?
2. How can you apply each of these motivation techniques to motivation theories?
   a. Training
   b. Employee recognition programs

c. Bonuses
d. Management training for your current managers
e. Profit sharing

---

[1] Dan Farrell and James C. Petersen, "Commitment, Absenteeism and Turnover of New Employees: A Longitudinal Study," Human Relations 37, no. 8 (August 1984): 681–692, accessed August 26, 2011,http://libres.uncg.edu/ir/uncg/f/J_Petersen_Commitment_1984.pdf .

[2] Elton Mayo, The Social Problems of an Industrial Civilization (1949; repr., New York: Arno Press, 2007).

[3] Abraham Maslow, Toward a Psychology of Being, 3rd ed. (New York: Wiley, 1999).

[4] Frederick Herzberg, Bernard Mausner, and Barbara Bloch Snyderman, The Motivation to Work (New Brunswick, NJ: Transaction Publishers, 1993).

[5] Douglas McGregor, The Human Side of Enterprise (1960; repr., New York: McGraw-Hill, 2006).

[6] "Job Descriptive Index," JDI Research Group, Bowling Green State University, accessed July 29, 2011, http://www.bgsu.edu/departments/psych/io/jdi/page54706.html.

[7] "Job Descriptive Index," JDI Research Group, Bowling Green State University, accessed July 29, 2011, http://www.bgsu.edu/departments/psych/io/jdi/page54706.html.

7.3 Implementing Retention Strategies

LEARNING OBJECTIVE

1. Explain the strategies and considerations in development of a retention plan.

As we have addressed so far in this chapter, retention and reduction of turnover is paramount to a healthy organization. Performing research, such as calculating turnover rates, doing exit interviews, and surveying employees' satisfaction, are the first steps. Once this is done, understanding motivational theories and the application of them in the retention plan can help reduce turnover. Next, we can apply specific retention strategies to include in our plans, while keeping our budget in mind. Some of the retention strategies discussed have already or will be discussed in their own chapters, but they are certainly worth a mention here as part of the overall plan.

Salaries and Benefits

A comprehensive compensation plan that includes not only pay but things such as health benefits and paid time off (PTO) is the first retention strategy that should be addressed. The compensation plan should not only help in recruitment of the right people but also help retain employees. Utilizing a pay banding system, in which the levels of compensation for jobs are clearly defined, is one way to ensure fairness exists within internal pay structures.

As we know from this chapter, compensation is not everything. An employee can be well paid and have great benefits but still not be satisfied with the organization. Some of the considerations surrounding pay as a way to retain employees include the following:

1. *Instituting a standard process.* Many organizations do not have set pay plans, which can result in unfairness when onboarding (the process of bringing someone "on board" with the organizational, including discussion and negotiation of compensation) or offering pay increases. Make sure the process for receiving pay raises is fair and defensible, so as not to appear to be discriminatory. This can be addressed in both your compensation planning process as well as your retention plan.
2. *A pay communication strategy.* Employees deserve to know how their pay rates are being determined. Transparency in the process of how raises are given and then communicating the process can help in your retention planning process.[1]
3. *Paid time off.* Is your organization offering competitive PTO? Consider implementing a PTO system that is based on the amount of hours an employee works. For example, rather than developing a policy based on hours worked for the organizational, consider revising the policy so that for every X number of hours worked, PTO is earned. This can create fairness for the salaried employee, especially for those employees who may work more than the required forty hours.

Please refer to Chapter 6 "Compensation and Benefits" for more information on pay and benefits, and analyze how your compensation plans could be negatively affecting your retention.

Training and Development

To meet our higher level needs, humans need to experience self-growth. HR professionals and managers can help this process by offering training programs within the organization and paying for employees to attend career skill seminars and programs. In addition, many organizations offer tuition reimbursement programs to help the employee earn a degree. Dick's Drive-In, a local fast food restaurant in Seattle, Washington, offers $18,000 in scholarships over four years to employees working twenty hours per week. There is a six-month waiting period, and the employee must continue to work twenty hours per week. In a high turnover industry, Dick's Drive-In boasts one of the highest retention rates around.

HOW WOULD YOU HANDLE THIS?

You work for a small organization in the HR department. One of your web developers schedules a meeting with you, and during the meeting she says that she doesn't see any career growth for her in the organization. As a result, she confides that she is planning to leave the organization as soon as she can find another job. She is one of the best developers you have and you would hate to lose her.
How Would You Handle This?

Performance Appraisals
The performance appraisal is a formalized process to assess how well an employee does his or her job. The effectiveness of this process can contribute to employee retention, in that employees can gain constructive feedback on their job performance, and it can be an opportunity for the manager to work with the employee to set goals within the organization. This process can help ensure the employee's upper level self-actualization needs are met, but it also can address some of the motivational factors discussed by Herzberg, such as achievement, recognition, and responsibility.

HUMAN RESOURCE RECALL

How important is PTO to you? How do you think the amount of PTO would affect your likelihood to accept one job over another?

Succession Planning
Succession planning is a process of identifying and developing internal people who have the potential for filling positions. As we know, many people leave organizations because they do not see career growth or potential. One way we can combat this in our retention plan is to make sure we have a clear succession planning process that is communicated to employees. Succession planning is sometimes called the talent bench, because successful organizations always have talented people "on the bench" or ready to do the job should a key position become vacant. The goals of most succession plans include the following:_[2]

- Identify high-potential employees capable of advancing to positions of higher responsibility.
- Ensure the development of these individuals to help them be "ready" to earn a promotion into a new position.
- Ensure diversity in the talent bench by creating a formal succession planning process.

Succession planning must be just that: planned. This allows clear communication to the employees on how they can further develop within the organization, and it helps them see what skills they should master before that time comes.

Flextime, Telecommuting, and Sabbaticals
According to a Salary.com survey, the ability to work from home and flexible work schedules are benefits that would entice an employee to stay in their job._[3] The ability to implement this type of retention strategy might be difficult, depending on the type of public organization. For example, a retailer may not be able to implement this, since the sales associate must be in the store to assist customers. However, for many professions, it is a viable option, worth including in the retention plan and part of work-life balance.

Some organizations, such as Recreational Equipment Inorganizationald, based in Seattle, offer twelve weeks of unpaid leave per year (beyond the twelve weeks required under the Family and Medical Leave Act) for the employee to pursue volunteering or traveling opportunities. In addition, with fifteen years of service with the organizational, paid sabbaticals are offered, which include four weeks plus already earned vacation time.

Management Training
A manager can affect an employee's willingness to stay on the job. In a recent Gallup poll of one million workers, a poor supervisor or manager is the number one reason why people leave their jobs._[4] Managers who bully, use the theory X approach, communicate poorly, or are incompetent may find it difficult to motivate employees to stay within the organization. While in HR we cannot control a manager's behavior, we can provide training to create better management. Training of managers to be better communicators and motivators is a way to handle this retention issue.

Conflict Management and Fairness
Perceptions on fairness and how organizations handle conflict can be a contributing factor to retention. Outcome fairness refers to the judgment that people make with respect to the outcomes they receive versus the outcomes received by others with whom they associate with. When people are deciding if something is fair, they will likely look at procedural justice, or the process used to determine the outcomes received. There are six main areas employees will use to determine the outcome fairness of a conflict:

1. Consistency. The employee will determine if the procedures are applied consistently to other persons and throughout periods of time.

2. Bias suppression. The employee perceives the person making the decision does not have bias or vested interest in the outcome.
3. Information accuracy. The decision made is based on correct information.
4. Correctability. The decision is able to be appealed and mistakes in the decision process can be corrected.
5. Representativeness. The employee feels the concerns of all stakeholders involved have been taken into account.
6. Ethicality. The decision is in line with moral societal standards.

For example, let's suppose JoAnn just received a bonus and recognition at the organizational party for her contributions to an important organizational project. Another employee, Sam, might compare his inputs and outputs and determine it was unfair that JoAnn was recognized because he had worked on bigger projects and not received the same recognition or bonus. When we look at how our retention strategies are developed, we want to be sure they can apply to everyone in the organization; otherwise it may cause retention problems. Some of the procedures questioned could include the following:

- How time off is requested
- How assignments of the "best" projects are given
- Division of work
- Promotion processes
- Pay processes

While some of these policies may seem minor, they can make a big difference in retention. Besides development of fair policies, we should be sure that the policies are clearly communicated and any processes are communicated as well. These types of policies should be revisited yearly and addressed in the retention plan if it appears they are causing employee dissatisfaction.

In addition to a sense of fairness within the organization, there should be a specific way (process) of managing conflict. If the organization is unionized, it is likely a grievance process is already in place to handle many types of conflicts. There are four basic steps to handle conflict. First, the individuals in conflict should try to handle the conflict by discussing the problem with one another. If this doesn't work, a panel of representatives from the organization should hear both sides of the dispute and make a recommendation. If this doesn't work, the organization may want to consider mediation and, in extreme cases, arbitration. Inmediation, a neutral third party from outside the organization hears both sides of a dispute and tries to get the parties to come to a resolution, while in arbitration, an outside person hears both sides and makes a specific decision about how things should proceed.

ORGANIZATIONAL FOCUS

With over nineteen thousand employees in sixty countries, Google has seen its share of retention problems._[5] In late 2010, Googlers left the organization en masse to work for Facebook or Twitter._[6] Many who left were looking for pre–initial public offering (IPO) organizations to work with, something that Google couldn't compete with, since it went IPO in April 2004. As a result of the high turnover, Google put its mathematical algorithms to work to determine which employees were most likely to leave, allowing HR to determine what departments to focus on in their retention plans. In 2011, Google gave every employee a 10 percent pay raise, and it continues to offer a variety of new and old perks, such as free food in any of its cafeterias, 20 percent of time to work on personal projects, and $175 peer spot bonuses. Google also offers free laundry services, climbing walls, tuition reimbursement, child-care centers, financial planning classes, and matching funds (up to $3,000 per employee) to nonprofit organizations. For all this, Google ranked number four on Fortune magazine's list of 100 best organizations to work for in 2011._[7] Some say it isn't the perks, high pay, or bonuses but the organizational culture that Google creates. A weekly all-hands meeting with the founders, where people are encouraged to ask the founders questions, and a team focus meeting where everyone shares ideas are examples of the organizational culture Google creates. Google exemplifies the importance of culture in retention of employees.

Job Design, Job Enlargement, and Empowerment

As we have discussed previously, one of the reasons for job dissatisfaction is the job itself. Ensuring we are appropriately matching skills with the job when we do our initial hiring is important. Revisiting the recruitment plan and selection process should be a consideration.

Job enrichment means to enhance a job by adding more meaningful tasks to make the employee's work more rewarding. For example, if a retail salesperson is good at creating eye-catching displays, allow him or her to practice this skill and assign tasks revolving around this. Job enrichment can fulfill the higher level of human needs while creating job satisfaction at the same time. In fact, research in this area by Richard Hackman and Greg Oldham_[8] found that employees need the following to achieve job satisfaction:

- Skill variety, or many different activities as part of the job

- Task identity, or being able to complete one task from beginning to end
- Task significance, or the degree to which the job has impact on others, internally or externally
- Autonomy, or freedom to make decisions within the job
- Feedback, or clear information about performance

In addition, job enlargement, defined as the adding of new challenges or responsibilities to a current job, can create job satisfaction. Assigning employees to a special project or task is an example of job enlargement. Be cautioned, though, that some employees may resent additional work, and job enlargement could actually be a demotivator. Otherwise, knowing the employee and his or her goals and adding work that can be an end to these goals is the best way to achieve retention through job enlargement.

Employee empowerment involves employees in their work by allowing them to make decisions and act upon those decisions, with the support of the organization. Employees who are not micromanaged and who have the power to determine the sequence of their own work day, for example, tend to be more satisfied than those who are not empowered. Empowerment can include the following:

- Encourage innovation or new ways of doing things.
- Make sure employees have the information they need to do their jobs; for example, they are not dependent on managers for information in decision making.
- Use management styles that allow for participation, feedback, and ideas from employees.

Pay-for-Performance Strategies

A pay-for-performance strategy means that employees are rewarded for meeting preset objectives within the organization. For example, in a merit-based pay system, the employee is rewarded for meeting or exceeding performance during a given time period. Rather than a set pay increase every year, the increase is based on performance. Some organizations offer bonuses to employees for meeting objectives, while some organizations offer team incentive pay if a team achieves a specific, predetermined outcome. For example, each player on the winning team of the 2010 NFL Super Bowl earned a team bonus of $83,000,[9] while the losing team of the Super Bowl took home $42,000. Players also earn money for each wild card game and payoff game. Some organizations also offer profit sharing, which is tied to a organizational's overall performance. Gain sharing, different from profit sharing, focuses on improvement of productivity within the organization. For example, the city of Loveland in Colorado implemented a gain-sharing program that defined three criteria that needed to be met for employees to be given extra compensation. The city revenues had to exceed expenses, expenses had to be equal to or less than the previous year's expenses, and a citizen satisfaction survey had to meet minimum requirements.

To make sure a pay-for-performance system works, the organization needs to ensure the following:

- Standards are specific and measureable.
- The system is applied fairly to all employees.
- The system is communicated clearly to employees.
- The best work from everyone in the organization is encouraged.
- Rewards are given to performers versus nonperformers.
- The system is updated as the public organization climate changes.
- There are substantial rewards for high performers.

As we have already addressed, pay isn't everything, but it certainly can be an important part of the employee retention plan and strategy.

Work-Life Balance

Work-life balance discussions originated during the 1960s and 1970s and pertained mostly to working mothers' meeting the demands of family and work. During the 1980s, the realization that meeting a work-life balance is important (for all, not just working mothers) resulted in organizations such as IBM implementing flextime and home-based work solutions. The growing awareness of the work-life balance problem continued into the 1990s, when policies were developed and implemented but not acted upon by managers and employees, according to Jim Bird in Employment Relations Today.[10] Today, work-life balance is considered an important topic, so much so that the World at Work Society offers special certifications in this area. The World at Work certification programs focus on creation of successful programs to attract, retain, and motivate employees.

Karol Rose, author of Work Life Effectiveness,[11] says that most organizations look at a systems approach of work-life balance, instead of a systems and individual approach. The systems approach to work-life balance includes policies and procedures that allow people flexibility, such as telecommuting and flextime options.

According to Rose, looking at the individual differences is equally as important as the systems approach. Brad

Harrington, the director of Boston College's Center for Work and Family, stresses this issue: "Work-life balance comes down, not to an organizational strategy, but to an individual strategy." For example, a single parent has a different work-life balance need than someone without children. In other words, as HR professionals, we can create work-life balance systems, but we should also look at individual approaches. For example, at Recreational Equipment Inorganizationald (REI),[12] they use the systems approach perspective and offer paid time off and sabbaticals, but their employee assistance program also offers access to services, referrals, and free consulting for the individual to find his or her perfect work-life balance. For this, REI receives a number nine ranking on Fortune's list of best organizations to work for in the area of work-life balance.

The organizational culture can contribute greatly to work-life balance. Some organizations have a culture of flexibility that fares well for workers who do not want to feel tethered to an office, while some workers prefer to be in the office where more informal socializing can occur. While some organizations promote work-life balance on paper, upper management needs to let employees know it is OK to take advantage of the alternatives to create a positive work-life balance. For example, organizations place different levels of value on work-life options such as telecommuting. An organization may have a telecommuting option, but the employees must feel it is OK to use these options. Even in a organizational that has work-life balance systems, a manager who sends e-mails at 10 p.m. on Saturday night could be sending the wrong message to employees about the expectations, creating an environment in which work-life balance is not practiced in reality. O'Neill, a surf gear organizational in California, sends a strong message to its employees by offering half-day Fridays during the summer,[13] so employees can get a head start on the weekend.

Jim Bird, in his work-life balance article in Employment Relations Today, suggests implementing a work-life balance training program that is dual purpose (can serve both personal interests and professional development). In other words, implement trainings in which the employee can develop both personal skills and interests that can translate into higher productivity at work.

Besides the training program, Bird suggests creating a monthly work-life newsletter as an educational tool to show the organizational's commitment to work-life balance. The newsletter can include interviews from respected employees and tips on how to create a work-life balance.

Finally, training managers on the importance of work-life balance and how to create a culture that embraces this is a key way to use work-life balance as a retention strategy.

Other Retention Strategies

According to Fortune's "100 Best Organizations to Work For,"[14] retention strategies that are more unusual might be part of your retention plan. Some strategies from the list might include the following:

- On-site daycare or daycare assistance
- Gym memberships or on-site gyms
- Concierge service to assist in party planning or dog grooming, for example
- On-site dry cleaning drop-off and pickup
- Car care, such as oil changes, on-site once a week
- On-site doggie daycare
- On-site yoga or other fitness classes
- "Summer Fridays," when all employees work half days on Fridays during the summer
- Various support groups for cancer survivors, weight loss, or support in caring for aging parents
- Allowance for fertility treatment benefits
- On-site life coaches
- Peer-to-peer employee recognition programs
- Management recognition programs

While some of these options may not work in your organization, we must remember to be creative when our goal is to retain our best employees and reduce turnover in our organizations. The bottom line is to create a plan and make sure the plan is communicated to all employees.

KEY TAKEAWAYS

- Once you determine the employee's level of satisfaction through exit interviews and surveys and understand motivational theories, you can begin to develop specific retention strategies.
- Of course, salary and benefits are a major component of retention strategies. Consistent pay systems and transparent processes as to how raises occur must be included in a retention plan (and compensation strategy).
- Training and development meets the higher level needs of the individual. Many organizations offer paid tuition programs, reimbursement programs,

and in-house training to increase the skills and knowledge of the employee.

- Performance appraisals provide an avenue for feedback and goal setting. They also allow for employees to be recognized for their contributions.
- Succession plans allow employees to see how they can continue their career with the organization, and they clearly detail what employees need to do to achieve career growth, without leaving your organization.
- Flextime and telecommuting options are worth considering as an addition to your retention plan. These types of plans allow the employee flexibility when developing his or her schedule and some control of his or her work. Some organizations also offer paid or unpaid sabbaticals after a certain number of years with the organizational to pursue personal interests.
- Since one of the reasons people are dissatisfied at their job is because of the relationship with their manager, providing in-house training to all management team members to help them become better communicators and better managers can trickle down to the employee level, creating better relationships and resulting in better retention and less turnover.
- Reviewing organizational policies to ensure they are fair can contribute to better retention. For example, how projects are assigned or the process for requesting vacation time can contribute to dissatisfaction if the employee feels the processes are not fair.
- Review the job design to ensure the employee is experiencing growth within their job. Changing the job through empowerment or job enlargement to help the growth of the employee can create better retention.
- Other, more unique ways of retaining employees might include offering services to make the employee's life easier, such as dry cleaning, daycare services, or on-site yoga classes.

EXERCISE

1. Research two different organizations you might be interested in working for. When reviewing their list of benefits, which ones are offered that might motivate someone to stay with the organization?

---

[1] "The Knowledge of Pay Study," WorldatWork and The LeBlanc Group LLC, 2010, accessed February 26, 2011, http://www.worldatwork.org/waw/Content/research/html/research-home.jsp.

[2] William J. Rothwell and H. C. Kazanas, Building In-House Leadership and Management Development Programs: Their Creation, Management, and Continuous Improvement(Westport, CT: Quorum Books, 1999), 131.

[3] "Employee Job Satisfaction and Retention Survey, 2007/2008," Salary.com, 2008, accessed February 26, 2011, http://www.salary.com/docs/resources/JobSatSurvey_08.pdf.

[4] "No. 1 Reason People Quit Their jobs," AOL News, Netscape, n.d., accessed July 28, 2011,http://webcenters.netscape.compuserve.com/whatsnew/package.jsp?name=fte/quitjobs/quitjobs&floc=wn-dx.

[5] "Our Philosophy," Google, n.d., accessed July 28, 2011,http://www.google.com/about/organizational/organizational/tenthings.html.

[6] Ben Popper, "Why Google's Retention Plan Backfired," CBS Public organization Network, September 16, 2010, accessed July 28, 2011, http://www.bnet.com/blog/high-tech/why-googles-retention-plan-backfired/1172.

[7] "100 Best Organizations to Work For," CNN Money, 2011, accessed July 28, 2011,http://money.cnn.com/magazines/fortune/bestorganizations/2011/snapshots/4.html.

[8] Robert N. Ford, Motivation through the Work Itself (New York: American Management Association, 1969); William J. Paul, Keith B. Robertson, and Frederick Herzberg, "Job Enrichment Pays Off," Harvard Public organization Review, March–April 1969, 61–78.

[9] Darren Rovell, "How Much Do Players Get Paid for Winning the Super Bowl?" CNBC Sports, January 18, 2011, accessed July 29, 2011,http://www.cnbc.com/id/41138354/How_Much_Do_Players_Get_Paid_For_Winning_the_Super_Bowl.

[10] Jim Bird, "Work-Life Balance: Doing It Right and Avoiding the Pitfalls," Employment Relations Today 33, no. 3 (2006), reprinted on WorkLifeBalance.com, accessed July 29, 2011,http://www.worklifebalance.com/assets/pdfs/article3.pdf.

[11] Karol Rose, Work-life Effectiveness: Bottom-line Strategies for Today's Workplace(Scottsdale, AZ: World at Work Press, 2006).

[12] "Pay and Benefits: Total Rewards at REI," Recreational Equipment Inorganizationald, n.d., accessed July 29, 2011, http://www.rei.com/jobs/pay.html.

[13] "Vans, Quiksilver, and California Top Skate Organizations Offer Dream Careers to FIDM's Graphic Design School Grads," Fashion News, June 4, 2011, accessed July 29, 2011,http://www.fashionnews.com/2011/06/04/vans-quiksilver-californias-top-skate-organizations-offer-dream-careers-to-fidms-graphic-design-school-grads.

[14] "100 Best Organizations to Work For," CNN Money, 2011, accessed February 26, 2011,http://money.cnn.com/galleries/2011/news/organizations/1101/gallery.bestorganizations_unusual_perks.fortune/5.html.

7.4 Cases and Problems

CHAPTER SUMMARY

- Retaining employees is an important component to a healthy organization. Losing an employee is called turnover.
- Direct turnover costs and indirect turnover costs can include the costs associated with employee replacement, declining employee morale, or lost customers.

- A high-performance work system (HPWS) is a set of systematic HR practices that create an environment where the employee has greater involvement and responsibility for the success of the organization. The overall organizational strategy should impact the HPWS HR develops in regard to retention.
- Retention plans are developed to address employee turnover, resulting in a more effective organization.
- Some of the reasons why employees leave can include a poor match between job and skills, no growth potential, pay inequity among employees, the fairness and communication style of management, and heavy workloads.
- The first step in developing a retention plan is to use exit interviews and/or surveys to find out the satisfaction level of employees. Once you have the data, you can begin to write the plan, making sure it is tied to the organizational objectives.
- A retention plan normally consists of survey and exit interview analysis, any current plans and strengths and weaknesses of those plans, the goal of the retention plan, and the specific strategies to be implemented.
- There are many motivation theories that attempt to explain people's motivation or lack of motivation at work.
- The Hawthorne studies were a series of studies beginning in 1927 that initially looked at physical environments but found that people tended to be more motivated when they felt cared about. The implications to retention are clear, in that employees should feel cared about and developed within the organization.
- Maslow's theory on motivation says that if someone already has a need met, giving them something to meet more of that need will no longer motivate. Maslow divided the needs into physiological, safety, social, esteem, and self-actualization needs. Many organizations only motivate based on the low-level needs, such as pay. Development of training opportunities, for example, can motivate employees on high-level self-actualization needs.
- Herzberg developed motivational theories based on actual motivation factors and hygiene factors. Hygiene factors are those things that are expected in the workplace and will demotivate employees when absent but will not actually motivate when present. If managers try to motivate only on the basis of hygiene factors, turnover can be high. Motivation on both factors is key to a good retention plan.
- McGregor's theory on motivation looked at managers' attitudes toward employees. He found that theory X managers had more of a negative view of employees, while theory Y managers had a more positive view. Providing training to the managers in our organization can be a key retention strategy, based on McGregor's theory.
- The carrot-and-stick approach means you can get someone to do something by prodding or offering some incentive to motivate them to do the work. This theory implies these are the only two methods to motivate, which we know isn't true. The implication of this in our retention plan is such that we must utilize a variety of methods to retain employees.
- Once you determine the employee's level of satisfaction through exit interviews and surveys and understand motivational theories, you can develop specific retention strategies.
- Of course, salary and benefits are a major component of retention strategies. Consistent pay systems and transparent processes as to how raises occur must be included in a retention plan (and compensation strategy).
- Training and development meets the higher level needs of the individual. Many organizations offer paid tuition programs, reimbursement programs, and in-house training to increase the skills and knowledge of the employee.
- Performance appraisals provide an avenue for feedback and goal setting. They also allow for employees to be recognized for their contributions.
- Succession plans allow employees to see how they can continue their career with the organization, and they clearly detail what employees need to do to achieve career growth-without leaving your organization.
- Flextime and telecommuting options are worth considering as an addition to your retention plan. These types of plans allow the employee flexibility when developing his or her schedule and some control of his or her work. Some organizations also offer paid or unpaid sabbaticals after a certain number of years with the organizational to pursue personal interests.
- Since one of the reasons people are dissatisfied at their job is because of the relationship with their manager, providing in-house training to all management team members to help them become better communicators and better managers can trickle down to the employee level, creating better relationships and resulting in better retention and less turnover.

- Reviewing organizational policies to ensure they are fair can contribute to better retention. For example, how projects are assigned or the process for requesting vacation time can contribute to dissatisfaction if the employee feels the processes are not fair.
- Review the job design to ensure the employee is experiencing growth within their job. Changing the job through empowerment or job enlargement to help the growth of the employee can create better retention.
- Other, more unique ways of retaining employees might include offering services to make the employee's life easier, such as dry cleaning, daycare services, or on-site yoga classes.

CHAPTER CASE

Turnover Analysis

You recently completed your organizational's new compensation plan. You are happy with the results but know there is more to retaining the employees than just pay, and you don't currently have a retention plan. Your organization is a large staffing firm, consisting of several offices on the West Coast. The majority of employees are staffing recruiters, and they fill full-time and temporary positions for a variety of clients. One of the challenges you face is a difference in geographical areas, and as a result, there are differences in what may motivate employees.

As you initially look at turnover numbers, you have the sense that turnover has increased over the last six months. Your initial thoughts are the need for a better retention strategy, utilizing a bonus structure as well as other methods of retention. Currently, your organization pays a straight salary to employees, does not offer flextime or telecommuting options, focuses on individual performance (number of staffing placements) rather than team performance, and provides five days of vacation for every two years with the organization.

Month	Separated Employees	Total Number of Employees Midmonth
March	12	552
April	14	541
May	16	539
June	20	548
July	22	545

1. Calculate monthly turnover for the past six months.
2. What are the possible reasons for turnover in your organization and other organizations?
3. What steps would you take to remedy the situation?

TEAM ACTIVITY

1. Following is a list of some possible retention strategies. Rank each one in order of importance to you as an employee (1 being the most important), then share your rankings with classmates:
   a. Salary
   b. Opportunity for bonuses, profit sharing
   c. Benefits
   d. Opportunity to grow professionally with the organization
   e. Team bonuses
   f. More paid time off
   g. Option to telecommute
   h. Flextime scheduling
   i. Sense of empowerment
   j. Tuition reimbursement
   k. Job satisfaction

NOTES:

NOTES:

Chapter 8: Training and Development in Public Organizations

Training: Not Like It Used to Be

Imagine this: You have a pile of work on your desk and as you get started, your Outlook calendar reminds you about a sexual harassment training in ten minutes. You groan to yourself, not looking forward to sitting in a conference room and seeing PowerPoint slide after PowerPoint slide. As you walk to the conference room, you run into a colleague who is taking the same training that day and commiserate on how boring this training is probably going to be. When you step into the conference room, however, you see something very different.

Computers are set up at every chair with a video ready to start on the computer. The HR manager greets you and asks you to take a seat. When the training starts, you are introduced (via video) on each of the computers to a series of sexual harassment example scenarios. The videos stop, and there is a recorded discussion about what the videos portrayed. Your colleagues in the Washington, DC, office are able to see the same training and, via video conferencing, are able to participate in the discussions. It is highly interactive and interesting. Once the training is finished, there are assignments to be completed via specific channels that have been set up for this training. You communicate about the material and complete the assignments in teams with members of your Washington, DC, office. If you want to review the material, you simply click on a review and the entire session or parts of the training can be reviewed. In fact, on your bus ride home from work, you access the channels on your iPhone, chatting with a colleague in your other office about the sexual harassment training assignment you have due next week. You receive an e-mail from your HR manager asking you to complete a training assessment located in a specific channel in the software, and you happily comply because you have an entirely new perspective on what training can be.

This is the training of today. No longer do people sit in hot, stuffy rooms to get training on boring content. Training has become highly interactive, technical, and interesting owing to the amount of multimedia we can use. Sun Microsystems, for example, has developed just the kind of software mentioned above, called Social Learning eXchange (SLX). This type of training allows people across the country to connect with each other, saving both money and time. In fact, Sun Microsystems received a Best Practices Award from Training Magazine for this innovative software in 2010._[1] The SLX software allows training to be delivered in an interactive manner in multiple locations. The implications of this type of software are numerous. For example, SLX is used at Sun Professional Services division by delivering instructional videos on tools and software, which employees can view at their own pace._[2] There is also a channel in the software that allows the vice president to communicate with employees on a regular basis to improve employee communications. In another example, this software can be used to quickly communicate product changes to the sales team, who then begin the process of positioning their products to consumers. Training videos, including breakout sessions, can save organizations money by not requiring travel to a session. These can even be accessed using application technology on cell phones. Employees can obtain the training they need in the comfort of their own city, office, or home. Someone is sick the day the training is delivered? No problem; they can review the recorded training sessions.

An estimated $1,400 per employee is spent on training annually, with training costs consuming 2.72 percent of the total payroll budget_[3] for the average organizational. With such a large amount of funds at stake, HR managers must develop the right training programs to meet the needs; otherwise, these funds are virtually wasted. This chapter is all about how to assess, develop, implement, and measure an effective training program.

---

[1] "2010 Top 25 Winners," Training Magazine, accessed July 25, 2010,http://www.trainingmag.com/article/2010-top-125-winners.

[2] "Video Community for the Enterprise," Social Learning eXchange, accessed July 25, 2010,http://www.slideshare.net/sociallearningexchange/social-learning-exchange-slx?from=share_email.

[3] See the American Society for Training and Development Trend Review, ASTD Website, accessed July 25, 2010, http://www.astd.org/.

8.1 Steps to Take in Training an Employee

LEARNING OBJECTIVE

1. Explain the four steps involved when training an employee.

Any effective organizational has training in place to make sure employees can perform his or her job. During the recruitment and selection process, the right person should be hired to begin with. But even the right person may need training in how your organizational does things. Lack of training can result in lost productivity, lost customers, and poor relationships between employees and managers. It can also result in dissatisfaction, which means retention problems and high turnover. All these end up being direct costs to the organization. In fact, a study performed by the American Society for Training and Development (ASTD) found that 41 percent of employees at organizations with poor training planned to leave within the year, but in organizations with excellent training, only 12 percent planned to leave.[1] To reduce some costs associated with not training or undertraining, development of training programs can help with some of the risk. This is what this chapter will address.

For effective employee training, there are four steps that generally occur. First, the new employee goes through an orientation, and then he or she will receive in-house training on job-specific areas. Next, the employee should be assigned a mentor, and then, as comfort with the job duties grows, he or she may engage in external training.Employee training and development is the process of helping employees develop their personal and organization skills, knowledge, and abilities.

Employee Orientation

The first step in training is an employee orientation. Employee orientation is the process used for welcoming a new employee into the organization. The importance of employee orientation is two-fold. First, the goal is for employees to gain an understanding of the organizational policies and learn how their specific job fits into the big picture. Employee orientation usually involves filling out employee paperwork such as I-9 and 401(k) program forms.

The goals of an orientation are as follows:

2. To reduce start-up costs. If an orientation is done right, it can help get the employee up to speed on various policies and procedures, so the employee can start working right away. It can also be a way to ensure all hiring paperwork is filled out correctly, so the employee is paid on time.
3. To reduce anxiety. Starting a new job can be stressful. One goal of an orientation is to reduce the stress and anxiety people feel when going into an unknown situation.
4. To reduce employee turnover. Employee turnover tends to be higher when employees don't feel valued or are not given the tools to perform. An employee orientation can show that the organization values the employee and provides tools necessary for a successful entry.
5. To save time for the supervisor and coworkers. A well-done orientation makes for a better prepared employee, which means less time having to teach the employee.
6. To set expectations and attitudes. If employees know from the start what the expectations are, they tend to perform better. Likewise, if employees learn the values and attitudes of the organization from the beginning, there is a higher chance of a successful tenure at the organizational.
7. Some organizations use employee orientation as a way to introduce employees not only to the organizational policies and procedures but also to the staff.

HUMAN RESOURCE RECALL

Have you ever participated in an orientation? What was it like? What components did it have?

In-House Training

In-house training programs are learning opportunities developed by the organization in which they are used. This is usually the second step in the training process and often is ongoing. In-house training programs can be training related to a specific job, such as how to use a particular kind of software. In a manufacturing setting, in-house training might include an employee learning how to use a particular kind of machinery.

Many organizations provide in-house training on various HR topics as well, meaning it doesn't always have to relate to a specific job. Some examples of in-house training include the following:

- Ethics training
- Sexual harassment training
- Multicultural training
- Communication training
- Management training
- Customer service training
- Operation of special equipment
- Training to do the job itself
- Basic skills training

As you can tell by the list of topics, HR might sometimes create and deliver this training, but often a supervisor or manager delivers the training.

Mentoring

After the employee has completed orientation and in-house training, organizations see the value in offering mentoring opportunities as the next step in training. Sometimes a mentor may be assigned during in-house training. A mentor is a trusted, experienced advisor who has direct investment in the development of an employee. A mentor may be a supervisor, but often a mentor is a colleague who has the experience and personality to help guide someone through processes. While mentoring may occur informally, a mentorship program can help ensure the new employee not only feels welcomed but is paired up with someone who already knows the ropes and can help guide the new employee through any on-the-job challenges.

To work effectively, a mentoring program should become part of the organizational culture; in other words, new mentors should receive in-house training to be a mentor. Mentors are selected based on experience, willingness, and personality. IBM's Integrated Supply Chain Division, for example, has successfully implemented a mentorship program. The organizational's division boasts 19,000 employees and half of IBM's revenues, making management of a mentorship program challenging. However, potential mentors are trained and put into a database where new employees can search attributes and strengths of mentors and choose the person who closely meets their needs. Then the mentor and mentee work together in development of the new employee. "We view this as a best practice," says Patricia Lewis-Burton, vice president of human resources, Integrated Supply Chain Division. "We view it as something that is not left to human resources alone. In fact, the program is imbedded in the way our group does public organization."[2]

Some organizations use short-term mentorship programs because they find employees training other employees to be valuable for all involved. Starbucks, for example, utilizes this approach. When it opens a new store in a new market, a team of experienced store managers and baristas are sent from existing stores to the new stores to lead the store-opening efforts, including training of new employees._[3]

External Training

External training includes any type of training that is not performed in-house. This is usually the last step in training, and it can be ongoing. It can include sending an employee to a seminar to help further develop leadership skills or helping pay tuition for an employee who wants to take a marketing class. To be a Ford automotive technician, for example, you must attend the Ford ASSET Program, which is a partnership between Ford Motor Organizational, Ford dealers, and select technical schools._[4]

HOW WOULD YOU HANDLE THIS?

To Train or Not to Train

Towanda Michaels is the human resource manager at a medium-size pet supply wholesaler. Casey Cleps is a salesperson at the organization and an invaluable member of the team. Last year, his sales brought in about 20 percent of the organizational revenue alone. Everybody likes Casey: he is friendly, competent, and professional.

Training is an important part of the organizational, and an e-mail was sent last month that said if employees do not complete the required safety training by July 1, they would be let go.

It is July 15, and it has just come to Towanda's attention that Casey has not completed the online safety training that is required for his job. When she approaches him about it, he says, "I am the best salesperson here; I can't waste time doing training. I already know all the safety rules anyway."

Would you let Casey go, as stated in the e-mail? How would you handle this?

How Would You Handle This?

KEY TAKEAWAYS

- Employee training and development is the framework for helping employees develop their personal and organizational skills, knowledge, and abilities. Training is important to employee retention.
- There are four steps in training that should occur. Employee orientation has the purpose of welcoming new employees into the organization. An effective employee orientation can help reduce start-up costs, reduce anxiety for the employee, reduce turnover, save time for the supervisor and colleagues, and set expectations and attitudes.
- An in-house training program is any type of program in which the training is delivered by someone who works for the organizational. This could include management or HR. Examples might include sexual harassment training or ethics training. In-house training can also include components specific to a job, such as how to use a specific kind of software. In-house training is normally done as a second and ongoing step in employee development.
- A mentor form of training pairs a new employee with a seasoned employee. This is usually the third step in employee training. A mentor program for training should include a formalized program and process.

- External training is any type of training not performed in-house; part of the last training step, external training can also be ongoing. It can include sending employees to conferences or seminars for leadership development or even paying tuition for a class they want to take.

EXERCISES

1. Why do you think some organizations do not follow the four training steps? What are the advantages of doing so?
2. What qualities do you think a mentor should have? List at least five.
3. Have you ever worked with a mentor in a job, at school, or in extracurricular activities? Describe your experience.

---

[1] Leigh Branham, The 7 Hidden Reasons Why Employees Leave (New York: American Management Association, 2005), 112–5.
[2] Blyde Witt, "Serious Leadership: IBM Builds a Successful Mentoring Program," Material Handling Management, December 1, 2005, accessed July 25, 2010,http://mhmonline.com/workforce-solutions/mhm_imp_4483/.
[3] Arthur Thompson, "Starbucks Corporation," July 24, 2011, accessed July 29, 2011,http://www.mhhe.com/public organization/management/thompson/11e/case/starbucks-2.html.
[4] "Automotive Technology/Ford ASSET Course," Sheridan Technical Center, accessed July 29, 2011, http://www.sheridantechnical.com/Default.aspx?tabid=692.

8.2 Types of Training

LEARNING OBJECTIVE

1. Be able to explain and give examples of the types of training that can be offered within an organization.

There are a number of different types of training we can use to engage an employee. These types are usually used in all steps in a training process (orientation, in-house, mentorship, and external training). The training utilized depends on the amount of resources available for training, the type of organizational, and the priority the organizational places on training. Organizations such as The Cheesecake Factory, a family restaurant, make training a high priority. The organizational spends an average of $2,000 per hourly employee. This includes everyone from the dishwasher and managers to the servers. For The Cheesecake Factory, this expenditure has paid off. They measure the effectiveness of its training by looking at turnover, which is 15 percent below the industry average._[1] Servers make up 40 percent of the workforce and spend two weeks training to obtain certification. Thirty days later, they receive follow-up classes, and when the menu changes, they receive additional training._[2] Let's take a look at some of the training we can offer our employees.

As you will see from the types of training below, no one type would be enough for the jobs we do. Most HR managers use a variety of these types of training to develop a holistic employee.

Technical or Technology Training

Depending on the type of job, technical training will be required. Technical trainingis a type of training meant to teach the new employee the technological aspects of the job. In a retail environment, technical training might include teaching someone how to use the computer system to ring up customers. In a sales position, it might include showing someone how to use the customer relationship management (CRM) system to find new prospects. In a consulting public organization, technical training might be used so the consultant knows how to use the system to input the number of hours that should be charged to a client. In a restaurant, the server needs to be trained on how to use the system to process orders. Let's assume your organizational has decided to switch to the newest version of Microsoft Office. This might require some technical training of the entire organizational to ensure everyone uses the technology effectively. Technical training is often performed in-house, but it can also be administrered externally.

Quality Training

In a production-focused public organization, quality training is extremely important.Quality training refers to familiarizing employees with the means of preventing, detecting, and eliminating nonquality items, usually in an organization that produces a product. In a world where quality can set your public organization apart from competitors, this type of training provides employees with the knowledge to recognize products that are not up to quality standards and teaches them what to do in this scenario. Numerous organizations, such as the International Organization for Standardization (ISO), measure quality based on a number of metrics. This organization provides the stamp of quality approval for organizations producing tangible products. ISO has developed quality standards for almost every field imaginable, not only considering product quality but also certifying organizations in environmental management quality. ISO9000 is the set of standards for quality management, while ISO14000 is the set of standards for environmental management. ISO has developed 18,000 standards over the last 60 years._[3] With the increase in globalization, these international quality standards are more important than ever for public organization development.

Some organizations, like 3M,_[4]choose to offer ISO training as external online training, employing organizations such as QAI to deliver the training both online and in classrooms to employees.

Training employees on quality standards, including ISO standards, can give them a competitive advantage. It can result in cost savings in production as well as provide an edge in marketing of the quality-controlled products. Some quality training can happen in-house, but organizations such as ISO also perform external training.

Skills Training

Skills training, the third type of training, includes proficiencies needed to actually perform the job. For example, an administrative assistant might be trained in how to answer the phone, while a salesperson at Best Buy might be trained in assessment of customer needs and on how to offer the customer information to make a buying decision. Think of skills training as the things you actually need to know to perform your job. A cashier needs to know not only the technology to ring someone up but what to do if something is priced wrong. Most of the time, skills training is given in-house and can include the use of a mentor. An example of a type of skills training is from AT&T and Apple,_[5] who in summer 2011 asked their managers to accelerate retail employee training on the iPhone 5, which was released to market in the fall.

Soft Skills Training

Our fourth type of training is called soft skills training. Soft skills refer to personality traits, social graces, communication, and personal habits that are used to characterize relationships with other people. Soft skills might include how to answer the phone or how to be friendly and welcoming to customers. It could include sexual harassment training and ethics training. In some jobs, necessary soft skills might include how to motivate others, maintain small talk, and establish rapport.

In a retail or restaurant environment, soft skills are used in every interaction with customers and are a key component of the customer experience. In fact, according to aComputerworld magazine survey, executives say there is an increasing need for people who have not only the skills and technical skills to do a job but also the necessary soft skills, such as strong listening and communication abilities._[6] Many problems in organizations are due to a lack of soft skills, or interpersonal skills, not by problems with the public organization itself. As a result, HR and managers should work together to strengthen these employee skills. Soft skills training can be administered either in-house or externally.

Professional Training and Legal Training

In some jobs, professional training must be done on an ongoing basis.Professional training is a type of training required to be up to date in one's own professional field. For example, tax laws change often, and as a result, an accountant for H&R Block must receive yearly professional training on new tax codes._[7] Lawyers need professional training as laws change. A personal fitness trainer will undergo yearly certifications to stay up to date in new fitness and nutrition information.

Some organizations have paid a high cost for not properly training their employees on the laws relating to their industry. In 2011, Massachusetts General Hospital paid over $1 million in fines related to privacy policies that were not followed._[8] As a result, the organization has agreed to develop training for workers on medical privacy. The fines could have been prevented if the organization had provided the proper training to begin with. Other types of legal training might include sexual harassment law training and discrimination law training.

Team Training

Do you know the exercise in which a person is asked to close his or her eyes and fall back, and then supposedly the team members will catch that person? As a team-building exercise (and a scary one at that), this is an example of team training. The goal of team training is to develop cohesiveness among team members, allowing them to get to know each other and facilitate relationship building. We can define team training as a process that empowers teams to improve decision making, problem solving, and team-development skills to achieve public organization results. Often this type of training can occur after an organization has been restructured and new people are working together or perhaps after a merger or acquisition. Some reasons for team training include the following:

- Improving communication
- Making the workplace more enjoyable
- Motivating a team
- Getting to know each other
- Getting everyone "onto the same page," including goal setting
- Teaching the team self-regulation strategies
- Helping participants to learn more about themselves (strengths and weaknesses)
- Identifying and utilizing the strengths of team members

- Improving team productivity
- Practicing effective collaboration with team members

Team training can be administered either in-house or externally. Ironically, through the use of technology, team training no longer requires people to even be in the same room.

HUMAN RESOURCE RECALL

What kind of team training have you participated in? What was it like? Do you think it accomplished what it was supposed to accomplish?

Managerial Training

After someone has spent time with an organization, they might be identified as a candidate for promotion. When this occurs, managerial training would occur. Topics might include those from our soft skills section, such as how to motivate and delegate, while others may be technical in nature. For example, if management uses a particular computer system for scheduling, the manager candidate might be technically trained. Some managerial training might be performed in-house while other training, such as leadership skills, might be performed externally.

For example, Mastek, a global IT solutions and services provider, provides a program called "One Skill a Month," which enables managers to learn skills such as delegation, coaching, and giving feedback. The average number of total training days at Mastek is 7.8 per employee [9] and includes managerial topics and soft skills topics such as e-mail etiquette. The goal of its training programs is to increase productivity, one of the organization's core values.

Safety Training

Safety training is a type of training that occurs to ensure employees are protected from injuries caused by work-related accidents. Safety training is especially important for organizations that use chemicals or other types of hazardous materials in their production. Safety training can also include evacuation plans, fire drills, and workplace violence procedures. Safety training can also include the following:

- Eye safety
- First aid
- Food service safety
- Hearing protection
- Asbestos
- Construction safety
- Hazmat safety

The Occupational Safety and Health Administration, or OSHA, is the main federal agency charged with enforcement of safety and health regulation in the United States. OSHA provides external training to organizations on OSHA standards. Sometimes in-house training will also cover safety training.

STARBUCKS TRAINING VIDEO

This is a short video Starbucks uses to train new employees on customer service.
Please view this video at http://www.youtube.com/watch?v=OAmftgYEWqU.

KEY TAKEAWAYS

- There are several types of training we can provide for employees. In all situations, a variety of training types will be used, depending on the type of job.
- Technical training addresses software or other programs that employees use while working for the organization.
- Quality training is a type of training that familiarizes all employees with the means to produce a good-quality product. The ISO sets the standard on quality for most production and environmental situations. ISO training can be done in-house or externally.
- Skills training focuses on the skills that the employee actually needs to know to perform their job. A mentor can help with this kind of training.
- Soft skills are those that do not relate directly to our job but are important. Soft skills training may train someone on how to better communicate and negotiate or provide good customer service.
- Professional training is normally given externally and might be obtaining certification or specific information needed about a profession to perform a job. For example, tax accountants need to be up to date on tax laws; this type of training is often external.
- Team training is a process that empowers teams to improve decision making, problem solving, and team-development skills. Team training can help improve communication and result in more productive public organizationes.
- To get someone ready to take on a management role, managerial training might be given.

- Safety training is important to make sure an organization is meeting OSHAstandards. Safety training can also include disaster planning.

EXERCISES

1. Which type of training do you think is most important for an administrative assistant? What about for a restaurant server? Explain your answer.
2. Research OSHA. What are some of the new standards and laws it has recently developed? Outline a training plan for the new standards.

[1] Gina Ruiz, "Cheesecake Factory Cooks Up a Rigorous Employee Training Program,"Workforce Management, April 24, 2006, accessed July 25, 2010,http://www.workforce.com/section/11/feature/24/35/18/.
[2] Gina Ruiz, "Cheesecake Factory Cooks Up a Rigorous Employee Training Program,"Workforce Management, April 24, 2006, accessed July 25, 2010,http://www.workforce.com/section/11/feature/24/35/18/.
[3] "The ISO Story," International Organization for Standards, accessed July 26, 2010,http://www.iso.org/iso/about/the_iso_story/iso_story_early_years.htm.
[4] QAI website, accessed July 30, 2011, http://www.trainingforquality.com/Content.aspx?id=26.
[5] Lance Whitney, "Apple, AT&T Reportedly Prepping Staff for iPhone 5 Launch," CNET, July 26, 2011, accessed July 29, 2011, http://news.cnet.com/8301-13579_3-20083435-37/apple-at-t-reportedly-prepping-staff-for-iphone-5-launch/.
[6] Thomas Hoffman, "Nine Nontechie Skills That Hiring Managers Wish You Had,"Computerworld, November 12, 2007, accessed July 26, 2010,http://www.computerworld.com/s/article/305966/Are_You_the_Complete_Package_.
[7] Jeannine Silkey, "Tax Preparer Certifications," Suite 101, January 28, 2010, accessed July 26, 2010, http://personal-tax-planning.suite101.com/article.cfm/tax-preparer-certifications.
[8] Julie Donnelly, "Mass. General to Pay $1M to Settle Privacy Claims," Boston Public organization Journal, February 24, 1011, accessed February 26, 2011,http://www.bizjournals.com/boston/news/2011/02/24/mass-general_to_pay_1m_to_settle.html.
[9] Mastek website, accessed July 30, 2011, http://www.mastek.com/careers/learning-development.html.

8.3 Training Delivery Methods

LEARNING OBJECTIVE

1. Explain the types of training delivery methods.

Depending on the type of training occurring, you may choose one delivery method over another. This section discusses the types of delivery methods we can use to execute the types of training. Keep in mind, however, that most good training programs will use a variety of delivery methods.

On-the-Job Coaching Training Delivery

On-the-job coaching is one way to facilitate employee skills training. On-the-job coaching refers to an approved person training an employee on the skills necessary to complete tasks. A manager or someone with experience shows the employee how to perform the actual job. The selection of an on-the-job coach can be done in a variety of ways, but usually the coach is selected based on personality, skills, and knowledge. This type of skills training is normally facilitated in-house. The disadvantage of this training revolves around the person delivering the training. If he or she is not a good communicator, the training may not work. Likewise, if this person has "other things to do," he or she may not spend as much time required to train the person and provide guidance. In this situation, training can frustrate the new employee and may result in turnover.

Mentoring and Coaching Training Delivery

Mentoring is also a type of training delivery. A mentor is a trusted, experienced advisor who has direct investment in the development of an employee. Mentoring is a process by which an employee can be trained and developed by an experienced person. Normally, mentoring is used as a continuing method to train and develop an employee. One disadvantage of this type of training is possible communication style and personality conflict. It can also create overdependence in the mentee or micromanagement by the mentor. This is more different than on-the-job coaching, which tends to be short term and focuses on the skills needed to perform a particular job.

Brown Bag Lunch Training Delivery

Brown bag lunches are a training delivery method meant to create an informal atmosphere. As the name suggests,brown bag lunch training is one in which the training occurs during lunchtime, employees bring their food, and someone presents training information to them. The trainer could be HR or management or even another employee showing a new technical skill. Brown bag lunches can also be an effective way to perform team training, as it brings people together in a more relaxed atmosphere. Some organizations offer brown bag lunch training for personal development as well. For example, HR might want to bring in a specialist on 401(k) plans, or perhaps an employee provides a slide presentation on a trip he or she has taken, discussing the things learned on the trip. One disadvantage to this type of training can be low attendance and garnering enough interest from employees who may not want to "work" during lunch breaks. There can also be inconsistency in messages if training is delivered and not everyone is present to hear the message.

HUMAN RESOURCE RECALL

What types of brown bag lunch training would employees be most willing to attend? Do you think this type of training should be required?

Web-Based Training Delivery

Web-based training delivery has a number of names. It could be called e-learning or Internet-based, computer-based, or technology-based learning. No matter what it is called, any web-based training involves the use of technology to facilitate training. There are two types of web-based learning. First, synchronous learning uses instructor-led facilitation. Asynchronous learning is self-directed, and there is no instructor facilitating the course. There are several advantages to web-based training. First, it is available on demand, does not require travel, and can be cost efficient. However, disadvantages might include an impersonal aspect to the training and limited bandwidth or technology capabilities._[1]

Web-based training delivery lends itself well to certain training topics. For example, this might be an appropriate delivery method for safety training, technical training, quality training, and professional training. However, for some training, such as soft-skills training, job skills training, managerial training, and team training, another more personalized method may be better for delivery. However, there are many different platforms that lend themselves to an interactive approach to training, such as Sun Microsystems' Social Learning eXchange (SLX) training system, which has real-time video and recording capabilities. Hundreds of platforms are available to facilitate web-based training. DigitalChalk, for example, allows for both synchronous and asynchronous training and allows the instructor or human relations manager to track training progress and completion._[2] Some organizations use SharePoint, an intranet platform, to store training videos and materials._[3] Blackboard and Angel (used primarily by higher education institutions) allows human resource managers to create training modules, which can be moderated by a facilitator or managed in a self-paced format. In any of the platforms available, media such as video and podcasts can be included within the training.

Considerations for selecting a web-based platform include the following:

- Is there a one-time fee or a per-user fee?
- Do the majority of your employees use a Mac or a PC, and how does the platform work with both systems?
- Is there enough bandwidth in your organization to support this type of platform?
- Is the platform flexible enough to meet your training needs?
- Does the software allow for collaboration and multimedia?
- Is there training for the trainer in adoption of this system? Is technical support offered?

Job Shadowing Training Delivery

Job shadowing is a training delivery method that places an employee who already has the skills with another employee who wants to develop those skills. Apprenticeships use job shadowing as one type of training method. For example, an apprentice electrician would shadow and watch the journeyman electrician perform the skills and tasks and learn by watching. Eventually, the apprentice would be able to learn the skills to do the job alone. The downside to this type of training is the possibility that the person job shadowing may learn "bad habits" or shortcuts to performing tasks that may not be beneficial to the organization.

ORGANIZATIONAL FOCUS

It takes a lot of training for the Walt Disney Organizational to produce the best Mickey Mouse, Snow White, Aladdin, or Peter Pan. In Orlando at Disneyworld, most of this training takes place at Disney University. Disney University provides training to its 42,000 cast members (this is what Disney calls employees) in areas such as culinary arts, computer applications, and specific job components. Once hired, all cast members go through a two-day Disney training program called Traditions, where they learn the basics of being a good cast member and the history of the organizational. For all practical purposes, Traditions is a new employee orientation.

Training doesn't stop at orientation, though. While all positions receive extensive training, one of the most extensive trainings are especially for Disney characters, since their presence at the theme parks is a major part of the customer experience. To become a character cast member, a character performer audition is required. The auditions require dancing and acting, and once hired, the individual is given the job of several characters to play. After a two-week intensive training process on character history, personalities, and ability to sign the names of the characters (for the autograph books sold at the parks for kids), an exam is given. The exam tests competency in character understanding, and passing the exam is required to become hired._[4]

While Disney University trains people for specific positions, it also offers an array of continuing development courses called Disney Development Connection. Disney says in 2010, more than 3,254,596 hours were spent training a variety of employees,[5] from characters to management. The training doesn't stop at in-house training, either. Disney offers tuition reimbursement up to $700 per credit and pays for 100 percent of books and $100 per course for cost of other materials. In 2010, Disney paid over $8 million in tuition expenses for cast members.[6]
Disney consistently ranks in "America's Most Admired Organizations" by Fortune Magazine, and its excellent training could be one of the many reasons.

Job Swapping Training Delivery
Job swapping is a method for training in which two employees agree to change jobs for a period of time. Of course, with this training delivery method, other training would be necessary to ensure the employee learns the skills needed to perform the skills of the new job. Job swap options can be motivational to employees by providing a change of scenery. It can be great for the organization as well to cross-train employees in different types of jobs. However, the time spent learning can result in unproductive time and lost revenue.

Vestibule Training Delivery
In vestibule training, training is performed near the worksite in conference rooms, lecture rooms, and classrooms. This might be an appropriate method to deliver orientations and some skills-based training. For example, to become a journeyman electrician, an apprentice performs job shadowing, on-the-job training, and vestibule training to learn the law and codes related to electricity installation. During the busy holiday season, Macy's uses vestibule training to teach new hires how to use the cash register system and provides skills training on how to provide great customer service.[7]

Many organizations use vestibule training for technical training, safety training, professional training, and quality training. It can also be appropriate for managerial training, soft skills training, and team training. As you can tell, this delivery method, like web-based training delivery, is quite versatile. For some jobs or training topics, this may take too much time away from performing the actual "job," which can result in lost productivity.

International Assignment Training
Since we are working within a global economy, it might be necessary to provide training to employees who are moving overseas or working overseas. Up to 40 percent of international assignments are terminated early because of a lack of international training.[8] Ensuring success overseas is reliant upon the local employee's learning how to navigate in the new country. The following topics might be included in this type of training:
1. Cultural differences and similarities
2. Insight and daily living in the country
3. Social norms and etiquette
4. Communication training, such as language skills

This training is best delivered by a professional in the region or area in which the employee will be working.

KEY TAKEAWAYS

- Training delivery methods are important to consider, depending on the type of training that needs to be performed.
- Most organizations do not use only one type of training delivery method; a combination of many methods will be used.
- On-the-job coaching delivery method is a training delivery method in which an employee is assigned to a more experienced employee or manager to learn the skills needed for the job. This is similar to the mentor training delivery method, except a mentor training method is less about skills training and more about ongoing employee development.
- Brown bag lunch training delivery is normally informal and can involve personal development as well as specific job-related skills.
- Web-based training is any type of training that is delivered using technology.
- There are numerous platforms that can be used for web-based training and considerations, such as cost, when selecting a platform for use.
- A synchronous training method is used for web-based training and refers to delivery that is led by a facilitator. An asynchronous training method is one that is self-directed.
- Job shadowing is a delivery method consisting of on-the-job training and the employee's learning skills by watching someone more experienced.
- To motivate employees and allow them to develop new skills, job swappingtraining delivery may be used. This occurs when two people change jobs for a set period of time to learn new skills. With this

method, it is likely that other methods will also be used, too.

- Vestibule training delivery is also known as "near site" training. It normally happens in a classroom, conference room, or lecture room and works well to deliver orientations and some skills-based training. Many organizations also use vestibule training for technical training, safety training, professional training, and quality training.
- Since many organizations operate overseas, providing training to those employees with international assignments can better prepare them for living and working abroad.

EXERCISES

1. Do an Internet search on web-based training. Discuss two of the platforms you found. What are the features and benefits?
2. Which training delivery method do you think you personally would prefer in a job and why?
3. What do you see as advantages and disadvantages to each type of training method?

---

[1] "Advantages and Disadvantages," Web Based Training Information Center, accessed July 27, 2010, http://www.webbasedtraining.com/primer_advdis.aspx.
[2] DigitalChalk website, accessed August 12, 2010, http://www.digitalchalk.com/.
[3] Microsoft's SharePoint website, accessed August 12, 2010,http://sharepoint.microsoft.com/en-us/Pages/default.aspx.
[4] Jim Hill, "Blood, Sweat, and Fur," Jim Hill Media, May 2005, accessed July 30, 2011,http://jimhillmedia.com/guest_writers1/b/rob_bloom/archive/2005/05/03/1703.aspx.
[5] "Training and Development," Disney, accessed July 30, 2011,http://organizational.disney.go.com/citizenship2010/disneyworkplaces/overview/traininganddevelopment/.
[6] "Training and Development," Disney, accessed July 30, 2011,http://organizational.disney.go.com/citizenship2010/disneyworkplaces/overview/traininganddevelopment/.
[7] Macy's website, accessed July 27, 2010, http://www.macysjobs.com/about/.
[8] Sherry E. Sullivan and Howard Tu, "Preparing Yourself for an International Assignment," Bnet, accessed September 15, 2011,http://findarticles.com/p/articles/mi_m1038/is_n1_v37/ai_14922926/.

8.4 Designing a Training Program

LEARNING OBJECTIVES

1. Be able to design a training program framework.
2. Understand the uses and applications of a career development program.

The next step in the training process is to create a training framework that will help guide you as you set up a training program. Information on how to use the framework is included in this section.

Training Program Framework Development

When developing your training plan, there are a number of considerations. Training is something that should be planned and developed in advance.

Figure 8.6 Training Program Development Model

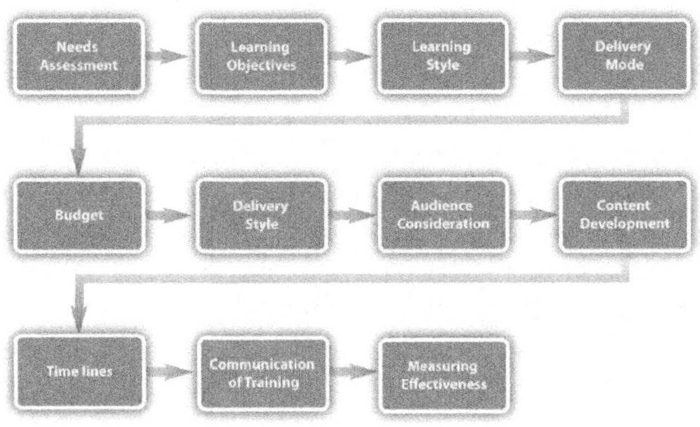

The considerations for developing a training program are as follows:

1. *Needs assessment and learning objectives.* This part of the framework development asks you to consider what kind of training is needed in your organization. Once you have determined the training needed, you can set learning objectives to measure at the end of the training.
2. *Consideration of learning styles.* Making sure to teach to a variety of learning styles is important to development of training programs.
3. *Delivery mode.* What is the best way to get your message across? Is web-based training more appropriate, or should mentoring be used? Can vestibule training be used for a portion of the training while job shadowing be used for some of the training, too? Most training programs will include a variety of delivery methods.
4. *Budget.* How much money do you have to spend on this training?
5. *Delivery style.* Will the training be self-paced or instructor led? What kinds of discussions and interactivity can be developed in conjunction with this training?
6. *Audience.* Who will be part of this training? Do you have a mix of roles, such as accounting people and marketing people? What are the job responsibilities of these individuals, and how can you make the training relevant to their individual jobs?

7. *Content.* What needs to be taught? How will you sequence the information?
8. *Timelines.* How long will it take to develop the training? Is there a deadline for training to be completed?
9. *Communication.* How will employees know the training is available to them?
10. *Measuring effectiveness of training.* How will you know if your training worked? What ways will you use to measure this?

HUMAN RESOURCE RECALL

Can you think of a time where you received training, but the facilitator did not connect with the audience? Does that ever happen in any of your classes (of course not this one, though)?

Needs Assessment

The first step in developing a training program is to determine what the organization needs in terms of training. There are three levels of training needs assessment:organizational assessment, occupational (task) as sessment, andindividual assessment:

1. *Organizational assessment.* In this type of needs assessment, we can determine the skills, knowledge, and abilities a organizational needs to meet its strategic objectives. This type of assessment considers things such as changing demographics and technological trends. Overall, this type of assessment looks at how the organization as a whole can handle its weaknesses while promoting strengths.
2. *Occupational (task) assessment.* This type of assessment looks at the specific tasks, skills knowledge, and abilities required to do jobs within the organization.
3. *Individual assessment.* An individual assessment looks at the performance of an individual employee and determines what training should be accomplished for that individual.

We can apply each of these to our training plan. First, to perform an organizational assessment, we can look at future trends and our overall organizational's strategic plan to determine training needs. We can also see how jobs and industries are changing, and knowing this, we can better determine the occupational and individual assessments.

Researching training needs can be done through a variety of ways. One option is to use an online tool such as SurveyMonkey to poll employees on what types of training they would like to see offered.

As you review performance evaluations turned in by your managers, you may see a pattern developing showing that employees are not meeting expectations. As a result, this may provide data as to where your training is lacking.

There are also types of training that will likely be required for a job, such as technical training, safety training, quality training, and professional training. Each of these should be viewed as separate training programs, requiring an individual framework for each type of training. For example, an employee orientation framework will look entirely different from an in-house technical training framework.

Training must be tied to job expectations. Any and all training developed should transfer directly to the skills of that particular employee. Reviewing the HR strategic plan and various job analyses may help you see what kind of training should be developed for specific job titles in your organization.

Learning Objectives

After you have determined what type of training should occur, learning objectives for the training should be set. A learning objective is what you want the learner to be able to do, explain, or demonstrate at the end of the training period. Good learning objectives are performance based and clear, and the end result of the learning objective can be observable or measured in some way. Examples of learning objectives might include the following:

1. Be able to explain the organizational policy on sexual harassment and give examples of sexual harassment.
2. Be able to show the proper way to take a customer's order.
3. Perform a variety of customer needs analyses using organizational software.
4. Understand and utilize the new expense-tracking software.
5. Explain the safety procedure in handling chemicals.
6. Be able to explain the types of communication styles and strategies to effectively deal with each style.
7. Demonstrate ethics when handling customer complaints.
8. Be able to effectively delegate to employees.

Once we have set our learning objectives, we can utilize information on learning styles to then determine the best delivery mode for our training.

Learning Styles

Understanding learning styles is an important component to any training program. For our purposes, we will utilize a widely accepted learning style model. Recent research has shown that classifying people into learning styles may not be the best way to determine a style, and most people have a different style depending on the information being taught. In a study by Pashler et al.,[1] the authors look at aptitude and personality as key traits when learning, as opposed to classifying people into categories of learning styles. Bearing this in mind, we will address a common approach to learning styles next.

An effective trainer tries to develop training to meet the three different learning styles:[2]

1. *Visual learner.* A visual learner usually has a clear "picture" of an experience. A visual learner often says things such as "I can see what you are saying" or "This looks good." A visual learner is best reached using graphics, pictures, and figures.
2. *Auditory learner.* An auditory learner learns by sound. An auditory learner might say, "If I hear you right" or "What do you hear about this situation?" The auditory learner will learn by listening to a lecture or to someone explaining how to do something.
3. *Kinesthetic learner.* A kinesthetic learner learns by developing feelings toward an experience. These types of learners tend to learn by doing rather than listening or seeing someone else do it. This type of learner will often say things such as "This feels right."

Most individuals use more than one type of learning style, depending on what kinds of information they are processing. For example, in class you might be a visual learner, but when learning how to change a tire, you might be a kinesthetic learner.

Delivery Mode

Depending on the type of training that needs to be delivered, you will likely choose a different mode to deliver the training. An orientation might lend itself best to vestibule training, while sexual harassment training may be better for web-based training. When choosing a delivery mode, it is important to consider the audience and budget constrictions. For example, Oakwood Worldwide, a provider of temporary housing, recently won the Top 125 Training Award for its training and development programs.[3] It offers in-class and online classes for all associates and constantly add to its course catalog. This is a major recruitment as well as retention tool for its employees. In fact, the organizational credits this program for retaining 25 percent of its workforce for ten years or more. Table 8.1 "Types of Training and Delivery" looks at each of the types of training and suggests appropriate options for delivery modes.

Table 8.1 Types of Training and Delivery

Delivery Method	Type of Training Suggested
	Technical training
	Skills training
	Managerial training
On-the-job coaching	Safety training
	Technical training
	Skills training
	Managerial training
Mentor	Safety training
	Quality training
	Soft skills training
	Professional training
Brown bag lunch	Safety training
	Technical training
	Quality training
	Skills training
	Soft skills training
	Professional training
	Team training
	Managerial training
Web-based	Safety training
	Technical training
	Quality training
	Skills training
Job shadowing	Safety training
	Technical training
Job swapping	Quality training

Delivery Method	Type of Training Suggested
	Skills training
	Professional training
	Team training
	Managerial training
	Safety training
	Technical training
	Quality training
	Skills training
	Soft skills training
	Professional training
	Team training
	Managerial training
Vestibule training	Safety training

Budget

How much money do you think the training will cost? The type of training performed will depend greatly on the budget. If you decide that web-based training is the right delivery mode, but you don't have the budget to pay the user fee for the platform, this wouldn't be the best option. Besides the actual cost of training, another cost consideration is people's time. If employees are in training for two hours, what is the cost to the organization while they are not able to perform their job? A spreadsheet should be developed that lists the actual cost for materials, snacks, and other direct costs, but also the indirect costs, such as people's time.

Delivery Style

Taking into consideration the delivery method, what is the best style to deliver this training? It's also important to keep in mind that most people don't learn through "death by PowerPoint"; they learn in a variety of ways, such as auditory, kinesthetic, or visual. Considering this, what kinds of ice breakers, breakout discussions, and activities can you inorganizational to make the training as interactive as possible? Role plays and other games can make the training fun for employees. Many trainers implement online videos, podcasts, and other interactive media in their training sessions. This ensures different learning styles are met and also makes the training more interesting.

Audience

Considering your audience is an important aspect to training. How long have they been with the organization, or are they new employees? What departments do they work in? Knowing the answers to these questions can help you develop a relevant delivery style that makes for better training. For example, if you know that all the people attending the training are from the accounting department, examples you provide in the training can be focused on this type of job. If you have a mixed group, examples and discussions can touch on a variety of disciplines.

Content Development

The content you want to deliver is perhaps one of the most important parts in training and one of the most time-consuming to develop. Development of learning objectives or those things you want your learners to know after the training makes for a more focused training. Think of learning objectives as goals—what should someone know after completing this training? Here are some sample learning objectives:

1. Be able to define and explain the handling of hazardous materials in the workplace.
2. Be able to utilize the team decision process model.
3. Understand the definition of sexual harassment and be able to recognize sexual harassment in the workplace.
4. Understand and be able to explain the organizational policies and structure.

After you have developed the objectives and goals, you can begin to develop the content of the training. Consideration of the learning methods you will use, such as discussion and role playing, will be outlined in your content area.

Development of content usually requires a development of learning objectives and then a brief outline of the major topics you wish to cover. With that outline, you can "fill in" the major topics with information. Based on this information, you can develop modules or PowerPoint slides, activities, discussion questions, and other learning techniques.

Timelines

For some types of training, time lines may be required to ensure the training has been done. This is often the case for safety training; usually the training should be done before the employee starts. In other words, in what time frame should an employee complete the training?

Another consideration regarding time lines is how much time you think you need to give the training. Perhaps one hour will be enough, but sometimes, training may take a day or even a week. After you have developed your training content, you will likely have a good idea as to how long it will take to deliver it. Consider the fact that most people do not have a lot of time for training and keep the training time realistic and concise.

From a long-term approach, it may not be cost effective to offer an orientation each time someone new is hired. One consideration might be to offer orientation training once per month so that all employees hired within that month are trained at the same time.

Development of a dependable schedule for training might be ideal, as in the following example:

1. Orientation is offered on the first Thursday of every month.
2. The second and third Tuesday will consist of vestibule training on management skills and communication.
3. Twice yearly, in August and March, safety and sexual harassment training will be given to meet the legal organizational requirements.

Developing a dependable training schedule allows for better communication to your staff, results in fewer communication issues surrounding training, and allows all employees to plan ahead to attend training.

Communication

Once you have developed your training, your next consideration is how you will communicate the available training to employees. In a situation such as an orientation, you will need to communicate to managers, staff, and anyone involved in the training the timing and confirm that it fits within their schedule. If it is an informal training, such as a brown bag lunch on 401(k) plans, this might involve determining the days and times that most people are in the office and might be able to participate. Because employees use Mondays and Fridays, respectively, to catch up and finish up work for the week, these days tend to be the worst for training.

Consider utilizing your organizational's intranet, e-mail, and even old-fashioned posters to communicate the training. Many organizations have Listservs that can relay the message to only certain groups, if need be.

HUMAN RESOURCE RECALL

What can happen if training is not communicated to employees appropriately?

Measuring Effectiveness

After we have completed the training, we want to make sure our training objectives were met. One model to measure effectiveness of training is the Kirkpatrick model,[4]developed in the 1950s. His model has four levels:

1. *Reaction:* How did the participants react to the training program?
2. *Learning:* To what extent did participants improve knowledge and skills?
3. *Behavior:* Did behavior change as a result of the training?
4. *Results:* What benefits to the organization resulted from the training?

Each of Kirkpatrick's levels can be assessed using a variety of methods. We will discuss those next.

Figure 8.7 Kirkpatrick's Four Levels of Training Evaluation

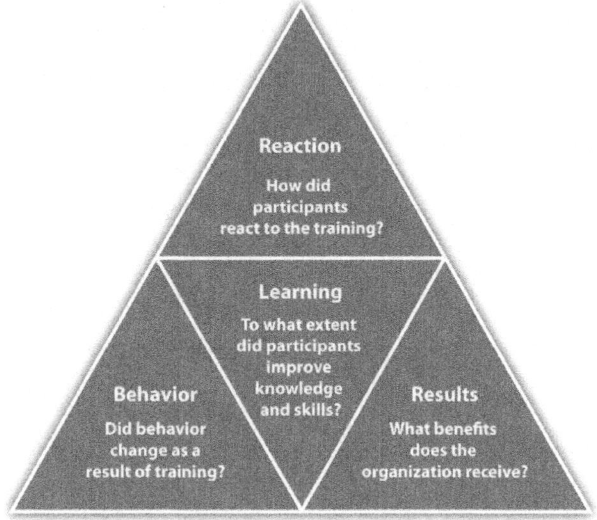

Review the performance of the employees who received the training, and if possible review the performance of those who did not receive the training. For example, in your orientation training, if one of the learning objectives was to be able to request time off using the organizational intranet, and several employees who attended the training come back and ask for clarification on how to perform this task, it may mean the training didn't work as well as you might have thought. In this case, it is important to go back and review the learning objectives and content of your training to ensure it can be more effective in the future.

Many trainers also ask people to take informal, anonymous surveys after the training to gauge the training. These types

of surveys can be developed quickly and easily through websites such as SurveyMonkey. Another option is to require a quiz at the end of the training to see how well the employees understand what you were trying to teach them. The quiz should be developed based on the learning objective you set for the training. For example, if a learning objective was to be able to follow OSHA standards, then a quiz might be developed specifically related to those standards. There are a number of online tools, some free, to develop quizzes and send them to people attending your training. For example, Wondershare QuizCreator_[5] offers a free trial and enables the manager to track who took the quiz and how well they did. Once developed by the trainer, the quiz can be e-mailed to each participant and the manager can see how each trainee did on the final quiz. After you see how participants do on the quiz, you can modify the training for next time to highlight areas where participants needed improvement.
It can be easy to forget about this step in the training process because usually we are so involved with the next task: we forget to ask questions about how something went and then take steps to improve it.

One way to improve effectiveness of a training program is to offer rewards when employees meet training goals. For example, if budget allows, a person might receive a pay increase or other reward for each level of training completed.

Career Development Programs and Succession Planning
Another important aspect to training is career development programs. Acareer development program is a process developed to help people manage their career, learn new things, and take steps to improve personally and professionally. Think of it as a training program of sorts, but for individuals. Sometimes career development programs are called professional development plans.

Career development programs are necessary in today's organizations for a variety of reasons. First, with a maturing baby-boom population, newer employees must be trained to take those jobs once baby boomers retire. Second, if an employee knows a particular path to career development is in place, this can increase motivation. A career development plan usually includes a list of short- and long-term goals that employees have pertaining to their current and future jobs and a planned sequence of formal and informal training and experiences needed to help them reach the goals. As this chapter has discussed, the organization can and should be instrumental in defining what types of training, both in-house and external, can be used to help develop employees.

To help develop this type of program, managers can consider a few components:_[6]

1. *Talk to employees.* Although this may seem obvious, it doesn't always happen. Talking with employees about their goals and what they hope to achieve can be a good first step in developing a formal career development program.
2. *Create specific requirements for career development.* Allow employees to see that if they do A, B, and C, they will be eligible for promotion. For example, to become a supervisor, maybe three years of experience, management training, and communication training are required. Perhaps an employee might be required to prove themselves in certain areas, such as "maintain and exceed sales quota for eight quarters" to be a sales manager. In other words, in career development there should be a clear process for the employees to develop themselves within the organization.
3. *Use cross-training and job rotation.* Cross-training is a method by which employees can gain management experience, even if for short periods of time. For example, when a manager is out of the office, putting an employee "in charge" can help the employee learn skills and abilities needed to perform that function appropriately. Through the use of job rotation, which involves a systematic movement of employees from job to job within an organization, employees can gain a variety of experiences to prepare them for upward movement in the organization.
4. *Utilize mentors.* Mentorship can be a great way for employees to understand what it takes to develop one's career to the next level. A formal mentorship program in place with willing mentees can add value to your career development program.

Figure 8.11 Career Development Planning Process

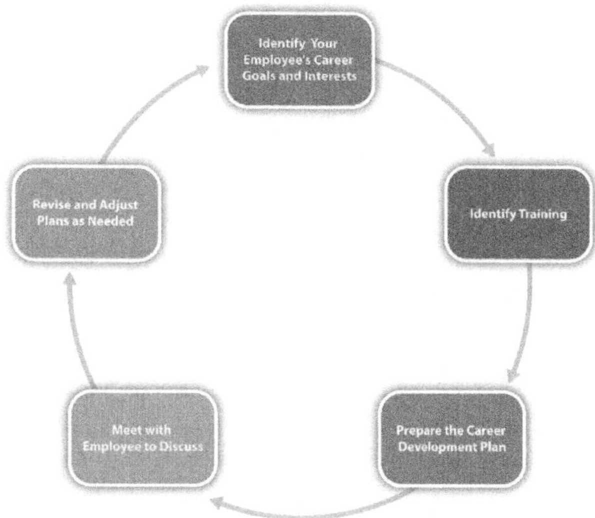

There are many tools on the web, including templates to help employees develop their own career development plans. Many organizations, in fact, ask employees to develop their own plans and use those as a starting point for understanding long-term career goals. Then hopefully the organization can provide them with the opportunities to meet these career goals. In the late 1980s, many employees felt that career opportunities at their current organizations dwindled after seeing the downsizing that occurred. It gave employees the feeling that organizations were not going to help develop them, unless they took the initiative to do so themselves. Unfortunately, this attitude means that workers will not wait for career opportunities within the organizational, unless a clear plan and guide is put into place by the organizational._[7] Here is an example of a process that can be used to put a career development program in place:_[8]

1. Meet individually with employees to identify their long-term career interests (this may be done by human resources or the direct manager).
2. Identify resources within the organization that can help employees achieve their goals. Create new opportunities for training if you see a gap in needs versus what is currently offered.
3. Prepare a plan for each employee, or ask them to prepare the plan.
4. Meet with the employee to discuss the plan.
5. During performance evaluations, revisit the plan and make changes as necessary.

Identifying and developing a planning process not only helps the employee but also can assist the managers in supporting employees in gaining new skills, adding value, and motivating employees.

KEY TAKEAWAYS

- There are a number of key considerations in developing a training program. Training should not be handled casually but instead developed specifically to meet the needs of the organization. This can be done by a needs assessment consisting of three levels: organizational, occupational, and individual assessments.
- The first consideration is the delivery mode; depending on the type of training and other factors, some modes might be better than others.
- Budget is a consideration in developing training. The cost of materials, but also the cost of time, should be considered.
- The delivery style must take into account people's individual learning styles. The amount of lecture, discussion, role plays, and activities are considered part of delivery style.
- The audience for the training is an important aspect when developing training. This can allow the training to be better developed to meet the needs and the skills of a particular group of people.
- The content obviously is an important consideration. Learning objectives and goals for the training should be developed before content is developed.
- After content is developed, understanding the time constraints is an important aspect. Will the training take one hour or a day to deliver? What is the time line consideration in terms of when people should take the training?
- Letting people know when and where the training will take place is part of communication.
- The final aspect of developing a training framework is to consider how it will be measured. At the end, how will you know if the trainees learned what they needed to learn?
- A career development process can help retain good employees. It involves creating a specific program in which employee goals are identified and new training and opportunities are identified and created to help the employee in the career development process.

EXERCISES

1. Develop a rough draft of a training framework using for a job you find on Monster.com.
2. Write three learning objectives you think would be necessary when developing orientation training for a receptionist in an advertising firm.

3. Why is a career development plan important to develop personally, even if your organizational doesn't have a formal plan in place? List at least three reasons and describe.

---

[1] Harold Pashler, Mark McDaniel, Doug Rohrer, and Robert Bjork, "Learning Styles: Concepts and Evidence," Psychological Science in the Public Interest 9, no. 3 (2008): 109–19, accessed February 26, 2011, http://www.psychologicalscience.org/journals/pspi/PSPI_9_3.pdf.
[2] "What's YOUR Learning Style?" adapted from Instructor Magazine, University of South Dakota, August 1989, accessed July 28, 2010, http://people.usd.edu/~bwjames/tut/learning-style/.
[3] "Oakwood Worldwide Honored by Training Magazine for Fifth Consecutive Year Training also Presents Oakwood with Best Practice Award," press release, February 25, 2011,Marketwire, accessed February 26, 2011, http://www.live-pr.com/en/oakwood-worldwide-honored-by-training-magazine-r1048761409.htm.
[4] Donald Kirkpatrick, Evaluating Training Programs, 3rd ed. (San Francisco: Berrett-Koehler, 2006).
[5] WonderShare QuizCreator, accessed July 29, 2010, http://www.sameshow.com/quiz-creator.html#172.
[6] Martha Heller, "Six Tips for Effective Employee Development Programs," CIO Magazine, June 15, 2005, accessed July 28, 2010,http://www.cio.com/article/29169/Six_Tips_for_Effective_Career_Development_Programs.
[7] Peter Capelli, "A Balanced Plan for Career Development," n.d., Microsoft, accessed July 29, 2010, http://office.microsoft.com/en-us/word-help/a-balanced-plan-for-career-development-HA001126815.aspx.
[8] Jose Trueba Adolfo, "The Career Development Plan: A Quick Guide for Managers and Supervisors," n.d., National Career Development Association, accessed July 29, 2010,http://associationdatabase.com/aws/NCDA/pt/sd/news_article/6420/_PARENT/layout_details/false.

8.5 Cases and Problems

CHAPTER SUMMARY

- Employee training and development is a necessity in today's work environment. Training and development can lead to lower turnover and increased motivation.
- There are four basic steps to employee training: employee orientation, in-house training, mentoring, and external training.
- Different types of training can be delivered, each falling into the steps of employee training. These include technical or technology training, quality training, skills training, soft skills training, professional training, team training, managerial training, and safety training.
- Within the types of training, we need to determine which method is best for the actual delivery of training. Options include on-the-job training, mentor training, brown bag lunches, web-based training, job shadowing, job swapping, and vestibule training.
- Development of a training development framework is the first step in solidifying the training.
- Considerations and steps to developing the training framework include determining the training needs, delivery modes, budget, delivery style, audience, content, time lines, communication of the training, and measurement of the training.
- Career development programs can be an essential piece to the training puzzle. A comprehensive program or plan, either developed by employees or administered by HR, can help with motivation and fill the gap when people in the organization leave or retire. It can also be used as a motivational tool.

CHAPTER CASE

New on the Job

JoAnn Michaels just started her job as human resources manager at In the Dog House, a retail chain specializing in dog apparel and accessories. She is a good friend of yours you met in college.

The organization has 35 stores with 250 employees in Washington, Idaho, and Oregon. As the chain has grown, the training programs have been conducted somewhat piecemeal. Upon visiting some of the stores in a three-week tour, JoAnn has realized that all the stores seem to have different ways of training their in-store employees.

When she digs further, she realizes even the organizational offices, which employ seventy-five people, have no formal training program. In the past, they have done informal and optional brown bag lunch training to keep employees up to date. As a result, JoAnn develops a survey using SurveyMonkey and sends it to all seventy-five organizational employees. She created a rating system, with 1 meaning strongly disagree and 5 meaning strongly agree. Employees were not required to answer all questions, hence the variation in the number of responses column. After this task, JoAnn creates a slightly different survey and sends it to all store managers, asking them to encourage their retail employees to take the survey. The results are shown here.

In the Dog House Organizational Employee Survey Results		
Question	Number of Responses	Average Rating
I am paid fairly.	73	3.9
I feel my group works well as a team.	69	2.63
I appreciate the amount of soft skills training offered at In the Dog House.	74	2.1

In the Dog House Organizational Employee Survey Results		
I can see myself growing professionally here.	69	1.95
I feel I am paid fairly.	74	3.8
I have all the tools and equipment I need to do my job.	67	4.2
I feel confident if there were an emergency at the office, I would know what to do and could help others.	73	2.67
I think my direct supervisor is an excellent manager.	55	2.41
The orientation training I received was helpful in understanding the expectations of the job.	75	3.1
I would take training related to my job knowing there would be a reward offered for doing so.	71	4.24

In the Dog House Retail Employee Survey Results		
Question	Number of Responses	Average Rating
I am content with the benefits I am receiving.	143	1.2
I feel my store works well as a team.	190	4.1
I appreciate the amount of product training and information offered at In the Dog House.	182	2.34
I can see myself growing professionally here.	158	1.99
I feel I am paid fairly.	182	3.2
My supervisor works with my schedule, so I work at times that are convenient for me.	172	3.67
I feel confident if I had to evacuate the store, I would know what to do and could help customers.	179	2.88
I think my store manager is a great manager.	139	3.34
The orientation training I received was helpful in understanding the expectations of the job.	183	4.3
I am interested in developing my career at In the Dog House.	174	1.69

Based on the information JoAnn received from her survey, she decided some changes need to be made. JoAnn asks you to meet for coffee and take a look at the results. After you review them, JoAnn asks you the following questions. How would you respond to each?

1. "Obviously, I need to start working on some training programs. Which topics do you think I should start with?"
2. "How do I go about developing a training program that will be really useful and make people excited? What are the steps I need to take?"
3. "How should I communicate the training program to the organizational and retail employees? Should the new training I develop be communicated in the same way?"
4. "Do you think that we should look at changing pay and benefits? Why or why not?"
5. "Can you please help me draft a training program framework for what we have discussed? Do you think I should design one for both the organizational offices and one for the retail stores?"

TEAM ACTIVITY

1. In teams of three to four, outline a two-hour training program for managers to better understand motivation for their employees. Use the training development model discussed in this chapter. Your training should address learning objectives, delivery modes, budget, delivery style, time line, communication, and measurement. Prepare a five-minute presentation to present in class.
2. Using the same plan above, plan and deliver the content to the rest of the class.

NOTES:

NOTES:

Chapter 9: Successful Employee Communication in Public Organizations

The Biggest Challenge

Casey is seated at his desk reviewing his human resource strategic plan when Lily walks in, obviously upset. Her facial expressions show she is upset, and after she enters, she crosses her arms while standing in front of Casey's desk. Casey thinks Lily is a very hard worker and does an excellent job managing people as the manager of her marketing department. Lately, she has been having trouble with some of her employees.

"Casey," she says, "I really need to vent. Can I sit down and talk with you?" Casey offers Lily a seat and she sits down. She tells Casey that Sam, a marketing manager, made snide and underhanded comments during a meeting this morning. "For example, when I asked the status on one of our projects, Sam said snidely, 'Why don't you ask one of your marketing assistants? They are doing such a great job, after all.' I suspect he is upset with something I wrote on my blog last week. As you know, I started the blog to continually let employees know of changes in the department and to provide feedback. In last week's blog, I wrote about what a great job the marketing assistants are doing in my department."

Lily goes on, "So I pulled him aside after the meeting and asked him about his comment. He said that he was upset that I had given feedback to the marketing assistants because he feels that as their manager, it is his job to do that. He felt I had stepped on his toes and the toes of other marketing managers."

Casey thinks about the situation and asks Lily if she apologized. Lily responds, "I didn't feel like I needed to. I do think the marketing assistants are doing a good job, and I don't need to apologize for mentioning that. I am just trying to raise morale among them. You know, two marketing assistants have quit in the last three months."

Casey leans back in his chair and gives some thought as to how to advise Lily. He suggests that Lily speak with Sam directly (not via e-mail) and tell him that her intention was only positive and not meant to be harmful, and see what happens. Lily thinks about that and says she will try to see Sam later today. When she leaves, Casey sits back and thinks about how communication is one of the biggest challenges in any job, but especially in human resources.

9.1 Communication Strategies

LEARNING OBJECTIVES

1. Explain the concept of emotional intelligence.
2. Describe the four types of communication in the workplace.
3. Explain the various communication styles and identify your own style.
4. Define nonverbal communication and describe the importance of it in an HR setting.

Communication, as you see in our opening scenario, is key to a successful career as a human resource manager (HRM) or as a manager. While communication is likely discussed in several of your public organization classes, it should also be addressed in an HRM book, since much of what we do in HR is based on effective communication.

How many times do miscommunications happen on a daily basis, either in your personal life or at your job? The good news is that we can all get better at communication. The first thing we need to do is learn how we can communicate with our employees. Then we will want to look at our own communication style and compare that with other styles. Have you ever spoken with someone you just didn't "get"? It is probably because you have different communication styles.

Body language is also a key contributor to communication; in fact, as was suggested in the late 1960s by researcher Albert Mehrabian, body language makes up 93 percent of our communication.[1] Part of communication is also looking at the way we manage people. Depending on our style of management, we may use a variety of management styles to communicate things we need done or to give performance feedback. One major way organizations communicate with employees is through the use of meetings. Some meetings can be very effective, but as you probably already know, many meetings aren't very productive. We will discuss some strategies to help you run a more effective meeting.

Communication and Emotional Intelligence (EI)

One of the most important aspects to good communication is emotional intelligence (EI). Emotional intelligence is different from IQ. First, EI predicts much of life success, much more than IQ, in fact.[2] The great thing about EI is that it can actually improve over time, unlike IQ, which stays the same over a lifetime. According to Daniel Goleman,[3] a researcher on EI, there are five main aspects or domains to EI:

1. Knowing your emotions
2. Managing your emotions
3. Motivating yourself
4. Recognizing and understanding other people's emotions
5. Managing relationships

First, let's discuss knowing your emotions. If we don't know how we feel about something, it can be difficult to communicate. It may seem obvious to know what we are feeling from moment to moment, but oftentimes we do not. How we feel impacts our body language as well as our verbal communication. For example, let's say you just got home from work and had a really crummy day. When you get home, you find that your spouse has not unloaded the dishwasher yet, as you had agreed. Tie this with a crummy day, and you might communicate differently about it than if you had a great day.

On the other hand, if you recognize that you are tired and a bit cranky, your awareness of these emotions allows you to manage them. The third aspect of EI, motivating yourself, goes without saying in a management or human resource role. This is the key not only to career success but also to personal success.

The last two domains of EI revolve around being able to see and understand emotions in other people, which in turn can benefit the relationship. Let's say, in the situation above, you get home and the dishwasher isn't unloaded, but you recognize immediately through body language and facial expressions that your spouse is extremely upset by something. Seeing this emotion in someone else may help you decide if you should mention the dishwasher—or not—at this specific time. But what if you didn't recognize this emotion and raised your voice to your spouse about the unloaded dishwasher? It will probably result in an argument. Using this example, I am sure you can see how this translates into the workplace. Emotional intelligence allows us to work better with people, understand them, and communicate with them.

HUMAN RESOURCE RECALL

Do you think you are a good communicator? What could you improve?

Communication Directions

As you already know, communication in organizations is key to having a successful organization. Those organizations who communicate well with their employees end up with more loyal and motivated workers. Those that don't communicate well, though, see increased turnover, absenteeism, dissatisfied customers, higher product defect rates, lack of focus on public organization objectives, and lack of innovation.[4] Proper communication can result in a sense of belonging and self-worth, leading to less turnover and absenteeism, which is mentioned in the opening scenario.

Four main types of communications occur within a organizational: upward communication, downward communication, diagonal communication, and horizontal communication. Each type of communication can serve a different purpose in human resources, and many messages may be sent in a variety of ways.

Upward communication is when the lower levels of an organization communicate with the upper levels of an organization. Some examples might be an employee satisfaction survey using online survey tools such as SurveyMonkey. These kinds of tools can be used to determine the changes that should occur in a organizational. Oftentimes human resource departments may develop a survey such as this to find out how satisfied the employees are with things such as benefits. Then the organization can make changes based on the satisfaction level of the employees. Employees might also engage in upward communication in a given work situation. They might tell their manager their plate is full and they can't take on any new projects. This is considered upward communication, too.

Downward communication is the opposite of upward communication, in that the communication occurs from the upper levels of an organization down to the lower levels of the organization. A manager explaining how to do a task to an employee would be considered downward communication. Development of training programs to communicate safety in the organization might be another example. A change in a pay or bonus structure would be communicated using the downward approach as well.
A diagonal communication approach occurs when interdepartmental communication occurs with people at different levels of the organization. When the human resources assistant speaks with the marketing manager about the hiring of a new employee in marketing, this would be considered diagonal communication.

Horizontal communication occurs when people of the same level in an organization, for example, a marketing manager and a human resource manager, communicate usually to coordinate work between departments. An accounting manager might share information with a production manager so the production manager knows how much budget they have left.

Within all the communication methods we discussed, there are a variety of approaches. Of course, the most obvious is the informal communication that occurs. An e-mail may be sent or a phone call made. Meetings are another way to communicate information. Organizations can also use more formal means to communicate. A blog would be an example. Many organizations use blogs to communicate information such as financial numbers, changes to policy, and other "state of the public organization" information. This type of information is often downward communication. However, blogs are not just for upper management anymore. Organizations are using microblogs more and more to ensure that people in various departments stay connected with each other, especially when tasks tend to be very interdependent.

Organizations also use social networking sites to keep in touch, such as Twitter and Facebook. For example, Alcatel-Lucent, a 77,000-employee telecommunications organizational in Europe, found that using social media keeps a large number of employees connected and tends to be a low or no-cost method of communicating. Rather than sending e-mail to their employees telling them to expect updates via these methods, the news is spread via word of mouth as most of the employees blog or use Facebook or other social media to communicate. In fact, Alcatel-Lucent has over eight hundred groups in its system, ranging from public organization related to ones social in nature.[5] Use of this type of technology can result in upward, downward, horizontal, and diagonal communication all at once.

Organizations also use intranets to communicate information to their employees. An intranet is an internal website, meaning that others generally cannot log in and see information there. The intranet may include information on pay and vacation time as well as recent happenings, awards, and achievements.

Communication Styles

In addition to the communication that occurs within organizations, each of us has our own individual communication style. Many organizations give tests that may indicate their candidate's preferred style, providing information on the best job fit.

Our communication styles can determine how well we communicate with others, how well we are understood, and even how well we get along with others. As you can imagine, our personality types and our communication styles are very similar. Keep in mind, though, that no one person is "always" one style. We can change our style depending on the situation. The more we can understand our own dominant communication style and pinpoint the styles of others, the better we can communicate. The styles are expresser, driver, relater, and analytical. Let's discuss each of these styles next. People with an expresser communication style tend to get excited. They like challenges and rely heavily on hunches and feelings. Depending on the type of public organization, this can be a downfall as sometimes hard data should be used for decision-making purposes. These people are easily recognized because they don't like too many facts or boring explanations and tend to be antsy if they feel their time is being wasted with too many facts.

People with a driver style like to have their own way and tend to be decisive. They have strong viewpoints, which they are not afraid to share with others. They like to take charge in their jobs but also in the way they communicate. Drivers usually get right to the point and not waste time with small talk.

People with a relater style like positive attention and want to be regarded warmly. They want others to care about them and treat them well. Because relaters value friendships, a good way to communicate well with them is to create a communication environment where they can feel close to others.

People with an analytical communication style will ask a lot of questions and behave methodically. They don't like to be pressured to make a decision and prefer to be structured. They are easily recognized by the high number of questions they ask.

Let's discuss an example of how these communication styles might interact. Let's assume an analytical communicator and a relater are beginning a meeting where the purpose is to develop a project time line. The analytical communicator will be focused on the time line and not necessarily the rapport building that the relater would be focused on. The conversation might go something like this:

Table 9.1 Which One of These Communication Styles Do You Tend to Use?

	Passive	Assertive	Aggressive
Definition	Communication style in which you put the rights of others before your own, minimizing your own self-worth	Communication style in which you stand up for your rights while maintaining respect for the rights of others	Communication style in which you stand up for your rights but you violate the rights of others
Implications to others	my feelings are not important	we are both important	your feelings are not important
	I don't matter	we both matter	you don't matter
	I think I'm inferior	I think we are equal	I think I'm superior
Verbal styles	apologetic	I statements	you statements
	overly soft or tentative voice	firm voice	loud voice
Nonverbal styles	looking down or away	looking direct	staring, narrow eyes
	stooped posture, excessive head nodding	relaxed posture, smooth and relaxed movements	tense, clenched fists, rigid posture, pointing fingers
Potential consequences	lowered self-esteem	higher self-esteem	guilt
	anger at self	self-respect	anger from others
	false feelings of inferiority	respect from others	lowered self-esteem
	disrespect from others	respect of others	disrespect from others
	pitied by others		feared by others

Table 9.12 Example 1 of How Styles Might Interact

Relater:	What are you doing this weekend? I am going to my son's baseball game. It is supposed to be hot—I am looking forward to it.
Analytical:	That's great. OK, so I was thinking a start date of August 1st for this project. I can get Kristin started on a to-do list for the project.
Relater:	That would be great. Kristin is a really hard worker, and I'm sure she won't miss any details.
Analytical:	Yes, she's OK. So, your team will need to start development now with a start day coming up. How are you going to go about this?

How do these two personality styles walk away from this conversation? First, the relater may feel ignored or rejected, because the analytical communicator didn't want to discuss weekend details. The analytical communicator may feel annoyed that the relater is wasting time talking about personal things when they have a goal to set a project time line. These types of small miscommunications in public organization are what can create low morale, absenteeism, and other workplace issues. Understanding which style we tend to use can be the key in determining how we communicate with others. Here is another, personal example of these communication styles and how a conversation might go:

Table 9.13 Example 2 of How Styles Might Interact

Expresser, to his partner:	I am really excited for our hiking trip this weekend.
Driver:	I still think we should leave on Thursday night rather than Friday.
Expresser:	I told you, I don't think I can get all day Friday off. Besides, we won't have much time to explore anyway, if we get there on Thursday, it will already be dark.
Driver:	It won't be dark; we will get there around 7, before anyone else, if we leave after work.
Expresser:	I planned the trip. I am the one who went and got our food and permits, I don't see why you have to change it.
Driver:	You didn't plan the trip; I am the one who applied for the permits.

In this situation, you can see that the expresser is just excited about the trip and brings up the conversation as such. The driver has a tendency to be competitive and wants to win,

hence his willingness to get there Thursday before everyone else. The expresser, on the other hand, tried to sell his ideas and didn't get the feedback he felt he deserved for planning the trip, which made the communication start to go south.
In addition to our communication personalities, people tend to communicate based on one of three styles. First, a passive communicator tends to put the rights of others before his or her own. Passive communicators tend to be apologetic or sound tentative when they speak. They do not speak up if they feel like they are being wronged.

An aggressive communicator, on the other hand, will come across as standing up for his or her rights, while possibly violating the rights of others. This person tends to communicate in a way that tells others they don't matter, or their feelings don't matter.

An assertive communicator respects his rights and the rights of others when communicating. This person tends to be direct but not insulting or offensive. The assertive communicator stands up for his or her own rights but makes sure the rights of others aren't affected.

Have you heard of a passive-aggressive communicator? This person tends to be passive but later aggressive by perhaps making negative comments about others or making snide or underhanded comments. This person might express his or her negative feelings in an indirect way, instead of being direct. For example, you are trying to complete a project for a client and the deadline is three days away. You and your team are working frantically to finish. You ask one of your employees to come in to work on Saturday morning to finish up the loose ends, so the project will be ready to present to the client on Monday. Your employee agrees, but when you show up on Monday, the project isn't ready to present. You find out that this person had plans on Saturday but wasn't direct with you about this. So the project didn't get completed, and you had to change the appointment with the client. Later, you also find out that this employee was complaining to everyone else that you had asked her to come in on Saturday. As you can see from this example, passive-aggressive behavior doesn't benefit anyone. The employee should have been direct and simply said, "I can't come in on Saturday, but I can come in Sunday or work late Friday night." Ideally, we want to be assertive communicators, as this shows our own self-esteem but at the same time respects others and isn't misleading to others, either.

When dealing with someone who exhibits passive-aggressive behavior, it is best to just be direct with them. Tell that person you would rather she be direct than not show up. Oftentimes passive-aggressive people try to play the martyr or the victim. Do not allow such people to press your buttons and get you to feel sorry for them. This gives them control and can allow them to take advantage.

Nonverbal Communication

Now that we have discussed the types of communication in organizations and different verbal communication styles, it is only appropriate to discuss body language as well. Most successful HR professionals are excellent at reading and understanding nonverbal language, especially during the interview process.

The interviewer's nonverbal language can also help or hinder a candidate, so we want to be careful of our nonverbal language when interviewing someone. Nonverbal language accounts for a large part of communication. Without seeing and hearing the nonverbal clues, it is easier to have misunderstandings. Nonverbal language can include facial expressions, eye contact, standing or sitting posture, and the position of our hands. Our tone of voice, loudness or softness, and gestures can also be part of body language. The better we can get at knowing what our own body language is telling others and reading others' body language, the better we can get at communicating well with others.

STRATEGIC HR COMMUNICATION STYLE IN ORGANIZATIONS

Consider the use of digital forms of communication, such as e-mail and text messaging. These forms of communication do not allow us to read another's body language, which can often result in misconceptions about what another is saying. Use of "smiley" icons can make this clearer, but often people cannot detect sarcasm and other nonverbal communication cues. If you have something important to communicate, it is better to communicate most of the time in person or via phone, so you can hear tone and see facial expressions.

HOW WOULD YOU HANDLE THIS?

She Said What?
As the HR manager, you have a meeting scheduled in a few minutes with Adeline. Adeline is the accounting manager for a small firm in Boise, Idaho. She has four people who report to her, Alan being one of them. Alan manages three people in his position as account director. Adeline just left a meeting with one of Alan's employees, who complained of Alan's communication style and threatened to quit. She said that Alan belittles them and withholds information. She also complained of

Alan making inappropriate comments, which were meant as a joke but were offensive. How would you handle this?

Another note to consider on body language is how body language can be different across cultures. For example, the OK sign (thumb and pointer figure put together to form a circle) means "great" or "fine" in the United States, but in Brazil, Germany, and Russia, this sign would be considered both rude and offensive. In Japan, this sign means you want the store to give you change in coins. When traveling, we often take for granted that gestures, and even interpersonal distance, or how far apart we stand from another person, are the same at home, but obviously this is not the case. Different nonverbal language can be different wherever you go, so reading up on the place you will visit can ensure you won't offend anyone while there. Having this information can also help us train our employees for overseas assignments.

Listening

Figure 9.3 Active listening involves four phases

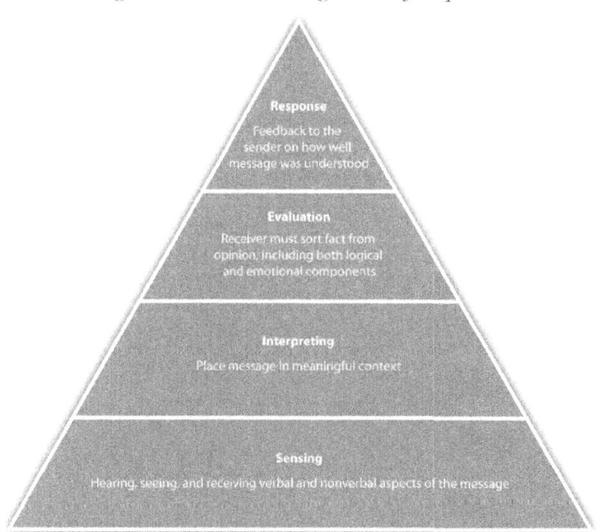

Listening is obviously an important part of communication. There are three main types of listening. Competitive or combative listening happens when we are focused on sharing our own point of view instead of listening to someone else. Inpassive listening, we are interesting in hearing the other person and assume we hear and understand what the person says correctly, without verifying. In active listening, we are interested in what the other person has to say and we are active in checking our understanding with the speaker. For example, we may restate what the person has said and then verify our understanding is correct. The feedback process is the main difference between passive listening and active listening.

KEY TAKEAWAYS

- Emotional intelligence can be improved over time, unlike IQ, which stays stable throughout life.
- Emotional intelligence includes knowing and managing your emotions, motivating yourself, recognizing and understanding other people's emotions, and managing relationships.
- There are four types of communication at work: downward, upward, horizontal, and diagonal. All types of communication can happen at once, especially with the use of blogs and social networking sites.
- Organizations that use good communication tend to have less turnover and less absenteeism.
- There are four main types of communication styles: expresser, driver, relater, andanalytical. The better we can understand our own style of communication and the communication styles of others, the easier it will be to communicate with them.
- Passive, aggressive, and passive-aggressive behaviors are not healthy ways of communicating. Assertive behavior, on the other hand, respects one's own rights and the rights of others.
- Nonverbal communication is one of the most important tools we can use to communicate how we feel. Watching others' body language can give us signals as to how they may really feel.
- Listening is also an important part of communication. Active listening occurs when we are interested in what the other person has to say, and we check with the speaker to make sure we understand what they have said. Competitive or combative listening is when we are focused on sharing our own point of view.Passive listening is when we listen to someone, but do not verify that we understand what someone is saying.

EXERCISES

1. Learn more about your EI by going tohttp://www.queendom.com/tests/access_page/index.htm?idRegTest=1121 and taking the test. Then answer the following questions:

a. What did the test say about your EI?

b. What are some things you can do to improve your EI? What strategies might you use to improve your EI?

Which communication style, the expresser, driver, relater, or analytical, do you typically use? How can you get better at understanding other people's style and get comfortable communicating in their style?

Do you tend to be passive, assertive, or aggressive? Give an example of when you used each style and discuss the result.

Take a few hours and watch the body language of the people in your workplace or personal life. Pay careful attention, really being aware of body language. What was the situation? What kinds of body language did they show?

---

[1] Albert Mehrabian and Susan R. Ferris, "Inference of Attitudes from Nonverbal Communication in Two Channels," Journal of Consulting Psychology 31, no. 3 (1967): 248–58.
[2] Daniel Goleman, Emotional Intelligence (New York: Bantam Books, 2005).
[3] Daniel Goleman, Emotional Intelligence (New York: Bantam Books, 2005).
[4] "Effective Communication in the Workplace," Public organization Performance, accessed July 19, 2010, http://www.public organizationperform.com/workplace-communication/workplace_communication.html.
[5] Sharon Gaudin, "Alcatel-Lucent Gets Social with Organizational Communication,"Computerworld, accessed July 19, 2010,http://www.computerworld.com/s/article/9179169/Alcatel_Lucent_gets_social_with_organizational_communication.
[6] Lyman Steil, Larry Barker, and Kittie Watson, "SIER Hierarchy of Active Listening," Provenmodels, accessed August 1, 2011, http://www.provenmodels.com/554.

9.2 Management Styles

LEARNING OBJECTIVES

1. Define the various types of management styles.
2. Explain how we can determine which style to use in a variety of situations.

Management style ties in very closely with communication style. There isn't necessarily one management style that is better than another; they are simply different and might be used in a variety of situations. HR managers can provide training on each of these areas since management style impacts the ability and motivation of employees to do their jobs.

ORGANIZATIONAL FOCUS

One of the most famous Organizational management styles is the GE Way, which has been discussed in numerous books and articles. In fact, GE has traditionally been the recruiting ground for other organizations' CEO searches. When Jack Welch, the famous GE CEO known for several books on his management style, includingWinning, retired and was replaced, it took less than a week for the two runners-up for his job to be offered jobs at other Organizational organizations. Home Depot recruited Robert Nardellia and 3M recruited W. James McNearney._[1] However, the command-and-control management style responsible for the success of GE did not work out well for several former GE executives. Command-and-control style is based on military management. The idea is to get people to do what you tell them to do, and if they don't, there are major penalties, similar to an autocratic style. Many say that Nardellia was unsuccessful at Home Depot because of this ingrained management style learned at GE._[2] For example, Nardellia insisted that shelves be stocked during off hours, and he instituted formal inventory control. Unfortunately, he didn't understand most employees were not looking to rise within the organization, so the extra work didn't provide any upside for the individuals, causing high turnover. An autocratic style may work well in some organizations, well enough for numerous books to be written, but management style isn't always transferable to other organizations, as Nardellia found out at Home Depot.

Management styles are one of the most challenging topics we can deal with in a work setting. Everyone is different; everyone has a preference for which style motivates them the best in a variety of situations. Oftentimes managers make the mistake of using the same style for everyone, regardless of ability or motivation. In this section, we will discuss some of the main management styles and how to know which one to use in a specific situation.

Task Style versus People-Centered Style

When we look at the styles of management, we see that most styles fall into one of two categories, a task-oriented management style or a people-centered style.

A manager with a task-oriented style will focus on the technical or task aspects of the job. The concern for this manager is that employees know what is expected of them and have the tools needed to do their job.

A people-oriented style is more concerned with the relationships in the workplace. The manager emphasizes the interpersonal relations, as opposed to the task. The manager

is most concerned about the welfare of the employee and tends to be friendly and trusting.
Understanding these two main differences in management style, we will now look at other possible styles a manager might use.

Participatory, Directing, or Teamwork Styles
Utilization of a participatory management style involves both a task-oriented style and a people-centered style. This style emphasizes how the employee's assigned task fits into the bigger picture. This style will provide support and input where needed. As a result, the focus is on the task but also on the person and the relationships required to get the task done. This style might be used when the employees are experienced and the deadlines reasonable enough to provide the time needed to focus both on the task and the person. If more hands-on management is required,[3] adirecting management style might be appropriate. Consider a very tight deadline or an emergency situation in which someone needs to be calling the shots. For example, in your doggie treats public organization, you just received an order for one hundred dog cookies by later this afternoon. You might consider using a directing style to make sure it gets done on time. This style doesn't focus on the person, but rather focuses on getting the task done; hence it tends to be more of a task-oriented style.

A manager who uses a teamwork management style believes there is a value (or necessity) in having people work in teams. As a result, this style tends to require a people-centered approach. Relationships are most important, and assuming the individuals work well together, the task will be successfully accomplished. The advantage to this style, given the type of task and situation, is that as a manager you are able to pool resources and abilities from several different people. Use of a team style can also provide big benefits for the organizational. For example, Google uses a teamwork approach it calls "grouplets." Google believes that individuals should be able to spend time on something that interests them and is also organizational related. Engineers at Google spend 20 percent of their time on this endeavor. As a result, grouplets are formed, and the grouplet works on their idea with no specific budget. Some of the best ideas from Google have come through this teamwork process. Gmail, in fact, was developed using a grouplet.[4]

Autocratic, Participative, and Free-Reign Styles
An autocratic style of management involves the task-oriented style. The focus is on getting things done, and relationships are secondary. This type of manager tends to tell people what to do and takes a "my way or the highway" approach. Another description for this type of manager is a taskmaster. This person uses his or her authority and makes all the decisions as to who does what, how it is done, and when it should get done.

On the other hand, a participative style constantly seeks input from the employees. Setting goals, making plans, and determining objectives are viewed as a group effort, rather than the manager making all the decisions.

At the other extreme, a free-rein style gives employees total freedom to make decisions on how things will get done. The manager may establish a few objectives, but the employees can decide how those objectives are met. In other words, the leader tends to be removed from the day-to-day activities but is available to help employees deal with any situation that may come up.

Path Goal Model for Leadership

Figure 9.4 Path Goal Model for Leadership

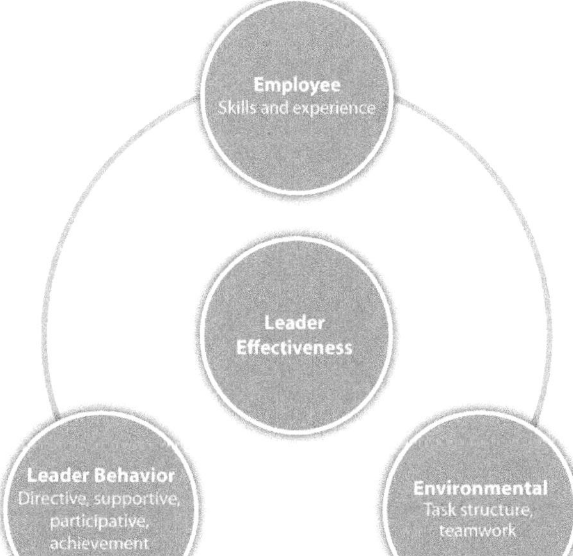

The path goal theory says that the role of a leader is to define goals and lay down the path for the employees to meet those goals. Aspects include clarification of the task and scope of the process. Clarification of the employee's role and clarification around how the success of the task will be measured are key aspects in this model. The leader also is involved in guidance and coaching surrounding the goal and removes obstacles for employees that might affect the completion of the task. The path goal theory says that if employees are satisfied by the leadership style, they will be motivated toward the goals of leadership. Part of the model also stresses that the skills, experience, and environmental contingencies of the job play a role in the success of the leader.

Applying Management Styles

It is great to talk about management style, but application of that management style, especially in an HR environment, is just as important as knowing the management styles. In this section, we will discuss how and when you might use each style when managing people.

Another way we can view leadership is through the situational leadership model.[5] This model, developed by Ken Blanchard (author of the One Minute Manager series of books), does a good job explaining how we might use one type of management style versus another.

Figure 9.5 Blanchard's Situational Leadership Model

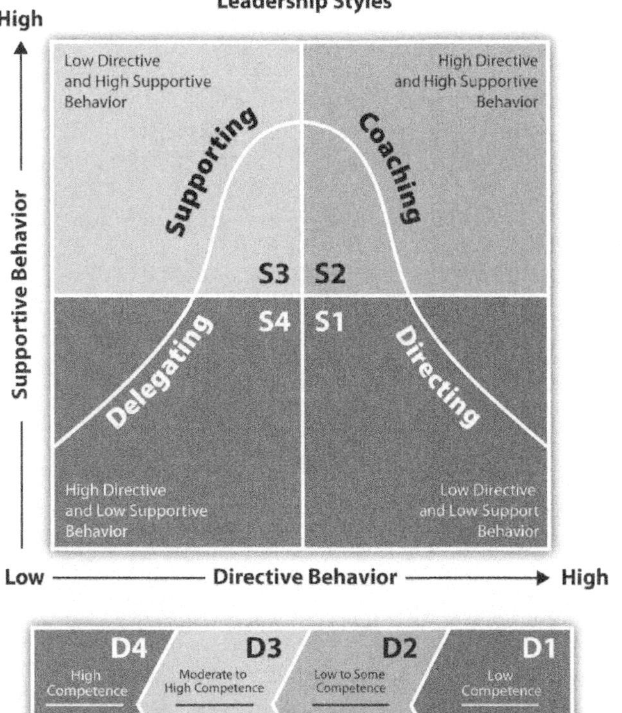

The model looks at three areas: the relationship behavior of the manager, the task behavior of the manager, and the readiness of employees. The relationship behavior means how supportive the manager needs to be in helping employees. Task behavior refers to the type of style the manager should use when managing employees, based on their readiness level. Readiness includes the willingness and skills to perform the task at hand. Depending on where the employees fall in each of these areas, you might use a different management style:

- D4—High Competence, High Commitment—Experienced at the job and comfortable with their own ability to do it well. May even be more skilled than the leader.
- D3—High Competence, Variable Commitment—Experienced and capable, but may lack the confidence to go it alone or the motivation to do it well/quickly.
- D2—Some Competence, Low Commitment—May have some relevant skills but won't be able to do the job without help. The task or the situation may be new to them.
- D1—Low Competence, High Commitment—Generally lacking the specific skills required for the job at hand but has the confidence and/or motivation to tackle it.

Based on the readiness and commitment of the employee, the leader can see what management style and level of support the employee should experience:[6]

- S1—Telling/Directing—High task focus, low relationship focus—Leaders define the roles and tasks of the "follower" and supervise them closely. Decisions are made by the leader and announced, so communication is largely one way. This style can be used with people who lack competence but are enthusiastic and committed and who need direction and supervision to get them started.
- S2—Selling/Coaching—High task focus, high relationship focus—Leaders still define roles and tasks but seek ideas and suggestions from the follower. Decisions remain the leader's prerogative, but communication is much more two-way. This approach can be used with people who have some competence but lack commitment and who need direction and supervision because they are still relatively inexperienced. These individuals may also need support and praise to build their self-esteem and involvement in decision making to restore their commitment.
- S3—Participating/Supporting—Low task focus, high relationship focus—Leaders pass day-to-day decisions, such as task allocation and processes, to the follower. The leader facilitates and takes part in decisions, but control is given to the follower. This style can be used with people who have the necessary competence but lack confidence or motivation. These individuals may need little direction because of their skills, but support is necessary to bolster their confidence and motivation.

- S4—Delegating—Low task focus, low relationship focus—Leaders are still involved in decisions and problem solving, but control is with the follower. The follower decides when and how the leader will be involved. This style would work with people who have both competence and commitment and who are able and willing to work on a project by themselves with little supervision or support.

The bottom line when discussing management style is that no one style works best in all situations. We may be more comfortable with one style versus another, but we need to change our management style depending on the person and task we are working with. For example, if you have an employee who is brand new, you will likely work with that person using a more directive style. As she develops, you might change to a participative style. Likewise, someone who does good work and has lots of experience may prefer a free-rein style. Many managers make the mistake of trying to use the same style with every person in every situation. To be a great manager, we must change our styles based on the situation and the individual involved.

How does this relate to human resources? First, in HR, we are the "go to" people when there are communication issues or issues between management and employees. By understanding these styles ourselves, it will be easier to communicate with and provide solutions for the people we work with. We might even be able to use this information to develop management training, which can result in better communication and higher productivity.

HUMAN RESOURCE RECALL

What kind of management style does your supervisor use? Is it effective?

KEY TAKEAWAYS

- Just like in communication, a different management style should be used depending on the employee.
- Task styles focus on getting the job done, while people-centered styles focus on relationships.
- A participatory style involves both task-oriented and people-centered styles. Adirecting style is focused on the task and doesn't allow for employee participation. A teamwork style focuses on teamwork and is a people-oriented style. The advantage of this style is the ability to use strengths from everyone on the team.
- An autocratic style doesn't allow much room for employee decision making; the focus is on getting the task done. A participative style constantly requires input from employees. The free-rein style gives employees freedom to make decisions on how things will get done.
- The situational leadership model, which looks at relationship behavior, task behavior, and the readiness of employees, is used to recommend different management styles.
- No one management style works in all situations. Just like with communication, you will likely want to vary your approach based on the situation to get the best results.

EXERCISES

1. Why is it important to understand management style if you are an HR professional or manager? Discuss at least three points.
2. What combinations of management style might you use in each of these situations and why?
   a. You are considering a major change in the way your organizational does public organization. Your staff has an excellent record of achieving goals, and your relationship with them is trusting and supportive.
   b. Your employees do a great job. A situation has developed in which you need to make quick decisions and finish a project by the end of the week.
   c. Your employees arehaving trouble getting the job done. Their performance as a whole is less than expected..
   d. You have an employee who is very motivated but has little experience.

---

[1] Claudia Deutsch, "The GE Way Isn't for Everyone," New York Times, January 7, 2007, accessed August 1, 2011,http://www.nytimes.com/2007/01/04/public organization/worldpublic organization/04iht-ge.4102488.html.
[2] Claudia Deutsch, "The GE Way Isn't for Everyone," New York Times, January 7, 2007, accessed August 1, 2011,http://www.nytimes.com/2007/01/04/public organization/worldpublic organization/04iht-ge.4102488.html.
[3] "Three Effective Management Styles," Dun & Bradstreet Credibility Corp., 2010, accessed February 5, 2010, http://smallpublic organization.dnb.com/human-resources/workforce-management/11438-1.html.
[4] Bharat Mediratta, as told to Julie Bick, "The Google Way: Give Engineers Room," New York Times, October 21, 2007, accessed February 15, 2010,http://www.nytimes.com/2007/10/21/jobs/21pre.html.

[5] Ken Blanchard, Patricia Zigarmi, and Drea Zigarmi, Leadership and the One Minute Manager (New York: HarperCollins Entertainment, 2000).
[6] Situational Leadership Grid, Chimaera Consulting, 2008, accessed February 4, 2010,http://www.chimaeraconsulting.com/sitleader.htm.

9.3 Cases and Problems

CHAPTER SUMMARY

- Emotional intelligence can be improved over time, unlike IQ, which stays stable throughout life.
- Emotional intelligence includes knowing and managing your emotions, motivating yourself, recognizing and understanding other people's emotions, and managing relationships.
- There are four types of communication at work: downward, upward,horizontal, and diagonal. All types of communication can happen at once, especially with the use of blogs and social networking sites.
- Organizations that use good communication tend to have less turnover and less absenteeism.
- There are four main types of communication styles: expresser, driver, relater, and analytical. The better we can understand our own style of communication and the communication styles of others, the easier it will be to communicate with them.
- Passive, aggressive, and passive-aggressive behaviors are not healthy ways of communicating. Assertive behavior, on the other hand, respects one's own rights and the rights of others.
- Nonverbal communication is one of the most important tools we can use to communicate how we feel. Watching others' body language can give us signals as to how they may really feel.
- Just like in communication, a different management style should be used depending on the employee.
- Task styles focus on getting the job done, while people-centered styles focus on relationships.
- A participatory style involves both task-oriented and people-centered styles. A directing style is focused on the task and doesn't allow for employee participation. A teamwork style focuses on teamwork and is a people-oriented style. The advantage of this style is the ability to use strengths from everyone on the team.
- An autocratic style doesn't allow much room for employee decision making; the focus is on getting the task done. A participative style constantly requires input from employees. The free-rein style gives employees freedom to make decisions on how things will get done.
- The situational leadership model, which looks at relationship behavior, task behavior, and the readiness of employees, is used to recommend different management styles.
- No one management style works in all situations. Just like with communication, you will likely want to vary your approach based on the situation to get the best results.

CHAPTER CASE

Management Style, Applied

You recently completely overhauled several aspects of employee benefits, including health insurance and compensation packages. You have also developed clear succession plans and career development plans to assist in the retention of your current employees. You are pretty excited about the changes and feel they are better for the employees, while costing your organization less money. These plans came from your development of a strategic plan and goals set last year. You think these plans will result in lower turnover. However, in four recent exit interviews, the former employees mentioned the lack of communication from your department on the changes you made. They said they did not feel well informed and are disappointed they were not notified. In addition, they complained of micromanagement on the part of two particular managers. They said they spend half of their day responding to their managers with project updates, instead of working on the projects themselves. As you begin to think about these exit interviews, you realize that development of the strategic plan and implementing it simply isn't enough; you must communicate the changes to employees as well. You also have a bit of concern about the management styles mentioned and think it might be a good time to offer training on effective management to your entire organizational.

1. Using concepts from this chapter and other HRM chapters, develop an outline for a training program on effective management.
2. Discuss some of the ways you can communicate the following topics to the employees: changes to benefits, training opportunities, compensation plans, and succession plans.

TEAM ACTIVITY

1. In groups of three to five, prepare a presentation you could give to a team of managers on management style and communication. In your presentation, address how management style affects employee retention.

NOTES:

NOTES:

Chapter 10:
Managing Employee Performance in Public Organizations

A Dilemma

You have been the store manager for a large coffee shop for three years but have never had this type of problem employee to handle before, and you schedule a meeting to speak with your HR manager about it. Jake, one of your best employees, has recently begun to have some problems. He is showing up to work late at least twice per week, and he missed the mandatory employee meeting on Saturday morning. When you ask him about it, he says that he is having some personal problems and will try to get better.

For a bit of time, Jake does get better, comes to work on time, and is his normal, pleasant self when helping customers. However, the situation gets more serious two weeks later when Jake comes to work smelling of alcohol and wearing the same clothes he wore to work the day before. You overhear some of the employees talking about Jake's drinking problem. You pull Jake aside and ask him what is happening. He says his wife kicked him out of the house last night and he stayed with a friend, but he didn't have time to gather any of his belongings when he left his house. You accept his answer and hope that things will get better.

A week later, when Jake arrives for his 10–7 shift, he is obviously drunk. He is talking and laughing loudly, smells of alcohol, and has a hard time standing up. You pull him aside and decide to have a serious talk with him. You confront him about his drinking problem, but he denies it, saying he isn't drunk, just tired from everything happening with his wife. You point out the smell and the inability to stand up, and Jake starts crying and says he quit drinking ten years ago but has recently started again with his impending divorce. He begs for you to give him another chance and promises to stop drinking. You tell him you will think about it, but in the meantime, you send him home.

The meeting with HR is this afternoon and you feel nervous. You want to do what is right for Jake, but you also know this kind of disruptive behavior can't continue. You like Jake as a person and he is normally a good employee, so you don't want to fire him. When you meet with the HR manager, he discusses your options. The options, he says, are based on a discipline process developed by HR, and the process helps to ensure that the firing of an employee is both legal and fair. As you review the process, you realize that ignoring the behavior early on has an effect on what you can do now. Since you didn't warn Jake earlier, you must formally document his behavior before you can make any decision to let him go. You hope that Jake can improve so it doesn't come down to that.

10.1 Handling Performance

LEARNING OBJECTIVES

1. Explain the types of performance issues that occur in the workplace, and the internal and external reasons for poor performance.
2. Understand how to develop a process for handling employee performance issues.
3. Be able to discuss considerations for initiating layoffs or downsizing.

As you know from reading this book so far, the time and money investment in a new employee is overwhelming. The cost to select, hire, and train a new employee is staggering. But what if that new employee isn't working out? This next section will provide some examples of performance issues and examples of processes to handle these types of employee problems.

Types of Performance Issues

One of the most difficult parts of managing others isn't when they are doing a great job—it is when they aren't doing a good job. In this section, we will address some examples of performance issues and how to handle them.

1. Constantly late or leaves early. While we know that flexible schedules can provide a work-life balance, managing this flexible schedule is key. Some employees may take advantage and, instead of working at home, perform nonwork-related tasks instead.
2. Too much time spent doing personal things at work. Most organizations have a policy about using a computer or phone for personal use. For most organizations, some personal use is fine, but it can become a problem if someone doesn't know where to draw the line.
3. Inability to handle proprietary information. Many organizations handle important client and patient information. The ability to keep this information private for the protection of others is important to the success of the organizational.
4. Family issues. Child-care issues, divorce, or other family challenges can cause absenteeism, but also poor work

quality. Absenteeism is defined as a habitual pattern of not being at work.

5. Drug and alcohol abuse. The US Department of Labor says that 40 percent of industrial fatalities and 47 percent of industrial injury can be tied to alcohol consumption. The US Department of Labor estimates that employees who use substances are 25–30 percent less productive and miss work three times more often than nonabusing employees._[1] Please keep in mind that when we talk about substance abuse, we are talking about not only illegal drugs but prescription drug abuse as well. In fact, the National Institute on Drug Abuse says that 15.2 million Americans have taken a prescription pain reliever, tranquilizer, or sedative for nonmedical purposes at least once._[2] Substance abuse can cause obvious problems, such as tardiness, absenteeism, and nonperformance, but it can also result in accidents or other more serious issues.
6. Nonperforming. Sometimes employees are just not performing at their peak. Some causes may include family or personal issues, but oftentimes it can mean motivational issues or lack of tools and/or ability to do their current job.
7. Conflicts with management or other employees. While it is normal to have the occasional conflict at work, some employees seem to have more than the average owing to personality issues. Of course, this affects an organization's productivity.
8. Theft. The numbers surrounding employee theft are staggering. The American Marketing Association estimates $10 billion is lost annually owing to employee theft, while the FBI estimates up to $150 billion annually._[3] Obviously, this is a serious employee problem that must be addressed.
9. Ethical breaches. The most commonly reported ethical breaches by employees include lying, withholding information, abusive behavior, and misreporting time or hours worked, according to a National Public organization Ethics study._[4] Sharing certain proprietary information when it is against organizational policy and violating noncompete agreements are also considered ethical violations. Many organizations also have a nonfraternization policy that restricts managers from socializing with nonmanagement employees.
10. Harassment. Engagement of sexual harassment, bullying, or other types of harassment would be considered an issue to be dealt with immediately and, depending on the severity, may result in immediate termination.
11. Employee conduct outside the workplace. Speaking poorly of the organization on blogs or Facebook is an example of conduct occurring outside the workplace that could violate organizational policy. Violating specific organizational policies outside work could also result in termination. For example, in 2010, thirteen Virgin Atlantic employees were fired after posting criticisms about customers and joking about the lack of safety on Virgin airplanes in a public Facebook group._[5]In another example, an NFL Indianapolis Colts cheerleader was fired after racy Playboy promotional photos surfaced (before she became a cheerleader) that showed her wearing only body paint._[6]

While certainly not exhaustive, this list provides some insight into the types of problems that may be experienced. As you can see, some of these problems are more serious than others. Some issues may only require a warning, while some may require immediate dismissal. As an HR professional, it is your job to develop policies and procedures for dealing with such problems. Let's discuss these next.

ORGANIZATIONAL FOCUS

To handle attendance problems at many organizations, a no-fault attendance plan is put into place. In this type of plan, employees are allowed a certain number of absences; when they exceed that number, a progressive discipline process begins and might result in dismissal of the employee. A no-fault attendance policy means there are no excused or unexcused absences, and all absences count against an employee. For example, a organizational might give one point for an absence that is called in the night before work, a half point for a tardy, and two points for a no-call and no-show absence. When an employee reaches a certain number determined by the organizational, he or she is disciplined. This type of policy is advantageous in industries in which unplanned absences have a direct effect on productivity, such as manufacturing and production. Another advantage is that managers do not need to make judgment calls on what is an excused versus an unexcused absence, and this can result in fairness to all employees.

One such organizational with a no-fault attendance policy is Verizon Communications. However, the Equal Employment Opportunity Commission (EEOC) investigated this policy and announced that Verizon will pay $20 million to resolve a disability discrimination lawsuit._[7] The lawsuit said that the organizational, through use of the no-fault attendance policy, denied reasonable accommodations required by the Americans with Disabilities Act (ADA). As a result, hundreds of Verizon employees were disciplined or fired. In this case, the EEOC cites paid or unpaid leave as one way for an employer to provide reasonable accommodations for an employee with a disability. The policy specified there would be no exceptions made to the no-fault attendance policy to accommodate employees with ADA disabilities. When discussing the case, the EEOC chair justified the agency's position by saying, "Flexibility on leave can enable a worker with a disability to remain employed and productive, a win for the worker, employer, and the economy. By contrast, an inflexible leave policy may deny workers with disabilities a reasonable accommodation."_[8] Part of the settlement also involved additional training to Verizon employees on ADA and how to administer the attendance plan. This successful lawsuit shows that even the most seemingly clear performance expectations must be flexible to meet legal obligations.

HUMAN RESOURCE RECALL

What would you do if you saw a coworker taking a box of pens home from the office?

What Influences Performance?

When an employee isn't performing as expected, it can be very disapointing. When you consider the amount of time it takes to recruit, hire, and train someone, it can be disappointing to find that a person has performance issues. Sometimes performance issues can be related to something personal, such as drug or alchol abuse, but often it is a combination of factors. Some of these factors can be internal while others may be external. Internal factors may include the following:

1. Career goals are not being met with the job.
2. There is conflict with other employees or the manager.
3. The goals or expectations are not in line with the employee's abilities.
4. The employee views unfairness in the workplace.
5. The employee manages time poorly.
6. The employee is dissatisfied with the job.
7. Some of the external factors may include the following:
8. The employee doesn't have correct equipment or tools to perform the job.
9. The job design is incorrect.
10. External motivation factors are absent.
11. There is a lack of management support.
12. The employee's skills and job are mismatched.

All the internal reasons speak to the importance once again of hiring the right person to begin with. The external reasons may be something that can be easily addressed and fixed. Whether the reason is internal or external, performance issues must be handled in a timely manner.

Defining Discipline

If an employee is not meeting the expectations, discipline might need to occur.Discipline is defined as the process that corrects undesirable behavior. The goal of a discipline process shouldn't necessarily be to punish, but to help the employee meet performance expectations. Often supervisors choose not to apply discipline procedures because they have not documented past employee actions or did not want to take the time to handle the situation. When this occurs, the organization lacks consistency among managers, possibility resulting in motivational issues for other employees and loss of productivity.

To have an effective discipline process, rules and policies need to be in place and communicated so all employees know the expectations. Here are some guidelines on creation of rules and organizational policies:

1. All rules or procedures should be in a written document.
2. Rules should be related to safety and productivity of the organization.
3. Rules should be written clearly, so no ambiguity occurs between different managers.
4. Supervisors, managers, and human resources should communicate rules clearly in orientation, training, and via other methods.
5. Rules should be revised periodically, as the organization's needs change.

Of course, there is a balance between too many "rules" and giving employees freedom to do their work. However, the point of written rules is to maintain consistency. Suppose, for example, you have a manager in operations and a manager in marketing. They both lead with a different style; the operations manager has a more rigid management style, while the marketing manager uses more of a laissez-faire approach. Suppose one employee in each of the areas is constantly late to work. The marketing manager may not do anything about it, while the operations manager may decide each tardy day merits a "write-up," and after three write-ups, the employee is let go. See how lack of consistency might be a problem? If this employee is let go, he or she might be able to successfully file a lawsuit for wrongful termination, since another employee with the same performance issue was not let go. Wrongful termination means an employer has fired or laid off an employee for illegal reasons, such as violation of antidiscrimination laws or violation of oral and/or written employee agreements. To avoid such situations, a consistent approach to managing employee performance is a crucial part of the human resources job.

The Role of the Performance Appraisal in Discipline

Figure 10.1 The Process for Handling

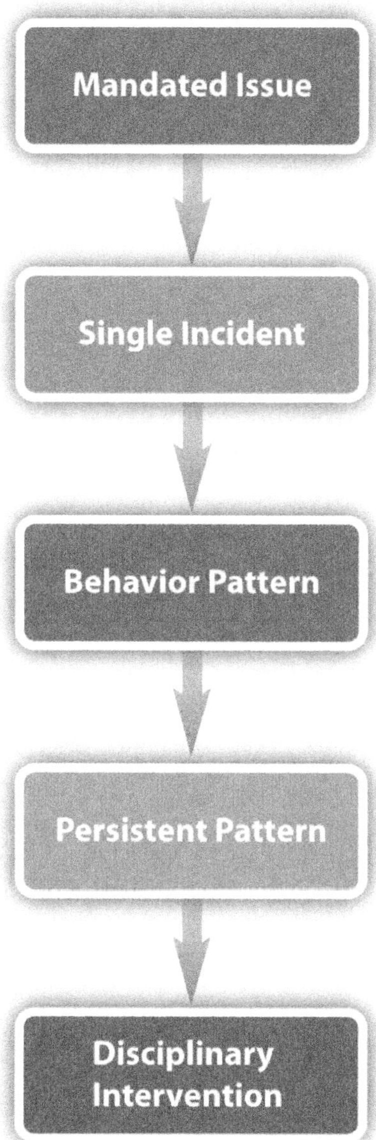

Besides the written rules, each individual job analysis should have rules and policies that apply to that specific job. The performance appraisal is a systematic process to evaluate employees on (at least) an annual basis. The organization's performance appraisal and general rules and policies should be the tools that measure the employee's overall performance. If an employee breaks the rules or does not meet expectations of the performance appraisal, the performance issue model, which we will discuss next, can be used to correct the behavior.

Performance Issue Model

Because of the many varieties of performance issues, we will not discuss how to handle each type in detail here. Instead, we present a model that can be used to develop policies around performance, for fairness and consistency.

We can view performance issues in one of five areas. First, the mandated issue is serious and must be addressed immediately. Usually, the mandated issue is one that goes beyond the organizational and could be a law. Examples of mandated issues might include an employee sharing information that violates privacy laws, not following safety procedures, or engaging in sexual harassment. For example, let's say a hospital employee posts something on his Facebook page that violates patient privacy. This would be considered a mandated issue (to not violate privacy laws) and could put the hospital in serious trouble. These types of issues need to be handled swiftly. A written policy detailing how this type of issue would be handled is crucial. In our example above, the policy may state that the employee is immediately fired for this type of violation. Or, it may mean this employee is required to go through privacy training again and is given a written warning. Whatever the result, developing a policy on how mandated issues will be handled is important for consistency.

The second performance issue can be called a single incident. Perhaps the employee misspeaks and insults some colleagues or perhaps he or she was over budget or late on a project. These types of incidents are usually best solved with a casual conversation to let the employee know what he or she did wasn't appropriate. Consider this type of misstep a development opportunity for your employee. Coaching and working with the employee on this issue can be the best way to nip this problem before it gets worse.

Often when single incidents are not immediately corrected, they can evolve into a behavior pattern, which is our third type of performance issue. This can occur when the employee doesn't think the incident is a big deal because he hasn't been correct before or may not even realize his is doing something wrong. In this case, it's important to talk with the employee and let him know what is expected.

If the employee has been corrected for a behavior pattern but continues to exhibit the same behavior, we call this a persistent pattern. Often you see employees correct the problem after an initial discussion but then fall back into old habits. If they do not self-correct, it could be they do not have the training or the skills to perform the job. In this phase of handling performance issues, it is important to let the employee know that the problem is serious and further action will be taken if it continues. If you believe the employee just doesn't have the skills or knowledge to perform the job, asking him or her about this could be helpful to getting to the root of the problem as well. If the employee continues to be nonperforming, you may consider utilizing the progressive discipline process before initiating an employee separation. However, investigating the performance issue should occur before implementing any sort of discipline.

Investigation of Performance Issues

When an employee is having a performance issue, often it is our responsibility as HR professionals to investigate the situation. Training managers on how to document performance failings is the first step in this process. Proper documentation is necessary should the employee need to be terminated later for the performance issue. The documentation should include the following information:

1. Date of incident
2. Time of incident
3. Location (if applicable) of incident
4. A description of the performance issue
5. Notes on the discussion with the employee on the performance issue
6. An improvement plan, if necessary
7. Next steps, should the employee commit the same infraction
8. Signatures from both the manager and employee

With this proper documentation, the employee and the manager will clearly know the next steps that will be taken should the employee commit the infraction in the future. Once the issue has been documented, the manager and employee should meet about the infraction. This type of meeting is called an investigative interview and is used to make sure the employee is fully aware of the discipline issue. This also allows the employee the opportunity to explain his or her side of the story. These types of meetings should always be conducted in private, never in the presence of other employees.

In unionized organizations, however, the employee is entitled to union representation at the investigative interview. This union representation is normally calledinterest based bargaining_[9] referring to a National Labor Relations Board case that went to the United States Supreme Court in 1975. Recently, Weingarten rights continued to be protected when Alonso and Carus Ironworks was ordered to cease and desist from threatening union representatives who attempted to represent an employee during an investigative interview._[10]

Options for Handling Performance Issues

Our last phase of dealing with employee problems would be a disciplinary intervention. Often this is called the progressive discipline process. It refers to a series of steps taking corrective action on nonperformance issues. The progressive discipline process is useful if the offense is not serious and does not demand immediate dismissal, such as employee theft. The progressive discipline process should be documented and applied to all employees committing the same offenses. The steps in progressive discipline normally are the following:

1. *First offense:* Unofficial verbal warning. Counseling and restatement of expectations.
2. *Second offense:* Official written warning, documented in employee file.
3. *Third offense: Second* official warning. Improvement plan (discussed later) may be developed. Documented in employee file.
4. *Fourth offense:* Possible suspension or other punishment, documented in employee file.
5. *Fifth offense:* Termination and/or alternative dispute resolution.

Alternative Dispute Resolution

Another option in handling disputes, performance issues, and terminations isalternative dispute resolution (ADR). This method can be effective in getting two parties to come to a resolution. In ADR, an unbiased third party looks at the facts in the case and tries to help the parties come to an agreement. In mediation, the third party facilitates the resolution process, but the results of the process are not binding for either party. This is different from arbitration, in which a person reviews the case and makes a resolution or a decision on the situation. The benefits of ADR are lower cost and flexibility, as opposed to taking the issue to court.

Some organizations use a step-review system. In this type of system, the performance issue is reviewed by consecutively higher levels of management, should there be disagreement by the employee in a discipline procedure. Some organizations also implement a peer resolution system. In this type of system, a committee of management and employees is formed to review employee complaints or discipline issues. In this situation, the peer review system normally involves the peer group reviewing the documentation and rendering a decision. Another type of ADR is called the ombudsman system. In this system, a person is selected (or elected) to be the designated individual for employees to go to should they have a complaint or an issue with a discipline procedure. In this situation, the ombudsman utilizes problem-solving approaches to resolve the issue. For example, at National Geographic Traveler Magazine an ombudsman handles employee complaints and issues and also customer complaints about travel organizations.

Employee Separation

Employee separation can occur in any of these scenarios. First, the employee resigns and decides to leave the organization. Second, the employee is terminated for one or more of the performance issues listed previously. Lastly, absconding is when the employee decides to leave the organization without resigning and following the normal process. For example, if an employee simply stops showing up to work without notifying anyone of his or her departure, this would be considered absconding. Let's discuss each of these in detail. Employee separation costs can be expensive. In the second quarter in 2011, for example, Halliburton reported $8 million in employee separation costs._[11]

Resignation means the employee chooses to leave the organization. First, if an employee resigns, normally he or she will provide the manager with a formal resignation e-mail. Then the HR professional usually schedules an exit interview, which can consist of an informal confidential discussion as to why the employee is leaving the organization. If HR thinks the issue or reasons for leaving can be fixed, he or she may discuss with the manager if the resignation will be accepted. Assuming the resignation is accepted, the employee will work with the manager to determine a plan for his or her workload. Some managers may prefer the employee leave right away and will redistribute the workload. For some jobs, it may make sense for the employee to finish the current project and then depart. This will vary from job to job, but two weeks' notice is normally the standard time for resignations.

If it is determined an employee should be terminated, different steps would be taken than in a resignation. First, documentation is necessary, which should have occurred in the progressive discipline process. Performance appraisals, performance improvement plans, and any other performance warnings the employee received should be readily available before meeting with the employee. It should be noted that the reliability and validity of performance appraisals should be checked before dismissing an employee based upon them. Questionable performance appraisals come from the real-world conditions common to rating situations, particularly because of limitations in the abilities of the raters._[12]

Remember that if the discipline process is followed as outlined prior, a termination for nonperformance should never be a surprise to an employee. Normally, the manager and HR manager would meet with the employee to deliver the news. It should be delivered with compassion but be direct and to the point. Depending on previous contracts, the employee may be entitled to a severance package. A severance package can include pay, benefits, or other compensation for which an employee is entitled when they leave the organization. The purpose of a severance plan is to assist the employee while he or she seeks other employment. The HR professional normally develops this type of package in conjunction with the manager. Some considerations in developing a severance package (preferably before anyone is terminated) might include the following:

1. How the severance will be paid (i.e., lump sum or in x equal increments)
2. Which situations will pay a severance and which will not. For example, if an employee is terminated for violation of a sexual harassment policy, is a severance still paid?
3. A formula for how severance will be paid, based on work group, years with the organization, etc.
4. Legal documents, such as legal releases and noncompete agreements
5. How accrued vacation and/or sick leave will be paid, if at all

The last topic that we should discuss in this section is the case of an absconded employee. If an employee stops showing up to work, a good effort to contact this person should be the first priority. If after three days this person has not been reachable and has not contacted the organizational, it would be prudent to stop pay and seek legal help to recover any organizational items he or she has, such as laptops or parking passes.

Sometimes rather than dealing with individual performance issues and/or terminations, we find ourselves having to perform layoffs of several to hundreds of employees. Let's address your role in this process next.

Rightsizing and Layoffs

Rightsizing refers to the process of reducing the total size of employees, to ultimately save on costs. Downsizing ultimately means the same thing as rightsizing, but the usage of the word has changed in that rightsizing seems to define the organization's goals better, which would be to reduce staff to save money, or rightsize. When a organizational decides to rightsize and, ultimately, engage in layoffs, some aspects should be considered.

First, is the downturn temporary? There is nothing worse than laying people off, only to find that as public organization increases, you need to hire again. Second, has the organization looked at other ways to cut expenses? Perhaps cutting expenses in other areas would be advisable before choosing to lay people off. Finally, consideration should be given to offering temporary sabbaticals, voluntary retirement, or changing from a full- to part-time position. Some employees may even be willing to take a temporary pay cut to reduce costs. Organizations find they can still keep good people by looking at some alternatives that may work for the employee and the organization, even on a temporary basis.

If the organizational has decided the only way to reduce costs is to cut full-time employees, this is often where HR should be directly involved to ensure legal and ethical guidelines are met. Articulating the reasons for layoffs and establishing a formalized approach to layoffs is the first consideration. Before it is decided who should get cut, criteria should be developed on how these decisions will be made. Similar to how selection criteria might be developed, the development of criteria that determines which jobs will be cut makes the process of cutting more fair, albeit still difficult. Establishing the criteria ahead of time can also help avoid managers' trying to "save" certain people from their own departments. After development of criteria, the next phase would be to sit down with management and decide who does or doesn't meet the criteria and who will be laid off. At this point, before the layoffs happen, it makes sense to discuss severance packages. Usually, when an employee signs for a severance package, the employee should also sign a form (the legal department can help with this) that releases the organization from all future claims made by the employee.

After criteria have been developed, people selected, and severance packages determined, it's key to have a solid communication plan as to how the layoffs will be announced. Usually, this involve an initial e-mail to all employees, letting them know of impending layoffs. Speak with each employee separately, then announce which positions were eliminated. The important thing to remember during layoffs is keeping your employees' dignity; they did not do anything wrong to lose their job—it was just a result of circumstances.

KEY TAKEAWAYS

- Performance issues in the workplace are common. Examples of performance issues might include constant tardiness, too much time at work handling personal issues, mishandling of proprietary information, family issues, drug and alcohol problems, nonperformance, theft, or conflicts in the workplace.
- Employees choose to leave organizations for internal and external reasons. Some of these may include a mismatch of career goals, conflict, too high expectations, time-management issues, and mismatch of job and skills.
- HR professionals should develop a set of policies that deal with performance issues in the workplace. The advantage of having such a policy is that it can eliminate wrongful termination legal action.
- A mandated issue is usually one that deals with safety or legal issues that go beyond the workplace. An infringement of this type of issue requires immediate attention.
- A single incident may include a misstep of the employee, and he or she should immediately be spoken with to ensure it doesn't happen again.
- A behavior pattern occurs when an employee consistently exhibits a performance issue. This type of issue should be discussed with the employee and plans taken, such as more training, to ensure it does not continue. A persistent pattern occurs when an employee consistently exhibits a performance issue and does not improve, despite HR's talking with him or her.
- At some point during the persistent pattern, disciplinary action will likely need to be taken. It is important to develop consistent procedures on how to record and handle disciplinary issues. Most employers use a progressive discipline process to accomplish this goal.
- Employee separation occurs in one of three ways. First, the employee resignsfrom the organization. Second, the employee is terminated for performance issues, and third, an employee absconds. Absconds means the employee abandons his or her job without submitting a formal resignation.
- In some cases, a severance package may be offered to the employee upon his or her departure from the organization.

- Rightsizing is a term used when an organization must cut costs through layoffs of employees. Development of criteria for layoffs, communication, and severance package discussion are all parts of this process.

EXERCISES

1. What are some considerations before developing a severance package? What are the advantages of offering a severance package to your departing employees?
2. What are some common performance issues? What is HR's role in handling these issues?
3. What process should you use to initiate layoffs?

---

[1] United States Department of Labor, "General Workplace Impact," 2011, accessed March 8, 2011, http://www.esrcheck.com/wordpress/2011/08/12/studies-show-drugs-in-workplace-cost-employers-billions- and-small-public organizationes-employ-more-drug-users-but-drug-test-less/.

[2] Barry Fisher, "Targeting Prescription Drug Abuse," Ventura County Star, March 6, 2011, accessed March 8, 2011, http://www.vcstar.com/news/2011/mar/06/targeting-prescription-drug-abuse/.

[3] "Employee Theft and Legal Aspects," Net Industries, accessed March 8, 2011,http://law.jrank.org/pages/1084/Employee-Theft-Legal-Aspects-Estimates-cost.html.

[4] "Careers By the Numbers," InfoWorld, October 2, 2000, accessed August 1, 2011,http://books.google.com/books?id=ST0EAAAAMBAJ&pg=PA93&lpg=PA93&dq=Careers+By+the+Numbers +InfoWorld+October+2,+2000&source=bl&ots=KU2eMTa3C3&sig=rU3s8ywYcc0Z kUbuydMO3wrO1Rc&hl=en&sa=X&ei=yoVsT6PfGYSw0QH11u3TBg&ved=0CCIQ6 AEwAA#v=onepage&q= Careers%20By%20the%20Numbers%20InfoWorld%20October %202%2C%202000&f=false.

[5] Catherine Smith, "Fired Over Facebook," Huffington Post, July 2010, accessed August 1, 2011, http://www.huffingtonpost.com/2010/07/26/fired-over-facebook-posts_n_659170.html#s115752&title=13_Virgin_Atlantic.

[6] Rick Chandler, "Ex-Colts Cheerleader Sues Team Over Dismissal for Playboy Pics," NBC Sports, May 11, 2011, accessed August 1, 2011,http://offthebench.nbcsports.com/2011/05/11/ex-colts-cheerleader-sues-team-over-dismissal-for-playboy-pics/.

[7] Jim Evans, "EEOC Finds Fault with Organizational's No Fault Attendance Plan," Zanesville Times, July 17, 2011, accessed August 1, 2011,http://www.public organizationmanagementdaily.com/19860/eeoc-finds-fault-with-no-fault-attendance-policies.

[8] Jim Evans, "EEOC Finds Fault with Organizational's No Fault Attendance Plan," Zanesville Times, July 17, 2011, accessed August 1, 2011,http://www.public organizationmanagementdaily.com/19860/eeoc-finds-fault-with-no-fault-attendance-policies.

[9] National Labor Relations Board website, "Administrative Law Judge Orders San Juan Organizational to Respect Employee Weingarten Rights," March 28, 2011, accessed August 17, 2011.

[10] National Labor Relations Board website, "Administrative Law Judge Orders San Juan Organizational to Respect Employee Weingarten Rights," March 28, 2011, accessed August 17, 2011.

[11] Brad Lemaire, "Halliburton Posts 54% Q2 Growth," Proactive Investors, July 18, 2011, accessed August 1, 2011,http://www.proactiveinvestors.com/organizations/news/16404/halliburton-posts-54-q2-profit-growth-16404.html.

[12] Jeff Weekley, Academy of Management Journal 32, no. 1 (1989): 213–22.

10.2 Employee Rights

LEARNING OBJECTIVES

1. Be able to explain employee rights.
2. Define unions and explain their relation to the HRM function.

Employee rights is defined as the ability to receive fair treatment from employers. This section will discuss employee rights surrounding job protection, privacy, and unionization.

Job Protection Rights

If HR doesn't understand or properly manage employee rights, lawsuits are sure to follow. It is the HR professional's job to understand and protect the rights of employees. In the United States, the employment-at-will principle (EAW) is the right of an employer to fire an employee or an employee to leave an organization at any time, without any specific cause. The EAW principle gives both the employee and employer freedom to terminate the relationship at any time. There are three main exceptions to this principle, and whether they are accepted is up to the various states:

1. *Public policy exception.* With a public policy exception, an employer may not fire an employee if it would violate the individual state's doctrine or statute. For example, in Borse v. Piece Goods Shop in Pennsylvania, a federal circuit court of appeals ruled that Pennsylvania law may protect at-will employees from being fired for refusing to take part in drug test programs if the employee's privacy is invaded. Borse contended that the free speech provisions of the state and of the First Amendment protected the refusal to participate. Some public policy exceptions occur when an employee is fired for refusing to violate state or federal law.
2. *Implied contract exception.* In a breach of an implied contract, the discharged employee can prove that the employer indicated that the employee has job security. The indication does not need to be formally written, only implied. InWright v. Honda, an Ohio employee was terminated but argued that the implied contract exception was relevant to the employment-at-will doctrine. She was able to prove that in orientation, Honda stressed to employees the importance of

attendance and quality work. She was also able to prove that the language in the associate handbook implied job security: "the job security of each employee depends upon doing your best on your job with the spirit of cooperation." Progress reports showing professional development further solidified her case, as she had an implied contract that Honda had altered the employment-at-will doctrine through its policies and actions.

3. *Good faith and fair dealing exception.* In thegood faith and fair dealing exception, the discharged employee contends that he was not treated fairly. This exception to the employment-at-will doctrine is less common than the first two. Examples might include firing or transferring of employees to prevent them from collecting commissions, misleading employees about promotions and pay increases, and taking extreme actions that would force the employee to quit.

When one of the exceptions can be proven, wrongful discharge accusations may occur. The United States is one of the few major industrial powers that utilize an employment-at-will philosophy. Most countries, including France and the UK, require employers to show just cause for termination of a person's employment.[1] The advantage of employment at will allows for freedom of employment; the possibility of wrongful discharge tells us that we must be prepared to defend the termination of an employee, as to not be charged with a wrongful discharge case.

Employees also have job protection if they engage in whistleblowing. Whistleblowing refers to an employee's telling the public about ethical or legal violations of his or her organization. This protection was granted in 1989 and extended through the Sarbanes-Oxley Act of 2002. Many organizations create whistleblowing policies and a mechanism to report illegal or unethical practices within the organization.[2]

Another consideration for employee job protection is that of an implied contract. It is in the best interest of HR professionals and managers alike to avoid implying an employee has a contract with the organization. In fact, many organizations develop employment-at-will policies and ask their employees to sign these policies as a disclaimer for the organization.

A constructive discharge means the employee resigned, but only because the work conditions were so intolerable that he or she had no choice. For example, if James is being sexually harassed at work, and it is so bad he quits, he would need to prove not only the sexual harassment but that it was so bad it required him to quit. This type of situation is important to note; should James's case go to court and sexual harassment and constructive discharge are found, James may be entitled to back pay and other compensation.

The Worker Adjustment and Retraining Notification Act (WARN) requires organizations with more than one hundred employees to give employees and their communities at least sixty days' notice of closure or layoff affecting fifty or more full-time employees. This law does not apply in the case of unforeseeable public organization circumstances. If an employer violates this law, it can be subject to back pay for employees.[3] This does not include workers who have been with the organization for less than six months, however.
Retaliatory discharge means punishment of an employee for engaging in a protected activity, such as filing a discrimination charge or opposing illegal employer practices. For example, it might include poor treatment of an employee because he or she filed a workers' compensation claim. Employees should not be harassed or mistreated should they file a claim against the organization.

Privacy Rights

Technology makes it possible to more easily monitor aspects of employees' jobs, although a policy on this subject should be considered before implementing it. In regard to privacy, a question exists whether an employer should be allowed to monitor an employee's online activities. This may include work e-mail, websites visited using organizational property, and also personal activity online.

Digital Footprints, Inc. is a organizational that specializes in tracking the digital movements of employees and can provide reports to the organization by tracking these footprints. This type of technology might look for patterns, word usage, and other communication patterns between individuals. This monitoring can be useful in determining violations of workplace policies, such as sexual harassment. This type of software and management can be expensive, so before launching it, it's imperative to address its value in the workplace.

Another privacy concern can include monitoring of employee postings on external websites. Organizations such as Social Sentry, under contract, monitor employee postings on sites such as Facebook, Twitter, LinkedIn, and YouTube.[4] Lawyers warn, however, that this type of monitoring should only be done if the employee has consented._[5] A monitoring organizational isn't always needed to monitor employees' movements on social networking. And sometimes employees don't even have to tweet something negative about their own organizational to lose their job. A case in point is when Chadd Scott, who does Atlanta sports updates for 680/The Fan, was fired for tweeting about Delta Airlines. In his tweet, he complained about a Delta delay and said they did not have enough de-icing fluid. Within a few hours, he was fired from his job, because Delta was a sponsor of 680/The Fan._[6]

The US Patriot Act also includes caveats to privacy when investigating possible terrorist activity. The Patriot Act requires organizations to provide private employee information when requested. Overall, it is a good idea to have a clear organizational policy and perhaps even a signed waiver from employees stating they understand their activities may be monitored and information shared with the US government under the Patriot Act.

Depending on the state in which you live, employees may be given to see their personnel files and the right to see and correct any incorrect information within their files. Medical or disability information should be kept separate from the employee's work file, per the Americans with Disabilities Act. In addition, the Health Insurance Portability and Accountability Act (HIPAA) mandates that health information should be private, and therefore it is good practice to keep health information in a separate file as well. Finally, drug testing and the right to privacy is a delicate balancing act. Organizations that implement drug testing often do so for insurance or safety reasons. Because of theDrug-Free Workplace Act of 1988, some federal contractors and all federal grantees must agree they will provide a drug free workplace, as a condition of obtaining the contract. The ADA does not view testing for illegal drug use as a medical examination (making them legal), and people using illegal drugs are not protected under the ADA;_[7] however, people covered under ADA laws are allowed to take medications directly related to their disability. In a recent case, Bates v. Dura Automotive Systems, an auto parts manufacturer had a high accident rate and decided to implement drug testing to increase safety. Several prescription drugs were banned because they were known to cause impairment. The plaintiffs in the case had been dismissed from their jobs because of prescription drug use, and they sued, claiming the drug-testing program violated ADA laws._[8] However, the Sixth Circuit Court reversed the case because the plaintiffs were not protected under ADA laws (they did not have a documented disability).

In organizations where heavy machinery is operated, a monthly drug test may be a job requirement. In fact, under the Omnibus Transportation Employee Testing Act of 1991, employers are legally required to test for drugs in transportation-related public organizationes such as airlines, railroads, trucking, and public transportation, such as bus systems. Medical marijuana is a relatively new issue that is still being addressed in states that allow its use. For example, if the organizational requires a drug test and the employee shows positive for marijuana use, does asking the employee to prove it is being used for medical purposes violate HIPAA privacy laws? This issue is certainly one to watch over the coming years.

HUMAN RESOURCE RECALL

What does the term retaliatory discharge mean?

Labor Unions

A union is an organization of employees formed to bargain with an employer. It is important to mention unions here, since labor contracts often guide the process for layoffs and discipline. Labor unions have been a part of the US workplace landscape since the late 1920s, but the Wagner Act of 1935 significantly impacted labor and management relations by addressing several unfair labor practices. The National Labor Relations Board is responsible for administering and enforcing the provisions outlined in the Wagner Act. The act made acts such as interfering with the formation of unions and discriminating on the basis of union membership illegal for employers. By the 1940s, 9 million people were members of a union, which spurred the passage of the Taft-Hartley Act. This act set a new set of standards for fair practices by the unions, within a unionized environment.

The purpose of a union is to give collective bargaining power to a group of individuals. For example, instead of one person negotiating salary, a union gives people the power to bargain as a group, creating a shift from the traditional power model. Issues to negotiate can include pay, health benefits, working hours, and other aspects relating to a job. People often decide to form a union if they perceive the organization or management of the organization is treating them unfairly. Some people also believe that belonging to a union means higher wages and better benefits.

Many employers feel it is not in the best interest of the organization to unionize, so they will engage in strategies to prevent unionization. However, the Taft-Hartley Act says that employers can express their views about unions but may not threaten employees with loss of job or other benefits if they unionize. Some of the talking points an organization might express about unions include the following:

1. Less ability to deal more informally with the organization
2. Possibility of strikes
3. Payment of union dues by employees
4. Emphasis on what positive aspects the employer has provided

If employees still unionize, managers and HR professionals alike will engage in the bargaining process. The collective bargaining process is the process of negotiating an agreement between management and employees. This process ultimately defines the contract terms for employees. In negotiating with the union, being prepared is important. Gathering data of what worked with the old contract and what didn't can be a good starting point. Understanding the union's likely requests and preparing a counteraction to these requests and possible compromises should be done before even sitting down to the bargaining table. One of the better strategies for negotiating a contract is called interest-based bargaining. In this type of bargaining, mutual interests are brought up and discussed, rather than each party coming to the table with a list of demands. This can create a win-win situation for both parties.

Once an agreement has been decided, the union members vote whether to accept the new contract. If the contract is accepted, the next task is to look at how to administer the agreement.

First, the HR professional must know the contract well to administer it well. For example, if higher pay is successfully negotiated, obviously it would be the job of HR to implement this new pay scale. The HR professional may need to develop new sets of policies and procedures when a new agreement is in place. One such procedure HR may have to work with occasionally is the grievance process. The grievance process is a formal way by which employees can submit a complaint regarding something that is not administered correctly in the contract. Usually, the grievance process will involve discussions with direct supervisors first, discussions with the union representative next, and then the filing of a formal, written grievance complaint. Management is then required to provide a written response to the grievance, and depending on the collective bargaining agreement, a formalized process is stated on how the appeals process would work, should the grievance not be solved by the management response. One such example is the dismissal of members of the National Air Traffic Controller Association (union). In 2011, of the 140 proposed dismissals of air traffic controllers, 58 had penalties rescinded, reduced, or deferred. [9] This is because of due-process protections used to prevent mass firings when a new administration comes to power. Federal workers, including controllers, can challenge disciplinary action penalties through a government panel called the Merit Systems Protection Board. The process is described in union contracts and mentions involvement of an arbitrator, if necessary.

HOW WOULD YOU HANDLE THIS?

To Join or Not to Join

As the HR manager for a two-hundred-person organizational, you have always worked hard to ensure that workers received competitive benefits and salaries. When you hear rumors of the workers' wanting to form a union, you are a little distressed, because you feel everyone is treated fairly. How would you handle this?

How Would You Handle This?

KEY TAKEAWAYS

- The employment-at-will principle means that an employer can separate from an employee without cause, and vice versa.
- Even though we have employment at will, a wrongful discharge can occur when there are violations of public policy, an employee has a contract with an employer, or an employer does something outside the boundaries of good faith.
- Whistleblowing is when an employee notifies organizations of illegal or unethical activity. Whistleblowers are protected from discharge due to their activity.
- A constructive discharge means the conditions are so poor that the employee had no choice but to leave the organization.
- The Worker Adjustment and Retraining Notification Act (WARN) is a law that requires organizations of one hundred or more employees to notify employees and the community if fifty or more employees are to be laid off.
- A retaliatory discharge is one that occurs if an employer fires or lays off an employee owing to a charge the employee filed. For example, if an employee files a workers' compensation claim and then is let go, this could be a retaliatory discharge.

- The privacy of employees is an issue that HR must address. It is prudent to develop policies surrounding what type of monitoring may occur within an organization. For example, some organizations monitor e-mail, computer usage, and even postings on social network sites.
- Drug testing is also a privacy issue, although in many industries requiring safe working conditions, drug testing can be necessary to ensure the safety of all employees.
- A union is a group of workers who decide to work together toward a collective bargaining agreement. This agreement allows workers to negotiate as one, rather than as individuals.
- The Wagner Act, passed in 1935, addresses many issues related to workers' unionization.
- The process of collective bargaining means to negotiate a contract between management and workers. HR is generally part of this process.
- Interest based bargaining occurs when mutual interests are discussed, rather than starting with a list of demands.
- Once an agreement is reached, HR is generally responsible for knowing the agreement and implementing any changes that should occur as a result of the agreement. One such example is understanding the grievance process.

EXERCISES

1. Perform an Internet search and find a union agreement. Discuss how the union agreement handles terminations and grievances.
2. Compare and contrast the differences between a retaliatory discharge and a constructive discharge.

---

[1] USLegal, "Employment at Will," accessed March 15, 2011,http://employment.uslegal.com/employment-at-will/.
[2] Lilanthi Ravishankar, "Encouraging Internal Whistle Blowing," Santa Clara University, accessed March 15, 2011,http://www.scu.edu/ethics/publications/submitted/whistleblowing.html.
[3] US Department of Labor, "WARN Fact Sheet," accessed March 15, 2011,http://www.doleta.gov/programs/factsht/warn.htm.
[4] Teneros Corporation, "Social Sentry Lets Employers Track Their Workers across the Internet," accessed March 17, 2011,http://www.readwriteweb.com/archives/social_sentry_track_employees_across_the_web.php.
[5] People Management, "Employers Should Have Monitoring Policy for Social Networks," accessed March 17, 2011,http://www.peoplemanagement.co.uk/pm/articles/2011/02/employers-should-have-monitoring-policy-for-social-networks.htm.
[6] Rodney Ho, "Chadd Scott Said He Was Fired for Tweets about Delta," Access Atlanta (blog), accessed March 16, 2011, http://blogs.ajc.com/radio-tv-talk/2011/03/15/680the-fans-chadd-scott-said-he-was-fired-for-tweets-about-delta-airlines/?cxntlid=thbz_hm.
[7] US Equal Employment Opportunity Commission, "The ADA, Your Responsibilities as an Employer," accessed August 1, 2011, http://www.eeoc.gov/facts/ada17.html.
[8] Jackson lewis, "Employees' ADA Claims on Prescription-Drug-Use Dismissals Rejected by Federal Court," December 1, 2010, accessed August 1, 2011,http://www.jacksonlewis.com/resources.php?NewsID=3478.
[9] John Hughes, "You're Fired Doesn't Mean Fired to Four of 10 Air Traffic Controllers,"Bloomberg News, July 24, 2011, accessed August 1, 2011,http://www.bloomberg.com/news/2011-07-25/-you-re-fired-doesn-t-mean-fired-to-four-of-10-air-controllers.html.

10.3 Cases and Problems

CHAPTER SUMMARY

- Performance issues in the workplace are common. Examples of performance issues include constant tardiness, too much time at work handling personal issues, mishandling of proprietary information, family issues, drug and alcohol problems, nonperformance, theft, and conflicts in the workplace.
- Employees choose to leave organizations for internal and external reasons. Some of these may include a mismatch of career goals, conflict, too high expectations, time-management issues, and a mismatch between job and skills.
- HR professionals should develop a set of policies that deal with performance issues in the workplace. The advantage to having such policies is that they can eliminate wrongful termination legal action.
- A mandated issue is usually one that deals with safety or legal issues that go beyond the workplace. An infringement of this type of issue requires immediate attention.
- A single incident may include a misstep of the employee, and the employee should immediately be spoken with about it, to ensure it doesn't happen again.
- A behavior pattern occurs when an employee consistently exhibits a performance issue. This type of issue should be discussed with the employee and actions taken, such as providing more training, to ensure it does not continue. A persistent pattern occurs when an employee consistently exhibits a performance issue and does not improve, despite HR's talking with him or her.
- At some point during the persistent pattern, disciplinary action will likely need to be taken. It is important to develop consistent procedures on how to record and handle disciplinary issues.

- Employee separation occurs in one of three ways. First, the employee resignsfrom the organization. Second, the employee is terminated for performance issues, and third, an employee absconds. Absconds means the employee abandons his or her job without submitting a formal resignation.
- In some cases, a severance package may be offered to the employee upon his or her departure from the organization.
- Rightsizing is a term used when an organization must cut costs through layoffs of employees. Development of criteria for layoffs, communication, and severance package discussion are all parts of this process.
- Employment at will means that an employer can separate from an employee without cause, and vice versa.
- Even though we have employment at will, a wrongful discharge can occur when there are violations of public policy, an employee has a contract with an employer, or an employer does something outside the boundaries of good faith.
- Whistleblowing is when an employee notifies organizations of illegal or unethical activity. Whistleblowers are protected from discharge due to their activity.
- A constructive discharge means the conditions are so poor that the employee has no choice but to leave the organization.
- The Worker Adjustment and Retraining Notification Act (WARN) is a law that requires organizations of one hundred or more employees to notify employees and the community if fifty or more employees are to be laid off.
- A retaliatory discharge is one that occurs if an employer fires or lays off an employee because of a charge the employee filed. For example, if an employee files a workers' compensation claim and then is let go, this could be a retaliatory discharge.
- The privacy of employees is an issue that HR must address. It is prudent to develop policies surrounding what type of monitoring may occur within an organization. For example, some organizations monitor e-mail, computer usage, and even postings on social network sites.
- Drug testing is also a privacy issue, although in many industries requiring safe working conditions, drug testing can be necessary to ensure the safety of all employees.
- A union is a group of workers who decide to work together toward a collective bargaining agreement. This agreement allows workers to negotiate as one, rather than as individuals.
- The Wagner Act, passed in 1935, addresses many issues related to workers' unionization.
- The process of collective bargaining means to negotiate a contract between management and workers. HR is generally part of this process.
- Interest based bargaining occurs when mutual interests are discussed, rather than starting with a list of demands.
- Once an agreement is reached, HR is generally responsible for knowing the agreement and implementing any changes that should occur as a result of the agreement. One such example is understanding the grievance process.

CHAPTER CASE

Who Goes, Who Stays?

The consulting firm you have worked for over the last year is having some financial troubles. The large contracts it once had are slowly going away, and as your organizational struggles to make payroll, it is clear that layoffs must occur. The sales staff has not been meeting the sales goals set for them, resulting in incorrect budgets.

It has been decided that at least three people in the sales department should be laid off. You create a spreadsheet with pertinent sales employee data:

Name	Title	Years with the organizational	Last overall rating on performance evaluation (1–5 scale, 5 being highest)	Last year's sales goal met?
Deb Waters	Sales Manager	1	3	N/A as her position is managerial
Jeff Spirits	Account Manager	5	3	Yes, 1% over
Orlando Chang	Account Manager	3	4	Yes, 10% over goal
Jake Toolmeyer	Account Manager	2	4	No, 2% under goal
Audrey Barnes	Account Manager	5	5	Yes, 15% over goal
Kelly Andrews	Account Manager	1	2	No, 20% under goal
Amir Saied	Account Manager	8	5	Yes, 5% over goal

Name	Title	Years with the organizational	Last overall rating on performance evaluation (1–5 scale, 5 being highest)	Last year's sales goal met?
Winfrey Jones	Account Manager	4	2	No, 10% under goal

1. Making reasonable assumptions, develop criteria for the layoffs in the sales department.
2. Develop a plan as to how layoffs will be communicated with the individual as well as within the organizational.
3. Discuss strategies to motivate those sales employees who stay with the organization.

TEAM ACTIVITIES

1. In a team of three to four people, discuss each of the situations and determine if you think the employee should receive immediate termination or a progressive discipline process, and provide justification for your responses:
    a. The employee stole one pack of office paper, stating he would be using it at home to perform his job.
    b. An employee posted how boring her job is on a Facebook status update. You know she is Facebook friends with several clients.
    c. The employee groped a colleague in the break room.
    d. You saw the employee's résumé posted on LinkedIn, stating she was looking for a new job.
    e. The manager has told you the employee is difficult to work with and not liked by his colleagues.

In teams of three to four, discuss the following situation: Your marketing manager has just told you she plans to dismiss her administrative assistant for nonperformance and needs help designing a severance package. The administrative assistant was with the organization for two-and-a-half years and his current salary is $35,670. What would you suggest he be offered? Discuss and be prepared to share your ideas wh the class.

NOTES:

NOTES:

Chapter 11:
Employee Assessment in Public Organizations

A Tough Conversation

As you wake up this morning, you think about the performance evaluation you will give one of your employees, Sean, later this morning. Sean has been with your organizational for two years, and over the last six months his performance has begun to slide. As the manager, it is your responsibility to talk with him about performance, which you have done on several occasions. However, the performance evaluation will make his nonperformance more formalized. You know that Sean has had some personal troubles that can account for some of the performance issues, but despite this, you really need to get his performance up to par. Your goal in the performance evaluation interview today is to create an improvement plan for Sean, while documenting his nonperformance.

When you arrive at work, you look over the essay rating part of Sean's evaluation. It details two client project deadlines that were missed, as well as the over-budget amounts of the two client projects. It was Sean's responsibility to oversee both aspects of this project. When Sean arrives at your office, you greet him, ask him to take a seat, and begin to discuss the evaluation with him.

"Sean, while you have always been a high performer, these last few months have been lackluster. On two of your projects, you were over budget and late. The client commented on both of these aspects when it filled out the client evaluation. As a result, you can see this is documented in your performance evaluation."

Using defensive nonverbal language, Sean says, "Missing the project deadlines and budget wasn't my fault. Emily said everything was under control, and I trusted her. She is the one who should have a bad performance review."

You say, "Ultimately, as the account director, you are responsible, as outlined in your job description. As you know, it is important to manage the accountability within your team, and in this case, you didn't perform. In fact, in your 360 reviews, several of your colleagues suggested you were not putting in enough time on the projects and seemed distracted."

"I really dislike those 360 reviews. It really is just a popularity contest, anyway," Sean says. "So, am I fired for these two mistakes?" You have worked with people who exhibited this type of defensive behavior before, and you know it is natural for people to feel like they need to defend themselves when having this type of conversation. You decide to move the conversation ahead and focus on future behavior rather than past behavior.

You say, "Sean, you normally add a lot of value to the organization. Although these issues will be documented in your performance evaluation, I believe you can produce high-quality work. As a result, let's work together to develop an improvement plan so you can continue to add value to the organization. The improvement plan addresses project deadlines and budgets, and I think you will find it helpful for your career development."

Sean agrees begrudgingly and you begin to show him the improvement plan document the organizational uses, so you can fill it out together.

When you head home after work, you think about the day's events and about Sean. As you had suspected, he was defensive at first but seemed enthusiastic to work on the improvement plan after you showed him the document. You feel positive that this performance evaluation was a step in the right direction to ensure Sean continues to be a high producer in the organizational, despite these mistakes.

11.1 Performance Evaluation Systems

LEARNING OBJECTIVES

1. Define the reasons for a formal performance evaluation system.
2. Explain the process to develop a performance review system.

A performance evaluation system is a systematic way to examine how well an employee is performing in his or her job. If you notice, the word systematic implies the performance evaluation process should be a planned system that allows feedback to be given in a formal—as opposed to informal—sense. Performance evaluations can also be called performance appraisals, performance assessments, or employee appraisals.

There are four reasons why a systematic performance evaluation system should be implemented. First, the evaluation process should encourage positive performance and behavior. Second, it is a way to satisfy employee curiosity as to how well they are performing in their job. It can also be used as a tool to develop employees. Lastly, it can provide a basis for pay raises, promotions, and legal disciplinary actions.

Designing a Performance Appraisal System

There are a number of things to consider before designing or revising an existing performance appraisal system. Some researchers suggest that the performance appraisal system is perhaps one of the most important parts of the organization,[1] while others suggest that performance appraisal systems are ultimately flawed,[2] making them worthless. For the purpose of this chapter, let's assume we can create a performance appraisal system that will provide value to the organization and the employee. When designing this process, we should recognize that any process has its limitations, but if we plan it correctly, we can minimize some of these.

The first step in the process is to determine how often performance appraisals should be given. Please keep in mind that managers should constantly be giving feedback to employees, and this process is a more formal way of doing so. Some organizations choose to give performance evaluations once per year, while others give them twice per year, or more. The advantage to giving an evaluation twice per year, of course, is more feedback and opportunity for employee development. The downside is the time it takes for the manager to write the evaluation and discuss it with the employee. If done well, it could take several hours for just one employee. Depending on your organization's structure, you may choose one or the other. For example, if most of your managers have five or ten people to manage (this is called span of control), it might be worthwhile to give performance evaluations more than once per year, since the time cost isn't high. If most of your managers have twenty or more employees, it may not be feasible to perform this process more than once per year. To determine costs of your performance evaluations, see Table 11.1 "Estimating the Costs of Performance Evaluations". Asking for feedback from managers and employees is also a good way to determine how often performance evaluations should be given.

Table 11.1 Estimating the Costs of Performance Evaluations

Narrow Span of Control	
Average span of control	8
Average time to complete one written review	1 hour
Average time to discuss with employee	1 hour
Administrative time to set up meetings with employees	1/2 hour

8 employees × 2 hours per employee + 1/2 hour administrative time to set up times to meet with employees = 16.5 hours of time for one manager to complete all performance reviews

Wider Span of Control	
Average span of control	25
Average time to complete one written review	1 hour
Average time to discuss with employee	1 hour
Administrative time to set up meetings with employees	1 hour

25 employees × 2 hours per employee + 1 hour administrative time to set up times to meet with employees = 51 hours

Once you have the number of hours it takes, you can multiply that by your manager's hourly pay to get an estimated cost to the organization

16 hours × $50 per hour = $85051 hours × $50 per hour = $2550

Should pay increases be tied to performance evaluations? This might be the second consideration before development of a performance evaluation process. There is research that shows employees have a greater acceptance of performance reviews if the review is linked to rewards.[3]

The third consideration should include goal setting. In other words, what goals does the organization hope to achieve with the performance appraisal process?

Once the frequency, rewards, and goals have been determined, it is time to begin to formalize the process. First, we will need to develop the actual forms that will be used to evaluate each job within the organization. Every performance evaluation should be directly tied with that employee's job description.

Determining who should evaluate the performance of the employee is the next decision. It could be their direct manager (most common method), subordinates, customers or clients, self, and/or peers. Table 11.2 "Advantages and Disadvantages of Each Source for Performance Evaluations" shows some of the advantages and disadvantages for each source of information for performance evaluations. Ultimately, using a variety of sources might garner the best results.

A 360-degree performance appraisal method is a way to appraise performance by using several sources to measure the employee's effectiveness. Organizations must be careful when using peer-reviewed information. For example, in the Mathewson v. Aloha Airlines case, peer evaluations were found to be retaliatory against a pilot who had crossed picket lines during the pilot's union strike against a different airline. Management of this process can be time-consuming for the HR professional. That's why there are many software programs available to help administer and assess 360 review feedback. Halogen 360, for example, is used by Princess Cruises and media organizations such as MSNBC.[4] This type of software allows the HR professional to set criteria and easily send links to customers, peers, or managers, who provide the information requested. Then the data are gathered and a report is automatically generated, which an employee can use for quick feedback. Other similar types of software include Carbon360 and Argos.

Performance Appraisal System Errors

Before we begin to develop our performance review process, it is important to note some of the errors that can occur during this process. First, halo effects can occur when the source or the rater feels one aspect of the performance is high and therefore rates all areas high. A mistake in rating can also occur when we compare one employee to another, as opposed to the job description's standards. Sometimes halo effects will occur because the rater is uncomfortable rating someone low on a performance assessment item. Of course, when this occurs, it makes the performance evaluation less valuable for employee development. Proper training on how to manage a performance appraisal interview is a good way to avoid this.

Validity issues are the extent to which the tool measures the relevant aspects of performance. The aspects of performance should be based on the key skills and responsibilities of the job, and these should be reviewed often to make sure they are still applicable to the job analysis and description.

Reliability refers to how consistent the same measuring tool works throughout the organization (or job title). When we look at reliability in performance appraisals, we ask ourselves if two raters were to rate an employee, how close would the ratings be? If the ratings would be far apart from one another, the method may have reliability issues. To prevent this kind of issue, we can make sure that performance standards are written in a way that will make them measurable. For example, instead of "increase sales" as a performance standard, we may want to say, "increase sales by 10 percent from last year." This performance standard is easily measured and allows us to ensure the accuracy of our performance methods.

Acceptability refers to how well members of the organization, manager and employees, accept the performance evaluation tool as a valid measure of performance. For example, let's assume the current measurement tools of Blewett Gravel, Inc. are in place and show validity for each job function. However, managers don't think the tool is useful because they take too much time. As a result, they spend minimal time on the evaluation. This could mean the current process is flawed because of acceptability error.

Another consideration is the specificity, which tells employees the job expectations and how they can be met. If they are not specific enough, the tool is not useful to the employee for development or to the manager to ensure the employee is meeting expectations. Finally, after we have developed our process, we need to create a time line and educate managers and employees on the process. This can be done through formal training and communicated through organizational blogs or e-mails. According to Robert Kent,[5] teaching people how to receive benefit from the feedback they receive can be an important part of the process as well.

Performance Appraisal Legal Considerations

The legality of performance appraisals was questioned in 1973 in Brito v. Zia, in which an employee was terminated based on a subjective performance evaluation. Following this important case, employers began to rethink their performance evaluation system and the legality of it.

The Civil Service Reform Act of 1978 set new standards for performance evaluation. Although these standards related only to public sector employees, the Reform Act began an important trend toward making certain performance evaluations were legal. The Reform Act created the following criteria for performance appraisals in government agencies:

1. All agencies were required to create performance review systems.
2. Appraisal systems would encourage employee participation in establishing the performance standards they will be rated against.
3. The critical elements of the job must be in writing.
4. Employees must be advised of the critical elements when hired.
5. The system must be based exclusively on the actual performance and critical elements of the job. They cannot be based on a curve, for example.
6. They must be conducted and recorded at least once per year.
7. Training must be offered for all persons giving performance evaluations.
8. The appraisals must provide information that can be used for decision making, such as pay decisions and promotion decisions.

Early performance appraisal research can provide us a good example as to why we should be concerned with the legality of the performance appraisal process. Holley and Field[6] analyzed sixty-six legal cases that involved discrimination and performance evaluation. Of the cases, defendants won thirty-five of the cases. The authors of the study determined that the cases that were won by the defendant had similar characteristics:

1. Appraisers were given written instructions on how to complete the appraisal for employees.
2. Job analysis was used to develop the performance measures of the evaluation.
3. The focus of the appraisal was actual behaviors instead of personality traits.
4. Upper management reviewed the ratings before the performance appraisal interview was conducted.
5. This tells us that the following considerations should be met when developing our performance appraisal process:
6. Performance standards should be developed using the job analysis and should change as the job changes.
7. Provide the employees with a copy of the evaluation when they begin working for the organization, and even consider having the employees sign off, saying they have received it.
8. All raters and appraisers should be trained.
9. When rating, examples of observable behavior (rather than personality characteristics) should be given.
10. A formal process should be developed in the event an employee disagrees with a performance review.

Now that we have discussed some of the pitfalls of performance appraisals, we can begin to discuss how to develop the process of performance evaluations.

Table 11.2 Advantages and Disadvantages of Each Source for Performance Evaluations

Source	Advantages	Disadvantages
Manager/Supervisor	Usually has extensive knowledge of the employee's performance and abilities	Bias
	Favoritism	
Self	Self-analysis can help with employee growth	In the employee's interest to inflate his or her own ratings
Peer	Works well when the supervisor doesn't always directly observe the employee	Relationships can create bias in the review
	Can bring a different perspective, since peers know the job well	If evaluations are tied to pay, this can put both the employee and the peer in an awkward situation
	If confidential, may create mistrust within the organization	
Customer/Client	Customers often have the best view of employee behavior	Can be expensive to obtain this feedback
	Can enhance long-term relationships with the customer by asking for feedback	Possible bias

Source	Advantages	Disadvantages
	Data garnered can include how well the manager treats employees	Possible retaliation if results are not favorable
	Can determine if employees feel there is favoritism within their department	
	Subordinates may not understand the "big picture" and rate low as a result	Rating inflation
	Can be used as a self-development tool for managers	
Subordinate	If nothing changes despite the evaluation, could create motivational issues among employees	If confidential, may create mistrust within the organization

HUMAN RESOURCE RECALL

What are the steps we should take when developing a performance review process?

KEY TAKEAWAYS

- A performance evaluation system is a systematic way to examine how well an employee is performing in his or her job.
- The use of the term systematic implies the process should be planned.
- Depending on which research you read, some believe the performance evaluation system is one of the most important to consider in HRM, but others view it as a flawed process, which makes it less valuable and therefore ineffective.
- The first step in designing a performance appraisal process is to determine how often the appraisals will be given. Consideration of time and effort to administer the evaluation should be a deciding factor.
- Many organizations offer pay increases as part of the system, while some organizations prefer to separate the process. Determine how this will be handled in the next step in the performance appraisal development process.
- Goals of the performance evaluation should be discussed before the process is developed. In other words, what does the organizational hope to gain from this process? Asking managers and employees for their feedback on this is an important part of this consideration.
- After determining how often the evaluations should be given, if pay will be tied to the evaluations and goals, you can now sit down and develop the process. First, determine what forms will be used to administer the process.
- After you have determined what forms will be used (or developed), determine who will be the source for the information. Perhaps managers, peers, or customers would be an option. A 360 review process combines several sources for a more thorough review.
- There are some errors that can occur in the process. These include halo effects or comparing an employee to another as opposed to rating employees only on the objectives. Other errors might include validity, reliability, acceptability, andspecificity.
- Performance evaluations should always be based on the actual job description.
- Our last step in development of this process is to communicate the process and train employees and managers on the process. Also, training on how best to use feedback is the final and perhaps most important step of the process.

EXERCISES

1. Perform an Internet search on 360 review software. Compare at least two types of software and discuss advantages and disadvantages of each.
2. Discuss the advantages and disadvantages of each type of performance evaluation source.

---

[1] J. Lawrie, "Prepare for a Performance Appraisal," Personnel Journal 69 (April 1990): 132–36.
[2] Marjorie Derven, "The Paradox of Performance Appraisals," Personnel Journal 69 (February 1990): 107–11.
[3] Brendan Bannister and David Balkin, "Performance Evaluation and Compensation Feedback Messages: An Integrated Model," Journal of Occupational Psychology 63 (June 1990): 97–111.
[4] Halogen Software, accessed March 22, 2011, http://www.halogensoftware.com.

[5] Robert Kent, "Why You Should Think Twice about 360 Performance Reviews," ManagerWise, accessed March 22, 2011, http://www.managerwise.com/article.phtml?id=128.
[6] Hubert Field and William Holley, "The Relationship of Performance Appraisal System Characteristics to Verdicts in Selected Employment Discrimination Cases," Academy of Management Journal 25, no. 2 (1982): 392–406.

11.2 Appraisal Methods

LEARNING OBJECTIVE

1. Be able to describe the various appraisal methods.

It probably goes without saying that different industries and jobs need different kinds of appraisal methods. For our purposes, we will discuss some of the main ways to assess performance in a performance evaluation form. Of course, these will change based upon the job specifications for each position within the organizational. In addition to industry-specific and job-specific methods, many organizations will use these methods in combination, as opposed to just one method. There are three main methods of determining performance. The first is the trait method, in which managers look at an employee's specific traits in relation to the job, such as friendliness to the customer. The behavioral method looks at individual actions within a specific job.Comparative methods compare one employee with other employees.Results methods are focused on employee accomplishments, such as whether or not employees met a quota.

Within the categories of performance appraisals, there are two main aspects to appraisal methods. First, the criteria are the aspects the employee is actually being evaluated on, which should be tied directly to the employee's job description. Second, the rating is the type of scale that will be used to rate each criterion in a performance evaluation: for example, scales of 1–5, essay ratings, or yes/no ratings. Tied to the rating and criteria is the weighting each item will be given. For example, if "communication" and "interaction with client" are two criteria, the interaction with the client may be weighted more than communication, depending on the job type. We will discuss the types of criteria and rating methods next.

Graphic Rating Scale

The graphic rating scale, a behavioral method, is perhaps the most popular choice for performance evaluations. This type of evaluation lists traits required for the job and asks the source to rate the individual on each attribute. A discrete scale is one that shows a number of different points. The ratings can include a scale of 1–10; excellent, average, or poor; or meets, exceeds, or doesn't meet expectations, for example. Acontinuous scale shows a scale and the manager puts a mark on the continuum scale that best represents the employee's performance. For example:

Poor	—	—	—	—	—	—	—	—	Excellent

The disadvantage of this type of scale is the subjectivity that can occur. This type of scale focuses on behavioral traits and is not specific enough to some jobs. Development of specific criteria can save an organization in legal costs. For example, in Thomas v. IBM, IBM was able to successfully defend accusations of age discrimination because of the objective criteria the employee (Thomas) had been rated on.

Many organizations use a graphic rating scale in conjunction with other appraisal methods to further solidify the tool's validity. For example, some organizations use amixed standard scale, which is similar to a graphic rating scale. This scale includes a series of mixed statements representing excellent, average, and poor performance, and the manager is asked to rate a "+" (performance is better than stated), "0" (performance is at stated level), or "−" (performance is below stated level). Mixed standard statements might include the following:

- The employee gets along with most coworkers and has had only a few interpersonal issues.
- This employee takes initiative.
- The employee consistently turns in below-average work.
- The employee always meets established deadlines.

Essay Appraisal

In an essay appraisal, the source answers a series of questions about the employee's performance in essay form. This can be a trait method and/or a behavioral method, depending on how the manager writes the essay. These statements may include strengths and weaknesses about the employee or statements about past performance. They can also include specific examples of past performance. The disadvantage of this type of method (when not combined with other rating systems) is that the manager's writing ability can contribute to the effectiveness of the evaluation. Also, managers may write less or more, which means less consistency between performance appraisals by various managers.

Checklist Scale

A checklist method for performance evaluations lessens the subjectivity, although subjectivity will still be present in this type of rating system. With a checklist scale, a series of questions is asked and the manager simply responds yes or no to the questions, which can fall into either the behavioral or the trait method, or both. Another variation to this scale is a check mark in the criteria the employee meets, and a blank in the areas the employee does not meet. The challenge with this format is that it doesn't allow more detailed answers and analysis of the performance criteria, unless combined with another method, such as essay ratings.

Critical Incident Appraisals

This method of appraisal, while more time-consuming for the manager, can be effective at providing specific examples of behavior. With a critical incident appraisal, the manager records examples of the employee's effective and ineffective behavior during the time period between evaluations, which is in the behavioral category. When it is time for the employee to be reviewed, the manager will pull out this file and formally record the incidents that occurred over the time period. The disadvantage of this method is the tendency to record only negative incidents instead of postive ones. However, this method can work well if the manager has the proper training to record incidents (perhaps by keeping a weekly diary) in a fair manner. This approach can also work well when specific jobs vary greatly from week to week, unlike, for example, a factory worker who routinely performs the same weekly tasks.

Work Standards Approach

For certain jobs in which productivity is most important, awork standards approach could be the more effective way of evaluating employees. With this results-focused approach, a minimum level is set and the employee's performance evaluation is based on this level. For example, if a sales person does not meet a quota of $1 million, this would be recorded as nonperforming. The downside is that this method does not allow for reasonable deviations. For example, if the quota isn't made, perhaps the employee just had a bad month but normally performs well. This approach works best in long-term situations, in which a reasonable measure of performance can be over a certain period of time. This method is also used in manufacuring situations where production is extremely important. For example, in an automotive assembly line, the focus is on how many cars are built in a specified period, and therefore, employee performance is measured this way, too. Since this approach is centered on production, it doesn't allow for rating of other factors, such as ability to work on a team or communication skills, which can be an important part of the job, too.

Ranking Methods

In a ranking method system (also called stack ranking), employees in a particular department are ranked based on their value to the manager or supervisor. This system is a comparative method for performance evaluations.The manager will have a list of all employees and will first choose the most valuable employee and put that name at the top. Then he or she will choose the least valuable employee and put that name at the bottom of the list. With the remaining employees, this process would be repeated. Obviously, there is room for bias with this method, and it may not work well in a larger organization, where managers may not interact with each employee on a day-to-day basis.

To make this type of evaluation most valuable (and legal), each supervisor should use the same criteria to rank each individual. Otherwise, if criteria are not clearly developed, validity and halo effects could be present. The Roper v. Exxon Corp case illustrates the need for clear guidelines when using a ranking system. At Exxon, the legal department attorneys were annually evaluated and then ranked based on input from attorneys, supervisors, and clients. Based on the feedback, each attorney for Exxon was ranked based on their relative contribution and performance. Each attorney was given a group percentile rank (i.e., 99 percent was the best-performing attorney). When Roper was in the bottom 10 percent for three years and was informed of his separation with the organizational, he filed an age discrimination lawsuit. The courts found no correlation between age and the lowest-ranking individuals, and because Exxon had a set of established ranking criteria, they won the case._[1]

Another consideration is the effect on employee morale should the rankings be made public. If they are not made public, morale issues may still exist, as the perception might be that management has "secret" documents.

ORGANIZATIONAL FOCUS

Critics have long said that a forced ranking system can be detrimental to morale; it focuses too much on individual performance as opposed to team performance. Some say a forced ranking system promotes too much competition in the workplace. However, many Organizational organizations use this system and have found it works for their culture. General Electric (GE) used perhaps one of the most well-known forced ranking systems. In this system, every year managers placed their employees into one of three categories: "A" employees are the top 20 percent, "B" employees are the middle 70 percent, and "C" performers are the bottom 10 percent. In GE's system, the bottom 10 percent are usually either let go or put on a performance plan. The top 20 percent are given more responsibility and perhaps even promoted. However, even GE has reinvented this stringent forced ranking system. In 2006, it changed the system to remove references to the 20/70/10 split, and GE now presents the curve as a guideline. This gives more freedom for managers to distribute employees in a less stringent manner._[2]

The advantages of a forced ranking system include that it creates a high-performance work culture and establishes well-defined consequences for not meeting performance standards. In recent research, a forced ranking system seems to correlate well with return on investment to shareholders. For example, the study[3] shows that organizations who use individual criteria (as opposed to overall performance) to measure performance outperform those who measure performance based on overall organizational success. To make a ranking system work, it is key to ensure managers have a firm grasp on the criteria on which employees will be ranked. Organizations using forced rankings without set criteria open themselves to lawsuits, because it would appear the rankings happen based on favoritism rather than quantifiable performance data. For example, Ford in the past used forced ranking systems but eliminated the system after settling class action lawsuits that claimed discrimination._[4] Conoco also has settled lawsuits over its forced ranking systems, as domestic employees claimed the system favored foreign workers._[5] To avoid these issues, the best way to develop and maintain a forced ranking system is to provide each employee with specific and measurable objectives, and also provide management training so the system is executed in a fair, quantifiable manner.

In a forced distribution system, like the one used by GE, employees are ranked in groups based on high performers, average performers, and nonperformers. The trouble with this system is that it does not consider that all employees could be in the top two categories, high or average performers, and requires that some employees be put in the nonperforming category.

In a paired comparison system, the manager must compare every employee with every other employee within the department or work group. Each employee is compared with another, and out of the two, the higher performer is given a score of 1. Once all the pairs are compared, the scores are added. This method takes a lot of time and, again, must have specific criteria attached to it when comparing employees.

HUMAN RESOURCE RECALL

How can you make sure the performance appraisal ties into a specific job description?

Management by Objectives (MBO)

Management by objectives (MBOs) is a concept developed by Peter Drucker in his 1954 book The Practice of Management._[6] This method is results oriented and similar to the work standards approach, with a few differences. First, the manager and employee sit down together and develop objectives for the time period. Then when it is time for the performance evaluation, the manager and employee sit down to review the goals that were set and determine whether they were met. The advantage of this is the open communication between the manager and the employee. The employee also has "buy-in" since he or she helped set the goals, and the evaluation can be used as a method for further skill development. This method is best applied for positions that are not routine and require a higher level of thinking to perform the job. To be efficient at MBOs, the managers and employee should be able to write strong objectives. To write objectives, they should be SMART:_[7]

1. *Specific.* There should be one key result for each MBO. What is the result that should be achieved?
2. *Measurable.* At the end of the time period, it should be clear if the goal was met or not. Usually a number can be attached to an objective to make it measurable, for example "sell $1,000,000 of new public organization in the third quarter."
3. *Attainable.* The objective should not be impossible to attain. It should be challenging, but not impossible.
4. *Result oriented.* The objective should be tied to the organizational's mission and values. Once the objective is made, it should make a difference in the organization as a whole.
5. *Time limited.* The objective should have a reasonable time to be accomplished, but not too much time.

SETTING MBOS WITH EMPLOYEES

To make MBOs an effective performance evaluation tool, it is a good idea to train managers and determine which job positions could benefit most from this type of method. You may find that for some more routine positions, such as administrative assistants, another method could work better.

Behaviorally Anchored Rating Scale (BARS)

A BARS method first determines the main performance dimensions of the job, for example, interpersonal relationships. Then the tool utilizes narrative information, such as from a critical incidents file, and assigns quantified ranks to each expected behavior. In this system, there is a specific narrative outlining what exemplifies a "good" and "poor" behavior for each category. The advantage of this type of system is that it focuses on the desired behaviors that are important to complete a task or perform a specific job. This method combines a graphic rating scale with a critical incidents system. The US Army Research Institute_[8] developed a BARS scale to measure the abilities of tactical thinking skills for combat leaders.

HOW WOULD YOU HANDLE THIS?

Playing Favorites

You were just promoted to manager of a high-end retail store. As you are sorting through your responsibilities, you receive an e-mail from HR outlining the process for performance evaluations. You are also notified that you must give two performance evaluations within the next two weeks. This concerns you, because you don't know any of the employees and their abilities yet. You aren't sure if you should base their performance on what you see in a short time period or if you should ask other employees for their thoughts on their peers' performance. As you go through the files on the computer, you find a critical incident file left from the previous manager, and you think this might help. As you look through it, it is obvious the past manager had "favorite" employees and you aren't sure if you should base the evaluations on this information. How would you handle this?
How Would You Handle This?

Table 11.3 Advantages and Disadvantages of Each Performance Appraisal Method

<table>
<tr><th>Type of Performance Appraisal Method</th><th>Advantages</th><th>Disadvantages</th></tr>
<tr><td rowspan="2">Graphic Rating Scale</td><td>Inexpensive to develop</td><td>Subjectivity</td></tr>
<tr><td>Easily understood by employees and managers</td><td>Can be difficult to use in making compensation and promotion decisions</td></tr>
<tr><td rowspan="3">Essay</td><td rowspan="3">Can easily provide feedback on the positive abilities of the employee</td><td>Subjectivity</td></tr>
<tr><td>Writing ability of reviewer impacts validity</td></tr>
<tr><td>Time consuming (if not combined with other methods)</td></tr>
<tr><td>Checklist scale</td><td>Measurable traits can point out specific behavioral expectations</td><td>Does not allow for detailed answers or explanations (unless combined with another method)</td></tr>
<tr><td rowspan="2">Critical Incidents</td><td>Provides specific examples</td><td rowspan="2">Tendency to report negative incidents</td></tr>
<tr><td>Time consuming for manager</td></tr>
<tr><td>Work Standards Approach</td><td>Ability to measure specific components of the job</td><td>Does not allow for deviations</td></tr>
<tr><td rowspan="3">Ranking</td><td>Can create a high-performance work culture</td><td rowspan="3">Possible bias</td></tr>
<tr><td>Validity depends on the amount of interaction between employees and manager</td></tr>
<tr><td>Can negatively affect teamwork</td></tr>
<tr><td rowspan="2">MBOs</td><td>Open communication</td><td rowspan="2">Many only work for some types of job titles</td></tr>
<tr><td>Employee may have more "buy-in"</td></tr>
<tr><td rowspan="3">BARS</td><td>Focus is on desired behaviors</td><td rowspan="3">Time consuming to set up</td></tr>
<tr><td>Scale is for each specific job</td></tr>
<tr><td>Desired behaviors are clearly outlined</td></tr>
<tr><td colspan="3">No one performance appraisal is best, so most organizations use a variety of methods to ensure the best results.</td></tr>
</table>

KEY TAKEAWAYS

- When developing performance appraisal criteria, it is important to remember the criteria should be job specific and industry specific.
- The performance appraisal criteria should be based on the job specifications of each specific job. General performance criteria are not an effective way to evaluate an employee.
- The rating is the scale that will be used to evaluate each criteria item. There are a number of different rating methods, including scales of 1–5, yes or no questions, and essay.
- In a graphic rating performance evaluation, employees are rated on certain desirable attributes. A variety of rating scales can be used with this method. The disadvantage is possible subjectivity.
- An essay performance evaluation will ask the manager to provide commentary on specific aspects of the employee's job performance.
- A checklist utilizes a yes or no rating selection, and the criteria are focused on components of the employee's job.
- Some managers keep a critical incidents file. These incidents serve as specific examples to be written about in a performance appraisal. The downside is the tendency to record only negative incidents and the time it can take to record this.
- The work standards performance appraisal approach looks at minimum standards of productivity and rates the employee performance based on minimum expectations. This method is often used for sales forces or manufacturing settings where productivity is an important aspect.
- In a ranking performance evaluation system, the manager ranks each employee from most valuable to least valuable. This can create morale issues within the workplace.
- An MBO or management by objectives system is where the manager and employee sit down together, determine objectives, then after a period of time, the manager assesses whether those objectives have been met. This can create great development opportunities for the employee and a good working relationship between the employee and manager.
- An MBO's objectives should be SMART: specific, measurable, attainable, results oriented, and time limited.
- A BARS approach uses a rating scale but provides specific narratives on what constitutes good or poor performance.

EXERCISE

1. Review each of the appraisal methods and discuss which one you might use for the following types of jobs, and discuss your choices.

a. Administrative Assistant
b. Chief Executive Officer
c. Human Resource Manager
d. Retail Store Assistant Manager

---

[1] Richard Grote, Forced Ranking: Making Performance Management Work (Boston: Harvard Public organization School Press, 2005).
[2] "The Struggle to Measure Performance," Public organizationWeek, January 9, 2006, accessed August 15, 2011, http://www.publicorganizationweek.com/magazine/content/06_02/b3966060.htm.
[3] Lisa Sprenkel, "Forced Ranking: A Good Thing for Public organization?" Workforce Management, n.d., accessed August 15, 2011, http://homepages.uwp.edu/crooker/790-iep-pm/Articles/meth-fd-workforce.pdf.
[4] Mark Lowery, "Forcing the Issue," Human Resource Executive Online, n.d., accessed August 15, 2011, http://www.hrexecutive.com/HRE/story.jsp?storyId=4222111&query=ranks.
[5] Mark Lowery, "Forcing the Issue," Human Resource Executive Online, n.d., accessed August 15, 2011, http://hre.lrp.com/HRE/story.jsp?query=ranking&storyId=4222111.
[6] Peter Drucker, The Practice of Management (New York: Harper, 2006).
[7] George T. Doran, "There's a S.M.A.R.T. Way to Write Management's Goals and Objectives,"Management Review 70, no. 11 (1981): 35.
[8] Jennifer Phillips, Jennifer Shafter, Karol Ross, Donald Cox, and Scott Shadrick, Behaviorally Anchored Rating Scales for the Assessment of Tactical Thinking Mental Models (Research Report 1854), June 2006, US Army Research Institute for the Behavioral and Social Sciences, accessed August 15, 2011, http://www.hqda.army.mil/ari/pdf/RR1854.pdf.

11.3 Completing and Conducting the Appraisal

LEARNING OBJECTIVES

1. Be able to discuss best practices in performance review planning.
2. Be able to write an improvement plan for an employee.

So far, we have discussed the necessity of providing formal feedback to employees through a systematic performance evaluation system. We have stressed the importance of making sure the HR professional knows how often performance evaluations should be given and if they are tied to pay increases.

The next step is to make sure you know the goals of the performance evaluation; for example, is the goal to improve performance and also identify people for succession planning? You will then determine the source for the performance evaluation data, and then create criteria and rating scales that relate directly to the employee's job description. Once this is done, the successful functioning of the performance evaluation system largely depends on the HR professional to implement and communicate the system to managers and employees. This will be the primary focus of our next section.

Best Practices in Performance Appraisals

Figure 11.6 Best Practices in Performance Appraisal Systems

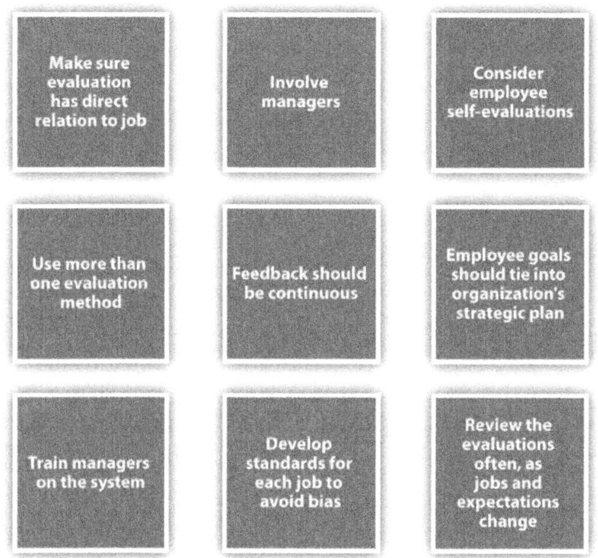

The most important things to remember when developing a performance evaluation system include the following:

1. Make sure the evaluation has a direct relationship to the job. Consider developing specific criteria for each job, based on the individual job specifications and description.
2. Involve managers when developing the process. Garner their feedback to obtain "buy-in" for the process.
3. Consider involving the employee in the process by asking the employee to fill out a self-evaluation.
4. Use a variety of methods to rate and evaluate the employee.
5. Avoid bias by standardizing performance evaluations systems for each job.
6. Give feedback on performance throughout the year, not just during performance review times.
7. Make sure the goals of the performance evaluation tie into the organizational and department goals.
8. Ensure the performance appraisal criteria also tie into the goals of the organization, for a strategic HRM approach.
9. Review the evaluation for each job title often, since jobs and expectations change.

As you can see from Figure 11.7 "Performance Review System", the performance appraisal aspect is just one part of the total process. We can call this a performance review system. The first step of the process is goal setting with the employee. This could mean showing the employee his or her performance appraisal criteria or sitting down with the employee to develop MBOs. The basic idea here is that the employee should know the expectations and how his or her job performance will be rated.

Figure 11.7 Performance Review System

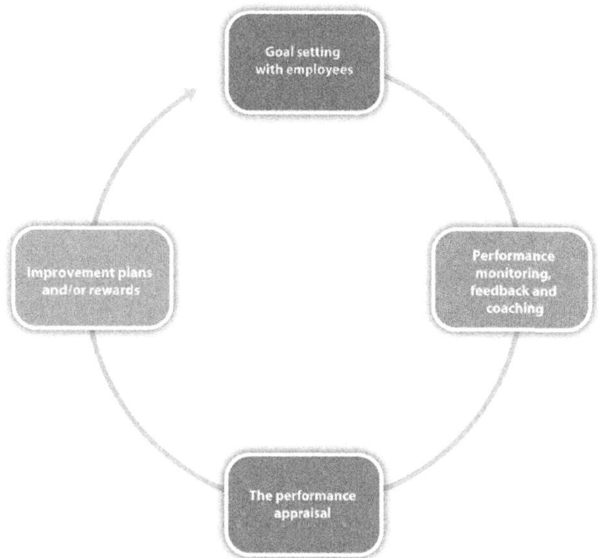

Constant monitoring, feedback, and coaching are the next step. Ensuring the employee knows what he or she is doing well and is not doing well in a more informal manner will allow for a more productive employee.

Next, of course, is the formal performance evaluation process. Choosing the criteria, rating scale, and source of the evaluation are steps we have already discussed. The next step is to work with the employee to develop improvement plans (if necessary) and offer any rewards as a result of excellent performance. The process then begins again, setting new goals with the employee.

Training Managers and Employees

As HR professionals, we know the importance of performance evaluation systems in developing employees, but this may not always be apparent to the managers we work with on a daily basis. It is our job to educate managers and employees on the standards for completing performance evaluation forms as well as train them on how to complete the necessary documents (criteria and ratings), how to develop improvement plans when necessary, and how to deliver the performance appraisal interview.

EMPLOYEE FEEDBACK

First, after you have developed the new performance appraisal system (or adjusted an old one), consider offering training on how to effectively use it. The training, if required, can save time later and make the process more valuable. What we want to avoid is making it seem as if the performance appraisal process is "just one more thing" for managers to do. Show the value of the system in your training or, better yet, involve managers in developing the process to begin with.

Set standards should be developed for managers filling out the performance ratings and criteria. The advantage of this is accuracy of data and limiting possible bias. Consider these "ground rules" to ensure that information is similar no matter which manager is writing the evaluation:

1. Use only factual information and avoid opinion or perception.
2. For each section, comments should be at least two sentences in length, and examples of employee behavior should be provided.
3. Reviews must be complete and shared with the employee before the deadline.
4. Make messages clear and direct.
5. Focus on observable behaviors.

Once your managers are trained, understand how to fill out the forms, and are comfortable with the ground rules associated with the process, we can coach them on how to prepare for performance evaluations. For example, here are the steps you may want to discuss with your managers who provide performance evaluations:

1. Review the employee's last performance evaluation. Note goals from the previous evaluation period.
2. Review the employee's file and speak with other managers who interface with this person. In other words, gather data about performance.
3. Fill out the necessary forms for this employee's appraisal. Note which areas you want to address in the appraisal interview with the employee.
4. If your organization bases pay increases on the performance evaluation, know the pay increase you are able to offer the employee.
5. Write any improvement plans as necessary.
6. Schedule a time and date with the employee.

Most people feel nervous about giving and receiving performance evaluations. One way to limit this is to show the employee the written evaluation before the interview, so the employee knows what to expect. To keep it a two-way conversation, many organizations have the employee fill out the same evaluation, and answers from the employee and manager are compared and discussed in the interview. When the manager meets with the employee to discuss the performance evaluation, the manager should be clear, direct, and to the point about positives and weaknesses. The manager should also discuss goals for the upcoming period, as well as any pay increases or improvement plans as a result of the evaluation. The manager should also be prepared for questions, concerns, and reasons for an employee's not being able to meet performance standards.

Improvement plans should not be punitive, but the goal of an improvement plan should be to help the employee succeed. Coaching and development should occur throughout the employee's tenure, and he or she should know before the performance evaluation whether expectations are not being met. This way, the introduction of an improvement plan is not a surprise. There are six main components to an employee improvement plan:

1. Define the problem.
2. Discuss the behaviors that should be modified, based on the problem.
3. List specific strategies to modify the behavior.
4. Develop long- and short-term goals.
5. Define a reasonable time line for improvements.
6. Schedule "check-in" dates to discuss the improvement plan.

An employee improvement plan works best if it is written with the employee, to obtain maximum buy-in. Once you have developed the process and your managers are comfortable with it, the process must be managed.

Organizing the Performance Appraisal Process

While it will be up to the individual manager to give performance appraisals to employees, as an HR professional, it will be up to you to develop the process (which we have already discussed) and to manage the process. Here are some things to consider to effectively manage the process:

1. Provide each manager with a job description for each employee. The job description should highlight the expectations of each job title and provide a sound basis for review.
2. Provide each manager with necessary documents, such as the criteria and rating sheets for each job description.
3. Give the manager instructions and ground rules for filling out the documents.
4. Work with the manager on pay increases for each employee, if your organization has decided to tie performance evaluations with pay increases.
5. Provide coaching assistance on objectives development and improvement plans, if necessary.
6. Give time lines to the manager for each performance review he or she is responsible for writing.

Most HR professionals will keep a spreadsheet or other document that lists all employees, their manager, and time lines for completion of performance evaluations. This makes it easier to keep track of when performance evaluations should be given.

Of course, the above process assumes the organization is not using software to manage performance evaluations. Numerous types of software are available that allow the HR professional to manage key job responsibilities and goals for every employee in the organization. This software tracks progress on those goals and allows the manager to enter notes (critical incidents files) online. The software can track 360 reviews and send e-mail reminders when it is time for an employee or manager to complete evaluations. This type of software can allow for a smoother, more streamlined process. Of course, as with any new system, it can be time-consuming to set up and train managers and employees on how to use the system. However, many organizations find the initial time to set up software or web-based performance evaluation systems well worth the easier recording and tracking of performance goals.

No matter how the system is managed, it must be managed and continually developed to meet the ultimate goal—continuing development of employees.

Performance Appraisal Interviews

Once a good understanding of the process is developed, it is time to think about the actual meeting with the employee. A performance review process could be intricately detailed and organized, but if the meeting with the employee doesn't go well, the overall strategic objective of performance reviews may not be met. In Norman R. F. Maier's famous book The Appraisal Interview, he addressed three types of appraisal interview styles. The first is the tell and sell interview. In this type of interview, the manager does most of the talking and passes his or her view to the employee. In thetell and listen type of interview, the manager communicates feedback and then addresses the employee's thoughts about the interview. In the problem-solving interview, the employee and the manager discuss the things that are going well and those that are not going well, which can make for a more productive discussion. To provide the best feedback to the employee, consider the following:

1. Be direct and specific. Use examples to show where the employee has room for improvement and where the employee exceeds expectations, such as, "The expectation is zero accidents, and you have not had any accidents this year."
2. Do not be personal; always compare the performance to the standard.For example, instead of saying, "You are too slow on the production line," say, the "expectations are ten units per hour, and currently you are at eight units."
3. Remember, it is a development opportunity. As a result, encourage the employee to talk. Understand what the employee feels he does well and what he thinks he needs to improve.
4. Thank the employee and avoid criticism. Instead of the interview being a list of things the employee doesn't do well (which may give the feeling of criticizing), thank the employee for what the employee does well, and work on action plans together to fix anything the employee isn't doing well. Think of it as a team effort to get the performance to the standard it needs to be.

The result of a completed performance evaluation usually means there are a variety of ramifications that can occur after evaluating employee performance:

1. The employee now has written, documented feedback on his or her performance.
2. The organization has documented information on low performance, in case the employee needs to be dismissed.
3. The employee has performed well and is eligible for a raise.
4. The employee has performed well and could be promoted.

5. Performance is not up to expectations, so an improvement plan should be put into place.
6. The employee hasn't done well, improvement plans have not worked (the employee has been warned before), and the employee should be dismissed.

In each of these cases, planning in advance of the performance appraisal interview is important, so all information is available to communicate to the employee. Consider Robin, an employee at Blewett Gravel who was told she was doing an excellent job. Robin was happy with the performance appraisal and when asked about promotion opportunities, the manager said none was available. This can devalue a positive review and impact employee motivation. The point, of course, is to use performance evaluations as a development tool, which will positively impact employee motivation.

KEY TAKEAWAYS

- There are many best practices to consider when developing, implementing, and managing a performance appraisal system. First, the appraisal system must always tie into organization goals and the individual employee's job description.
- Involvement of managers in the process can initiate buy-in.
- Consider using self-evaluation tools as a method to create a two-way conversation between the manager and the employee.
- Use a variety of rating methods to ensure a more unbiased result. For example, using peer evaluations in conjunction with self- and manager evaluations can create a clearer picture of employee performance.
- Be aware of bias that can occur with performance appraisal systems.
- Feedback should be given throughout the year, not just at performance appraisal time.
- The goals of a performance evaluation system should tie into the organization's strategic plan, and the goals for employees should tie into the organization's strategic plan as well.
- The process for managing performance evaluations should include goal setting, monitoring and coaching, and doing the formal evaluation process. The evaluation process should involve rewards or improvement plans where necessary. At the end of the evaluation period, new goals should be developed and the process started over again.
- It is the HR professional's job to make sure managers and employees are trained on the performance evaluation process.
- Standards should be developed for filling out employee evaluations, to ensure consistency and avoid bias.
- The HR professional can assist managers by providing best practices information on how to discuss the evaluation with the employee.
- Sometimes when performance is not up to standard, an improvement plan may be necessary. The improvement plan identifies the problem, the expected behavior, and the strategies needed to meet the expected behavior. The improvement plan should also address goals, time lines to meet the goals, and check-in dates for status on the goals.
- It is the job of the HR professional to organize the process for the organization. HR should provide the manager with training, necessary documents (such as criteria and job descriptions), instructions, pay increase information, and coaching, should the manager have to develop improvement plans.
- Some HR professionals organize the performance evaluation information in an Excel spreadsheet that lists all employees, job descriptions, and due dates for performance evaluations.
- There are many types of software programs available to manage the process. This software can manage complicated 360 review processes, self-evaluations, and manager's evaluations. Some software can also provide time line information and even send out e-mail reminders.
- The performance evaluation process should be constantly updated and managed to ensure the results contribute to the success of the organization.
- A variety of ramifications can occur, from the employee's earning a raise to possible dismissal, all of which should be determined ahead of the performance appraisal interview.

EXERCISES

1. What are the important aspects of an improvement plan? Why are these so important?
2. Name and describe three best practices for a performance evaluation system.

11.4 Cases and Problems

CHAPTER SUMMARY

- A performance evaluation system is a systematic way to examine how well an employee is performing in his or her job.
- The use of the term systematic implies the process should be planned.
- Depending on which research you read, some believe the performance evaluation system is one of the most important to consider in HRM, but others view it as a flawed process, which makes it less valuable and therefore ineffective.
- The first step in designing a performance appraisal process is to determine how often the appraisals will be given. Consideration of time and effort to administer the evaluation should be a deciding factor.
- Many organizations offer pay increases as part of the system, while some organizations prefer to separate the process. Determining how this will be handled is the next step in the performance appraisal development process.
- Goals of the performance evaluation should be discussed before the process is developed. In other words, what does the organizational hope to gain from this process? Asking managers and employees for their feedback on this is an important part of this consideration.
- After determining how often the evaluations should be given, and if pay will be tied to the evaluations and goals, you can now sit down and develop the process. First, determine what forms will be used to administer the process.
- After you have determined what forms will be used (or developed), determine who will be the source for the information. Managers, peers, and customers are options. A 360 review process combines several sources for a more thorough review.
- There are some errors that can occur in the process. These include halo effectsor comparing an employee to another as opposed to rating them only on the objectives.
- Performance evaluations should always be based on the actual job description.
- Our last step in the development of this process is to communicate the process and train our employees and managers on the process. Also, training on how best to use feedback is the final and perhaps most important step of the process.
- When developing performance appraisal criteria, it is important to remember the criteria should be job specific and industry specific.
- The performance appraisal criteria should be based on the job specifications of each specific job. General performance criteria are not an effective way to evaluate an employee.
- The rating is the scale that will be used to evaluate each criteria item. There are a number of different rating methods, including scales of 1–5, yes or no questions, and essay.
- In a graphic rating performance evaluation, employees are rated on certain desirable attributes. A variety of rating scales can be used with this method. The disadvantage is possible subjectivity.
- An essay performance evaluation will ask the manager to provide commentary on specific aspects of the employee's job performance.
- A checklist utilizes a yes or no rating selection, and the criteria are focused on components of the employee's job.
- Some managers keep a critical incidents file. These incidents serve as specific examples to be written about in a performance appraisal. The downside is the tendency to record only negative incidents and the time it can take to record this.
- The work standards performance appraisal approach looks at minimum standards of productivity and rates the employee performance based on minimum expectations. This method is often used for sales forces or manufacturing settings where productivity is an important aspect.
- In a ranking performance evaluation system, the manager ranks each employee from most valuable to least valuable. This can create morale issues within the workplace.
- An MBO or management by objectives system is where the manager and employee sit down together, determine objectives, then after a period of time, the manager assesses whether those objectives have been met. This can create great development opportunities for the employee and a good working relationship between the employee and manager.
- An MBO's objectives should be SMART: specific, measurable, attainable, results oriented, and time limited.
- A BARS approach uses a rating scale but provides specific narratives on what constitutes good or poor performance.

- There are many best practices to consider when developing, implementing, and managing a performance appraisal system. First, the appraisal system must always tie into organization goals and the individual employee's job description.
- Involvement of managers in the process can initiate buy-in for the process.
- Consider using self-evaluation tools as a method to create a two-way conversation between the manager and the employee.
- Use a variety of rating methods to ensure a more unbiased result. For example, using peer evaluations in conjunction with self and manager evaluations can create a clearer picture of employee performance.
- Be aware of bias that can occur with performance appraisal systems.
- Feedback should be given throughout the year, not just at performance appraisal time.
- The goals of a performance evaluation system should tie into the organization's strategic plan, and the goals for employees should tie into the organization's strategic plan as well.
- The process for managing performance evaluations should include goal setting, monitoring and coaching, and doing the formal evaluation process. The evaluation process should involve rewards or improvement plans where necessary. At the end of the evaluation period, new goals should be developed and the process started over again.
- It is the HR professional's job to make sure managers and employees are trained on the performance evaluation process.
- Standards should be developed for filling out employee evaluations, to ensure consistency and avoid bias.
- The HR professional can assist managers by providing best practices information on how to discuss the evaluation with the employee.
- Sometimes when performance is not up to standard, an improvement plan may be necessary. The improvement plan identifies the problem, the expected behavior, and the strategies needed to meet the expected behavior. The improvement plan should also address goals, time lines to meet the goals, and check-in dates for status on the goals.
- It is the job of the HR professional to organize the process for the organization. HR should provide the manager with training, necessary documents (such as criteria and job descriptions), instructions, pay increase information, and coaching, should the manager have to develop improvement plans.
- Some HR professionals organize the performance evaluation information in an Excel spreadsheet that lists all employees, job descriptions, and due dates for performance evaluations.
- There are many types of software available to manage the process. This software can manage complicated 360 review processes, self-evaluations, and manager's evaluations. Some software can also provide time line information and even send out e-mail reminders.
- The performance evaluation process should be constantly updated and managed to ensure the results contribute to the success of the organization.

CHAPTER CASE

Revamping the System

It is your first six months at your new job as an HR assistant at Groceries for You, a home delivery grocery service. When you ask the HR director, Chang, about performance evaluations, he just rolls his eyes and tells you to schedule a meeting in his Outlook calendar to discuss them. In the meantime, you gather some data that might be helpful in your discussion with Chang.

<table>
<tr><td>Number of managers</td><td>4</td></tr>
<tr><td>Number of employees</td><td>82</td></tr>
<tr><td rowspan="3">Average span of control</td><td>Delivery—38</td></tr>
<tr><td>Warehouse—24</td></tr>
<tr><td>Marketing/technology—16</td></tr>
<tr><td rowspan="8">Job types</td><td>11—customer service</td></tr>
<tr><td>1—delivery manager</td></tr>
<tr><td>1—warehouse manager</td></tr>
<tr><td>1—marketing and technology manager</td></tr>
<tr><td>38—delivery drivers</td></tr>
<tr><td>24—warehouse workers</td></tr>
<tr><td>1—tech support</td></tr>
<tr><td>5—marketing and website design</td></tr>
</table>

When you meet, Chang is very forward with you about the current process. "Right now, managers groan when they are told they need to complete evaluations. The evaluations are general—we use the same form for all jobs in the organization. It appears that promotion decisions are not based on the evaluations but instead tend to be based on subjective criteria, such as how well the manager likes the individual. We really need to get a handle on this system, but I haven't had the time to do it. I am hoping you can make some recommendations for our system and present them to me and then to the managers during next month's meeting. Can you do this?"

1. Detail each step you will take as you develop a new performance evaluation system.
2. Identify specifics such as source, type of rating system, and criteria plans for each job category. Discuss budget for each performance evaluation. Address how you will obtain management buy-in for the new process.
3. Develop PowerPoint slides for your presentation to management about your proposed process and forms.

TEAM ACTIVITY

1. In a group of three to four, develop a performance evaluation sheet, using at least two methods, for the following job description, and present to the class:

Job Class Specification for:
ACCOUNTANT, City of Seattle
Class Specification Schematic Number: 2000504
Class Summary:
Performs a variety of professional accounting functions and tasks for a city department or utility. Audits, monitors, researches, and recommends revisions to accounting procedures and operations. Performs and coordinates the maintenance and production of accounting reports and records and ensures compliance with established accounting procedures and practices.
Distinguishing Characteristics of the Class:
The accountant class is capable of performing a range of professional accounting functions and tasks within the established guidelines of the department/city and according to generally accepted accounting practices, procedures, and methods. This class is supervised by a higher level accountant or manager and supervises accounting support personnel as required.
Assignments are performed under moderate supervision within established guidelines, generally accepted accounting principles, standards, and methods. Receives direction on special projects or where guidelines and rules are unclear. Knowledge of accounting practices, methods, laws, rules, ordinances, and regulations is required to determine the most appropriate accounting methods and procedures to apply and to ensure appropriate compliance.
Personal contacts are with department employees, other departments, agencies, or the public to provide information, coordinate work activities, and resolve problems.
Examples of Work:

- Analyzes and prepares cash flow forecasts and updates forecasts based on actual revenues and expenditures.
- Prepares financial reports, statements, and schedules.
- Audits and reconciles assigned accounts in the general ledger.
- Monitors and controls accounting activities in the recording of financial transactions, that is, accounts receivables, accounts payables, collections, and fixed assets.
- Verifies and reviews accounting transactions. Makes appropriate corrections, entries, and adjustments to ensure accuracy of reports.
- Researches, analyzes, and prepares journals for financial transactions.
- Analyzes and maintains subsidiary ledgers (i.e., investments). Monitors and maintains investment ledger entries and investment schedules.
- Prepares variance reports required by outside auditors and program summaries explaining variances.
- Coordinates, trains, and monitors the work of accounting support personnel to ensure proper work operations.
- Assists in development and modification of internal accounting control policies, procedures, and practices.
- Assists in special projects such as research and analysis of financial information, long-term debt schedules, investment security reports, and reports for special information requested by departmental personnel.
- Performs other related duties of a comparable level/type as assigned.

Work Environment/Physical Demands:
Work is performed in an office environment.
Minimum Qualifications:
Bachelor's Degree in Accounting (or a combination of education and/or training and/or experience that provides an equivalent background required to perform the work of the class).

NOTES:

NOTES:

Chapter 12: Working with Labor Unions and Employee Relations in Public Organizations

Unhappy Employees Could Equal Unionization

As the HR manager for a two-hundred-person organizational, you tend to have a pretty good sense of employee morale. Recently, you are concerned because it seems that morale is low, because of pay and the increasing health benefit costs to employees. You discuss these concerns with upper-level management, but owing to financial pressures, the organizational is not able to give pay raises this year.

One afternoon, the manager of the marketing department comes to you with this concern, but also with some news. She tells you that she has heard talk of employees unionizing if they do not receive pay raises within the next few months. She expresses that the employees are very unhappy and productivity is suffering as a result. She says that employees have already started the unionization process by contacting the National Labor Relations Board and are in the process of proving 30 percent worker interest in unionization. As you mull over this news, you are concerned because the organization has always had a family atmosphere, and a union might change this. You are also concerned about the financial pressures to the organization should the employees unionize and negotiate higher pay. You know you must take action to see that this doesn't happen. However, you know you and all managers are legally bound by rules relating to unionization, and you need a refresher on what these rules are. You decide to call a meeting first with the CEO and then with managers to discuss strategy and inform them of the legal implications of this process. You feel confident that a resolution can be developed before the unionization happens.

12.1 The Nature of Unions

LEARNING OBJECTIVES

1. Be able to discuss the history of labor unions.
2. Explain some of the reasons for a decline in union membership over the past sixty years.
3. Be able to explain the process of unionization and laws that relate to unionization.

A labor union, or union, is defined as workers banding together to meet common goals, such as better pay, benefits, or promotion rules. In the United States, 11.9 percent of American workers belong to a union, down from 20.1 percent in 1983._[1] In this section, we will discuss the history of unions, reasons for decline in union membership, union labor laws, and the process employees go through to form a union. First, however, we should discuss some of the reasons why people join unions.

People may feel their economic needs are not being met with their current wages and benefits and believe that a union can help them receive better economic prospects. Fairness in the workplace is another reason why people join unions. They may feel that scheduling, vacation time, transfers, and promotions are not given fairly and feel that a union can help eliminate some of the unfairness associated with these processes. Let's discuss some basic information about unions before we discuss the unionization process.

History and Organization of Unions

Trade unions were developed in Europe during the Industrial Revolution, when employees had little skill and thus the entirety of power was shifted to the employer. When this power shifted, many employees were treated unfairly and underpaid. In the United States, unionization increased with the building of railroads in the late 1860s. Wages in the railroad industry were low and the threat of injury or death was high, as was the case in many manufacturing facilities with little or no safety laws and regulations in place. As a result, the Bortherhood of Locomotive Engineers and several other brotherhoods (focused on specific tasks only, such as conductors and brakemen) were formed to protect workers' rights, although many workers were fired because of their membership.

The first local unions in the United States were formed in the eighteenth century, in the form of the National Labor Union (NLU).

The National Labor Union, formed in 1866, paved the way for other labor organizations. The goal of the NLU was to form a national labor federation that could lobby government for labor reforms on behalf of the labor organizations. Its main focus was to limit the workday to eight hours. While the NLU garnered many supporters, it excluded Chinese workers and only made some attempts to defend the rights of African-Americans and female workers. The NLU can be credited with the eight-hour workday, which was passed in 1862. Because of a focus on government reform rather than collective bargaining, many workers joined the Knights of Labor in the 1880s.

The Knights of Labor started as a fraternal organization, and when the NLU dissolved, the Knights grew in popularity as the labor union of choice. The Knights promoted the social and cultural spirit of the worker better than the NLU had. It originally grew as a labor union for coal miners but also covered several other types of industries. The Knights of Labor initiated strikes that were successful in increasing pay and benefits. When this occurred, membership increased. After only a few years, though, membership declined because of unsuccessful strikes, which were a result of a too autocratic structure, lack of organization, and poor management. Disagreements between members within the organization also caused its demise.

The American Federation of Labor (AFL) was formed in 1886, mostly by people who wanted to see a change from the Knights of Labor. The focus was on higher wages and job security. Infighting among union members was minimized, creating a strong organization that still exists today. In the 1930s, the Congress of Industrial Organizations (CIO) was formed as a result of political differences in the AFL. In 1955, the two unions joined together to form the AFL-CIO.

Currently, the AFL-CIO is the largest federation of unions in the United States and is made up of fifty-six national and international unions. The goal of the AFL-CIO isn't to negotiate specific contracts for employees but rather to support the efforts of local unions throughout the country.

Currently in the United States, there are two main national labor unions that oversee several industry-specific local unions. There are also numerous independent national and international unions that are not affiliated with either national union:

1. *AFL-CIO:* local unions include Airline Pilots Association, American Federation of Government Employees, Associated Actors of America, and Federation of Professional Athletes
2. *CTW (Change to Win Federation):* includes the Teamsters, Service Employees International Union, United Farm Workers of America, and United Food and Commercial Workers
3. *Independent unions:* Directors Guild of America, Fraternal Order of Police, Independent Pilots Association, Major League Baseball Players Association

The national union plays an important role in legislative changes, while the local unions focus on collective bargaining agreements and other labor concerns specific to the area. Every local union has a union steward who represents the interests of union members. Normally, union stewards are elected by their peers.

A national union, besides focusing on legislative changes, also does the following:

1. Lobbies in government for worker rights laws
2. Resolves disputes between unions
3. Helps organize national protests
4. Works with allied organizations and sponsors various programs for the support of unions

For example, in 2011, the national Teamsters union organized demonstrations in eleven states to protest the closing of an Ontario, California, parts distribution center. Meanwhile, Teamster Local 495 protested at the Ontario plant.[2]

Current Union Challenges

The labor movement is currently experiencing several challenges, including a decrease in union membership, globalization, and employers' focus on maintaining nonunion status. As mentioned in the opening of this section, the United States has seen a steady decline of union membership since the 1950s. In the 1950s, 36 percent of all workers were unionized,[3] as opposed to just over 11 percent today.

HUMAN RESOURCE RECALL

When you are hired for your first job or your next job, do you think you would prefer to be part of a union or not?

Claude Fischer, a researcher from University of California Berkeley, believes the shift is cultural. His research says the decline is a result of American workers preferring individualism as opposed to collectivism.[4] Other research says the decline of unions is a result of globalization, and the fact that many jobs that used to be unionized in the manufacturing arena have now moved overseas. Other reasoning points to management, and that its unwillingness to work with unions has caused the decline in membership. Others suggest that unions are on the decline because of themselves. Past corruption, negative publicity, and hard-line tactics have made joining a union less favorable.

To fully understand unions, it is important to recognize the global aspect of unions. Statistics on a worldwide scale show unions in all countries declining but still healthy in some countries. For example, in eight of the twenty-seven

European Union member states, more than half the working population is part of a union. In fact, in the most populated countries, unionization rates are still at three times the unionization rate of the United States.[5] Italy has a unionization rate of 30 percent of all workers, while the UK has 29 percent, and Germany has a unionization rate of 27 percent.

In March 2011, Wisconsin governor Scott Walker proposed limiting the collective bargaining rights of state workers to save a flailing budget. Some called this move "union busting" and said this type of act is illegal, as it takes away the basic rights of workers. The governor defended his position by saying there is no other choice, since the state is in a budget crisis. Other states such as Ohio are considering similar measures. Whatever happens, there is a clear shift for unions today.

Globalization is also a challenge in labor organizations today. As more and more goods and services are produced overseas, unions lose not only membership but union values in the stronghold of worker culture. As globalization has increased, unions have continued to demand more governmental control but have been only somewhat successful in these attempts. For example, free trade agreements such as the North American Free Trade Agreement (NAFTA) have made it easier and more lucrative for organizations to manufacture goods overseas. For example, La-Z-Boy and Whirlpool closed production facilities in Dayton and Cleveland, Ohio, and built new factories in Mexico to take advantage of cheaper labor and less stringent environmental standards. Globalization creates options for organizations to produce goods wherever they think is best to produce them. As a result, unions are fighting the globalization trend to try and keep jobs in the United States.

There are a number of reasons why organizations do not want unions in their organizations, which we will discuss in greater detail later. One of the main reasons, however, is increased cost and less management control. As a result, organizations are on a quest to maintain a union-free work environment. In doing so, they try to provide higher wages and benefits so workers do not feel compelled to join a union. Organizations that want to stay union free constantly monitor their retention strategies and policies.

Labor Union Laws

The Railway Labor Act (RLA) of 1926 originally applied to railroads and in 1936 was amended to cover airlines. The act received support from both management and unions. The goal of the act is to ensure no disruption of interstate commerce. The main provisions of the act include alternate dispute resolution, arbitration, and mediation to resolve labor disputes. Any dispute must be resolved in this manner before a strike can happen. The RLA is administered by the National Mediation Board (NMB), a federal agency, and outlines very specific and detailed processes for dispute resolution in these industries.

Figure 12.3 Major Acts Regarding Unions, at a Glance

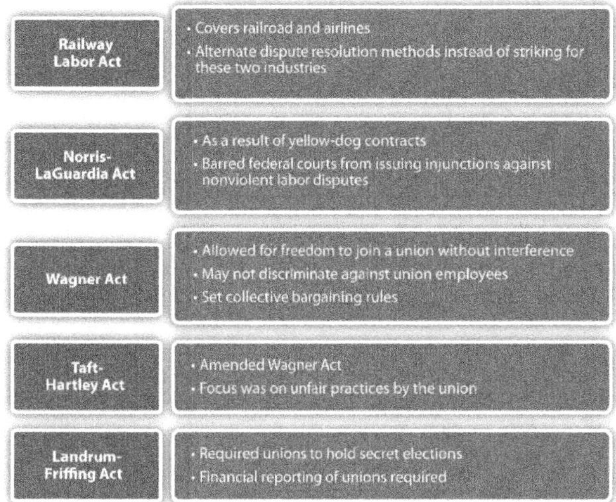

The Norris-LaGuardia Act of 1932 (also known as the anti-injunction bill), barred federal courts from issuing injunctions (a court order that requires a party to do something or refrain from doing something) against nonviolent labor disputes and barred employers from interfering with workers joining a union. The act was a result of common yellow-dog contracts, in which a worker agreed not to join a union before accepting a job. The Norris-LaGuardia Act made yellow-dog contracts unenforceable in courts and established that employees were free to join unions without employer interference.

Figure 12.5 Things That Shouldn't Be Said to Employees during a Unionization Process

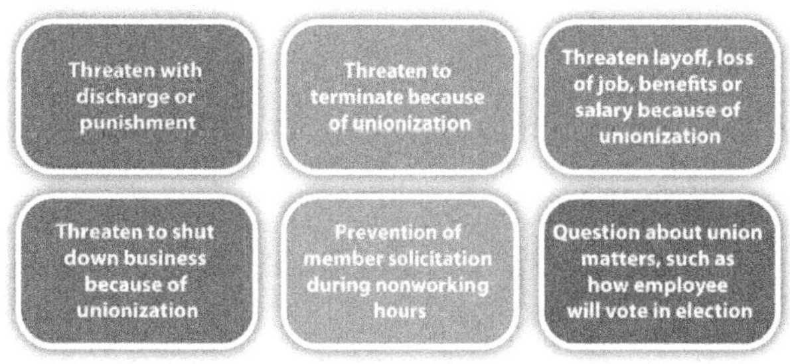

In 1935, the Wagner Act (sometimes called the National Labor Relations Act) was passed, changing the way employers can react to several aspects of unions. The Wagner Act had a few main aspects:

1. Employers must allow freedom of association and organization and cannot interfere with, restrain, or coerce employees who form a union.
2. Employers may not discriminate against employees who form or are part of a union, or those who file charges.
3. An employer must bargain collectively with representation of a union.

The National Labor Relations Board (NLRB) oversees this act, handling any complaints that may arise from the act. For example, in April 2011, the NLRB worked with employees at Ozburn-Hessey Logistics in Tennessee after they had been fired because of their involvement in forming a union. The organizational was also accused of interrogating employees about their union activities and threatened employees with loss of benefits should they form a union. The NLRB utilized their attorney to fight on behalf of the employees, and a federal judge ordered the organizational to rehire the fired employees and also to desist in other antiunion activities._[6]

The Taft-Hartley Act also had major implications for unions. Passed in 1947, Taft-Hartley amended the Wagner Act. The act was introduced because of the upsurge of strikes during this time period. While the Wagner Act addressed unfair labor practices on the part of the organizational, the Taft-Hartley Act focused on unfair acts by the unions. For example, it outlawed strikes that were not authorized by the union, calledwildcat strikes. It also prohibited secondary actions(or secondary boycotts) in which one union goes on strike in sympathy for another union. The act allowed the executive branch of the federal government to disallow a strike should the strike affect national health or security. One of the most famous injunctions was made by President Ronald Reagan in 1981. Air traffic controllers had been off the job for two days despite their no-strike oath, and Reagan ordered all of them (over eleven thousand) discharged because they violated this federal law.

The Landrum Griffin Act, also known as the Labor Management Reporting and Disclosure (LMRDA) Act, was passed in 1959. This act required unions to hold secret elections, required unions to submit their annual financial reports to the U.S. Department of Labor, and created standards governing expulsion of a member from a union. This act was created because of racketeering charges and corruptions charges by unions. In fact, investigations of the Teamsters Union found they were linked to organized crime, and the Teamsters were banned from the AFL-CIO. The goal of this act was to regulate the internal functioning of unions and to combat abuse of union members by union leaders.

The Unionization Process

Figure 12.4 The Unionization Process

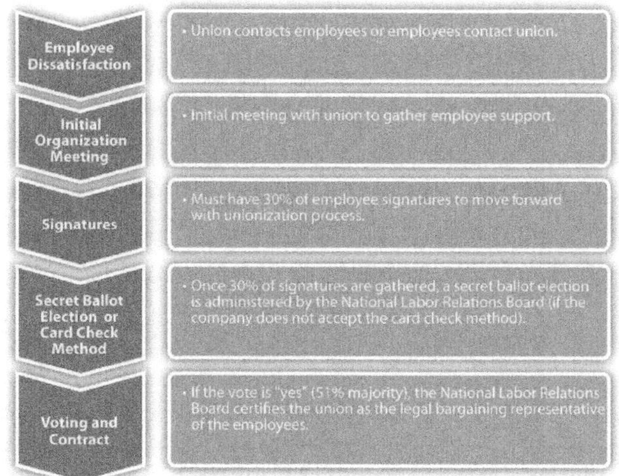

There are one of two ways in which a unionization process can begin. First, the union may contact several employees and discuss the possibility of a union, or employees may contact a union on their own. The union will then help employees gather signatures to show that the employees want to be part of a union. To hold an election, the union must show signatures from over 30 percent of the employees of the organization.

Once the signatures are gathered, the National Labor Relations Board is petitioned to move forward with a secret-ballot election. An alternative to the secret-ballot election is the card check method, in which the union organizer provides the organizational with authorization cards signed by a simple majority (half plus one). The employer can accept the cards as proof that the employees desire a union in their organization. The NLRB then certifies the union as the employees' collective bargaining representative.

If the organization does not accept the card check method as authorization for a union, the second option is via a secret ballot. Before this method is used, a petition must be filed by the NLRB, and an election is usually held two months after the petition is filed. In essence, the employees vote whether to unionize or not, and there must be a simple majority (half plus one). The NLRB is responsible for election logistics and counting of ballots. Observers from all parties can be present during the counting of votes. Once votes are counted, a

decision on unionization occurs, and at that time, the collective bargaining process begins.
Once the NLRB is involved, there are many limits as to what the employer can say or do during the process to prevent unionization of the organization. It is advisable for HR and management to be educated on what can legally and illegally be said during this process. It is illegal to threaten or intimidate employees if they are discussing a union. You cannot threaten job, pay, or benefits loss as a result of forming a union. Figure 12.5 "Things That Shouldn't Be Said to Employees during a Unionization Process" includes information on what should legally be avoided if employees are considering unionization.

Obviously, it is in the best interest of the union to have as many members as possible. Because of this, unions may use many tactics during the organizing process. For example, many unions are also politically involved and support candidates who they feel best represent labor. They provide training to organizers and sometimes even encourage union supporters to apply for jobs in nonunion environments to actively work to unionize other employees when they are hired. This practice is calledunion salting. Unions, especially on the national level, can be involved in organizational campaigns that boycott certain products or organizations because of their labor practices. The United Food and Commercial Workers (UFCW), for example, has a "Wake Up Walmart Campaign" that targets the labor practices of this organization.

Strategies Organizations Use to Avoid Unionization

Most organizations feel the constraints of having a union organization are too great. It affects the cost to the organization and operation efficiency. Collective bargaining at times can put management at odds with its employees and cost more to produce products and services. Ideally, organizations will provide safe working conditions, fair pay, and benefits so the employees do not feel they need to form a union. There are three main phases of unionization:

1. *Phase 1:* Your organization is union free and there is little or no interest in unionizing.
2. *Phase 2:* You learn that some employees are discussing unionization or you learn about specific attempts by the union to recruit employees.
3. *Phase 3:* You receive a petition from the National Labor Relations Board filed by a union requesting a unionization vote.

Because of increased costs and operational efficiency, it is normally in a organizational's best interest to avoid unionization. While in phase 1, it is important to review employee relations programs including pay, benefits, and other compensation. Ensure the compensation plans are fair so employees feel fairly treated and have no reason to seek the representation of a union.

Despite your best efforts, you could hear of unionization in your organization. The goal here is to prevent the union from gaining support to ask for a National Labor Relations Board election. Since only 30 percent of employees need to sign union cards for a vote to take place, this phase to avoid unionization is very important. During this time, HR professionals and managers should respond to the issues the employees have and also develop a specific strategy on how to handle the union vote, should it get that far.

In phase 3, familiarization with all the National Labor Relations Board rules around elections and communications is important. With this information, you can organize meetings to inform managers on these rules. At this time, you will likely want to draw up an antiunion campaign and communicate that to managers, but also make sure it does not violate laws. To this end, develop specific strategies to encourage employees to vote "no" for the union. Some of the arguments that might be used include talking with the employee and mentioning the following:

1. Union dues are costly.
2. Employees could be forced to go on strike.
3. Employees and management may no longer be able to discuss matters informally and individually.
4. Unionization can create more bureaucracy within the organizational.
5. Individual issues may not be discussed.
6. Many decisions within a union, such as vacation time, are based on seniority only.

With unionization in decline, it is likely you may never need to handle a new union in your organization. However, organizations such as Change to Win are in the process of trying to increase union membership. This organization has four affiliated unions, with a goal to strengthen the labor movement. Teamsters, United Food and Commercial Workers, United Farm Workers, and Service Employees International Union are all unions affiliated with this organization.[7] The next few years will be telling as to the fate of unions in today's organizations.

ORGANIZATIONAL FOCUS

Perhaps no organization is better known for its antiunion stance than Walmart. Walmart has over 3,800 stores in the

United States and over 4,800 internationally with $419 billion in sales.[8] Walmart employs more than 2 million associates worldwide.[9] The billions of dollars Walmart earns do not immunize the organizational to trouble. In 2005, the organizational's vice president, Tom Coughlin, was forced to resign after admitting that between $100,000 and $500,000 was spent for undeclared purposes, but it was eventually found that the money was spent to keep the United Food and Commercial Workers union (UFCW) out of Walmart[10](he was found guilty and sentenced to two years of house arrest).

Other claims surrounding union busting are the closing of stores, such as the Walmart Tire and Lube Express in Gatineau, Quebec,[11] when discussions of unionization occurred. Other reports of union busting include the accusation that organizational policy requires store managers to report rumors of unionizing to organizational headquarters. Once the report is made, all labor decisions for that store are handled by the organizational offices instead of the store manager. According to labor unions in the United States, Walmart is willing to work with international labor unions but continues to fiercely oppose unionization in the United States. In one example, after butchers at a Jacksonville, Texas, Walmart voted to unionize, Walmart eliminated all US meat-cutting departments.

A group called OUR Walmart (Organization United for Respect), financed by the United Food and Commercial Workers* (UFCW) union, has stemmed from the accusations of union busting. Walmart spokesperson David Tovar says he sees the group as a Trojan horse assembled by labor organizations to lay the groundwork for full-fledged unionization and seek media attention to fulfill their agenda. While the organization's activities may walk a fine line between legal and illegal union practices under the Taft-Hartley Act, this new group will certainly affect the future of unionization at Walmart in its US stores.
*Note: UFCW was part of the AFL-CIO until 2005 and now is an independent national union.

The Impact of Unions on Organizations

You may wonder why organizations are opposed to unions. As we have mentioned, since union workers do receive higher wages, this can be a negative impact on the organization. Unionization also impacts the ability of managers to make certain decisions and limits their freedom when working with employees. For example, if an employee is constantly late to work, the union contract will specify how to discipline in this situation, resulting in little management freedom to handle this situation on a case-by-case basis. In 2010, for example, the Art Institute of Seattle faculty filed signatures and voted on unionization.[12] Some of the major issues were scheduling issues and office space, not necessarily pay and benefits. While the particular National Labor Relations Board vote was no to unionization, a yes vote could have given less freedom to management in scheduling, since scheduling would be based on collective bargaining contracts. Another concern about unionization for management is the ability to promote workers. A union contract may stipulate certain terms (such as seniority) for promotion, which means the manager has less control over the employees he or she can promote.

KEY TAKEAWAYS

- Union membership in the United States has been slowly declining. Today, union membership consists of about 11.9 percent of the workforce, while in 1983 it consisted of 20 percent of the workforce.
- The reasons for decline are varied, depending on whom you ask. Some say the moving of jobs overseas is the reason for the decline, while others say unions' hard-line tactics put them out of favor.
- Besides declining membership, union challenges today include globalization and organizations' wanting a union-free workplace.
- The United States began its first labor movement in the 1800s. This was a result of low wages, no vacation time, safety issues, and other issues.
- Many labor organizations have disappeared, but the American Federation of Labor (AFL) still exists today, although it merged with the Congress of Industrial Organizations (CIO) and is now known as the AFL-CIO. It is the largest labor union and represents local labor unions in a variety of industries.
- The United States has a low number of union members compared with other countries. Much of Europe, for example, has over 30 percent of their workforce in labor unions, while in some countries as much as 50 percent of the workforce are members of a labor union.
- Legislation has been created over time to support both labor unions and the organizations who have labor unions. The Railway Labor Act applies to airlines and railroads and stipulates that employees may not strike until they have gone through an extensive dispute resolution process. The Norris-LaGuardia Act madeyellow-dog contracts illegal and barred courts from issuing injunctions.

- The Wagner Act was created to protect employees from retaliation should they join a union. The Taft-Hartley Act was developed to protect organizations from unfair labor practices by unions.
- The National Labor Relations Board is the overseeing body for labor unions, and it handles disputes between organizations as well as facilitates the process of new labor unions in the developing stages. Its job is to enforce both the Wagner Act and the Taft-Hartley Act.
- The Landrum Griffin Act was created in 1959 to combat corruption in labor unions during this time period.
- To form a union, the organizer must have signatures from 30 percent of the employees. If this occurs, the National Labor Relations Board will facilitate a card check to determine more than 50 percent of the workforce at that organizational is in agreement with union representation. If the organizational does not accept this, then the NLRB holds secret elections to determine if the employees will be unionized. A collective bargaining agreement is put into place if the vote is yes.
- Organizations prefer to not have unions in their organizations because it affects costs and operational productivity. Organizations will usually try to prevent a union from organizing in their workplace.
- Managers are impacted when a organizational does unionize. For example, management rights are affected, and everything must be guided by the contract instead of management prerogative.

EXERCISES

1. Visit the National Labor Relations Board website. View the "weekly case summary" and discuss it in at least two paragraphs, stating your opinion on this case.
2. Do you agree with unionization within organizations? Why or why not? List the advantages and disadvantages of unions to the employee and the organizational.

---

[1] "Union Members: 2010," Bureau of Labor Statistics, US Department of Labor, news release, January 21, 2011, accessed April 4, 2011, http://www.bls.gov/news.release/pdf/union2.pdf.
[2] "Teamsters Escalate BMW Protests across America," PR Newswire, August 2, 2011, accessed August 15, 2011, http://www.teamster.org/content/teamsters-escalate-bmw-protests-across-america.
[3] Gerald Friedman, "Labor Unions in the United States," Economic History Association, February 2, 2010, accessed April 4, 2011,http://eh.net/encyclopedia/article/friedman.unions.us.
[4] Claude Fischer, , "Why Has Union Membership Declined?" Economist's View, September 11, 2010, accessed April 11, 2011,http://economistsview.typepad.com/economistsview/2010/09/why-has-union-membership-declined.html.
[5] Federation of European Employers, "Trade Unions across Europe," accessed April 4, 2011,http://www.fedee.com/tradeunions.html.
[6] "Federal Judge Orders Employer to Reinstate Three Memphis Warehouse Workers and Stop Threatening Union Supporters While Case Proceeds at NLRB," Office of Public Affairs, National Labor Relations Board, news release, April 7, 2011, accessed April 7, 2011,http://www.nlrb.gov/news/federal-judge-orders-employer-reinstate-three-memphis-warehouse-workers- and-stop-threatening-un.
[7] Change to Win website, accessed April 7, 2011, http://www.changetowin.org.
[8] "Investors," Walmart Organizational, 2011, accessed August 15, 2011,http://investors.walmartstores.com/phoenix.zhtml?c=112761&p=irol-irhome.
[9] "Investors," Walmart Organizational, 2011, accessed August 15, 2011,http://investors.walmartstores.com/phoenix.zhtml?c=112761&p=irol-irhome.
[10] Los AngelesTimes Wire Services, "Wal-Mart Accused of Unfair Labor Practices," accessed September 15, 2011, http://articles.latimes.com/2005/apr/13/public organization/fi-walmart13.
[11] UFCW Canada, "Want a Union? You're Fired," n.d., accessed August 15, 2011,http://www.ufcw.ca/index.php?option=com multicategories&view=article&id=1935&Itemid=98&lang=en.
[12] "Union Push in For-Profit Higher Ed," Inside Higher Ed, May 24, 2010, accessed August 15, 2011, http://www.insidehighered.com/news/2010/05/24/union.

12.2 Collective Bargaining

LEARNING OBJECTIVES

1. Be able to describe the process of collective bargaining.
2. Understand the types of bargaining issues and the rights of management.
3. Discuss some strategies when working with unions.

When employees of an organization vote to unionize, the process for collective bargaining begins. Collective bargaining is the process of negotiations between the organizational and representatives of the union. The goal is for management and the union to reach a contract agreement, which is put into place for a specified period of time. Once this time is up, a new contract is negotiated. In this section, we will discuss the components of the collective bargaining agreement.

The Process of Collective Bargaining

In any bargaining agreement, certain management rights are not negotiable, including the right to manage and operate the public organization, hire, promote, or discharge employees. However, in the negotiated agreement there may be a process outlined by the union for how these processes should work. Management rights also include the ability of the organization to direct the work of the employees and to establish operational policies. As an HR professional sits at the bargaining table, it is important to be strategic in the process and tie the strategic plan with the concessions the organization is willing to make and the concessions the organization will not make.

Another important point in the collective bargaining process is the aspect of union security. Obviously, it is in the union's best interest to collect dues from members and recruit as many new members as possible. In the contract, a checkoff provision may be negotiated. This provision occurs when the employer, on behalf of the union, automatically deducts dues from union members' paychecks. This ensures that a steady stream of dues is paid to the union.

Figure 12.6 Map of Right-to-Work States

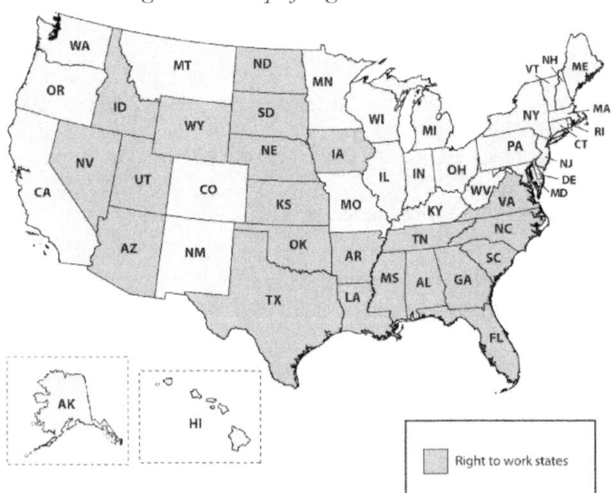

To recruit new members, the union may require something called a union shop. Aunion shop requires a person to join the union within a certain time period of joining the organization. In right-to-work states a union shop may be illegal. Twenty-two states have passed right-to-work laws, as you can see in Figure 12.6 "Map of Right-to-Work States". These laws prohibit a requirement to join a union or pay dues and fees to a union. To get around these laws, agency shops were created. An agency shop is similar to a union shop in that workers do not have to join the union but still must pay union dues. Agency shop union fees are known as agency fees and may be illegal in right-to-work states. A closed shop used to be a mechanism for a steady flow of membership. In this arrangement, a person must be a union member to be hired. This, however, was made illegal under the Taft-Hartley Act. According to a study by CNBC, all twenty-two right-to-work states are in the top twenty-five states for having the best workforces.[1] However, according to the AFL-CIO, the average worker in a right-to-work state makes $5,333 less per year than other workers.[2]

Figure 12.7 Steps in Collective Bargaining

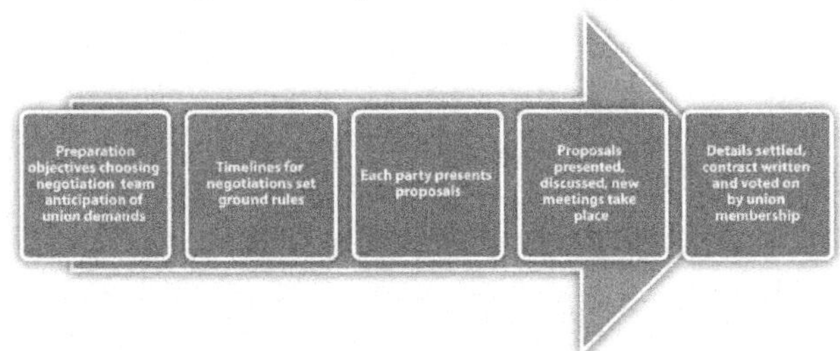

In a collective bargaining process, both parties are legally bound to bargain in good faith. This means they have a mutual obligation to participate actively in the deliberations and indicate a desire to find a basis for agreement. There are three main classification of bargaining topics: mandatory, permissive, and illegal. Wages, health and safety, management rights, work conditions, and benefits fall into themandatory category. Permissive topics are those that are not required but may be brought up during the process. An example might include the requirement of drug testing for candidates or the required tools that must be provided to the employee to perform the job, such as a cellular phone or computer. It is important to note that while management is not required by labor laws to bargain on these issues, refusing to do so could affect employee morale. We can also classify bargaining issues as illegal topics, which obviously cannot be discussed. These types of illegal issues may be of a discriminatory nature or anything that would be considered illegal outside the agreement.

EXAMPLES OF BARGAINING TOPICS

- Pay rate and structure
- Health benefits
- Incentive programs
- Job classification
- Performance assessment procedure
- Vacation time and sick leave
- Health plans
- Layoff procedures
- Seniority
- Training process
- Severance pay

- Tools provided to employees
- Process for new applicants

The collective bargaining process has five main steps; we will discuss each of these steps next. The first step is the preparation of both parties. The negotiation team should consist of individuals with knowledge of the organization and the skills to be an effective negotiator. An understanding of the working conditions and dissatisfaction with working conditions is an important part of this preparation step. Establishing objectives for the negotiation and reviewing the old contract are key components to this step. The management team should also prepare and anticipate union demands, to better prepare for compromises.

The second step of the process involves both parties agreeing on how the time lines will be set for the negotiations. In addition, setting ground rules for how the negotiation will occur is an important step, as it lays the foundation for the work to come.

In the third step, each party comes to the table with proposals. It will likely involve initial opening statements and options that exist to resolve any situations that exist. The key to a successful proposal is to come to the table with a "let's make this work" attitude. An initial discussion is had and then each party generally goes back to determine which requests it can honor and which it can't. At this point, another meeting is generally set up to continue further discussion.

Once the group comes to an agreement or settlement (which may take many months and proposals), a new contract is written and the union members vote on whether to accept the agreement. If the union doesn't agree, then the process begins all over again.

Ramifications of a Bargaining Impasse

When the two parties are unable to reach consensus on the collective bargaining agreement, this is called a bargaining impasse. Various kinds of strikes are used to show the displeasure of workers regarding a bargaining impasse. Aneconomic strike is a strike stemming from unhappiness about the economic conditions during contract negotiations. For example, 45,000 Verizon workers rallied in the summer of 2011 when contract negotiations failed._[3] The two unions, Communications Workers of America and the International Brotherhood of Electric Workers, claim that the new contract is unfair, as it asks Verizon workers to contribute more to health plans, and the organizational is also looking to freeze pensions at the end of the year and reduce sick time._[4] Verizon says the telecommunications public organization is changing, and it cannot afford these expenses. An unfair labor practices strike can happen during negotiations. The goal of an unfair labor practices strike is to get the organization to cease committing what the union believes to be an unfair labor practice. A bargaining impasse could mean the union goes on strike or a lockout occurs. The goal of a lockout, which prevents workers from working, is to put pressure on the union to accept the contract. A lockout can only be legally conducted when the existing collective bargaining agreement has expired and there is truly an impasse in contract negotiations. In summer 2011, the National Basketball Association locked out players when the collective bargaining agreement expired, jeopardizing the 2011–12 season_[5] while putting pressure on the players to accept the agreement. Similarly, the goal of a strike is to put pressure on the organization to accept the proposed contract. Some organizations will impose a lockout if workers engage in slowdowns, an intentional reduction in productivity. Some unions will engage in a slowdown instead of a strike, because the workers still earn pay, while in a strike they do not. A sick-outis when members of a union call in sick, which may be illegal since they are using allotted time, while a walk-out is an unannounced refusal to perform work. However, this type of tactic may be illegal if the conduct is irresponsible or indefensible, according to a judge. Jurisdictional strikes are used to put pressure on an employer to assign work to members of one union versus another (if there are two unions within the same organization) or to put pressure on management to recognize one union representation when it currently recognizes another. The goal of a sick-out strike is to show the organization how unproductive the organizational would be if the workers did go on strike. As mentioned under the Taft-Hartley Act, wildcat strikes are illegal, as they are not authorized by the union and usually violate a collective bargaining agreement.Sympathy strikes are work stoppages by other unions designed to show support for the union on strike. While they are not illegal, they may violate the terms of the collective bargaining agreement.

HUMAN RESOURCE RECALL

How would you feel about going on strike? What kinds of situations may cause you to do so?

Working with Labor Unions

First and foremost, when working witih labor unions, a clear understanding of the contract is imperative for all HR professionals and managers. The contract (also called the collective bargaining agreement) is the guiding document for all decisions relating to employees. All HR professionals and managers should have intimate knowledge of the document and be aware of the components of the contract that can affect dealings with employees. The agreement outlines all requirements of managers and usually outlines how discipline, promotion, and transfers will work.

Because as managers and HR professionals we will be working with members of the union on a daily basis, a positive relationship can not only assist the day-to-day operations but also create an easier bargaining process. Solicitation of input from the union before decisions are made can be one step to creating this positive relationship. Transparent communication is another way to achieve this goal.

HOW WOULD YOU HANDLE THIS?

Union Busting

The employees in your organization are unhappy with several aspects of their job, includingpay. You have tried to solve this issue by creating new compensation plans, but with no avail. You hear talk of unionizing. When you bring this issue to your CEO, she vehemently opposes unions and tells you to let the employees know that if they choose to unionize, they will all lose their jobs. Knowing the CEO's threat is illegal, and knowing you may lose your job if the workers decide to unionize, how would you handle this?

How Would You Handle This?

KEY TAKEAWAYS

- A union has two goals: to add new members and to collect dues. A check-off provision of a contract compels the organization to take union dues out of the paycheck of union members.
- In a union shop, people must join the union within a specified time period after joining the organization. This is illegal in right-to-work states. An agency shop is one where union membership is not required but union dues are still required to be paid. This may also be illegal in right-to-work states.
- Made illegal by the Taft-Hartley Act, a closed shop allows only union members to apply and be hired for a job.
- Collective bargaining is the process of negotiating the contact with union representatives. Collective bargaining, to be legal, must always be done in good faith.
- There are three categories of collective bargaining issues. Mandatory issues might include pay and benefits. Permissive bargaining items may include things such as drug testing or the required equipment the organization must supply to employees. Illegal issues are those things that cannot be discussed, which can include issues that could be considered discriminatory.
- The collective bargaining process can take time. Both parties prepare for the process by gathering information and reviewing the old contract. They then set time lines for the bargaining and reveal their wants and negotiate those wants. Abargaining impasse occurs when members cannot come to an agreement.
- When a bargaining impasse occurs, a strike or lockout of workers can occur. Aneconomic strike occurs during negotiations, while an unfair labor practices strikecan occur anytime, and during negotiations. A sick-out can also be used, when workers call in sick for the day. These strategies can be used to encourage the other side to agree to collective bargaining terms.
- Some tips for working with unions include knowing and following the contract, involving unions in organizational decisions, and communicating with transparency.

EXERCISES

1. Research negotiation techniques, then list and describe the options. Which do you think would work best when negotiating with unions?
2. Of the list of bargaining issues, which would be most important to you and why?

---

[1] "Best Workforces Are in Right to Work States," Redstate, June 30, 2011, accessed August 14, 2011, http://www.redstate.com/laborunionreport/2011/06/30/best-workforces-are-in-right-to-work-states-survey-finds/.

[2] "Right to Work for Less," AFL-CIO, accessed August 14, 2011,http://www.aflcio.org/issues/legislativealert/stateissues/work/.

[3] Dan Goldberg, "Verizon Strike Could Last Months," New Jersey News, August 7, 2011, accessed August 15, 2011,http://www.nj.com/news/index.ssf/2011/08/verizon_workers_outline_differ.html.

[4] Dan Goldberg, "Verizon Strike Could Last Months," New Jersey News, August 7, 2011, accessed August 15, 2011,http://www.nj.com/news/index.ssf/2011/08/verizon_workers_outline_differ.html.

[5] Steve Kyler, "Division among Owners?" HoopsWorld, August 8, 2011, accessed August 15, 2011, http://www.hoopsworld.com/Story.asp?story_id=20549.

12.3 Administration of the Collective Bargaining Agreement

LEARNING OBJECTIVE

1. Be able to explain how to manage the grievance process.

A grievance procedure or process is normally created within the collective bargaining agreement. The grievance procedure outlines the process by which grievances over contract violations will be handled. This will be the focus of our next section.

Procedures for Grievances

A violation of the contract terms or perception of violation normally results in a grievance. The process is specific to each contract, so we will discuss the process in generalities. A grievance is normally initiated by an employee and then handled by union representatives. Most contracts specify how the grievance is to be initiated, the steps to complete the procedure, and identification of representatives from both sides who will hear the grievance. Normally, the HR department is involved in most steps of this process. Since HRM has intimate knowledge of the contract, it makes sense for them to be involved. The basic process is shown in Figure 12.8 "A Sample Grievance Process".

Figure 12.8 A Sample Grievance Process

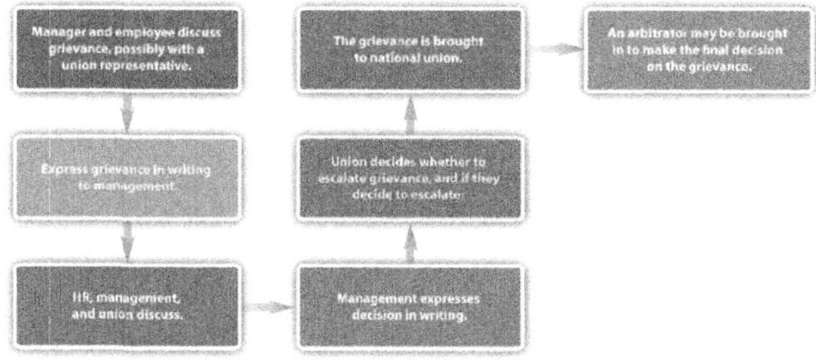

The first step is normally an informal conversation with the manager, employee, and possibly a union representative. Many grievances never go further than this step, because often the complaint is a result of a misunderstanding.

If the complaint is unresolved at this point, the union will normally initiate the grievance process by formally expressing it in writing. At this time, HR and management may discuss the grievance with a union representative. If the result is unsatisfactory to both parties, the complaint may be brought to the organizational's union grievance committee. This can be in the form of an informal meeting or a more formal hearing.
After discussion, management will then submit a formalized response to the grievance. It may decide to remedy the grievance or may outline why the complaint does not violate the contract. At this point, the process is escalated.

Further discussion will likely occur, and if management and the union cannot come to an agreement, the dispute will normally be brought to a national union officer, who will work with management to try and resolve the issue. A mediator may be called in, who acts as an impartial third party and tries to resolve the issue. Any recommendation made by the mediator is not binding for either of the parties involved. Mediators can work both on grievance processes and collective bargaining issues. For example, when the National Football League (NFL) and its players failed to reach a collective bargaining agreement, they agreed to try mediation.[1] In this case, the agreement to go to mediation was a positive sign after several months of failed negotiations. In the end, the mediation worked, and the NFL players started the 2011–12 season on time. In Washington State (as well as most other states), a nonprofit organization is available to assist in mediations (either grievance or collective bargaining related) and arbitrations. The goal of such an organization is to avoid disruptions to public services and to facilitate the dispute resolution process. In Washington, the organization is called the Public Employment Relations Commission (PERC).

If no resolution develops, an arbitrator might be asked to review the evidence and make a decision. An arbitrator is an impartial third party who is selected by both parties and who ultimately makes a binding decision in the situation. Thus arbitration is the final aspect of a grievance.
Some examples of grievances might include the following:

2. One employee was promoted over another, even though he had seniority.
3. An employee doesn't have the tools needed to perform his or her job, as outlined in the contract.
4. An employee was terminated, although the termination violated the rules of the contract.
5. An employee was improperly trained on chemical handling in a department.

Most grievances fall within one of four categories. There are individual/personal grievances, in which one member of the union feels he or she has been mistreated. A group grievance occurs if several union members have been mistreated in the same way. Aprinciple grievance deals with basic contract issues surrounding seniority or pay, for example. If an employee or group is not willing to formally file a grievance, the union may file a union or policy grievance on behalf of that individual or group.

The important things to remember about a grievance are that it should not be taken personally and, if used correctly can be a fair, clear process to solving problems within the organization.

KEY TAKEAWAYS

- The grievance process is a formal process to address any complaints about contract violations.
- The grievance process varies from contract to contract. It is an important part of the contract that ensures a fair process for both union members and management.
- HR is normally involved in this process, since it has intimate knowledge of the contract and laws that guide the contract.
- The grievance process can consist of any number of steps. First, the complaint is discussed with the manager, employee, and union representative. If no solution occurs, the grievance is put into writing by the union. Then HR, management, and the union discuss the process, sometimes in the form of a hearing in which both sides are able to express their opinion.
- Management then expresses its decision in writing to the union.
- If the union decides to escalate the grievance, the grievance may be brought to the national union for a decision. At this point, an arbitrator may be brought in, suitable to both parties, to make the final binding decision.
- There are four main types of grievances. First, the individual grievance is filed when one member of the union feels mistreated. A group grievance occurs when several members of the union feel they have been mistreated and file a grievance as a group. A principle grievance may be filed on behalf of the union and is usually based on a larger issue, such as a policy or contract issue. A union or policy grievance may be filed if the employee does not wish to file individually.
- Grievances should not be taken personally and should be considered a fair way in which to solve problems that can come up between the union and management.

EXERCISE

1. What are the advantages of a grievance process? What disadvantages do you see with a formalized grievance process?

---

[1] Associated Press, "NFL, Union Agree to Mediation," February 17, 2011, accessed August 15, 2011, http://msn.foxsports.com/nfl/story/NFL-players-union-agree-to-mediation-federal-for-labor-talks-CBA-021711.

12.4 Cases and Problems

CHAPTER SUMMARY

- Union membership in the United States has been slowly declining. Today, union membership consists of about 11.9 percent of the workforce, while in 1983 it consisted of 20 percent of the workforce.
- The reasons for decline are varied, depending on who you ask. Some say the moving of jobs overseas is the reason for the decline, while others say unions' hard-line tactics put them out of favor.
- The United States began its first labor movement in the 1800s. This was a result of low wages, no vacation time, safety issues, and other issues.
- Many labor organizations have disappeared, but the American Federation of Labor (AFL) still exists today, although it merged with the Congress of Industrial Organizations (CIO) and is now known as the AFL-CIO. It is the largest labor union and represents local labor unions in a variety of industries.
- The United States has a low number of union members compared with other countries. Much of Europe, for example, has over 30 percent of their workforce in labor unions, while in some countries as much as 50 percent of the workforce are members of a labor union.
- Legislation has been created over time to support both labor unions and the organizations who have labor unions. The Wagner Act was created to protect employees from retaliation should they join a union. The Taft-Hartley Actwas developed to protect organizations from unfair labor practices by unions.
- The National Labor Relations Board is the overseeing body for labor unions, and it handles disputes between organizations as well as facilitates the process of certifying new labor unions. Its job is to enforce the Wagner and Taft-Hartley acts.
- The Landrum Griffin Act was created in 1959 to combat corruption in labor unions during this time period.
- To form a union, the organizer must have signatures from 30 percent of the employees. If this occurs, the National Labor Relations Board will facilitate a card check to determine whether more than 50 percent of the workforce at that organizational is in agreement with union representation. If the organizational does not accept this, then the NLRB holds secret elections to determine if the employees will be unionized.
- A union has two goals: to add new members and to collect dues. The checkoff provision of a contract compels the organization to take union dues out of the paycheck of union members.
- In a union shop, people must join the union within a specified time period of joining the organization. This is illegal in right-to-work states.
- Made illegal by the Taft-Hartley Act, a closed shop allows only union members to apply and be hired for a job.
- Collective bargaining is the process of negotiating the contact with union representatives. Collective bargaining, to be legal, must always be done in good faith.
- There are three categories of collective bargaining issues. Mandatory issuesmight include pay and benefits. Permissive bargaining items may include things such as drug testing or the required equipment the organization must supply to employees. Illegal issues are those things that cannot be discussed, which can include issues that could be considered discriminatory.
- The collective bargaining process can take time. Both parties prepare for the process by gathering information and reviewing the old contract. They then set time lines for the bargaining and reveal their wants and negotiate those wants. A bargaining impasse occurs when members cannot come to an agreement.
- When a bargaining impasse occurs, a strike or lockout of workers can occur. These are both strategies that can be used to encourage the other side to agree to collective bargaining terms.
- Some tips for working with unions include knowing and following the contract, involving unions in organizational decisions, and communicating with transparency.
- The grievance process is a formal process that addresses any complaints about contract violations.
- The grievance process varies from contract to contract. It is an important part of the contract that ensures a fair process for both unions members and management.
- HRM is normally involved in the grievance process, since it has intimate knowledge of the contract and laws guiding the contract.
- The grievance process can consist of any number of steps. First, the complaint is discussed with the manager, employee, and union representative. If no solution occurs, the grievance is put into writing by the union. Then HR, management, and the union discuss the process, sometimes in the form of a hearing in which both sides are able to express their opinion.
- Management then expresses its decision in writing to the union.
- If the union decides to escalate the grievance, the grievance may be brought to the national union for a

decision. At this point, an arbitrator may be brought in, suitable to both parties, to make the final binding decision.

- There are four main types of grievances. First, the individual grievance is filed when one member of the union feels mistreated. A group grievance occurs when several members of the union feel they have been mistreated and file a grievance as a group. A principle grievance may be filed on behalf of the union and is usually based on a larger issue, such as a policy or contract issue. A union or policy grievance may be filed if the employee does not wish to file the grievance individually.
- Grievances should not be taken personally and should be considered a fair way in which to solve problems that can come up between the union and management.

CHAPTER CASE

But I Didn't Know

After a meeting with the operations manager of your organization, you close the door to your office so you can think of strategies to resolve an issue that has come up. The operations manager casually mentioned he had just finished a performance review of one of his employees and offered the employee a large raise because of all the hours the employee was putting in. The raise was equal to 11 percent of the employee's salary. The operations manager, being new both to the organizational and to a union shop, wasn't aware of the contract agreement surrounding pay increases. An employee must receive a minimum of a 2 percent pay increase per year and a maximum of 6 percent per year based on the contract. You worry that if the union gets wind of this, everyone at that employee's pay level may file a grievance asking for the same pay raise. Of course, the challenge is that the manager already told this person he would be receiving the 11 percent raise. You know you need to act fast to remedy this situation.

1. As an HR professional, what should you have done initially to prevent this issue from happening?
2. Outline a specific strategy to implement stating how you will prevent this from happening in the future.
3. What would you do about the 11 percent pay raise that was already promised to the employee?
4. If the union files a grievance, what type of grievance do you think it would be? Provide reasoning for your answer.
5. If the union does file a grievance, draft a response to the grievance to share with your upper-level managers as a starting point for discussion on how to remedy the situation.

TEAM ACTIVITY

1. Break into teams of four or five. Please choose the following roles for each of your team members:
   a. Mediator
   b. Manager
   c. HR professional
   d. Employee

Once roles are chosen, please determine a solution or make a recommendation for the following situation (remember, this is a role play; you may make reasonable assumptions): The employee believes the performance evaluation the manager gave was unfair and has filed a grievance about it. The employee shows proof of a good attendance record and three letters from colleagues stating the high quality of her work. The manager contends the employee does not use time wisely at work, hence the 3 out of 5 rating. The manager is able to show several examples of poor time usage.

Chapter 13:
Safety and Health at Work in Public Organizations

Training for Safety

As the HR manager of a large construction organizational, your workers' health and safety is of paramount concern. Last week, you reported an incidence rate of 7.5 accidents per 100 employees to the Occupational Safety and Health Administration (OSHA). When you compared these numbers to last year, you found the number had significantly increased, as it was 4.2. This is concerning, because you know an unsafe workplace is not only bad for employees and bad for public organization, but it could result in fines from OSHA. You ask your operations managers to meet with you about the situation. When you bring this to his attention, he doesn't seem at all concerned about the almost double increase in accidents over the last year. He says the increase in accidents is a result of scaffolding falling during a building project where several workers were hurt. He says this one accident skewed the numbers. He mentions that the supervisor responsible for the scaffolding had been let go six months ago for other reasons, and he assures you that there is no reason to be concerned. A few weeks after this conversation, two of your workers spend time in the hospital because of a falling scaffolding injury. Again, you approach the operations manager and he assures you that those employees were just new and he will implement proper procedures. You know the incident will result in another high incident percentage, even if there isn't another accident the rest of the year. You consider your options.

You look back over ten years of accident reports and find there are three areas for which your organizational seems to have 90 percent of all accidents. You decide you will develop a training program to address these safety issues in your workplace. You refer to your HRM textbook for tips on how to prepare and communicate this training to your employees. When you present this option to your operations manager, he says that employees don't have the time to take from their jobs to go through this training and suggests you just let it go. You are prepared for this response, and you give him the dollar figure of money lost owing to worker injury in your organization. This gets his attention, especially when you compare it to the small cost of doing a two-hour training for all employees. Both of you check your Outlook schedules to find the best day of the week to schedule the training, for minimum impact on employees' work.

13.1 Workplace Safety and Health Laws

LEARNING OBJECTIVES

1. Be able to explain OSHA laws.
2. Understand right-to-know laws.

Workplace safety is the responsibility of everyone in the organization. HR professionals and managers, however, play a large role in developing standards, making sure safety and health laws are followed, and tracking workplace accidents.

Occupational Safety and Health Administration (OSHA) Laws

In 2009 (the most recent data available at the time of this writing), 4,340 fatalities and 3.3 million injuries were reported.[1] This staggering number represents not only the cost to employees' well-being but also financial and time costs to the organizational. This is why health and safety is a key component of any human resource management (HRM) strategic plan.

What Is OSHA About?

The Occupational Safety and Health Act (OSHA), passed in 1970, created the Occupational Safety and Health Administration, which oversees health and safety in the workplace. The organization's mission is to ensure safe and healthful working conditions for working men and women by setting and enforcing standards and by providing training, outreach, education, and assistance. For example, OSHA offers ten- and thirty-hour courses on workplace hazards and also provides assistance to ensure organizations are in compliance with standards. OSHA is part of the US Department of Labor, with the main administrator being the assistant secretary of labor for occupational safety and health. This person reports to the labor secretary, who is a member of the president's cabinet.

Although OSHA applies to all organizations, health and safety standards are specifically mentioned for the following types of public organizationes:

2. Construction
3. Shipyard
4. Marine terminals

Although OSHA standards may appear to apply only to organizations in production, manufacturing, or construction, even organizations with primarily an office function are required to abide by the laws set by OSHA. Examples (not at all an exhaustive list) of the types of safety laws (for all types of public organizationes) that are overseen by OSHA are as follows:

1. *Regulations on walking/working surfaces.* According to OSHA, slips, trips, and falls constitute the majority of general industry accidents and 15 percent of all accidental deaths. The standards apply to all permanent places of employment. The provision says that "all passageways, storerooms, and service rooms shall be kept clean and orderly. Every floor and working space shall be kept free of protruding nails, splinters, holes, or loose boards." These are a few examples included in this provision.
2. *Means of egress (exiting), which includes emergency evacuation plans.* "Every building or structure shall be arranged and maintained as to provide free and unobstructed egress from all part of the buildings. No lock or fastening to prevent free escape from inside the building should be installed (except in penal or corrective institutions)." The provision also says that exits shall be marked by a visible sign.
3. *Occupational noise exposure.* "Protection against the effects of noise exposure shall be provided when the sound levels reach a specified level. Controls should be used to control the sound, and protective equipment should be provided."
4. *Hazardous handling of materials.* OSHA regulates exposure to four hundred substances and requires communication about the possible chemical hazards to employees.
5. *Protective equipment, such as eye, face, and respiratory protection.* OSHA requires the use of personal protective equipment to reduce employee exposure to hazards. For example, head protection is required when workers are in an area where there is potential for falling, and eye and face protection is required when workers are exposed to eye or face hazards such as flying particles and molten metal.
6. *Sanitation.* Some examples of these OSHA requirements include the following: Potable water should be provided in all places of employment. Vermin control is required in all enclosed workplaces. Toilet facilities must be provided, separate for each sex. The number of toilets provided depends on the number of employees.
7. *Requirement of first aid supplies on-site.* First aid kits are mandatory and should include gauze pads, bandages, gauze roller bandages, and other required items.
8. *Standards for fire equipment.* Fire extinguishers are required to be on-site for use by employees, unless there is a written fire policy that requires the immediate and total evacuation of employees.
9. *Standards for machine guards and other power tools.* Moving machine parts require safeguards (depending upon the industry) to prevent crushed fingers, hands, amputations, burns, or blindness. Safeguards might include a guard attached to the machine.
10. *Electrical requirements and standards.* OSHA electrical standards are designed to protect employees from electric shock, fires, and explosions. Electrical protective devices are required to cover wiring. OSHA also addresses the installation of electrical wiring.
11. *Commercial diving operation requirements.* OSHA provides information on the safety aspects of commercial diving such as pre- and postdive procedures, mixed-gas diving, and necessary qualifications of the dive team.

HR professionals and managers should have a good understanding of these laws and make sure, no matter which industry, that all these standards are followed in the workplace. These standards are normally part of the overall strategic HRM plan of any organization and are even more crucial to organizations involved in manufacturing.

There exist many examples of OSHA violations. For example, in a Queensbury, Pennsylvania, Dick's Sporting Goods store, OSHA found six violations, including blocked access to a fire extinguisher and workers' entering a trash compactor with the power supply on. Dick's was fined $57,300 by OSHA and told it had fifteen days to comply or contest the findings. [2]

THE MOST FREQUENTLY VIOLATED AND CITED OSHA STANDARDS

1. 1926.451—Scaffolding
2. 1926.501—Fall Protection
3. 1910.1200—Hazard Communication
4. 1910.134—Respiratory Protection
5. 1926.1053—Ladders
6. 1910.147—Lockout/Tagout
7. 1910.305—Electrical, Wiring Methods
8. 1910.178—Powered Industrial Trucks
9. 1910.303—Electrical, General Requirements
10. 1910.212—Machine Guarding

Right-to-Know Laws

The Emergency Planning and Community Right to Know A ct (EPCRA) or more simply, right-to-know laws, were established by Congress in 1986. The purpose of this act was to require local and state governments to provide emergency response plans to respond to a chemical emergency._[3] The other requirement is that these plans must be reviewed on an annual basis. Organizations that handleextremely hazardous substances (EHSs) in large quantities must develop response plans as well. In addition, any organization that manufactures, processes, or stores certain hazardous chemicals must make available to local fire departments and state and local officials material data safety sheets. The material data safety sheet should also be provided to employees, as the data lists not only the chemical components but health risks of the substance, how to handle the material safely, and how to administer first aid in the case of an accident. This requirement also states that inventories of all on-site chemicals must be reported to local and state governments, but the data sheets must also be made public, too.

This law and how it will be reported should be facilitated by the HR professional. Although the HRM may not know the chemical makeup of the materials used, he or she is responsible for facilitating the process to ensure that reporting is done timely and accurately. For organizations that use EHSs often, it is worthwhile to include the reporting process within the orientation training and provide ongoing training as the law changes. The A-Treat Bottling facility in Allentown, Pennsylvania, was cited by OSHA for repeat violations of lacking material safety data sheets for the chemicals it uses in manufacturing, among other infractions such as blocked exits and forklift violations. The fines totaled $110,880, and the organizational had fifteen days to comply or contest the allegations._[4]

It is also important to note that some state standards are different from federal standards, which means the HR professional will need to be aware of the laws in the individual state in which the organizational is operating.

HUMAN RESOURCE RECALL

How do you think the OSHA requirements apply to office work settings?

OSHA Enforcement

The record-keeping aspect of OSHA is perhaps as important as following the laws. Organizations having fewer than ten employees in some industries are not required to keep records. The purpose of the record keeping does not imply that the employee or the organizational is at fault for a illness or injury. In addition, just because a record is kept doesn't mean the employee will be eligible for workersworker's compensation#8217; compensation. The record-keeping aspect normally refers to the keeping of incidence rates, or the number of illnesses or injuries per one hundred full-time employees per year, as calculated by the following formula

- incidence rate=number of injuries and illness × 200,000total hours worked by all employees in the period

Two hundred thousand is the standard figure used, as it represents one hundred full-time employees who work forty hours per week for fifty weeks per year. An HR professional can then use this data and compare it to other organizations in the same industry to see how its public organization is meeting safety standards compared with other public organizationes. This calculation provides comparable information, no matter the size of the organizational. If the incidence rate is higher than the average, the HR professional might consider developing training surrounding safety in the workplace.

Additionall, knowing what should be reported and what shouldn't be reported is an important component to OSHA.

As mentioned earlier, OSHA is responsible for enforcing standards. Besides requiring reporting, OSHA also performs inspections. OSHA is responsible for 7 million worksites across the country and so, of course, has to prioritize which ones it visits. OSHA has five main priorities for inspecting sites. First, it will inspect imminent danger situations. These are serious dangers that could cause death or serious harm. The second priority is for those sites where three or more employees were harmed, suffered illness, or were killed. These events are classified as fatalities or catastrophes and must be reported within an eight-hour time frame. The next priority is responding to complaints, which employees are allowed to file anonymously. Organizations that have had previous violations are prioritized next, and finally, planned programs. A planned program might be an organization that has had safety problems in the past and is working with OSHA to remedy the problem.

Most site visits are unannounced and begin with the inspector introducing himself or herself. Prior to this, the inspector has performed research on the organization to be inspected. Once this occurs, a representative of the organization is assigned to acorganizational the inspector and the inspector discusses the reasons for the site visit. The HR professional is normally responsible for this task.

The inspector then walks around, pointing out any obvious violations, and then the inspector and representative discuss the findings. Within six months a complete report is sent, along with any citations or fines based on what the inspector found. If the organization is in disagreement with the violation or citation, a follow-up meeting with the OSHA director is scheduled and some fines may be reduced if the organization can show how it has improved and met the standards since the original visit.

OSHA has several penalties (per violation) it can assess on organizations, ranging from $7,000 to $70,000. The higher penalties often are a result of very serious offenses, in which an employee could have been killed, but also are imposed for willful offenses that the employer was aware could cause serious injury or death and did nothing about them. This is considered blatant indifference to the law. For example, Northeastern Wisconsin Wood Products was issued $378,620 in fines for willful violations in the summer of 2011. The violations stemmed from repeat visits and citations to the facility, where no safety changes had been made. Some of the willful violations included lack of guards on dangerous machine belts and band saw blades and open-sided floors without a guardrail to prevent falls. Michael Connors, OSHA's regional administrator in Chicago, said, "Northeastern Wisconsin Wood Products has a history of failing to comply with OSHA standards. The organizational has yet to abate many violations cited in previous inspections and are unduly placing their workers at risk."_[5] While any violation of OSHA is serious, a willful violation is more serious, and the fines associated with it represent this.

ORGANIZATIONAL FOCUS

PepsiCo is the world's largest manufacturer, seller, and distributor of Pepsi-Cola products and generates $119 billion in sales every year._[6] Tropicana juice is owned by Pepsi-Co. In October of 2005, a spark triggered an explosion at a Tropicana juice processing plant in Bradenton, Florida, causing burns to two-thirds of a worker's body. While the worker survived, he underwent multiple surgeries to treat his burns. In this case, OSHA concluded that the fire could have been prevented if Tropicana had followed basic safety requirements such as risk evaluation, given tools to workers that did not produce sparks, and monitored for a buildup of flammable vapors and ventilated the area. OSHA inspectors tallied up a dozen violations, including two serious ones. Vice president of operations Mike Haycock said the plant has an incidence rate that is far lower than others in the industry, and plants around the country have immediately addressed many of the problems and are constantly working to correct other problems._[7]

The irony is that although the Tropicana factory paid $164,250 in fines to OSHA, the organizational was part of the VPP or Voluntary Protection Program, whose membership benefits include exemption from regular inspections. Even after the fire, in 2007, OSHA formally reapproved the plant as a "star site," the highest level in VPP, meaning the plant pledged to exceed OSHA standards._[8] OSHA contends the VPP program isn't perfect but is still a useful model to all employers of what can be achieved. For admission into the VPP program, workplaces must show they have fewer accidents and missed work days than average for their industry. According to Robert Tuttle, president of the local Teamsters union representing Tropicana workers, accidents are more common when employees are shifted out of their normal responsibilities, which is more common as the weak economy has led to staff cuts._[9] Tropicana plants have had more than eighty deaths since 2000, varying from preventable explosions to chemical releases to crane accidents._[10]PepsiCo and Tropicana have taken a hard stance on these types of accidents, as each of the plants now has a safety manager trained on OSHA standards to prevent accidents. In addition, strict operating procedures have been implemented to prevent future problems.

KEY TAKEAWAYS

- Every year, 4,340 fatalities and 3.3 million injuries occur in the workplace in the United States.
- The Occupational Safety and Health Act was passed in 1970, with the goal of providing a safe and healthy work environment for all US workers.
- The Occupational Safety and Health Administration is part of the US Department of Labor and was created as a result of the act in 1970.
- OSHA applies to some specific industries, such as construction, shipyards, and marine terminals. However, some of the OSHA regulations apply to all industries.
- Some states may also have safety requirements that may be more stringent than federal laws.
- Right-to-know laws refer to a material data safety sheet, which discusses the types of chemicals, proper handling and storage, and first aid in case of an accident. These data sheets should be made available to the general public and employees.
- Right-to-know laws also require specific reporting to local and state agencies on chemicals used in certain quantities for some industries.
- OSHA requires recording keeping for all workplace accidents or illness. Record keeping is usually the

responsibility of HR, and reports are made via OSHA Form 300.

- OSHA can inspect any site without prior notification. Usually, OSHA will gather information, visit the site, and ask for a representative. The representative is normally the HR person. The site visit will be performed, followed by discussion with the organizational representative. Within six months of the visit, a report and any penalties will be communicated.

EXERCISES

1. Research the Internet for recent OSHA violations and write two paragraphs describing one.
2. Research possible strategies to reduce OSHA violations and write a paragraph on at least two methods.

---

[1] "Workplace Injuries and Illnesses: 2009," Bureau of Labor Statistics, US Department of Labor, news release, October 21, 2010, accessed April 14, 2011,http://www.bls.gov/news.release/archives/osh_10212010.pdf.
[2] Chris Churchill, "OSHA Finds Violations at Queensbury Retailer," Union Times, August 8, 2011, accessed August 21, 2011, http://www.timesunion.com/public organization/article/OSHA-finds-violations-at-Queensbury-retailer-1779404.php.
[3] "Emergency Planning and Community Right-to-Know Act (EPCRA)," United States Environmental Protection Agency, accessed April 15, 2011,http://www.epa.gov/epahome/r2k.htm.
[4] "OSHA Cites Allentown Soft Drink Organizational," NewsWire.com, August 4, 2011, accessed August 21, 2011, http://www.mmdnewswire.com/us-labor-departmen-57793.html.
[5] "$378,620 in Fines Issued for Willful Violations," Occupational Health and Safety, July 31, 2011, accessed August 21, 2011, http://ohsonline.com/articles/2011/07/31/378620-in-fines-issued-to-wisconsin-wood-firm-for-willful-violations.aspx? admgarea=news.
[6] "PepsiCo Annual Report," accessed September 15, 2011,http://www.pepsico.com/Download/PepsiCo_Annual_Report_2010_Full_Annual_Report.pdf.
[7] Just-drinks editorial team, "US: Tropicana in Safety Hazards Payout," just-drinks, April 18, 2006, accessed August 21, 2011, http://www.just-drinks.com/news/tropicana-in-safety-hazards-payout_id86183.aspx.
[8] Chris Hamby, "Model Workforce Not Always Safe," Massachusetts Coalition for Occupational Safety and Health, July 7, 2011, accessed August 21, 2011,http://www.masscosh.org/node/721.
[9] David Gulliver, "Employees Not Always Safe in Model Workplaces," Florida Center for Investigative Reporting, July 22, 2011, KitchenAid Mixer Review, accessed August 21, 2011,http://kitchenaidmixereview.com/2011/07/22/employees-not-always-safe-in-model-workplaces/.
[10] Chris Hamby, "Model Workplaces Not Always Safe," Iwatchnews, July 7, 2011, accessed August 21, 2011, http://www.iwatchnews.org/2011/07/07/5130/model-workplaces-not-always-so-safe.

13.2 Health Hazards at Work

LEARNING OBJECTIVE

1. Be able to explain health concerns that can affect employees at work.

While OSHA covers many areas relating to health and safety at work, a few other areas are also important to mention. Stress management, office-related injuries such as carpal tunnel syndrome, and no-fragrance areas are all contemporary issues surrounding employee health and safety. We will discuss these issues in this section.

Stress

In its annual survey on stress in America,[1] the American Psychological Association found that money (76 percent), work (70 percent), and the economy (65 percent) remain the most oft-cited sources of stress for Americans. Job instability is on the rise as a source of stress: nearly half (49 percent) of adults reported that job instability was a source of stress in 2010 (compared to 44 percent in 2009). At the same time, fewer Americans are satisfied with the ways their employers help them balance work and nonwork demands (36 percent in 2010 compared to 42 percent in 2009). The implications of these findings are obviously important for HRM professionals.

Before we discuss what HR professionals can do, let's discuss some basic information about stress. As it is currently used, the term stress was coined by Hans Selye in 1936, who defined it as "the nonspecific response of the body to any demand for change." [2]In other words, we can say that stress is the reaction we have to a stressor. Astressor is some activity, event, or other stimulus that causes either a positive or negative reaction in the body. Despite what people may think, some stress is actually good. For example, receiving a promotion at work may cause stress, but this kind of stress is considered to be positive. Stress is very much a personal thing, and depending on individual personalities, people may have different opinions about what is a stressor and what is not. For example, a professor does not normally find public speaking to be a stressor, while someone who does not do it on a daily basis may be very stressed about having to speak in public.

STRESS MANAGEMENT

Selye recognized that not all stress is negative. Positive stress is called eustress. This type of stress is healthy and gives a feeling of fulfillment and other positive feelings. Eustress can cause us to push ourselves harder to meet an end goal. On the other hand,distress is the term used for negative stress.

While eustress can push us, distress does not produce positive feelings and can go on for a long time without relief. We can further classify distress by chronic stress, which is prolonged exposure to stress, and acute stress, which is short-term high stress. For example, someone who receives little or no positive result from stress and is continuously stressed may experience chronic stress. Acute stress occurs in shorter bursts and may be experienced while someone is on a tight deadline for a project.

Two other terms related to stress are hyperstress and hypostress. Hyperstress is a type of stress in which there are extremes with little or no relief for a long period of time. This type of stress often results in burnout. Hypostress is the lack of eustress or distress in someone's life. Remember, some stress can be good and pushes us to work harder. We see this type of stress with people who may work in a factory or other type of repetitive job. The effect of this type of stress is usually feelings of restlessness.

As you have already guessed, stress on the job creates productivity issues, which is why it concerns HR professionals. We know that stress can cause headaches, stomach issues, and other negative effects that can result in lost productivity but also result in less creative work. Stress can raise health insurance costs and cause employee turnover. Because of this, according to HR Magazine,[3] many employers are taking the time to identify the chief workplace stressors in employees' lives. With this information, steps can be taken to reduce or eliminate such stress.

PricewaterhouseCoopers, for example, implemented several strategies to reduce stress in its workplace. The firm restructured its work teams so that rather than having one employee work with one client, teams of employees work with groups of clients. Rather than having an employee say, "I can't go to my son's baseball game because I need to wait for this client call," this arrangement allows employees to cover for each other.

The organization also requires employees to take vacation time and even promotes it with posters throughout the office. In fact, even weekends are precious at PricewaterhouseCoopers. If an employee sends an e-mail on the weekend, a popup screen reminds her or him it is the weekend and it is time to disconnect.

BEING A STUDENT CAN BE STRESSFUL

Here are the most common stressors for college students:

- Death of a loved one
- Relocating to a new city or state
- Divorce of parents
- Encounter with the legal system
- Transfer to a new school
- Marriage
- Lost job
- Elected to leadership position
- New romantic relationship
- Serious argument with close friend
- Increase in course load or difficulty of courses
- Change in health of family member
- First semester in college
- Failed important course
- Major personal injury or illness
- Change in living conditions
- Argument with instructor
- Outstanding achievement
- Change in social life
- Change in sleeping habits
- Lower grades than expected
- Breakup of relationship
- New job
- Financial problems
- Change in eating habits
- Chronic car trouble
- Pregnancy
- Too many missed classes
- Long commute to work/school
- Working more than one job
- Impending graduation
- Argument with family member
- Sexual concerns
- Changes in alcohol and/or drug use
- Roommate problems
- Raising children

scheduling, according to Von Madsen, HR manager at ARUP Laboratories,[4] allows employees to work around a schedule that suits them best. Other creative ways to reduce stress might be to offer concierge services, on-site child care, wellness initiatives, and massage therapy. All these options can garner loyalty and higher productivity from employees.

HUMAN RESOURCE RECALL

What does your organization do to reduce stress? What should it do that it is not doing?

Cumulative Trauma Disorders

Cumulative trauma disorders (CTDs) are injuries to the fingers, hands, arms, or shoulders that result from repetitive motions such as typing.

Carpal tunnel syndrome, or CTS, is a common cumulative disorder in which the hand and wrist is particularly affected. CTS is a disabling syndrome that fortunately can be prevented or at least minimized. According to one study of CTS,_[5] the percentage of a workday at a computer, posture while at the workstation, and the individual's body features all contribute to this workplace issue. More recently, CTD can be found in people who text a lot or use their smartphones to type or surf the Internet.

There are a number of keyboards, chairs, and other devices that can help limit or prevent CTD issues. CTD disorders cost organizations money through higher health-care costs and workersworker's compensation#8217; compensation payments. CTD is a required recordable case under OSHA. OSHA has voluntary employer guidelines for reducing CTD in specific industries such as poultry processing, shipyards, retail grocery, and nursing homes. OSHA is currently developing standards for industry-specific and task-specific jobs._[6]

Microsoft is attempting to relieve CTD by developing "surface" technology. First introduced in 2007, the system is controlled through intuitive touch rather than the traditional mouse and keyboard. Microsoft and Samsung in early 2011 introduced the newest consumer-ready product, which looks like a large tablet (or iPad) used to perform the same functions as one normally would on her computer._[7]

HOW WOULD YOU HANDLE THIS?

To Tell or Not?

You work for a large multinational organization as a manager on the factory floor. One of your employees was moving large barrels of chemicals from one workstation to another, when the barrel burst and gave him mild burns. When you talk with him about it, he says it was his own fault, and he doesn't want to take any days off or see a doctor. How would you handle this?

How Would You Handle This?

Video Display Terminals (VDTs)

In 1984, only 25 percent of people used computers at work, and today that number is 68 percent._[8] Awareness of the effects of computer monitors and other similar terminals are necessary to ensure a healthy workplace. Vision problems; fatigue; eye strain; and neck, back, arm, and muscle pain are common for frequent users of VDTs. OSHA recommands taking a break after every hour on a computer screen and reducing glare on screens. Proper posture and seat adjustment also limits the amount of injuries due to VDTs.

Chemical and Fragrance Sensitivities

The EEOC defines a disability as a physical or mental impairment that substantially limits one or more of the major life activities of individuals and the ability to provide evidence of such an impairment._[9] Because of this definition, people who have multiple chemical sensitivity (MCS) or environmental illness (EI) are eligible for reasonable accommodations in the workplace. MCS or EI is the inability to tolerate an environmental chemical or class of foreign chemicals. Symptoms can include headache, dizziness, inability to breathe, muscle pain, and many more depending on the person. As a result, implementing policies surrounding MCS may be not only a legal requirement but a best practice to keep employees safe and healthy in the workplace. Some examples of such policies might include the following:

- Institute a fragrance-free workplace policy (e.g., no scented lotions, hair products, or perfumes).
- Limit use of restroom air fresheners, cleaning agents, and candles.
- Ensure the ventilation system is in good working order.
- Provide a workspace with windows where possible.
- Consider providing an alternate workspace.
- Be cautious of remodels, renovations, and other projects that may cause excessive dust and odors.

If an organization is going to implement a fragrance-free work policy, this is normally addressed under the dress code area of the organization's employee manual. However, many employers are reluctant to require employees to refrain from wearing or using scented products. In this case, rather than creating a policy, it might be worthwhile to simply request a fragrance-free zone from employees through e-mail and other means of communication.

We recognize that exposure to strong scents and fragrances in the environment can cause discomfort, as well as directly impact the health of some individuals. Since we hope to support a healthful environment for employees, physicians, and visitors, it is the intent of Quality and Operations Support to strive for a fragrance-controlled workplace. Therefore, for the comfort and health of all, use of scents and fragrant products by QOS employees, other than minimally scented personal care products, is strongly discouraged. [10]

Chemicals and Substances

OSHA, as we mentioned earlier, has certain standards for how chemicals should be handled and how they should be labeled. Chemicals should be labeled in English, and employees must be able to cross-reference the chemicals to the materials safety data sheet, which describes how the chemicals should be handled.

It is estimated that 1,200 new chemicals are developed in North America alone every year.[11] For many of these chemicals, little is known about their immediate or long-term effects on the health of workers who come into contact with them. As a result, policies should be developed on how chemicals should be handled, and proper warnings should be given as to the harmful effects of any chemicals found in a job site.

In the United States, twenty-six of the fifty states have smoking bans in enclosed public spaces. These smoking bans are designed to protect workers' health from the dangers of secondhand smoke. A recent report released by the Centers for Disease Control and Prevention[12] says that state or local smoke-free laws cover 47.8 percent of workplaces. The report says if the trend continues, the United States will be 100 percent smoke free by 2020. Many organizations implement no-smoking policies because of health-care costs, and some organizations, such as Humana, Inc., say their no-tobacco policy is simply setting a good example (since they are a health-care organization). Humana tests all applicants for tobacco in a preemployment screening that applies to all tobacco products.[13] Most workplaces have no-smoking policies, and some even prefer not to hire smokers because of the higher cost of health care. Policies dealing with substances and chemicals are an important part of any employee training and orientation.

BENEFITS TO A SMOKE-FREE WORK ENVIRONMENT AND SAMPLE POLICY

For the employees

- A smoke-free environment helps create a safer, healthier workplace.
- Workers who are bothered by smoke will not be exposed to it at work.
- Smokers who want to quit may have more of a reason to do so.
- Smokers may appreciate a clear organizational policy about smoking at work.
- Managers are relieved when there is a clearly defined process for dealing with smoking in the workplace.
- For the employer
- A smoke-free environment helps create a safer, healthier workplace.
- Direct health-care costs to the organizational may be reduced.
- A clear plan that is carefully put into action by the employer to lower employees' exposure to secondhand smoke shows the organizational cares.
- Employees may be less likely to miss work due to smoking-related illnesses.
- Maintenance costs go down when smoke, matches, and cigarette butts are taken out of work facilities.
- Office equipment, carpets, and furniture last longer.
- The risk of fires is lower.
- It may be possible to get lower rates on health, life, and disability insurance coverage as fewer employees smoke.

Sample smoking policy

Because we recognize the hazards caused by exposure to environmental tobacco smoke, it shall be the policy of ____________ to provide a smoke-free environment for all employees and visitors. This policy covers the smoking of any tobacco product and the use of oral tobacco products or "spit" tobacco, and it applies to both employees and nonemployee visitors of ____________.

Source: American Cancer Society, http://www.cancer.org/Healthy/StayAwayfromTobacco/Smoke-freeCommunities/CreateaSmoke-freeWorkplace/smoking-in-the-workplace-a-model-policy (accessed August 20, 2011).

Substance abuse in the workplace can cause many problems for the organization. Not only does it create impaired ability to perform a job—resulting in more accidents—but it results in more sick days and less productivity, and substance abusers are more likely to file workersworker's compensation#8217; compensation claims. Keep in mind that taking prescription drugs, if not used in the proper amounts or used long after the prescribed use, is considered substance abuse. A drug-free policy, according to OSHA,[14] has five parts:

1. A policy
2. Supervisor training
3. Employee education
4. Employee assistance
5. Drug testing

According to the National Clearinghouse for Alcohol and Drug Information, substance abuse costs organizations over $100 billion in the United States alone.[15]This staggering figure alone makes it worthwhile for organizations to implement a policy and training on substance abuse.

Workplace Violence and Bullying

According to OSHA, 2 million American workers are victims of workplace violence every year.[16] OSHA addresses some of the workers who are at increased risk for workplace violence:

1. Workers who exchange money with the public
2. Workers who deliver goods, passengers, or services
3. People who work alone or in small groups
4. Workers who work late at night or early in the morning
5. Workers who work in high-crime areas

It is up to the organization and human resources to implement policies to ensure the safety of workers and provide a safe working environment. OSHA provides tips to provide a safer workplace:

1. Establish a workplace violence prevention policy, with a zero tolerance policy.
2. Provide safety education.
3. Secure the workplace with cameras, extra lighting, and alarm systems.
4. Provide a drop safe to limit the amount of cash on hand.
5. Provide cell phones to workers.
6. Require employees to travel in groups using a "buddy system."

Development of workplace policies surrounding these items is important. Ongoing training and development in these areas are key to the creation of a safe workplace. While outside influences may affect employee safety, it is also important to be aware of the employee's safety from other employees. There are several indicators of previolence as noted by the Workplace Violence Research Institute:[17]

1. Increased use of alcohol and/or illegal drugs
2. Unexplained increase in absenteeism
3. Noticeable decrease in attention to appearance and hygiene
4. Depression and withdrawal
5. Explosive outbursts of anger or rage without provocation
6. Threats or verbal abuse to coworkers and supervisors
7. Repeated comments that indicate suicidal tendencies
8. Frequent, vague physical complaints
9. Noticeably unstable emotional responses
10. Behavior indicative of paranoia
11. Preoccupation with previous incidents of violence
12. Increased mood swings
13. Has a plan to "solve all problems"
14. Resistance and overreaction to changes in procedures
15. Increase of unsolicited comments about firearms and other dangerous weapons
16. Repeated violations of organizational policies
17. Escalation of domestic problems

WORKPLACE VIOLENCE

A video on workplace violence training.
Please view this video at http://www.youtube.com/watch?v=oiuWLkdUZ5o.

Anyone exhibiting one or more of these preincident indicators should get the attention of HRM. The HR professional should take appropriate action such as discussing the problem with the employee and offering counseling.

Workplace bullying is defined as a tendency of individuals or groups to use persistent or repeated aggressive or unreasonable behavior against a coworker or subordinate. The Workplace Bullying Institute found that 35 percent of workers have reported being bullied at work. This number is worth considering, given that workplace bullying reduces productivity with missed work days and turnover. The Workplace Bullying Institute found that litigation and settlement of bullying lawsuits can cost organizations $100,000 to millions of dollars, in addition to the bad publicity that may be created. Examples of workplace bullying include the following:

1. Unwarranted or invalid criticism
2. Blame without factual information
3. Being treated differently than the rest of your work group
4. Humiliation
5. Unrealistic work deadlines
6. Spreading rumors
7. Undermining or deliberately impeding a person's work

In an Indiana Supreme court case, a hospital employee who was repeatedly bullied by a surgeon sued for emotional distress and won. This ruling drew national attention because it was an acknowledgment by the courts of the existence of workplace bullying as a phenomenon.[18] Prevention of workplace bullying means creating a culture in which employees are comfortable speaking with HR professionals and managers (assuming they are not the ones bullying) about these types of situations. Similar to traditional bullying, cyberbullying is defined as use of the Internet or technology used to send text that is intended to hurt or embarrass another person. Examples include using Facebook to post negative comments or setting up a fake e-mail account to send out fake e-mails from that person. Comments or blogs and posts that show the victim in a bad light are other examples of cyberbullying. Similar to workplace bullying, cyberbullying is about power and control in workplace relationships. Elizabeth Carll's research on cyberbullying shows that people who experience this type of harassment are more likely to experience heightened anxiety, fear, shock, and helplessness, which can result in lost productivity at work and retention issues,[19] a major concern for the HR professional. The US Justice Department shows that some 850,000 adults have been targets of online harassment.[20] Many states, including New York, Missouri, Rhode Island, and Maryland, have passed laws against digital harassment as far back as 2007.[21] In a recent cyberbullying case, a US Court of Appeals upheld a school's discipline of a student for engaging in off-campus cyberbullying of another student.[22]In the case, the victim said a MySpace profile was created that included inappropriate pictures of her, and the page's creator invited other people to join. The student who created the page sued the school after she was disciplined for it, saying it violated her right to free speech, but courts found that students do not have the right to cyberbully other students. While it seems that cyberbullying is for young people, as mentioned earlier, 35 percent of American workers feel they have been bullied. Bullying should be identified immediately and handled, as it affects workplace productivity, customer satisfaction, and eventually, profits.

Employee Privacy

In today's world of identity theft, it is important that HR professionals work to achieve maximum security and privacy for employees. When private information is exposed, it can be costly. For example, in March of 2011, the Texas Comptroller's office inadvertently disclosed on a public website the names, addresses, and social security numbers of 3.5 million state workers.[23] The state has already spent $1.8 million to remedy this problem by sending letters to affected parties and hiring technology consultants to review office procedures. While keeping employee information private is the responsibility of all management in an organization, ensuring privacy remains the job of the HR professional.

Some of the things to combat employee identity theft include the following:

1. Conduct background and criminal checks on employees who will have access to sensitive data.
2. Restrict access to areas where data is stored, including computers.
3. Provide training to staff who will have access to private employee information.
4. Keep information in locked files or in password-protected files.
5. Use numbers other than social security numbers to identify employees.

Another privacy issue that comes up often is the monitoring of employee activities on devices that are provided to them by the organization. Case law, for the most part, has decided that employees do not have privacy rights if they are using the organization's equipment, with a few exceptions. As a result, more than half of all organizations engage in some kind of monitoring. According to an American Management Association[24]survey, 73 percent of employers monitor e-mail messages and 66 percent monitor web surfing. If your organization finds it necessary to implement monitoring policies, ensuring the following is important to employee buy-in of the monitoring:

1. Develop a policy for monitoring.
2. Communicate what will be monitored.
3. Provide public organization reasons for why e-mail and Internet must be monitored.

Working with your IT department to implement standards and protect employee data kept on computers is a must in today's connected world. Communication of a privacy policy is an important step as well. Agrium, a Canadian-based supplier of agricultural products in North America, states its employee privacy policy on its website and shares with employees the tactics used to prevent security breaches.[25]

At Agrium we are committed to maintaining the accuracy, confidentiality, and security of your personal information. This Privacy Policy describes the personal information that Agrium collects from or about you, and how we use and to whom we disclose that information.

Terrorism

Since the 9/11 attacks, terrorism and its effect on the workplace are in the forefront of the HR professional's mind. Planning for evacuations is the job of everyone in an organization, but HR should initiate this discussion. OSHA provides free assistance in implementing plans and procedures in case of a terror attack. OSHA also provides a fill-in-the-blank system (http://www.osha.gov/SLTC/etools/evacuation/expertsystem/default.htm) to help organizations write a comprehensive report for evacuations and terrorist attacks.

Promoting a Culture of Safety and Health

Employee health and safety is a must in today's high-stress work environments. Although some may see employee health as something that shouldn't concern HR, the increasing cost of health benefits makes it in the best interest of the organizational to hire and maintain healthy employees. In fact, during the recession of the late 2000s, when cutbacks were common, 50 percent of all workplaces increased or planned to increase investments in wellness and health at their organization.[26]

EXAMPLE OF HEALTH AND SAFETY POLICY

Cordis (A Johnson & Johnson Organizational) Environmental, Health, and Safety Policy
Cordis Corporation is committed to global Environmental, Health, and Safety (EHS) performance and leadership with respect to its associates, customers, suppliers, contractors, visitors, and communities. To fulfill this commitment, Cordis Corporation conducts its public organization emphasizing regulatory compliance and collaboration.
We strive for:

- Comprehensive risk management
- Pollution prevention
- Healthy lifestyle culture
- Continuous improvement and sustainability
- Engaging partnerships
- Possession of outstanding EHS capabilities and skill sets
- We affirm that EHS is:
- A core public organization value and a key indicator of organizational excellence
- Considered in every task we perform and in every decision we make
- We believe that:
- All incidents and injuries are preventable
- Process Excellence is the driver for continuous improvement and sustainable results in all aspects of EHS
- Every associate is responsible and accountable for complying with all aspects of EHS, creating a safe and healthy work environment while leaving the smallest environmental footprint

A safe culture doesn't happen by requiring training sessions every year; it occurs by creating an environment in which people can recognize hazards and have the authority and ability to fix them. Instead of safety being a management focus only, every employee should take interest by being alert to the safety issues that can exist. If an employee is unable to handle the situation on his or her own, the manager should then take suggestions from employees seriously; making the change and then communicating the change to the employee can be an important component of a safe and healthy workplace.

A culture that promotes safety is one that never puts cost or production numbers ahead of safety. You do not want to create a culture in which health and safety priorities compete with production speedup, which can lead to a dangerous situation.

Another option to ensure health and safety is to implement anemployee assistance program (EAP). This benefit is intended to help employees with personal problems that could affect their performance at work. The EAP usually includes covered counseling and referral services. This type of program can assist employees with drug or alcohol addictions, emotional issues such as depression, stress management, or other personal issues. Sometimes these programs are outsourced to organizations that can provide in-house training and referral services to employees. For example, REI (Recreation Equipment Inc.), based in Seattle, has a comprehensive EAP for its employees in both retail stores and organizational offices.

Possible techniques you can implement to have a safe and healthy work environment include the following:

1. Know OSHA and other safety laws.
2. Provide training to employees on OSHA and safety laws.
3. Have a written policy for how violations will be handled.
4. Commit the resources (time and money) necessary to ensure a healthy work environment.
5. Involve employees in safety and health discussions, as they may have good ideas as to how the organization can improve.
6. Make safety part of an employee's job description; in other words, hold employees accountable for always practicing safety at work.
7. Understand how the health (or lack of health) of your employees contributes to or takes away from the bottom line and implement policies and programs to assist in this effort.

KEY TAKEAWAYS

- Stress is a major concern for organizations, since it can decrease productivity in the workplace. There are several types of stress.
- Eustress is a positive type of stress that can cause people to work harder toward a goal. Distress, on the other hand, is a type of negative stress.

- Acute stress occurs in short bursts, such as when finishing a project, while chronic stress tends to persist for long periods of time.
- Hyperstress is stress that is unrelieved for long periods of time and can often result in employee burnout. Hypostress is the lack of eustress in one's life, which can be as damaging as other types of stress, since stress is sometimes what pushes people harder.
- HR professionals can encourage employees to take vacation time, offer flextime, and encourage employees to take weekends off to help reduce stress.
- Cumulative trauma disorder (CTD) affects the hands, fingers, arms, or shoulders as a result of continuous repetitive motions. Carpel tunnel syndrome (CTS) is a type of CTD that affects the hand and wrist. People with these disorders often work in a factory or at a desk where they are doing repetitive motions constantly, such as typing or cashiering.
- OSHA has voluntary guidelines for reducing CTD in the workplace. HR can assist by ensuring employees are provided with proper equipment and training.
- Multiple chemical sensitivity (MCS) or environmental illness (EI) is extreme sensitivity to chemicals found in products such as hairsprays or lotions. Some individuals are extremely sensitive to other types of chemicals, such as those used in the manufacturing of carpets.
- MCS can be considered a disability if it limits one or more life activities. In this case, reasonable accommodations must be made, such as implementing fragrance-free zones as part of a workplace dress code.
- OSHA has specific guidelines on how to handle chemicals, but other chemicals, such as those from secondhand smoke, are an important consideration in workplace safety. Twenty-six states, for example, have implemented no-smoking policies to help protect the health of workers.
- Workplace violence affects 2 million Americans every year. A number of groups, such as those who deliver goods, people, or services, are at greatest risk. However, workplace violence can occur internally, which is why we must be aware of the warning signs.
- Workplace bullying is when a person is aggressive and unreasonable in his or her behavior toward another individual. Cyberbullying is similar, except technology is used to humiliate and intimidate the employee.
- Keeping employee information private is the job of HR and IT. In addition, some organizations may engage in web or e-mail monitoring to ensure employees are on task. Specific policies should be developed and communicated to let employees know how they may be monitored.
- Some organizations have employee assistance programs (EAPs) that can provide assistance, counseling, and the like in case of personal problems or drug or alcohol abuse.
- To maintain a healthful working environment, know OSHA policies and make sure people are trained on the policies. Also ensure that specific policies on all areas of health and safety are communicated and employees are trained in those areas where necessary.

EXERCISES

1. Visit http://www.osha.gov/SLTC/etools/evacuation/expertsystem/default.htm and create your own evacuation plan using the tool on the OSHA website. (Note: web addresses sometimes change, so you may have to search further for the tool.) Bring your plan to class to share.
2. Research examples of workplace bullying, write two paragraphs about two examples, and share your findings with the class.

---

[1] American Psychological Association, "Key Findings," news release, n.d., accessed April 17, 2011, http://www.apa.org/news/press/releases/stress/key-findings.aspx.
[2] The American Institute of Stress, accessed September 15, 2011,http://www.stress.org/topic-definition-stress.htm.
[3] Kathryn Tyler, "Stress Management," HR Magazine, September 1, 2006, accessed April 19, 2011, http://www.shrm.org/Publications/hrmagazine/EditorialContent/Pages/0906tyler.aspx.
[4] Kathryn Tyler, "Stress Management," HR Magazine, September 1, 2006, accessed April 19, 2011, http://www.shrm.org/Publications/hrmagazine/EditorialContent/Pages/0906tyler.aspx.
[5] A. C. Matias, G. Salvendy, and T. Kuczek, Ergonomics Journal 41, no. 2 (1998): 213–26, accessed April 19, 2011, http://www.ncbi.nlm.nih.gov/pubmed/9494433.
[6] "OSHA Protocol for Developing Industry-Specific and Task-Specific Ergonomics Guidelines," Occupational Safety and Health Administration, accessed April 25, 2011,http://www.osha.gov/SLTC/ergonomics/protocol.html.
[7] Microsoft News Center, "Microsoft and Samsung Unveil the Next Generation of Surface," news release, January 2011, accessed August 21, 2011,http://www.microsoft.com/presspass/press/2011/jan11/01-06mssurfacesamsungpr.mspx.
[8] "Survey Shows Widespread Enthusiasm for High Technology," NPR Online, n.d., accessed August 20, 2011, http://www.npr.org/programs/specials/poll/technology/.
[9] "Section 902: Definition of the Term Disability," Equal Employment Opportunity Commission, accessed April 25, 2011, http://www.eeoc.gov/policy/docs/902cm.html#902.1.
[10] Kaiser Permanente Fragrance Policy, accessed September 15, 2011,http://users.lmi.net/wilworks/ehnlinx/k.htm.
[11] International Labor Organization, "Your Safety and Health at Work: Chemicals in the Workplace," accessed April 25,

2011, http://actrav.itcilo.org/actrav-english/telearn/osh/kemi/ciwmain.htm.
[12] Julie Steenhuysen, "26 US States Have Comprehensive Smoking Bans," Reuters, April 21, 2011, accessed April 25, 2011, http://www.reuters.com/article/2011/04/21/usa-smoking-idUSN2128332820110421.
[13] "Insurer Humana Inc. Won't Hire Smokers in Arizona," Associated Press, June 30, 2011, accessed August 20, 2011, http://finance.yahoo.com/news/Insurer-Humana-Inc-wont-hire-apf-961910618.html?x=0&.v=1.
[14] "Workplace Substance Abuse," Occupational Safety and Health Administration, accessed August 20, 2011, http://www.osha.gov/SLTC/substanceabuse/index.html.
[15] T. Buddy, "Substance Abuse in the Workplace," About.com, November 20, 2011, accessed August 20, 2011, http://alcoholism.about.com/cs/work/a/aa990120.htm.
[16] "Workplace Violence" (OSHA Fact Sheet), Occupational Safety and Health Administration, accessed April 25, 2011, http://www.osha.gov/OshDoc/data_General_Facts/factsheet-workplace-violence.pdf.
[17] Jurg Mattman, "Pre-Incident Indicators," Workplace Violence Research Institute, June 2010, accessed April 27, 2011, http://www.nesdis.noaa.gov/RESPECT/pdf/RESPECT-Pre-IncidentIndicators24Jun09.pdf.
[18] Karen Klein, "Employers Can't Ignore Workplace Bullies," Bloomberg Public organizationweek, May 7, 2008, accessed August 20, 2011,http://www.public organizationweek.com/smallbiz/content/may2008/sb2008057_530667.htm.
[19] Madeleine White, "Are Cyber Bullies Worse for Victims than Real Bullies?" Globe and Mail, August 8, 2011, accessed August 20, 2011, http://www.theglobeandmail.com/life/the-hot-button/are-cyber-bullies-worse-for-victims-than-real-bullies/article2122943/
[20] Madeleine White, "Are Cyber Bullies Worse for Victims than Real Bullies?" Globe and Mail, August 8, 2011, accessed August 20, 2011, http://www.theglobeandmail.com/life/the-hot-button/are-cyber-bullies-worse-for-victims-than-real-bullies/article2122943/.
[21] National Conference of State Legislatures, "State Cyberstalking, Cyberharassment, and Cyberbullying Laws," January 26, 2011, accessed August 20, 2011,http://www.ncsl.org/default.aspx?tabid=13495.
[22] Daniel Solove, "Off Campus Cyberbullying and the First Amendment," Huffington Post, July 28, 2011, accessed August 20, 2011, http://www.huffingtonpost.com/daniel-j-solove/offcampus-cyberbullying-a_b_911654.html.
[23] Patricia Hart, "Attorneys Seek to Question Texas Comptroller Over Exposed Info,"Houston Chronicle, April 26, 2011, accessed April 27, 2011,http://www.chron.com/disp/story.mpl/metropolitan/7537769.html.
[24] "Electronic Monitoring and Surveillance Survey," American Management Association, 2007, accessed April 27, 2011, http://press.amanet.org/press-releases/177/2007-electronic-monitoring-surveillance-survey/.
[25] "Employee Privacy Policy," Agrium Inc., accessed August 21, 2011,http://www.agrium.com/employee_privacy.jsp.
[26] Donald Sears, "Gym Memberships and Wellness Programs Remain Standard Employee Benefits," The Ladders Career Line, July 21, 2009, accessed April 27, 2011, http://www.career-line.com/job-search/gym-memberships-and-wellness-programs-remain-standard-employee-benefits/.

13.3 Cases and Problems

CHAPTER SUMMARY

- Every year, 4,340 fatalities and 3.3 million injuries occur in the workplace in the United States.
- The Occupational Safety and Health Act was passed in 1970, with the goal of providing a safe and healthy work environment for all US workers.
- The Occupational Safety and Health Administration is part of the US Department of Labor and was created as a result of the act in 1970.
- OSHA applies to some specific industries such as construction, shipyards, and marine terminals. However, some of the regulations of OSHA apply to all industries.
- Some states may also have safety requirements, which may be more stringent than federal Laws.
- Right-to-know laws refer to a material data safety sheet, which discusses the types of chemicals, proper handling and storage, and first aid in case of an accident. These data sheets should be made available to the general public and employees.
- Right-to-know laws also require specific reporting to local and state agencies on chemicals used in certain quantities for some industries.
- OSHA requires recording keeping for all workplace accidents or illness. The record keeping is usually the responsibility of HR; OSHA Form 300 is used for reporting purposes.
- OSHA can inspect any site without prior notification. Usually, it will gather information, visit the site, and ask for a representative. The representative is normally the HR person. The site visit will be performed, followed by discussion with the organizational representative. Within six months of the visit a report and any penalties will be communicated.
- Stress is a major concern for organizations, since it can decrease productivity in the workplace. There are several types of stress.
- Eustress is a positive type of stress that can cause people to work harder toward a goal. Distress, on the other hand, is a type of negative stress.
- Acute stress occurs in short bursts, such as when finishing a project, whilechronic stress tends to persist for long periods of time.
- Hyperstress is stress that is unrelieved for long periods of time and can often result in employee burnout. Hypostress is the lack of eustress in one's life, which can be as damaging as other types of stress, since stress is sometimes what pushes people harder.
- HR professionals can encourage employees to take vacation time, offer flextime, and encourage employees to take weekends off to help reduce stress.

- Cumulative trauma disorder (CTD) affects the hands, fingers, arms, or shoulders as a result of continuous repetitive motions. Carpel tunnel syndrome (CTS) is a type of CTD that affects the hand and wrist. People with these disorders often work in a factory or at a desk where they are doing repetitive motions constantly, such as typing or cashiering.
- OSHA has voluntary guidelines for reducing CTD in the workplace. HR can assist by ensuring employees are provided with proper equipment and training.
- Multiple chemical sensitivity (MCS) or environmental illness (EI) is extreme sensitivity to chemicals found in products such as hairsprays or lotions. Some individuals are extremely sensitive to other types of chemicals, such as those used in the manufacturing of carpets.
- MCS can be considered a disability if it limits one or more of life activities. In this case, reasonable accommodations must be made, such as implementing fragrance-free zones as part of a workplace dress code.
- OSHA has specific guidelines on how to handle chemicals, but other chemicals, such as those from secondhand smoke, are an important consideration in workplace safety. Twenty-six states, for example, have implemented no-smoking policies to help protect the health of workers.
- Workplace violence affects 2 million Americans every year. A number of groups, such as those that deliver goods, people, or services, are at greatest risk. However, workplace violence can occur internally, which is why we must be aware of the warning signs.
- Workplace bullying is when a person is aggressive and unreasonable in his or her behavior toward another individual. Cyberbullying is similar, except technology is used to humiliate and intimidate the employee.
- Keeping employee information private is the job of HR and IT. In addition, some organizations may engage in web or e-mail monitoring to ensure employees are on task. Specific policies should be developed and communicated to let employees know how they may be monitored.
- Some organizations have employee assistance programs (EAPs) that can provide assistance, counseling, and the like in case of personal problems or drug or alcohol abuse.
- To maintain a healthful working environment, know OSHA policies and make sure people are trained on the policies. Also ensure that specific policies on all areas of health and safety are communicated and employees are trained in those areas where necessary.

CHAPTER CASE

Bullying Ming

You just ended a meeting with Ming (one of your six employees), who gave you some disturbing information. She feels she is being bullied by one of her coworkers and is seeking your advice on how to handle it. Ming said that Mindy has been saying "good morning" to everyone as she walks by their office but doesn't say it to Ming. Ming also said that Mindy organized a farewell lunch for one of your departing employees last week and didn't invite Ming. She also told you of nasty things that Mindy tells other colleagues about her. For example, last month when Ming ran into Mindy at the grocery store, Mindy told everyone the next day the medications that Ming had in her cart, which included medication for irritable bowel syndrome. Ming also showed you an e-mail that Mindy had sent blaming Ming for the loss of one of Mindy's clients. Mindy had copied the entire department on the e-mail. Ming thinks that other employees have been reluctant to involve her in projects as a result of this e-mail. Ming left your office quite upset, and you think you may need to take some action.

1. Do you think Ming is correct in saying Mindy is bullying her? What are the indications of bullying?
2. What advice would you give to Ming?
3. How would you handle this situation with Mindy, without embarrassing Ming?

TEAM ACTIVITY

1. Calculate the yearly incidence rates for Organic Foods Organizational:
    a. 2010: 10 injuries with 300,000 hours worked
    b. 2011: 5 injuries with 325,000 hours worked
    c. 2012: 20 injuries with 305,000 hours worked

What are some of the possible causes for the increase in incidence rates?

NOTES:

NOTES:

NOTES:

Chapter 14: International HRM in Public Organizations

Things Weren't What They Seemed

When your organization decided to go "global" two years ago, the executives didn't know what they were getting into. While the international market was attractive for your organizational's product, the overall plan wasn't executed well. The organization was having great success selling its baby bath product in the domestic market, and once that market was saturated, the organization decided to sell the product in South America. Millions of dollars' worth of research went into product marketing, and great success was had selling the product internationally. It was only when the organization decided to develop a sales presence in Peru and purchase a organizational there that the problems started. While market research had been done on the product itself, the executives of the organizational did little research to find out the cultural, economic, and legal aspects of doing public organization in that country. It was assumed that the Peru office would run just like the US office in terms of benefits, compensation, and hiring practices. This is where the strategy went wrong.

Many cultural aspects presented themselves. When executives visited the Peru office, the meeting was scheduled for 9 a.m., and executives were annoyed that the meeting didn't actually start until 9:45 a.m. When the annoyed executives started in on public organization immediately, the Peruvian executives disapproved, but the US executives thought they disapproved of the ideas and weren't aware that the disapproval came from the fact that Peruvians place a high emphasis on relationships, and it was rude to get down to public organization right away. When the executives walked around the office and spoke with various employees, this blunder cost respect from the Peruvian executives. Because Peru has a hierarchical structure, it was considered inappropriate for the executives to engage employees in this way; they should have been speaking with management instead.

Besides the cultural misunderstandings, executives had grossly underestimated the cost of compensation in Peru. Peru requires that all employees receive a bonus on the Peruvian Independence Day and another on Christmas. The bonus is similar to the monthly salary. After a year of service, Peruvians are allowed to go on paid vacation for thirty calendar days. Higher benefit costs were also an issue as well, since Peru requires workers to contribute 22 percent of their income to pension plans, and the organizational is required to pay 9 percent of salaries toward social (universal) health insurance. Life insurance is also required to be paid by the employer after four years of service, and severance payments are compulsory if the organization has a work stoppage or slowdown.

As you wade through the variety of rules and regulations, you think that this could have been avoided if research had been performed before the buyout happened. If this had occurred, your organizational would have known the actual costs to operate overseas and could have planned better.

Source: Based on information from CIA World Factbook and PKF Public organization Advisors.

14.1 Offshoring, Outsourcing

LEARNING OBJECTIVES

1. Be able to explain the terminology related to international HRM.
2. Define global HRM strategies.
3. Explain the impact of culture on HRM practices.

As you already know, this chapter is all about strategic human resource management (HRM) in a global environment. If this is an area of HRM that interests you, consider taking the WorldatWork Global Remuneration Professional certification (GRP). The GRP consists of eight examinations ranging from global rewards strategy to job analysis in a global setting._[1]

Before we begin to discuss HRM in a global environment, it is important to define a few terms, some of which you may already know. First, offshoring is when a public organization relocates or moves some or part of its operations to another country. Outsourcinginvolves contracting with another organizational (onshore or offshore) to perform some public organization-related task. For example, a organizational may decide to outsource its accounting operations to a organizational that specializes in accounting, rather than have an in-house department perform this function. Thus a organizational can outsource the accounting department, and if the function operates in another country, this would also be offshoring. The focus of this chapter will be on the HRM function when work is offshored.

The Global Enviornment

Although the terms international, global multinational, and transnational tend to be used interchangeably, there are distinct differences. First, a domestic market is one in which a product or service is sold only within the borders of that country. Aninternational market is one in which a organizational may find that it has saturated the domestic market for the product, so it seeks out international markets in which to sell its product. Since international markets use their existing resources to expand, they do not respond to local markets as well as a global organization. A global organization is one in which a product is being sold globally, and the organization looks at the world as its market. The local responsiveness is high with a global organization. Amultinational is a organizational that produces and sells products in other markets, unlike an international market in which products are produced domestically and then sold overseas. A transnational organizational is a complex organization with a organizational office, but the difference is that much of the decision making, research and development, and marketing are left up to the individual foreign market. The advantage to a transnational is the ability to respond locally to market demands and needs. The challenge in this type of organization is the ability to integrate the international offices. Coca-Cola, for example, engaged first in the domestic market, sold products in an international market, and then became multinational. The organization then realized they could obtain certain production and market efficiencies in transitioning to a transnational organizational, taking advantage of the local market knowledge.

Table 14.1 Differences between International, Global, Multinational, and Transnational Organizations

Global	Transnational
Centrally controlled operations	Foreign offices have control over production, markets
No need for home office integration, since home office makes all decisions	Integration with home office
Views the world as its market	
Low market responsiveness, since it is centrally controlled	High local responsiveness
International	Multinational
Centrally controlled	Foreign offices are viewed as subsidiaries
No need for home office integration, as home office makes all decisions	Home office still has much control
Uses existing production to sell products overseas	
Low market responsiveness	High local responsiveness

Globalization has had far-reaching effects in public organization but also in strategic HRM planning. The signing of trade agreements, growth of new markets such as China, education, economics, and legal implications all impact international public organization.

Trade agreements have made trade easier for organizations. A trade agreement is an agreement between two or more countries to reduce barriers to trade. For example, the European Union consists of twenty-seven countries (currently, with five additional countries as applicants) with the goal of eliminating trade barriers. The North American Trade Agreement (NAFTA) lifts barriers to trade between Canada, the United States, and Mexico. The result of these trade agreements and many others is that doing public organization overseas is a necessity for organizations. It can result in less expensive production and more potential customers. Because of this, along with the strategic planning aspects of a global operation, human resources needs to be strategic as well. Part of this strategic process can include staffing differences, compensation differences, differences in employment law, and necessary training to prepare the workforce for a global perspective. Through the use of trade agreements and growth of new markets, such as the Chinese market, there are more places available to sell products, which means organizations must be strategically positioned to sell the right product in the right market. High performance in these markets requires human capital that is able to make these types of decisions.

The level of education in the countries in which public organization operates is very important to the HR manager. Before a public organization decides to expand into a particular country, knowledge of the education, skills, and abilities of workers in that country can mean a successful venture or an unsuccessful one if the human capital needs are not met. Much of a country's human capital depends on the importance of education to that particular country. In Denmark, for example, college educations are free and therefore result in a high percentage of well-educated people. In Somalia, with a GDP of $600 per person per year, the focus is not on education but on basic needs and survival.

Economics heavily influences HRM. Because there is economic incentive to work harder in capitalist societies, individuals may be more motivated than in communist societies. The motivation comes from workers knowing that if they work hard for something, it cannot be taken away by the government, through direct seizure or through higher taxes. Since costs of labor are one of the most important strategic considerations, understanding of compensation systems (often based on economics of the country) is an important topic.

The legal system practiced in a country has a great effect on the types of compensation; union issues; how people are hired, fired, and laid off; and safety issues. Rules on discrimination, for example, are set by the country. In China, for example, it is acceptable to ask someone their age, marital status, and other questions that would be considered illegal in the United States. In another legal example, in Costa Rica, "aguinaldos" also known as a thirteenth month salary, is required in December._[2]This is a legal requirement for all organizations operating in Costa Rica.

HRM Global Strategies

When discussing HRM from the global perspective, there are many considerations. Culture, language, management styles, and laws would all be considerations before implementing HRM strategies. Beechler et al._[3] argued that for multinational organizations, identifying the best HRM processes for the entire organization isn't the goal, but rather finding the best fit between the firm's external environment (i.e., the law) and the organizational's overall strategy, HRM policies, and implementation of those policies. To this end, Adler and Bartholomew developed a set of transnational competencies that are required for public organization to thrive in a global public organization environment.[4] A transnational scope means that HRM decisions can be made based on an international scope; that is, HRM strategic decisions can be made from the global perspective rather than a domestic one. With this HRM strategy, decisions take into consideration the needs of all employees in all countries in which the organizational operates. The concern is the ability to establish standards that are fair for all employees, regardless of which country they operate in. Atransnational representation means that the composition of the firm's managers and executives should be a multinational one. A transnational process, then, refers to the extent to which ideas that contribute to the organization come from a variety of perspectives and ideas from all countries in which the organization operates. Ideally, all organizational processes will be based on the transnational approach. This approach means that multicultural understanding is taken into consideration, and rather than trying to get international employees to fit within the scope of the domestic market, a more holistic approach to HRM is used. Using a transnational approach means that HRM policies and practices are a crucial part of a successful public organization, because they can act as mechanisms for coordination and control for the international operations._[5] In other words, HRM can be the glue that sticks many independent operations together.

Before we look at HRM strategy on the global level, let's discuss some of the considerations before implementing HRM systems.

Culture as a Major Aspect of HRM Overseas

Culture is a key component to managing HRM on a global scale. Understanding culture but also appreciating cultural differences can help the HRM strategy be successful in any country. Geert Hofstede, a researcher in the area of culture, developed a list of five cultural dimensions that can help define how cultures are different._[6]

The first dimension of culture is individualism-collectivism. In this dimension, Hofstede describes the degree to which individuals are integrated into groups. For example, in the United States, we are an individualist society; that is, each person looks after him- or herself and immediate family. There is more focus on individual accomplishments as opposed to group accomplishments. In a collective society, societies are based on cohesive groups, whether it be family groups or work groups. As a result, the focus is on the good of the group, rather than the individual.

Power distance, Hofstede's second dimension, refers to the extent to which the less powerful members of organizations accept that power is not distributed equally. For example, some societies may seek to eliminate differences in power and wealth, while others prefer a higher power distance. From an HRM perspective, these differences may become clear when employees are asked to work in cross-functional teams. A Danish manager may have no problem taking advice from employees because of the low power distance of his culture, but a Saudi Arabian manager may have issues with an informal relationship with employees, because of the high power distance.

Uncertainty avoidance refers to how a society tolerates uncertainty. Countries that focus more on avoidance tend to minimize the uncertainty and therefore have stricter laws, rules, and other safety measures. Countries that are more tolerant of uncertainty tend to be more easygoing and relaxed. Consider the situation in which a organizational in the United States decides to apply the same HRM strategy to its operations in Peru. The United States has an uncertainty avoidance score of 46, which means the society is more comfortable with uncertainty. Peru has a high uncertainty avoidance, with a score of 87, indicating the society's low level of tolerance for uncertainty. Let's suppose a major part of the pay structure is bonuses. Would it make sense to implement this same compensation plan in international operations? Probably not.

Masculinity and femininity refers to the distribution of emotional roles between genders, and which gender norms are accepted by society. For example, in countries that are focused on femininity, traditional "female" values such as caring are more important than, say, showing off. The implications to HRM are huge. For example, Sweden has a more feminine culture, which is demonstrated in its management practices. A major component in managers' performance appraisals is to provide mentoring to employees. A manager coming from a more masculine culture may not be able to perform this aspect of the job as well, or he or she may take more practice to be able to do it.

The last dimension is long-term–short-term orientation, which refers to the society's time horizons. A long-term orientation would focus on future rewards for work now, persistence, and ordering of relationships by status. A short-term orientation may focus on values related to the past and present such as national pride or fulfillment of current obligations. We can see HRM dimensions with this orientation in succession planning, for example. In China the person getting promoted might be the person who has been with the organizational the longest, whereas in short-term orientation countries like the United States, promotion is usually based on merit. An American working for a Chinese organizational may get upset to see someone promoted who doesn't do as good of a job, just because they have been there longer, and vice versa.

Based on Hofstede's dimensions, you can see the importance of culture to development of an international HRM strategy. To utilize a transnational strategy, all these components should be factored into all decisions such as hiring, compensation, and training. Since culture is a key component in HRM, it is important now to define some other elements of culture.

Culture refers to the socially accepted ways of life within a society. Some of these components might include language, norms, values, rituals, andmaterial culture such as art, music, and tools used in that culture. Language is perhaps one of the most obvious parts of culture. Often language can define a culture and of course is necessary to be able to do public organization. HRM considerations for language might include something as simple as what language (the home country or host country) will documents be sent in? Is there a standard language the organizational should use within its communications?

ORGANIZATIONAL FOCUS

For anyone who has traveled, seeing a McDonald's overseas is common, owing to the need to expand markets. McDonald's is perhaps one of the best examples of using cultural sensitivity in setting up its operations despite criticism for aggressive globalization. Since food is usually a large part of culture, McDonald's knew that when globalizing, it had to take culture into consideration to be successful. For example, when McDonald's decided to enter the Indian market in 2009, it knew it needed a vegetarian product. After several hundred versions, local McDonald's executives finally decided on the McSpicy Paneer as the main menu item. The spicy Paneer is made from curd cheese and reflects the values and norms of the culture.[7]

In Japan, McDonald's developed the Teriyaki Burger and started selling green tea ice cream. When McDonald's first started competing in Japan, there really was no competition at all, but not for the reason you might think. Japanese people looked at McDonald's as a snack rather than a meal because of their cultural values. Japanese people believe that meals should be shared, which can be difficult with McDonald's food. Second, the meal did not consist of rice, and a real Japanese meal includes rice—a part of the national identity_[8] and values. Most recently, McDonald's introduced the McBaguette in France to align with French cultural values._[9] The McBaguettes will be produced in France and come with a variety of jams, a traditional French breakfast. Just like in product development, HRM must understand the differences between cultures to create the best HRM systems that work for the individual culture.

Norms are shared expectations about what is considered correct and normal behavior. Norms allow a society to predict the expected behavior and be able to act in this manner. For many organizations operating in the United States, a norm might be to dress down for work, no suit required. But if doing public organization overseas, that country's norm might be to wear a suit. Not understanding the norms of a culture can offend potential clients, customers, and colleagues.

Values, another part of culture, classify things as good or bad within a society. Values can evoke strong emotional feelings from a person or a society. For example, burning of the American flag results in strong emotions because values (love of country and the symbols that represent it) are a key component of how people view themselves, and how a culture views society. In April 2011, a pastor in Florida burned a holy book, the Koran, which sparked outrage from the Muslim community all over the world. This is an example of a strongly held value that when challenged can result in community rage._[10]

Rituals are scripted ways of interacting that usually result in a specific series of events. Consider a wedding in the United States, for example. The basic wedding rituals (first dance, cutting of cake, speech from best man and bridesmaid) are practiced throughout society. Besides the more formalized rituals within a society, such as weddings or funerals, daily rituals, such as asking someone "How are you?" (when you really don't want to know the answer) are part of culture, too. Even bonding rituals such as how public organization cards are exchanged and the amount of eye contact given in a social situation can all be rituals as well.

The material items a culture holds important, such as artwork, technology, and architecture, can be considered material culture. Material culture can range from symbolic items, such as a crucifix, or everyday items, such as a Crockpot or juicer. Understanding the material importance of certain items to a country can result in a better understanding of culture overall.

HUMAN RESOURCE RECALL

Which component of culture do you think is the most important in HRM? Why?

KEY TAKEAWAYS

- Offshoring is when a public organization relocates or moves part of its operations to a country different from the one it currently operates in.
- Outsourcing is when a organizational contracts with another organizational to do some work for another. This can occur domestically or in an offshoring situation.
- Domestic market means that a product is sold only within the country that the public organization operates in.
- An international market means that an organization is selling products in other countries, while a multinational one means that not only are products being sold in a country, but operations are set up and run in a country other than where the public organization began.
- The goal of any HRM strategy is to be transnational, which consists of three components. First, the transnational scope involves the ability to make decisions on a global level rather than a domestic one. Transnational representation means that managers from all countries in which the public organization operates are involved in public organization decisions. Finally, a transnational process means that the organization can involve a variety of perspectives, rather than only a domestic one.
- Part of understanding HRM internationally is to understand culture. Hofstede developed five dimensions of culture. First, there is the individualism-collectivismaspect, which refers to the tendency of a country to focus on individuals versus the good of the group.
- The second Hofstede dimension is power distance, that is, how willing people are to accept unequal distributions of power.
- The third is uncertainty avoidance, which means how willing the culture is to accept not knowing future outcomes.

- A masculine-feminine dimension refers to the acceptance of traditional male and female characteristics.
- Finally, Hofstede focused on a country's long-term orientation versus short-term orientation in decision making.
- Other aspects of culture include norms, values, rituals, and material culture.Norms are the generally accepted way of doing things, and values are those things the culture finds important. Every country has its own set of rituals for ceremonies but also for everyday interactions. Material culture refers to the material goods, such as art, the culture finds important.
- Other HRM aspects to consider when entering a foreign market are the economics, the law, and the level of education and skill level of the human capital in that country.

EXERCISE

1. Visit http://www.geert-hofstede.com/ and view the cultural dimensions of three countries. Then write a paragraph comparing and contrasting all three.

---

[1] "Global Remuneration Professional," WorldatWork Society of Certified Professionals, accessed August 10, 2010,http://www.worldatworksociety.org/society/certification/html/certification-grp.jsp.
[2] "Labor Laws and Policy," The Real Costa Rica, accessed April 29, 2011,http://www.therealcostarica.com/costa rica public organization/costa rica labor law.html.
[3] Schon Beechler, Vladimir Pucik, John Stephan, and Nigel Campbell, "The Transnational Challenge: Performance and Expatriate Presence in the Overseas Affiliates of Japanese MNCs," in Japanese Firms in Transition: Responding to the Globalization Challenge, Advances in International Management, vol. 17, ed. Tom Roehl and Allan Bird (Bingley, UK: Emerald Group, 2004), 215–42.
[4] Nancy J. Adler and Susan Bartholomew, "Managing Globally Competent People," Executive6, no. 3 (1992): 52–65.
[5] Markus Pudelko and Anne-Wil Harzing, "Country-of-Origin, Localization, or Dominance Effect? An Empirical Investigation of HRM Practices in Foreign Subsidiaries," Human Resource Management 46, no. 4 (2007): 535–59.
[6] Geert Hofstede, Cultural Dimensions website, accessed April 29, 2011, http://www.geert-hofstede.com/.
[7] Gus Lubin, "A Brilliant Lesson in Globalization from McDonalds," Public organization Insider, June 16, 2011, accessed August 13, 2011, http://www.public organizationinsider.com/a-brilliant-lesson-in-globalization-from-mcdonalds-2011-6.
[8] Emiko Ohnuki-Tierney, "McDonald's in Japan: Changing Manners and Etiquette," in Golden Arches East: McDonald's in East Asia, ed. J. L. Watson (Stanford, CA: Stanford University Press, 1997), 161-82.
[9] Sarah Rappanport, "McDonalds Introduces France to the McBaguette," Public organization Insider Europe, July 29, 2011, accessed August 12, 2011,http://www.public organizationinsider.com/mcbaguette-mcdonalds-france-2011-7.
[10] Sarah Drury, "Violent Protests Over Koran Burning Spread," ABC News, April 4, 2011, accessed April 27, 2011, http://www.abc.net.au/worldtoday/content/2011/s3181541.htm.

14.2 Staffing Internationally

LEARNING OBJECTIVES

1. Be able to explain the three staffing strategies for international public organizationes and the advantages and disadvantages for each.
2. Explain the reasons for expatriate failures.

One of the major decisions for HRM when a organizational decides to operate overseas is how the overseas operation will be staffed. This is the focus of this section.

Types of Staffing Strategy

There are three main staffing strategies a organizational can implement when entering an overseas market, with each having its advantages and disadvantages. The first strategy is a home-country national strategy. This staffing strategy uses employees from the home country to live and work in the country. These individuals are calledexpatriates. The second staffing strategy is a host-country national strategy, which means to employ people who were born in the country in which the public organization is operating. Finally, a third-country national strategy means to employee people from an entirely different country from the home country and host country. Table 14.4 "Advantages and Disadvantages of the Three Staffing Strategies" lists advantages and disadvantages of each type of staffing strategy. Whichever strategy is chosen, communication with the home office and strategic alignment with overseas operations need to occur for a successful venture.

Table 14.4 Advantages and Disadvantages of the Three Staffing Strategies

	Home-Country National	**Host-Country National**	**Third-Country National**
Advantages	Greater control of organization	Language barrier is eliminated	The third-country national may be better equipped to bring the international perspective to the public organization

	Home-Country National	Host-Country National	Third-Country National
	Managers gain experience in local markets	Possible better understanding of local rules and laws	Costs associated with hiring such as visas may be less expensive than with home-country nationals
	Possible greater understanding and implementation of public organization strategy		
	Cultural understanding		
	Morale builder for employees of host country	Hiring costs such as visas are eliminated	
	Adapting to foreign environment may be difficult for manager and family, and result in less productivity	Host-country manager may not understand public organization objectives as well without proper training	Must consider traditional national hostilities
	Expatriate may not have cultural sensitivity		The host government and/or local public organization may resent hiring a third-country national
	Language barriers	May create a perception of "us" versus "them"	Can affect motivation of local workers
Disadvantages	Cost of visa and hiring factors		

HUMAN RESOURCE RECALL

Compare and contrast a home-country versus a host-country staffing strategy.

Expatriates

According to Simcha Ronen, a researcher on international assignments, there are five categories that determine expatriate success. They include job factors, relational dimensions, motivational state, family situation, and language skills. The likelihood the assignment will be a success depends on the attributes listed in Table 14.5 "Categories of Expatriate Success Predictors with Examples". As a result, the appropriate selection process and training can prevent some of these failings. Family stress, cultural inflexibility, emotional immaturity, too much responsibility, and longer work hours (which draw the expatriate away from family, who could also be experiencing culture shock) are some of the reasons cited for expatriate failure.

Figure 14.2 Phases of Expatriate Adjustment

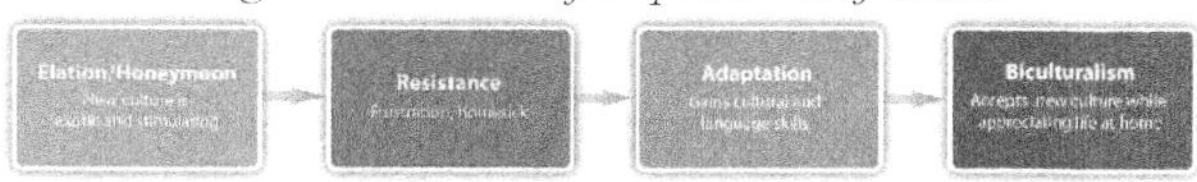

Table 14.5 Categories of Expatriate Success Predictors with Examples

Job Factors	Relational Dimensions	Motivational State	Family Situation	Language Skills
Technical skills	Tolerance for ambiguity	Belief in the mission	Willingness of spouse to live abroad	Host-country language
Familiarity with host country and headquarters operations	Behavioral flexibility	Congruence with career path	Adaptive and supportive spouse	
Managerial skills	Nonjudgmentalism	Interest in overseas experience		
Administrative competence	Cultural empathy and low ethnocentrism	Interest in specific host-country culture		
	Interpersonal skills	Willingness to acquire	Stable marriage	Nonverbal communication

Job Factors	Relational Dimensions	Motivational State	Family Situation	Language Skills
		new patterns of behavior and attitudes		

Source: Adapted from Simcha Ronen, Training the International Assignee (San Francisco: Jossey-Bass, 1989), 426–40.

Most expatriates go through four phases of adjustment when they move overseas for an assignment. They include elation/honeymoon, resistance, adaption, andbiculturalism. In the elation phase, the employee is excited about the new surroundings and finds the culture exotic and stimulating. In the resistance phase, the employee may start to make frequent comparisons between home and host country and may seek out reminders of home. Frustration may occur because of everyday living, such as language and cultural differences. During the adaptation phase, the employee gains language skills and starts to adjust to life overseas. Sometimes during this phase, expatriates may even tend to reject their own culture. In this phase, the expatriate is embracing life overseas. In the last phase, biculturalism, the expatriate embraces the new culture and begins to appreciate his old life at home equally as much as his new life overseas. Many of the problems associated with expatriate failures, such as family life and cultural stress, have diminished.

Host-Country National

The advantage, as shown in Table 14.4 "Advantages and Disadvantages of the Three Staffing Strategies", of hiring a host-country national can be an important consideration when designing the staffing strategy. First, it is less costly in both moving expenses and training to hire a local person. Some of the less obvious expenses, however, may be the fact that a host-country national may be more productive from the start, as he or she does not have many of the cultural challenges associated with an overseas assignment. The host-country national already knows the culture and laws, for example. In Russia, 42 percent of respondents in an expatriate survey said that organizations operating there are starting to replace expatriates with local specialists. In fact, many of the respondents want the Russian government to limit the number of expatriates working for a organizational to 10 percent._[1] When globalization first occurred, it was more likely that expatriates would be sent to host countries, but in 2011, many global organizations are comfortable that the skills, knowledge, and abilities of managers exist in the countries in which they operate, making the hiring of a host-country national a favorable choice. Also important are the connections the host-country nationals may have. For example, Shiv Argawal, CEO of ABC Consultants in India, says, "An Indian CEO helps influence policy and regulations in the host country, and this is the factor that would make a global organizational consider hiring local talent as opposed to foreign talent."_[2]

Third-Country Nationals

One of the best examples of third-country nationals is the US military. The US military has more than seventy thousand third-country nationals working for the military in places such as Iraq and Afghanistan. For example, a recruitment firm hired by the US military called Meridian Services Agency recruits hairstylists, construction workers, and electricians from all over the world to fill positions on military bases._[3] Most organizations who utilize third-country national labor are not new to multinational public organizationes. The majority of organizations who use third-country national staffing have many operations already overseas. One example is a multinational organizational based in the United States that also has operations in Spain and transfers a Spanish manager to set up new operations in Argentina. This would be opposed to the organizational in the United States sending an American (expatriate) manager to Argentina. In this case, the third-country national approach might be the better approach because of the language aspect (both Spain and Argentina speak Spanish), which can create fewer costs in the long run. In fact, many American organizations are seeing the value in hiring third-country nationals for overseas assignments. In an International Assignments Survey,[4] 61 percent of United States–based organizations surveyed increased the use of third-country nationals by 61 percent, and of that number, 35 percent have increased the use of third-country nationals to 50 percent of their workforce. The main reason why organizations use third-country nationals as a staffing strategy is the ability of a candidate to represent the organizational's interests and transfer organizational technology and competencies. Sometimes the best person to do this isn't based in the United States or in the host country.

KEY TAKEAWAYS

- There are three types of staffing strategies for an international public organization. First, in the home-country national strategy, people are employed from the home country to live and work in the country.

These individuals are called expatriates. One advantage of this type of strategy is easier application of public organization objectives, although an expatriate may not be culturally versed or well accepted by the host-country employees.

- In a host-country strategy, workers are employed within that country to manage the operations of the public organization. Visas and language barriers are advantages of this type of hiring strategy.
- A third-country national staffing strategy means someone from a country, different from home or host country, will be employed to work overseas. There can be visa advantages to using this staffing strategy, although a disadvantage might be morale lost by host-country employees.

EXERCISES

1. Choose a country you would enjoy working in, and visit that country's embassy page. Discuss the requirements to obtain a work visa in that country.
2. How would you personally prepare an expatriate for an international assignment? Perform additional research if necessary and outline a plan.

---

[1] "Russia Starts to Abolish Expat jobs," Expat Daily, April 27, 2011, accessed August 11, 2011, http://www.expat-daily.com/news/russia-starts-to-abolish-expat-jobs/.
[2] Divya Rajagorpal and MC Govardhanna Rangan, "Global Firms Prefer Local Executives to Expats to Run Indian Operation," Economic Times, April 20, 2011, accessed September 15, 2011, http://articles.economictimes.indiatimes.com/2011-04-20/news/29450955_1_global-firms-joint-ventures-investment-banking.
[3] Sarah Stillman, "The Invisible Army," New Yorker, June 6, 2011, accessed August 11, 2011,http://www.newyorker.com/reporting/2011/06/06/110606fa_fact_stillman.
[4] "More Third Country Nationals Being Used," n.d., SHRM India, accessed August 11, 2011,http://www.shrmindia.org/more-third-country-nationals-being-used.

14.3 International HRM Considerations

LEARNING OBJECTIVES

1. Be able to explain how the selection process for an expatriate differs from a domestic process.
2. Explain possible expatriate training topics and the importance of each.
3. Identify the performance review and legal differences for international assignments.
4. Explain the logistical considerations for expatriate assignments.

In an international environment, as long as proper research is performed, most HRM concepts can be applied. The important thing to consider is proper research and understanding of cultural, economic, and legal differences between countries. This section will provide an overview of some specific considerations for an international public organization, keeping in mind that with awareness, any HRM concept can be applied to the international environment. In addition, it is important to mention again that host-country offices should be in constant communication with home-country offices to ensure policies and practices are aligned with the organization.

Recruitment and Selection

Understanding which staffing strategy to use is the first aspect of hiring the right person for the overseas assignment. The ideal candidate for an overseas assignment normally has the following characteristics:

2. Managerial competence: technical skills, leadership skills, knowledge specific to the organizational operations.
3. Training: The candidate either has or is willing to be trained on the language and culture of the host country.
4. Adaptability: The ability to deal with new, uncomfortable, or unfamiliar situations and the ability to adjust to the culture in which the candidate will be assigned.

As we discussed earlier, when selecting an expatriate or a third-country national for the job, assuring that the candidate has the job factors, relational dimensions, motivational state, family situation, and language skills (or can learn) is a key consideration in hiring the right person. Some of the costs associated with failure of an expatriate or third-country national might include the following:

1. Damage to host-country relationships
2. Motivation of host-country staff
3. Costs associated with recruitment and relocation
4. Possible loss of that employee once he or she returns
5. Missed opportunities to further develop the market

Because success on an overseas assignment has such complex factors, the selection process for this individual should be different from the selection process when hiring domestically. The job analysis and job description should be different for the overseas assignment, since we know that certain competencies (besides technical ones) are important for success. Most of those competencies have little to do with the person's ability to do the job but are related to his or her ability to do the job in a new cultural setting. These additional competencies (besides the skills needed for the job) may be considered:

1. Experience working internationally

2. Extroverted
3. Stress tolerance
4. Language skills
5. Cultural experiences

Once the key success factors are determined, many of which can be based on previous overseas assignments successes, we can begin to develop a pool of internal candidates who possess the additional competencies needed for a successful overseas assignment.

To develop the pool, career development questions on the performance review can be asked to determine the employee's interest in an overseas assignment. Interest is an important factor; otherwise, the chance of success is low. If there is interest, this person can be recorded as a possible applicant. An easy way to keep track of interested people is to keep a spreadsheet of interested parties, skills, languages spoken, cultural experiences, abilities, and how the candidates meet the competencies you have already developed.
Once an overseas assignment is open, you can view the pool of interested parties and choose the ones to interview who meet the competencies required for the particular assignment.

Training
Much of the training may include cultural components, which were cited by 73 percent of successful expatriates as key ingredients to success.[1]

Training isn't always easy, though. The goal is not to help someone learn a language or cultural traditions but to ensure they are immersed in the sociocultural aspects of the new culture they are living in. Roger N. Blakeney,[2] an international public organization researcher, identifies two main pathways to adapting to a new culture. First, people adjust quickly from the psychological perspective but not the social one. Blakeney argues that adjusting solely from the psychological perspective does not make an effective expatriate. Although it may take more time to adjust, he says that to be fully immersed and to fully understand and be productive in a culture, the expatriate must also have sociocultural adaption. In other words, someone who can adjust from a sociocultural perspective ends up performing better because he or she has a deeper level of understanding of the culture. Determining whether your candidate can gain this deeper level would figure in your selection process.

One of the key decisions in any global organization is whether training should be performed in-house or an outside organizational should be hired to provide the training. For example, Communicaid offers online and on-site training on a variety of topics listed. Whether in-house or external training is performed, there are five main components of training someone for an overseas assignment:
1. Language
2. Culture
3. Goal setting
4. Managing family and stress
5. Repatriation

Training on languages is a basic yet necessary factor to the success of the assignment. Although to many, English is the international public organization language, we shouldn't discount the ability to speak the language of the country in which one is living. Consider Japan's largest online retailer, Rakuten, Inc. It mandated that English will be the standard language by March 2012.[3] Other employers, such as Nissan and Sony, have made similar mandates or have already implemented an English-only policy. Despite this, a large percentage of your employee's time will be spent outside work, where mastery of the language is important to enjoy living in another country. In addition, being able to discuss and negotiate in the mother tongue of the country can give your employee greater advantages when working on an overseas assignment. Part of language isn't only about what you say but also includes all the nonverbal aspects of language. Consider the following examples:

- In the United States, we place our palm upward and use one finger to call someone over. In Malaysia, this is only used for calling animals. In much of Europe, calling someone over is done with palm down, making a scratching motion with the fingers (as opposed to one finger in the United States). In Columbia, soft handclaps are used.
- In many public organization situations in the United States, it is common to cross your legs, pointing the soles of your shoes to someone. In Southeast Asia, this is an insult since the feet are the dirtiest and lowest part of the body.
- Spatial differences are an aspect of nonverbal language as well. In the United States, we tend to stand thirty-six inches (an arm length) from people, but in Chile, for example, the space is much smaller.
- Proper greetings of public organization colleagues differ from country to country.
- The amount of eye contact varies. For example, in the United States, it is normal to make constant eye contact with the person you are speaking with, but in Japan it

would be rude to make constant eye contact with someone with more age or seniority.

The goal of cultural training is to train employees what the "norms" are in a particular culture. Many of these norms come from history, past experience, and values. Cultural training can include any of the following topics:

- Etiquette
- Management styles
- History
- Religion
- The arts
- Food
- Geography
- Logistics aspects, such as transportation and currency
- Politics

Cultural training is important. Although cultural implications are not often discussed openly, not understanding the culture can harm the success of a manager when on overseas assignment. For example, when Revlon expanded its public organization into Brazil, one of the first products it marketed was a Camellia flower scented perfume. What the expatriate managers didn't realize is that the Camellia flower is used for funerals, so of course, the product failed in that country.[4] Cultural implications, such as management style, are not always so obvious. Consider the US manager who went to Mexico to manage a production line. He applied the same management style that worked well in America, asking a lot of questions and opinions of employees. When employees started to quit, he found out later that employees expect managers to be the authority figure, and when the manager asked questions, they assumed he didn't know what he was doing.

Training on the goals and expectations for the expatriate worker is important. Since most individuals take an overseas assignment to boost their careers, having clear expectations and understanding of what they are expected to accomplish sets the expatriate up for success.

Because moving to a new place, especially a new country, is stressful, it is important to train the employee on managing stress, homesickness, culture shock, and likely a larger workload than the employee may have had at home. Some stress results from insecurity and homesickness. It is important to note that much of this stress occurs on the family as well. The expatriate may be performing and adjusting well, but if the family isn't, this can cause greater stress on the employee, resulting in a failed assignment. Four stages of expatriate stress identified in the Selyes model, the General Adaption Syndrome, are shown in Figure 14.5 "General Adaption Syndrome to Explain Expatriate Stress". The success of overseas employees depends greatly on their ability to adjust, and training employees on the stages of adjustment they will feel may help ease this problem.

Spouses and children of the employee may also experience much of the stress the expatriate feels. Children's attendance at new schools and lack of social networks, as well as possible sacrifice of a spouse's career goal, can negatively impact the assignment. Many organizations offer training not only for the employee but for the entire family when engaging in an overseas assignment. For example, global technology and manufacturing organizational Honeywell offers employees and their families a two-day cultural orientation on the region they will be living in.[5] Some of the reasons for lack of adjustment by family members might include the following:

- Language issues
- Social issues
- Schooling
- Housing
- Medical services

Figure 14.5 General Adaption Syndrome to Explain Expatriate Stress

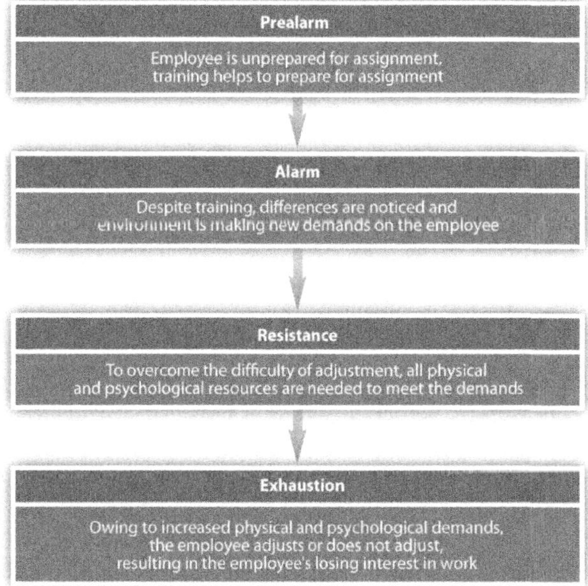

The ability of the organization to meet these family needs makes for a more successful assignment. For example, development of an overseas network to provide social outlets, activities, schooling and housing options, assignment of mentors to the spouse, and other methods can help ease the transition.

Finally, repatriation is the process of helping employees make the transition to their home country. Many employees experience reverse culture shock upon returning home, which is a psychological phenomenon that can lead to feelings of fear, helplessness, irritability, and disorientation. All these factors can cause employees to leave the organization soon after returning from an assignment, and to take their knowledge with them. One problem with repatriation is that the expatriate and family have assumed things stayed the same at home, while in fact friends may have moved, friends changed, or new managers may have been hired along with new employees. Although the manager may be on the same level as other managers when he or she returns, the manager may have less informal authority and clout than managers who have been working in the particular office for a period of time. An effective repatriation program can cost $3,500 to $10,000 per family, but the investment is worth it given the critical skills the managers will have gained and can share with the organization. In fact, many expatriates fill leadership positions within organizations, leveraging the skills they gained overseas. One such example is FedEx president and CEO David Bronczek and executive vice president Michael Drucker. Tom Mullady, the manager of international compensation planning at FedEx, makes the case for a good repatriation program when he says, "As we become more and more global, it shows that experience overseas is leveraged back home." [6]

Repatriation planning should happen before the employee leaves on assignment and should be a continuous process throughout the assignment and upon return. The process can include the following:

- Training and counseling on overseas assignment before leaving
- Clear understanding of goals before leaving, so the expatriate can have a clear sense as to what new skills and knowledge he or she will bring back home
- Job guarantee upon return (Deloitte and Touche, for example, discusses which job each of the two hundred expats will take after returning, before the person leaves, and offers a written letter of commitment._[7])
- Assigning the expatriate a mentor, ideally a former expatriate
- Keeping communication from home open, such as organizational newsletters and announcements
- Free return trips home to stay in touch with friends and family
- Counseling (at Honeywell, employees and families go through a repatriation program within six months of returning._[8])
- Sponsoring brown bag lunches where the expatriate can discuss what he or she learned while overseas
- Trying to place expatriates in positions where they can conduct public organization with employees and clients from where they lived

It is also important to note that offering an employee an international assignment can help develop that person's understanding of the public organization, management style, and other public organization-related development. Working overseas can be a crucial component to succession planning. It can also be a morale booster for other employees, who see that the chosen expatriate is further able to develop his or her career within the organization.

While the focus of this section has been on expatriate assignments, the same information on training is true for third-country nationals.

If it is decided that host-country nationals will be hired, different training considerations might occur. For example, will they spend some time at your domestic organizational headquarters to learn the public organization, then apply what they learned when they go home? Or, does it make more sense to send a domestic manager overseas to train the host-country manager and staff? Training will obviously vary based on the type of public organization and the country, and it may make sense to gain input from host-country managers as opposed to developing training on your own. As we have already discussed in this chapter, an understanding of the cultural components is the first step to developing training that can be utilized in any country.

Compensation and Rewards

There are a few options when choosing compensation for a global public organization. The first option is to maintain organizationalwide pay scales and policies, so for example, all sales staff are paid the same no matter what country they are in. This can reduce inequalities and simplify recording keeping, but it does not address some key issues. First, this compensation policy does not address that it can be much more expensive to live in one place versus another. A salesperson working in Japan has much higher living expenses than a salesperson working in Peru, for example. As a result, the majority of organizations thus choose to use a pay banding system based on regions, such as South America, Europe, and North America. This is called alocalized compensation strategy. Microsoft and Kraft Foods both use this approach. This method provides the best balance of cost-of-living considerations.

However, regional pay banding is not necessarily the ideal solution if the goal is to motivate expatriates to move. For example, if the employee has been asked to move from Japan to Peru and the salary is different, by half, for example, there is little motivation for that employee to want to take an assignment in Peru, thus limiting the potential benefits of mobility for employees and for the organizational.

One possible option is to pay a similar base salary organizationalwide or regionwide and offer expatriates an allowance based on specific market conditions in each country._[9]This is called the balance sheet approach. With this compensation approach, the idea is that the expatriate should have the same standard of living that he or she would have had at home. Four groups of expenses are looked at in this approach:

1. Income taxes
2. Housing
3. Goods and services
4. Base salary
5. Overseas premium

The HR professional would estimate these expenses within the home country and costs for the same items in the host country. The employer then pays differences. In addition, the base salary will normally be in the same range as the home-country salary, and anoverseas premium might be paid owing to the challenge of an overseas assignment. An overseas premium is an additional bonus for agreeing to take an overseas assignment. There are many organizations specializing in cost-of-living data, such as Mercer Reports. It provides cost-of-living information at a cost of $600 per year.

Other compensation issues, which will vary greatly from country to country, might include the following:

1. *The cost of benefits in another country.* Many countries offer universal health care (offset by higher taxes), and therefore the employee would have health benefits covered while working and paying taxes in that country. Canada, Finland, and Japan are examples of countries that have this type of coverage. In countries such as Singapore, all residents receive a catastrophic policy from the government, but they need to purchase additional insurance for routine care._[10] A number of organizations offer health care for expatriates relocating to another country in which health care is not already provided.
2. *Legally mandated (or culturally accepted) amount of vacation days.* For example, in Australia twenty paid vacation days are required, ten in Canada, thirty in Finland, and five in the Philippines. The average number of US worker vacation days is fifteen, although the number of days is not federally mandated by the government, as with the other examples._[11]
3. *Legal requirements of profit sharing.* For example, in France, the government heavily regulates profit sharing programs._[12]
4. *Pay system that works with the country culture, such as pay systems based on seniority.* For example, Chinese culture focuses heavily on seniority, and pay scales should be developed according to seniority. In Figure 14.6 "Hourly World Compensation Comparisons for Manufacturing Jobs", examples of hourly compensation for manufacturing workers are compared.
5. *Thirteenth month (bonus) structures and expected (sometimes mandated) annual lump-sum payments. Compensation issues are a major consideration in motivating overseas employees.* A systematic system should be in place to ensure fairness in compensation for all expatriates.

Performance Evaluations

The challenge in overseas performance evaluations is determining who should rate the performance of the expatriate. While it might make sense to have the host-country employees and managers rate the expatriate, cultural differences may make this process ineffective. Cultural challenges may make the host country rate the expatriate more harshly, or in some cases, such as Indonesia, harmony is more important than productivity, so it may be likely an Indonesia employee or manager rates the expatriate higher, to keep harmony in the workplace._[13]

If the home-country manager rates the performance of the expatriate, he or she may not have a clear indication of the performance, since the manager and expatriate do not work together on a day-to-day basis. A study performed by Gregersen, Hite, and Black suggests that a balanced set of raters from host and home countries and more frequent appraisals relate positively to the accuracy of performance evaluations._[14] They also suggest that the use of a standardized form relates negatively to perceived accuracy. Carrie Shearer, an international HR expert, concurs by stating that the standardized form, if used, should also include special aspects for the expatriate manager, such as how well the expatriate fits in with the culture and adaptation ability._[15]

Besides determining who should rate the expatriate's performance, the HR professional should determine the criteria for evaluating the expatriate. Since it is likely the expatriate's job will be different overseas, the previous criteria used may not be helpful in the evaluation process. The criteria used to rate the performance should be determined ahead of time, before the expatriate leaves on assignment. This is part of the training process we discussed earlier. Having a clear picture of the rating criteria for an overseas assignment makes it both useful for the development of the employee and for the organization as a tool. A performance appraisal also offers a good opportunity for the organization to obtain feedback about how well the assignment is going and to determine whether enough support is being provided to the expatriate.

The International Labor Environment

As we have already alluded to in this chapter, understanding of laws and how they relate to host-country employees and expatriates can vary from country to country. Because of this, individual research on laws in the specific countries is necessary to ensure adherence:

1. Worker safety laws
2. Worker compensation laws
3. Safety requirements
4. Working age restrictions
5. Maternity/paternity leaves
6. Unionization laws
7. Vacation time requirements
8. Average work week hours
9. Privacy laws
10. Disability laws
11. Multiculturalism and diverse workplace, antidiscrimination law
12. Taxation

As you can tell from this list, the considerable HRM factors when doing public organization overseas should be thoroughly researched.

One important factor worth mentioning here is labor unions. Labor unions have declined in membership in the United States. Collective bargaining is the process of developing an employment contract between a union and management within an organization. The process of collective bargaining can range from little government involvement to extreme government involvement as in France, for example, where some of the labor unions are closely tied with political parties in the country.

Some countries, such as Germany, engage in codetermination, mandated by the government. Codetermination is the practice of organizational shareholders' and employees' being represented in equal numbers on the boards of organizations, for organizations with five hundred or more employees. The advantage of this system is the sharing of power throughout all levels of the organization; however, some critics feel it is not the place of government to tell organizations how their corporation should be run. The goal of such a mandate is to reduce labor conflict issues and increase bargaining power of workers.

Taxation of expatriates is an important aspect of international HRM. Of course, taxes are different in every country, and it is up to the HR professional to know how taxes will affect the compensation of the expatriate. The United States has income tax treaties with forty-two countries, meaning taxing authorities of treaty countries can share information (such as income and foreign taxes paid) on residents living in other countries. US citizens must file a tax return, even if they have not lived in the United States during the tax year. US taxpayers claim over $90 billion in foreign tax credits on a yearly basis.[16] Foreign tax credits allow expatriates working abroad to claim taxes paid overseas on their US tax forms, reducing or eliminating double taxation. Many organizations with expatriate workers choose to enlist the help of tax accountants for their workers to ensure workers are paying the correct amount of taxes both abroad and in the United States.

Logistics of International Assignments

As you learned earlier, providing training for the expatriate is an important part of a successful assignment. However, many of the day-to-day aspects of living are important, too.

One of the most important logistical aspects is to make sure the employee can legally work in the country where you will be sending him or her, and ensuring his or her family has appropriate documentation as well. A visa is permission from the host country to visit, live, or work in that country. Obtaining visas is normally the job of an HR professional. For example, the US Department of State and the majority of countries require that all US citizens have a valid passport to travel to a foreign country. This is the first step to ensuring your host-country national or third-country national can travel and work in that country.

Next, understanding the different types of visas is a component to this process. For example, the United States offers a Visa Waiver Program (VWP) that allows some nationals of thirty-six participating countries to travel to the United States for stays of less than ninety days. Iceland, Singapore, and France are examples of countries that participate in this program. For most host-national assignments, however, this type of visa may not be long enough, which then requires research of the individual country. It is important to mention that most countries have several types of visas, such as the following:

1. Visas for crew members working on ships or airlines
2. Tourist visas
3. Student visas
4. Employment visas for long-term employment at a foreign organizational
5. Public organization visas

The visa process and time line can vary greatly depending on the country for which the visa is required. For example, obtaining a visa to work in China may take six months or longer. The best place to research this topic is on the country's embassy website.

Besides ensuring the expatriate can legally work in the country, other considerations are worth mentioning as well:

1. *Housing.* Where will I live is one of the most important questions that an expatriate may ask. The HR professional can help this process by outsourcing a leasing or rental organizational in the city where the expatriate will live to find a rental that meets the expectations of the expatriate. Choosing a place to live ahead of time can reduce stress (one of the causes of failure for assignments) for the expatriate and his or her family. Allowances may be made for housing costs, as discussed in the compensation section.
2. *Moving belongings.* Determination of how belongings left behind will be stored at home or if those items will be brought to the host country is another logistical consideration. If items will be brought, beyond what can be carried in a suitcase, the HR professional may want to consider hiring a moving logistics organizational that specializes in expatriate moves to help with this process.
3. *The possibility of return trips home.* As part of the initial discussion, the option of offering return trips home can make repatriation and performance reviews with home-country managers easier. This also gives the expatriate and his or her family the opportunity to visit with family and friends, reducing reverse culture shock upon return.
4. *Schooling.* Some organizations may want to provide information on the schooling system to the expatriate, if he or she has children. Schools begin at different times of the year, and this information can make the registration process for school easier on the family.
5. *Spousal job.* We know already from earlier in this chapter that one of the biggest challenges facing expatriates (and reasons for failure) is unhappiness of the spouse. He or she may have had a career at home and given that up while the spouse takes an assignment. HR professionals might consider offering job search services as part of the allowance discussed earlier in this chapter. Lockheed Martin, for example, offers job search services to spouses moving overseas.[17]

In any situation, support from the HR professional will help make the assignment a success, which shows that HRM practices should be aligned with organizational goals.

HOW WOULD YOU HANDLE THIS?

Visa Blues

Your manager has just notified you that one of your marketing managers has taken an assignment in China to work for one year. You tell your manager you will begin the visa process for employment. She disagrees and tells you it will be quicker to just get a tourist visa. You mention this is illegal and could get the employee and organizational in trouble, but she insists on your getting a tourist visa so the employee can leave within the month. How would you handle this?

How Would You Handle This?

KEY TAKEAWAYS

- Personality traits are a key component to determining whether someone is a good fit for an overseas assignment. Since 73 percent of overseas assignments fail, ensuring the right match up front is important.
- The ideal expatriate is able to deal with change, is flexible, and has the support of his or her family. Ideal expatriates are also organized, take risks, and are good at asking for help.
- The adjustment period an expatriate goes through depends on his or her initial preparation. Blakeney said there are two levels of adjustment: psychological adjustment and sociocultural adjustment. Although the psychological may take less time, it is the sociocultural adjustment that will allow the assignment to be successful.
- Training is a key component in the HRM global plan, whether expatriates or host-country nationals are to be hired. Both will require a different type of training. Training can reduce culture shock and stress.

- Consideration of the expatriate's family and their ability to adjust can make a more successful overseas assignment
- Compensation is another consideration of a global public organization. The balance sheet approach pays the expatriate extra allowances, such as living expenses, for taking an international assignment.
- Other considerations such as vacation days, health-care benefits, and profit-sharing programs are important as well.
- Laws of each country should be carefully evaluated from an HRM strategic perspective. Laws relating to disabilities, pregnancy, and safety, for example, should be understood before doing public organization overseas.
- Labor unions have different levels of involvement in different parts of the world. For example, Germany has codetermination, a policy that requires organizations to have employees sit on various boards.
- The United States has treaties with forty-two countries to share information about expatriates. The United States offers foreign tax credits to help expatriates avoid double taxation. However, US citizens must file taxes every year, even if they have not lived in the United States during that year.
- Logistical help can be important to ensuring the success of an overseas assignment. Help with finding a place to live, finding a job for a spouse, and moving can make the difference between a successful assignment and an unsuccessful one.
- The Visa Waiver Program (VWP) is a program in which nationals of thirty-six countries can enter the United States for up to a ninety-day period. This type of visa may not work well for expatriates, so it is important to research the type of visa needed from a particular country by using that country's embassy website.

EXERCISE

1. Research the country of your choice. Discuss at least five of the aspects you should know as an HRM professional about doing public organization in that country.

---

[1] The Economist Intelligence Unit, Up or Out: Next Moves for the Modern Expatriate, 2010, accessed April 28, 2011, http://graphics.eiu.com/upload/eb/LON_PL_Regus_WEB2.pdf.

[2] Roger Blakeney, "Psychological Adjustment and Sociocultural Adaptation: Coping on International Assignments" (paper, Annual Meeting of Academy of Management, Atlanta, GA, 2006).

[3] Jeff Thredgold, "English Is Increasingly the International Language of Public organization," Deseret News, December 14, 2010, accessed August 11, 2011,http://www.deseretnews.com/article/700091766/English-is-increasingly-the-international-language-of-public organization.html.

[4] Sudipta Roy, "Brand Failures: A Consumer Perspective to Formulate a MNC Entry Strategy" (postgraduate diploma, XLRI School of Public organization and Human Resources, 1998), accessed August 12, 2011, http://sudiptaroy.tripod.com/dissfin.pdf.

[5] Leslie Gross Klaff, "The Right Way to Bring Expats Home," BNET, July 2002, accessed August 12, 2011, http://findarticles.com/p/articles/mi_m0FXS/is_7_81/ai_89269493/.

[6] Leslie Gross Klaff, "The Right Way to Bring Expats Home," BNET, July 2002, accessed August 12, 2011, http://findarticles.com/p/articles/mi_m0FXS/is_7_81/ai_89269493/

[7] Leslie Gross Klaff, "The Right Way to Bring Expats Home," BNET, July 2002, accessed August 12, 2011, http://findarticles.com/p/articles/mi_m0FXS/is_7_81/ai_89269493/

[8] Leslie Gross Klaff, "The Right Way to Bring Expats Home," BNET, July 2002, accessed August 12, 2011, http://findarticles.com/p/articles/mi_m0FXS/is_7_81/ai_89269493/

[9] J. Cartland, "Reward Policies in a Global Corporation," Public organization Quarterly, Autumn 1993, 93–96.

[10] Countries with Universal Healthcare (no date), accessed August 11, 2011,http://truecostblog.com/2009/08/09/countries-with-universal-healthcare-by-date/.

[11] Jeanne Sahadi, "Who Gets the Most (and Least) Vacation" CNN Money, June 14, 2007, accessed August 11, 2011, http://money.cnn.com/2007/06/12/pf/vacation_days_worldwide/.

[12] Wilke, Maack, und Partner, "Profit-Sharing," Country Reports on Financial Participation in Europe, 2007, worker-participation.eu, 2007, accessed August 12, 2011, http://www.worker-participation.eu/National-Industrial-Relations/Across-Europe/Financial-Participation/Profit-sharing.

[13] George Whitfield, "Do as I Say, Not as I Do: Annual Performance Appraisal and Evaluation in Indonesia" n.d., Living in Indonesia, accessed August 11, 2011,http://www.expat.or.id/public organization/annualperformanceappraisal.html.

[14] Hal Gregersen, Julie Hite, and Steward Black, "Expatriate Performance Appraisal in US Multinational Firms," Journal of International Public organization Studies 27, no. 4 (1996): 711–38.

[15] Carrie Shearer, "Expat Performance Appraisal: A Two Tier Process?" October 8, 2004, Expatrica.com, accessed August 12, 2011, http://www.expatica.com/hr/story/expat-performance-appraisal-a-two-tier-process-10529.html.

[16] Internal Revenue Service, "Foreign Tax Credit," accessed August 13, 2011,http://www.irs.gov/public organizationes/article/0,,id=183263,00.html.

[17] Maureen Minehan, "Six Job Search Tips for Expatriate Spouses," n.d., Expatica, accessed August 12, 2011, http://www.expatica.com/nl/essentials_moving_to/essentials/six-job-search-tips-for-expatriate-spouses-327_9125.html.

14.4 Cases and Problems

CHAPTER SUMMARY

- Offshoring is when a public organization relocates or moves part of its operations to a country different from the one it currently operates in.
- Outsourcing is when a organizational contracts with another organizational to do some work for another. This can occur domestically or in an offshoring situation.
- Domestic market means that a product is sold only within the country that the public organization operates in.
- An international market means that an organization is selling products in other countries, while a multinational one means that not only are products being sold in a country, but operations are set up and run in a country other than where the public organization began.
- The goal of any HRM strategy is to be transnational, which consists of three components. First, the transnational scope involves the ability to make decisions on a global level rather than a domestic one. Transnational representation means that managers from all countries in which the public organization operates are involved in public organization decisions. Finally, a transnational processmeans that the organization can involve a variety of perspectives, rather than only a domestic one.
- Part of understanding HRM internationally is to understand culture. Hofstede developed five dimensions of culture. First, there is the individualism-collectivism aspect, which refers to the tendency of a country to focus on individuals versus the good of the group.
- The second Hofstede dimension is power distance, that is, how willing people are to accept unequal distributions of power.
- The third is uncertainty avoidance, which means how willing the culture is to accept not knowing future outcomes.
- A masculine-feminine dimension refers to the acceptance of traditional male and female characteristics.
- Finally, Hofstede focused on a country's long-term orientation versus short-term orientation in decision making.
- Other aspects of culture include norms, values, rituals, and material culture.Norms are the generally accepted way of doing things, and the values are those things the culture finds important. Every country has its own set ofrituals for ceremonies but also for everyday interactions. Material culturerefers to the material goods, such as art, the culture finds important.
- Other HRM aspects to consider when entering a foreign market are the economics, the law, and the level of education and skill level of the human capital in that country.
- There are three types of staffing strategies for an international public organization. First, in the home-country national strategy, people are employed from the home country to live and work in the country. These individuals are calledexpatriates. One advantage of this type of strategy is easier application of public organization objectives, although an expatriate may not be culturally versed or well accepted by the host-country employees.
- In a host-country strategy, workers are employed within that country to manage the operations of the public organization. Visas and language barriers are advantages of this type of hiring strategy.
- A third-country national staffing strategy means someone from a country, different from home or host country, will be employed to work overseas. There can be visa advantages to using this staffing strategy, although a disadvantage might be morale lost by host-country employees.
- Personality traits are a key component to determining whether someone is a good fit for an overseas assignment. Since 73 percent of overseas assignments fail, ensuring the right match up front is important.
- The ideal expatriate is able to deal with change, is flexible, and has the support of his or her family. Ideal expatriates are also organized, take risks, and are good at asking for help.
- The adjustment period an expatriate goes through depends on his or her initial preparation. Blakeney said there are two levels of adjustment: psychological adjustment and sociocultural adjustment. Although the psychological adjustment may take less time, it is the sociocultural adjustment that will allow the assignment to be successful.
- Training is a key component in the HRM global plan, whether expatriates or host-country nationals are to be hired. Both will require a different type of training. The expatriate should receive extensive training on culture, language, and adjustment.
- Compensation is another consideration of a global public organization. Most organizations keep a standard regional salary but may offer allowances for some expenses. Cost of living, taxes, and other considerations are important.

- Performance should be evaluated by both host-country and home-country managers and employees. The criteria should be determined ahead of time.
- Laws of each country should be carefully evaluated from an HRM strategic perspective. Laws relating to disabilities, pregnancy, and safety, for example, should be understood before doing public organization overseas.
- Logistical help can be important to ensuring the successful overseas assignment. Help with finding a place to live, finding a job for a spouse, and moving can make the difference between a successful assignment and an unsuccessful one.
- The Visa Waiver Program (VWP) is a program in which nationals of thirty-six countries can enter the United States for up to a ninety-day period. This type of visa may not work well for expatriates, so it is important to research the type of visa needed from a particular country by using that country's embassy website.

CHAPTER CASE

Fish to Go Is Going Places

Your organizational, Fish to Go, is a quick service restaurant specializing in fish tacos. Your success in the United States has been excellent, and your organizational has decided to develop an international strategy to further develop your market share. As the vice president for human resources, you have been asked to develop an international staffing strategy. The organization has decided that it makes the most sense to hire host-country nationals to manage the restaurants. Your current Fish to Go managers earn upwards of $45,000 per year, plus 2 percent profit sharing. The organization is also looking to you to determine and develop a comprehensive training program for your host-country managers. A training program is also needed for employees, but you have decided to wait and develop this with input from the host-country managers. Fish to Go has identified Mexico and the UK as the first two countries that will be entered. Perform the necessary research to prepare a PowerPoint presentation to the board of directors.

1. What are the advantages of choosing a host-country national staffing strategy?
2. Develop a compensation plan for each of the two countries, revising the current compensation for managers in the United States, if necessary. The compensation plan should include salary, benefits, and any fringe benefits to attract the most qualified people. The plan should also address any legal compensation requirements for both countries.
3. Develop an outline for a training plan, making reasonable assumptions about the information a new manager would need to know at Fish to Go.

TEAM ACTIVITY

1. What are four major considerations for aligning the HRM strategy with an overall globalization strategy? Discuss each and rank them in order of importance.
2. Find a team with an even number of members. Split each team into "reasons for localized compensation" and "reasons for regional or global compensation." Be prepared to debate the issue with prepared points.

NOTES:

Chapter 15: Leading an Ethical Public Organization

LEARNING OBJECTIVES

After reading this chapter, you should be able to understand and articulate answers to the following questions:

1. What are the key elements of effective organizational governance?
2. How do individuals and firms gauge ethical behavior?
3. What influences and biases might impact and impede decision making?

TOMS SHOES: DOING PUBLIC ORGANIZATION WITH SOUL

In 2002, Blake Mycoskie competed with his sister Paige on The Amazing Race—a reality show where groups of two people with existing relationships engage in a global race to win valuable prizes, with the winner receiving a coveted grand prize. Although Blake's team finished third in the second season of the show, the experience afforded him the opportunity to visit Argentina, where he returned in 2006 and developed the idea to build a organizational around the alpargata—a popular style of shoe in that region.

The premise of the organizational Blake started was a unique one. For every shoe sold, a pair will be given to someone in need. This simple public organization model was the basis for TOMS Shoes, which has now given away more than one million pairs of shoes to those in need in more than twenty countries worldwide. [1]

The rise of TOMS Shoes has inspired other organizations that have adopted the "buy-one-give-one" philosophy. For example, the Good Little Organizational donates a meal for every package purchased. [2] This public organization model has also been successfully applied to selling (and donating) other items such as glasses and books.

The social initiatives that drive TOMS Shoes stand in stark contrast to the criticisms that plagued Nike Corporation, where claims of human rights violations, ranging from the use of sweatshops and child labor to lack of compliance with minimum wage laws, were rampant in the 1990s. [3] While Nike struggled to win back confidence in buyers that were concerned with their public organization practices, TOMS social initiatives are a source of excellent publicity in pride in those who purchase their products. As further testament to their popularity, TOMS has engaged in partnerships with Nordstrom, Disney, and Element Skateboards.

Although the idea of social entrepreneurship and the birth of firms such as TOMS Shoes are relatively new, a push toward social initiatives has been the source of debate for executives for decades. Issues that have sparked particularly fierce debate include CEO pay and the role of today's modern corporation. More than a quarter of a century ago, famed economist Milton Friedman argued, "The social responsibility of public organization is to increase its profits." This notion is now being challenged by firms such as TOMS and their entrepreneurial CEO, who argue that serving other stakeholders beyond the owners and shareholders can be a powerful, inspiring, and successful motivation for growing public organization.

This chapter discusses some of the key issues and decisions relevant to understanding organizational and public organization ethics. Issues include how to govern large corporations in an effective and ethical manner, what behaviors are considered best practices in regard to organizational social performance, and how different generational perspectives and biases may hold a powerful influence on important decisions. Understanding these issues may provide knowledge that can encourage effective organizational leadership like that of TOMS Shoes and discourage the criticisms of many firms associated with the organizational scandals of the late 1990s and early 2000s.

15.1 Boards of Directors

LEARNING OBJECTIVES

1. Understand the key roles played by boards of directors.
2. Know how CEO pay and perks impact the landscape of organizational governance.
3. Explain different terms associated with organizational takeovers.

The Many Roles of Boards of Directors

"You're fired!" is a commonly used phrase most closely associated with Donald Trump as he dismisses candidates on his reality show, The Apprentice. But who would have the power to utter these words to today's CEOs, whose paychecks are on par with many of the top celebrities and athletes in the world? This honor belongs to the board of directors—a group of individuals that oversees the activities of an organization or corporation.

Potentially firing or hiring a CEO is one of many roles played by the board of directors in their charge to provide effective organizational governance for the firm. An effective board plays many roles, ranging from the approval of financial objectives, advising on strategic issues, making the firm aware of relevant laws, and representing stakeholders who have an interest in the long-term performance of the firm. Effective boards may help bring prestige and important resources to the organization. For example, General Electric's board often has included the CEOs of other firms as well as former senators and prestigious academics. Blake Mycoskie of TOMS Shoes was touted as an ideal candidate for an "all-star" board of directors because of his ability to fulfill his organizational's mission "to show how together we can create a better tomorrow by taking compassionate action today." [1]

The key stakeholder of most corporations is generally agreed to be the shareholders of the organizational's stock. Most large, publicly traded firms in the United States are made up of thousands of shareholders. While 5 percent ownership in many ventures may seem modest, this amount is considerable in publicly traded organizations where such ownership is generally limited to other organizations, and ownership in this amount could result in representation on the board of directors.

The possibility of conflicts of interest is considerable in public corporations. On the one hand, CEOs favor large salaries and job stability, and these desires are often accompanied by a tendency to make decisions that would benefit the firm (and their salaries) in the short term at the expense of decisions considered over a longer time horizon. In contrast, shareholders prefer decisions that will grow the value of their stock in the long term. This separation of interest creates an agency problem wherein the interests of the individuals that manage the organizational (agents such as the CEO) may not align with the interest of the owners (such as stockholders).

The composition of the board is critical because the dynamics of the board play an important part in resolving the agency problem. However, who exactly should be on the board is an issue that has been subject to fierce debate. CEOs often favor the use of board insiders who often have intimate knowledge of the firm's public organization affairs. In contrast, many institutional investors such as mutual funds and pension funds that hold large blocks of stock in the firm often prefer significant representation by board outsiders that provide a fresh, nonbiased perspective concerning a firm's actions.

One particularly controversial issue in regard to board composition is the potential for CEO duality, a situation in which the CEO is also the chairman of the board of directors. This has also been known to create a bitter divide within a corporation.

For example, during the 1990s, The Walt Disney Organizational was often listed in Public organizationWeek's rankings for having one of the worst boards of directors. [2] In 2005, Disney's board forced the separation of then CEO (and chairman of the board) Michael Eisner's dual roles. Eisner retained the role of CEO but later stepped down from Disney entirely. Disney's story reflects a changing reality that boards are acting with considerably more influence than in previous decades when they were viewed largely as rubber stamps that generally folded to the whims of the CEO.

Managing CEO Compensation

One of the most visible roles of boards of directors is setting CEO pay. The valuation of the human capital associated with the rare talent possessed by some CEOs can be illustrated in a story of an encounter one tourist had with the legendary artist Pablo Picasso. As the story goes, Picasso was once spotted by a woman sketching. Overwhelmed with excitement at the serendipitous meeting, the tourist offered Picasso fair market value if he would render a quick sketch of her image. After completing his commission, she was shocked when he asked for five thousand francs, responding, "But it only took you a few minutes." Undeterred, Picasso retorted, "No, it took me all my life." [3]

This story illustrates the complexity associated with managing CEO compensation. On the one hand, large corporations must pay competitive wages for the scarce talent that is needed to manage billion-dollar corporations. In addition, like celebrities and sport stars, CEO pay is much more than a function of a day's work for a day's pay. CEO compensation is a function of the competitive wages that other corporations would offer for a potential CEO's services.

On the other hand, boards will face considerable scrutiny from investors if CEO pay is out of line with industry norms. From the year 1980 to 2000, the gap between CEO pay and worker pay grew from 42 to 1 to 475 to 1. [4] Although efforts to close this gap have been made, as recently as 2008 reports indicate the ratio continues to be as high as 344 to 1, much higher than other countries, where an 80 to 1 ratio is common, or in Japan where the gap is just 16 to 1. [5] Meanwhile, shareholders need to be aware that research studies have found that CEO pay is positively correlated with the size of firms—the bigger the firm, the higher the CEO's compensation. [6] Consequently, when a CEO tries to grow a organizational, such as by acquiring a rival firm, shareholders should question whether such growth is in the organizational's best interest or whether it is simply an effort by the CEO to get a pay raise.

In most publicly traded firms, CEO compensation generally includes guaranteed salary, cash bonus, and stock options. But perks provide another valuable source of CEO compensation. In addition to the controversy surrounding CEO pay, such perks associated with holding the position of CEO have also come under considerable scrutiny. The term perks, derived from perquisite, refers to special privileges, or rights, as a function of one's position. CEO perks have ranged in magnitude from the sweet benefit of ice cream for life given to former Ben & Jerry's CEO Robert Holland, to much more extreme benefits that raise the ears of investors while outraging employees. One such perk was provided to John Thain, who, as former head of NYSE Euronext, received more than $1 million to renovate his office. While such perks may provide powerful incentives to stay with a organizational, they may result in considerable negative press and serve only to motivate vigilant investors wary of the value of such investments to shop elsewhere.

The Market for Organizational Governance

An old investment cliché encourages individuals to buy low and sell high. When a publicly traded firm loses value, often due to lack of vigilance on the part of the CEO and/or board, a organizational may become a target of a takeover wherein another firm or set of individuals purchases the organizational. Generally, the top management team is charged with revitalizing the firm and maximizing its assets.

In some cases, the takeover is in the form of a leveraged buyout (LBO) in which a publicly traded organizational is purchased and then taken off the stock market. One of the most famous LBOs was of RJR Nabisco, which inspired the book (and later film) Barbarians at the Gate. LBOs historically are associated with reduction in workforces to streamline processes and decrease costs. The managers who instigate buyouts generally bring a more entrepreneurial mind-set to the firm with the hopes of creating a turnaround from the same fate that made the organizational an attractive takeover target (recent poor performance). [7]

Many takeover attempts increase shareholder value. However, because most takeovers are associated with the dismissal of previous management, the terminology associated with change of ownership has a decidedly negative slant against the acquiring firm's management team. For example, individuals or firms that hope to conduct a takeover are often referred to as organizational raiders. An unsolicited takeover attempt is often dubbed a hostile takeover, with shark repellent as the potential defenses against such attempts. Although the poor management of a targeted firm is often the reason such public organizationes are potential takeover targets, when another firm that may be more favorable to existing management enters the picture as an alternative buyer, a white knight is said to have entered the picture.

The negative tone of takeover terminology also extends to the potential target firm. CEOs as well as board members are likely to lose their positions after a successful takeover occurs, and a number of antitakeover tactics have been used by boards to deter a organizational raid. For example, many firms are said to pay greenmail by repurchasing large blocks of stock at a premium to avoid a potential takeover. Firms may threaten to take a poison pill where additional stock is sold to existing shareholders, increasing the shares needed for a viable takeover. Even if the takeover is successful and the previous CEO is dismissed, a golden parachute that includes a lucrative financial settlement is likely to provide a soft landing for the ousted executive.

KEY TAKEAWAY

- Firms can benefit from superior organizational governance mechanisms such as an active board that monitors CEO actions, provides strategic advice, and helps to network to other useful resources. When such mechanisms are not in place, CEO excess may go unchecked, resulting in negative publicity, poor firm performance, and potential takeover by other firms.

EXERCISES

1. Divide the class into teams and see who can find the most egregious CEO perk in the last year.
2. Find a listing of members of a board of directors for a Organizational firm. Does the board seem to be composed of individuals who are likely to fulfill all the board roles effectively?
3. Research a hostile takeover in the past five years and examine the long-term impact on the firm's stock market performance. Was the takeover beneficial or harmful for shareholders?
4. Examine the AFL-CIO Executive Paywatch website (http://www.aflcio.org/organizationalwatch/paywatch) and select a organizational of interest to see how many years you would need to work to earn a year's pay enjoyed by the firm's CEO.

15.2 Organizational Ethics and Social Responsibility

LEARNING OBJECTIVES

1. Know the three levels and six stages of moral development suggested by Kohlberg.
2. Describe famous organizational scandals.
3. Understand how the Sarbanes-Oxley Act of 2002 provides a check on organizational ethical behavior in the United States.
4. Know the dimensions of organizational social performance tracked by KLD.

Stages of Moral Development

How do ethics evolve over time? Psychologist Lawrence Kohlberg suggests that there are six distinct stages of moral development and that some individuals move further along these stages than others. [1] Kohlberg's six stages were grouped into three levels: (1) preconventional, (2) conventional, and (3) postconventional.

The preconventional level of moral reasoning is very egocentric in nature, and moral reasoning is tied to personal concerns. In stage 1, individuals focus on the direct consequences that their actions will have—for example, worry about punishment or getting caught. In stage 2, right or wrong is defined by the reward stage, where a "what's in it for me" mentality is seen.

In the conventional level of moral reasoning, morality is judged by comparing individuals' actions with the expectations of society. In stage 3, individuals are conformity driven and act with the goal of fulfilling social roles. Parents that encourage their children to be good boys and girls use this form of moral guidance. In stage 4, the importance of obeying laws, social conventions, or other forms of authority to aid in maintaining a functional society is encouraged. You might witness encouragement under this stage when using a cell phone in a restaurant or when someone is chatting too loudly in a library.

The postconventional level, or principled level, occurs when morality is more than simply following social rules or norms. Stage 5 considers different values and opinions. Thus laws are viewed as social contracts that promote the greatest good for the greatest number of people. Following democratic principles or voting to determine an outcome is common when this stage of reasoning is invoked. In stage 6, moral reasoning is based on universal ethical principles. For example, the golden rule that you should do unto others as you would have them do unto you illustrates one such ethical principle. At this stage, laws are grounded in the idea of right and wrong. Thus individuals follow laws because they are just and not because they will be punished if caught or shunned by society. Consequently, with this stage there is an idea of civil disobedience that individuals have a duty to disobey unjust laws.

Organizational Scandals and Sarbanes-Oxley

In the 1990s and early 2000s, several organizational scandals were revealed in the United States that showed a lack of board vigilance. Perhaps the most famous involves Enron, whose executive antics were documented in the film The Smartest Guys in the Room. Enron used accounting loopholes to hide billions of dollars in failed deals. When their scandal was discovered, top management cashed out millions in stock options while preventing lower-level employees from selling their stock. The collective acts of Enron led many employees to lose all their retirement holdings, and many Enron execs were sentenced to prison.

In response to notable organizational scandals at Enron, WorldCom, Tyco, and other firms, Congress passed sweeping new legislation with the hopes of restoring investor confidence while preventing future scandals. Signed into law by President George W. Bush in 2002, Sarbanes-Oxley contained eleven aspects that represented some of the most far-reaching reforms since the presidency of Franklin

Roosevelt. These reforms create improved standards that affect all publicly traded firms in the United States. The key elements of each aspect of the act are summarized as follows:

1. Because accounting firms were implicated in organizational scandal, an oversight board was created to oversee auditing activities.
2. Standards now exist to ensure auditors are truly independent and not subject to conflicts of interest in regard to the organizations they represent.
3. Enron executives claimed that they had no idea what was going on in their organizational, but Sarbanes-Oxley requires senior executives to take personal responsibility for the accuracy of financial statements.
4. Enhanced reporting is now required to create more transparency in regard to a firm's financial condition.
5. Securities analysts must disclose potential conflicts of interest.
6. To prevent CEOs from claiming tax fraud is present at their firms, CEOs must personally sign the firm's tax return.
7. The Securities and Exchange Commission (SEC) now has expanded authority to censor or bar securities analysts from acting as brokers, advisers, or dealers.
8. Reports from the comptroller general are required to monitor any consolidations among public accounting firms, the role of credit agencies in securities market operations, securities violations, and enforcement actions.
9. Criminal penalties now exist for altering or destroying financial records.
10. Significant criminal penalties now exist for white-collar crimes.
11. The SEC can freeze unusually large transactions if fraud is suspected.

The changes that encouraged the creation of Sarbanes-Oxley were so sweeping that comedian Jon Stewart quipped, "Did Wall Street have any rules before this? Can you just shoot a guy for looking at you wrong?" Despite the considerable merits of Sarbanes-Oxley, no legislation can provide a cure-all for organizational scandal. As evidence, the scandal by Bernard Madoff that broke in 2008 represented the largest investor fraud ever committed by an individual. But in contrast to some previous scandals that resulted in relatively minor punishments for their perpetrators, Madoff was sentenced to 150 years in prison.

Measuring Organizational Social Performance

TOMS Shoes' commitment to donating a pair of shoes for every shoe sold illustrates the concept of social entrepreneurship, in which a public organization is created with a goal of bettering both public organization and society. [2] Firms such as TOMS exemplify a desire to improve organizational social performance (CSP) in which a commitment to individuals, communities, and the natural environment is valued alongside the goal of creating economic value. Although determining the level of a firm's social responsibility is subjective, this challenge has been addressed in detail by Kinder, Lydenberg and Domini & Co. (KLD), a Boston-based firm that rates firms on a number of stakeholder-related issues with the goal of measuring CSP. KLD conducts ongoing research on social, governance, and environmental performance metrics of publicly traded firms and reports such statistics to institutional investors. The KLD database provides ratings on numerous "strengths" and "concerns" for each firm along a number of dimensions associated with organizational social performance. The results of their assessment are used to develop the Domini social investments fund, which has performed at levels roughly equivalent to the S&P 500.

Assessing the community dimension of CSP is accomplished by assessing community strengths, such as charitable or innovative giving that supports housing, education, or relations with indigenous peoples, as well as charitable efforts worldwide, such as volunteer efforts or in-kind giving. A firm's CSP rating is lowered when a firm is involved in tax controversies or other negative actions that affect the community, such as plant closings that can negatively affect property values.

CSP diversity strengths are scored positively when the organizational is known for promoting women and minorities, especially for board membership and the CEO position. Employment of the disabled and the presence of family benefits such as child or elder care would also result in a positive score by KLD. Diversity concerns include fines or civil penalties in conjunction with an affirmative action or other diversity-related controversy. Lack of representation by women on top management positions—suggesting that a glass ceiling is present at a organizational—would also negatively impact scoring on this dimension.

The employee relations dimension of CSP gauges potential strengths such as notable union relations, profit sharing and employee stock-option plans, favorable retirement benefits, and positive health and safety programs noted by the US Occupational Health and Safety Administration. Employee relations concerns would be evident in poor union relations, as well as fines paid due to violations of health and safety standards. Substantial workforce reductions as well as concerns about adequate funding of pension plans also warrant concern for this dimension.

The environmental dimension records strengths by examining engagement in recycling, preventing pollution, or using alternative energies. KLD would also score a firm positively if profits derived from environmental products or services were a part of the organizational's public organization. Environmental concerns such as penalties for hazardous waste, air, water, or other violations or actions such as the production of goods or services that could negatively impact the environment would reduce a firm's CSP score.

Product quality/safety strengths exist when a firm has an established and/or recognized quality program; product quality safety concerns are evident when fines related to product quality and/or safety have been discovered or when a firm has been engaged in questionable marketing practices or paid fines related to antitrust practices or price fixing.

Organizational governance strengths are evident when lower levels of compensation for top management and board members exist, or when the firm owns considerable interest in another organizational rated favorably by KLD; organizational governance concerns arise when executive compensation is high or when controversies related to accounting, transparency, or political accountability exist.

STRATEGY AT THE MOVIES

Thank You for Smoking

Does smoking cigarettes cause lung cancer? Not necessarily, according to a fictitious lobbying group called the Academy of Tobacco Studies (ATS) depicted in Thank You for Smoking (2005). The ATS's ability to rebuff the critics of smoking was provided by a three-headed monster of disinformation: scientist Erhardt Von Grupten Mundt who had been able to delay finding conclusive evidence of the harms of tobacco for thirty years, lawyers drafted from Ivy League institutions to fight against tobacco legislation, and a spin control division led by the smooth-talking Nick Naylor.

The ATS was a promotional powerhouse. In just one week, the ATS and its spin doctor Naylor distracted the American public by proposing a $50 million campaign against teen smoking, brokered a deal with a major motion picture producer to feature actors and actresses smoking after sex, and bribed a cancer-stricken advertising spokesman to keep quiet. But after the ATS's transgressions were revealed and cigarette organizations were forced to settle a long-standing class-action lawsuit for $246 billion, the ATS was shut down. Although few organizations promote a product as harmful as cigarettes, the lessons offered in Thank You for Smoking have wide application. In particular, the film highlights that choosing between ethical and unethical public organization practices is not only a moral issue, but it can also determine whether an organization prospers or dies.

KEY TAKEAWAY

- The work of Lawrence Kohlberg examines how individuals can progress in their stages of moral development. Lack of such development by many CEOs led to a number of scandals, as well as legislation such as the Sarbanes-Oxley Act of 2002 that was enacted with the hope of deterring scandalous behavior in the future. Firms such as KLD provide objective measures of both positive and negative actions related to organizational social performance.

EXERCISES

1. How would your college or university fare if rated on the dimensions used by KLD?
2. Do you believe that executives will become more ethical based on legislation such as Sarbanes-Oxley?

15.3 Understanding Thought Patterns: A Key to Organizational Leadership?

LEARNING OBJECTIVES

1. Know the three major generational influences that make up the majority of the current workforce and their different perspectives and influences.
2. Understand how decision biases may impede effective decision making.

Generational Influences on Work Behavior

Psychologist Kurt Lewin, known as the "founder of social psychology," created a well-known formula $B = f(P,E)$ that states behavior is a function of the person and their environment. One powerful environmental influence that can be seen in organizations today is based on generational differences. Currently, four generations of workers (traditionalists, baby boomers, Generation X, Generation Y) coexist in many organizations. The different backgrounds and behaviors create challenges for leading these individuals that often have similar shared experiences within their generation but different sets of values, motivations, and preferences in contrast to other generations. Effective management of these four different generations involves a realization of their differences and preferred communication styles. [1]

The generation born between 1925 and 1946 that fought in World War II and lived through the Great Depression are referred to as traditionalists. The perseverance of this generation has led journalist Tom Brokaw to dub this group "The Greatest Generation." As a reflection of a generation that was molded by contributions to World War II, members of this generation value personal communication, loyalty, hierarchy, and are resistant to change. This group now makes up roughly 5 percent of the workforce.

The generation known as baby boomers was born between 1946 and 1964, corresponding with a population "boom" following the end of World War II. This group witnessed Beatlemania, Vietnam, and the Watergate scandal. College graduates should be aware that this group makes up the majority of the workforce and that boomer managers often view face time as an important contribution to a successful work environment. [2] In addition, a realization that this generation wants to be included in office activities and values recognition is important to achieving cohesiveness between generations.

Generation X, born between 1965 and 1980, is marked by an X symbolizing their unknown nature. In contrast to the baby boomer's value on office face time, Gen X members prize flexibility in their jobs and dislike the feeling that they are being micromanaged. [3] Because of the desire for independence as well as adaptability associated with this generation, you should try to answer the "What's in it for me?" question to avoid the risk of Gen X members moving on to other employment opportunities.

The generation that followed Generation X is known as Generation Y or millennials. This generation is highlighted by positive attributes such as the ability to embrace technology. More than previous generations, this group prizes job and life satisfaction highly, so making the workplace an enjoyable environment is key to managing Generation Y.

Wise members of this generation will also be aware of the negative attributes surrounding them. For example, millennials are associated with their "helicopter" parents who are often too comfortably involved in the lives of their children. For example, such parents have been known to show up to their children's job orientations, often attempting to interfere with other workplace experiences such as pay and promotion discussions that may be unwelcome by older generations. In addition, this generation is viewed as needing more feedback than previous groups. Finally, the trend toward discouraging some competitive activities among individuals in this age group has led millennials to be dubbed "Trophy Kids" by more cynical writers.

Rational Decision Making

Understanding generational differences can provide valuable insight into the perspectives that shape the behaviors of individuals born at different periods of time. But such knowledge does not answer a more fundamental question of interest to students of strategic management, namely, why do CEOs make bad, unethical, or other questionable decisions with the potential to lead their firms to poor performance or firm failure? Part of the answer lies in the method by which CEOs and other individuals make decisions. Ideally, individuals would make rational decisions for important choices such as buying a car or house, or choosing a career or place to live. The process of rational decision making involves problem identification, establishment and weighing of decision criteria, generation and evaluation of alternatives, selection of the best alternative, decision implementation, and decision evaluation.

Rational Decision-Making Model

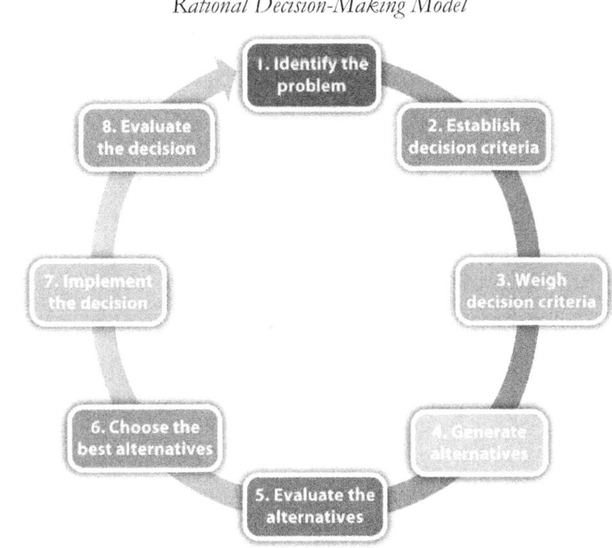

While this model provides valuable insights by providing an ideal approach by which to make decisions, there are several problems with this model when applied to many complex decisions. First, many strategic decisions are not presented in obvious ways, and many CEOs may not be aware their firms are having problems until it's too late to create a viable solution. Second, rational decision making assumes that options are clear and that a single best solution exists. Third, rational decision making assumes no time or cost constraints. Fourth, rational decision making assumes accurate information is available. Because of these challenges, some have joked that marriage is one of the least rational decisions a person can make because no one can seek out and pursue every possible alternative—even with all the online dating and social networking services in the world.

Decision Biases

In reality, decision making is not rational because there are limits on our ability to collect and process information. Because of these limitations, Nobel Prize-winner Herbert Simon argued that we can learn more by examining scenarios where individuals deviate from the ideal. These decision biases provide clues to why individuals such as CEOs make decisions that in retrospect often seem very illogical—especially when they lead to actions that damage the firm and its performance. A number of the most common biases with the potential to affect public organization decision making are discussed next.

Anchoring and adjustment bias occurs when individuals react to arbitrary or irrelevant numbers when setting financial or other numerical targets. For example, it is tempting for college graduates to compare their starting salaries at their first career job to the wages earned at jobs used to fund school. Comparisons to siblings, friends, parents, and others with different majors are also very tempting while being generally irrelevant. Instead, research the average starting salary for your background, experience, and other relevant characteristics to get a true gauge. This bias could undermine firm performance if executives make decisions about the potential value of a merger or acquisition by making comparisons to previous deals rather than based on a realistic and careful study of a move's profit potential.

The availability bias occurs when more readily available information is incorrectly assessed to also be more likely. For example, research shows that most people think that auto accidents cause more deaths than stomach cancer because auto accidents are reported more in the media than deaths by stomach cancer at a rate of more than 100 to 1. This bias could cause trouble for executives if they focus on readily available information such as their own firm's performance figures but fail to collect meaningful data on their competitors or industry trends that suggest the need for a potential change in strategic direction.

The idea of "throwing good money after bad" illustrates the bias of escalation of commitment, when individuals continue on a failing course of action even after it becomes clear that this may be a poor path to follow. This can be regularly seen at Vegas casinos when individuals think the next coin must be more likely to hit the jackpot at the slots. The concept of escalation of commitment was chronicled in the 1990 book Barbarians at the Gate: The Rise and Fall of RJR Nabisco. The book follows the buyout of RJR Nabisco and the bidding war that took place between then CEO of RJR Nabisco F. Ross Johnson and leverage buyout pioneers Henry Kravis and George Roberts. The result of the bidding war was an extremely high sales price of the organizational that resulted in significant debt for the new owners.

Fundamental attribution error occurs when good outcomes are attributed to personal characteristics but undesirable outcomes are attributed to external circumstances. Many professors lament a common scenario that, when a student does well on a test, it's attributed to intelligence. But when a student performs poorly, the result is attributed to an unfair test or lack of adequate teaching based on the professor. In a similar vein, some CEOs are quick to take credit when their firm performs well, but often attribute poor performance to external factors such as the state of the economy.

Hindsight bias occurs when mistakes seem obvious after they have already occurred. This bias is often seen when second-guessing failed plays on the football field and is so closely associated with watching National Football League games on Sunday that the phrase Monday morning quarterback is a part of our public organization and sports vernacular. The decline of firms such as Kodak as victims to the increasing popularity of digital cameras may seem obvious in retrospect. It is easy to overlook the poor quality of early digital technology and to dismiss any notion that Kodak executives had good reason not to view this new technology as a significant competitive threat when digital cameras were first introduced to the market.

Judgments about correlation and causality can lead to problems when individuals make inaccurate attributions about the causes of events. Three things are necessary to determine cause—or why one element affects another. For example, understanding how marketing spending affects firm performance involves (1) correlation (do sales increase when marketing increases), (2) temporal order (does marketing spending occur before sales increase), and (3) ruling out other potential causes (is something else causing sales to increase: better products, more employees, a recession, a competitor went bankrupt, etc.). The first two items can be tracked easily, but the third is almost impossible to isolate because there are always so many changing factors. In economics, the expression ceteris paribus (all things being equal or constant) is the basis of many economic models; unfortunately, the only constant in reality is change. Of course, just because determining causality is difficult and often inconclusive does not mean that firms should be slow to take strategic action. As the old public organization saying goes, "We know we always waste half of our marketing budget, we just don't know which half."

Misunderstandings about sampling may occur when individuals draw broad conclusions from small sets of observations instead of more reliable sources of information derived from large, randomly drawn samples. Many CEOs have been known to make major financial decisions based on their own instincts rather than on careful number crunching.

Overconfidence bias occurs when individuals are more confident in their abilities to predict an event than logic suggests is actually possible. For example, two-thirds of lawyers in civil cases believe their side will emerge victorious. But as the famed Yankees player/manager Yogi Berra once noted, "It's hard to make predictions, especially about the future." Such overconfidence is common in CEOs that have had success in the past and who often rely on their own intuition rather than on hard data and market research.

Representativeness bias occurs when managers use stereotypes of similar occurrences when making judgments or decisions. In some cases, managers may draw from previous experiences to make good decisions when changes in the environment occur. In other cases, representativeness can lead to discriminatory behaviors that may be both unethical and illegal.

Framing bias occurs when the way information is presented alters the decision an individual will make. Poor framing frequently occurs in organizations because employees are often reluctant to bring bad news to CEOs. To avoid an unpleasant message, they might be tempted to frame information in a more positive light than reality, knowing that individuals react differently to news that a glass is half empty versus half full.

Satisficing occurs when individuals settle for the first acceptable alternative instead of seeking the best possible (optimal) decision. While this bias might actually be desirable when others are waiting behind you at a vending machine, research shows that CEOs commonly satisfice with major decisions such as mergers and takeovers.

KEY TAKEAWAY

- Generational differences provide powerful influences on the mind-set of employees that should be carefully considered to effectively manage a diverse workforce. Wise managers will also be aware of the numerous decision biases that could impede effective decision making.

EXERCISES

1. Explain how a specific decision bias mentioned in this chapter led to poor decision making by a firm.
2. Are there negative generational tendencies in your age group that you have worked to overcome?

15.4 Conclusion

This chapter explains the role of boards of directors in the organizational governance of organizations such as large, publicly traded corporations. Wise boards work to manage the agency problem that creates a conflict of interest between top managers such as CEO and other groups with a stake in the firm. When boards fail to do their duties, numerous scandals may ensue. Organizational scandals became so widespread that new legislation such as the Sarbanes-Oxley Act of 2002 has been developed with the hope of impeding future actions by executives associated with unethical or illegal behavior. Finally, firms should be aware of generational influences as well as other biases that may lead to poor decisions.

EXERCISES

1. Divide your class into four or eight groups, depending on the size of the class. Each group should select a different industry. Find positive and negative examples of organizational social performance based on the dimensions used by KLD.

2. This chapter discussed Blake Mycoskie and TOMS Shoes. What other opportunities exist to create new organizations that serve both social and financial goals?

NOTES:

Printed in Great Britain
by Amazon

37741161R00132